# Beginning Dynamic Websites
# with ASP.NET Web Matrix

David Sussman
with
James Greenwood
Alex Homer
Colt Kwong
John West

Programmer to Programmer

D1314721

# Beginning Dynamic Websites with ASP.NET Web Matrix

Published by
**Wiley Publishing, Inc.**
10475 Crosspoint Boulevard
Indianapolis, IN 46256
www.wiley.com

Copyright © 2003 by Wiley Publishing, Inc., Indianapolis, Indiana

Published simultaneously in Canada

Library of Congress Card Number: 2003107076

ISBN: 0-7645-4374-1

Manufactured in the United States of America

10 9 8 7 6 5 4 3 2 1

1B/QZ/QW/QT/IN

For general information on our other products and services or to obtain technical support, please contact our Customer Care Department within the U.S. at (800) 762-2974, outside the U.S. at (317) 572-3993 or fax (317) 572-4002.

Wiley also publishes its books in a variety of electronic formats. Some content that appears in print may not be available in electronic books.

**Trademarks:** Wiley, the Wiley Publishing logo, Wrox, the Wrox logo, the Wrox Programmer to Programmer logo and related trade dress are trademarks or registered trademarks of Wiley in the United States and other countries, and may not be used without written permission. All other trademarks are the property of their respective owners. Wiley Publishing, Inc., is not associated with any product or vendor mentioned in this book.

# TABLE OF CONTENTS

## Trademark Acknowledgments

## Credits

**Authors**
David Sussman
James Greenwood
Alex Homer
Colt Kwong
John West

**Additional Material**
David Barnes
Chris Hart

**Technical Editors**
Mankee Cheng
Chris Hart
Michelle Everitt

**Commissioning Editor**
David Barnes

**Publisher**
Dominic Shakeshaft

**Project Manager**
Darren Murphy

**Managing Editor**
Joanna Mason

**Series Editor**
John Collin

**Technical Reviewers**
Martin Beaulieu
John Collin
Slavomir Furman
Ben Galbraith
Jay Glynn
Brad Maiani
Johan Normen
Teri Radichel
Ranga Raghunathan
Larry Schoeneman
Scott Watermasysk

**Production Coordinator**
Sarah Hall

**Cover Design**
Natalie O'Donnell

**Index**
John Collin

**Proofreader**
Chris Smith

**Music**
Adequate 7
www.adequate7.co.uk

# From David...

This book will teach you all the things you need to know to turn your design idea into a dynamic website. You will still need to bring the creativity, but you can leave the programming to us.

Over the course of this book, you'll build some powerful website features, but that's just the start. Almost all of the advanced, commercial websites you see today are based on principles you'll learn from this book – online magazines and newspapers, e-commerce sites, discussion forums, and games will all be within your grasp by the time you finish.

Want to provide an online news service? Then you'll need a database to store the stories, a login screen to update them, some pages to display the news to visitors, and maybe a web service to let other sites display your stories. It's all in here, and once you've had the idea, it will come together easily and quickly using Web Matrix as the tool for the development process.

Web Matrix is about community. Although it was developed by Microsoft employees, it really was a labor of love. I was talking to the Microsoft ASP.NET team as they were working on it in their spare time, and got the chance to play with some top-secret betas. I could tell they were onto something: fast, friendly, simple, and a price tag few could argue with – it was free!

It's come a long way since then, but at the core, it's still the same – a great tool that lets you do everything you want, but nothing you don't.

I hope you can say the same thing about my book!

David

# About the Authors

### David Sussman

David Sussman has spent the majority of his professional life as a developer, using both Unix-based and Microsoft-based products. After writing his first two books while in full time employment, he realized that being an author sounded more glamorous than being a programmer. The reality is somewhat different. He now spends most of his time writing books for Wrox Press, speaking at conferences, and playing with most beta products that Microsoft ships.

### James Greenwood

James Greenwood is a technical architect and author based in West Yorkshire, England. He spends his days (and most of his nights) designing and implementing .NET solutions from Government knowledge-management systems to mobile integration platforms, all the while waxing lyrical on the latest Microsoft technologies. His professional interests include research into distributed interfaces, the automation of application development, and human-machine convergence.

When he can be prised away from the keyboard, James can be found out and about, indulging in his other great loves – British sports cars and Egyptology.

You can reach James at jsg@altervisitor.com.

## Alex Homer

Alex Homer is a software developer and technical author living and working in the idyllic rural surroundings of the Derbyshire Dales in England. He came to computing late in life – in fact, while he was at school people still thought that the LED wristwatch was a really cool idea. Since then, he has obtained a Bachelor of Arts degree in Mathematics, and so, looked destined for a career painting computers. Instead, while not busy developing ASP components for Stonebroom Software (http://www.stonebroom.com), he prefers to install and play with the latest and flakiest beta code he can find – and then write about it. You can contact him at alex@stonebroom.com or alex@stonebroom.co.uk.

## Colt Kwong

Colt Kwong is a Microsoft .NET MVP, software developer, technical writer, and addict of all things about .NET. He's one of the top posters and a moderator on the Microsoft official ASP.NET forums at http://www.asp.net/Forums/. He also contributes on other popular websites and newsgroups as well. He spends a great deal of his free time providing help to budding ASP.NET developers. He is a guest speaker for Microsoft Hong Kong TechEd and a freelancer for Microsoft Hong Kong. He's in the Winner's Circle for Microsoft's Asia Student .NET Online Challenge, earning perfect scores in advanced, intermediate, and basic levels of .NET, ASP.NET, XML web services, XML, Visual Basic .NET, Visual Studio .NET, and HailStorm. Moreover, he was also recognized as one of the Level 2 AspElite members and is a Moderator of AspFriends.com .

*I would like to thank David Barnes, Darren Murphy, and the Wrox Editorial Team. Without their kindness, care, and support, I don't think I could have completed this book in such a smooth way!*

## John West

John West is a Principal Consultant at Intellinet (www.intellinet.com), based out of Atlanta, Georgia. He specializes in leading Microsoft .NET application development efforts. Intellinet provides infrastructure and business intelligence solutions. Intellinet's Intelligent Enterprise integration solution helps clients to benefit from systems that meet current needs and can scale to future demands. Often, .NET applications become the glue to integrate the Intelligent Enterprise, which consists of networking, security, messaging, collaboration, custom applications, data, and mobility solutions.

When not working, he usually spends his time reading, hanging out with friends from church, and boating. John can be reached at wrox@johnwest.com.

# Table of Contents

**vii**

# INTRODUCTION

# Introduction

Programming web applications is a great way to start your programming career. Using Web Matrix as your entry point makes even more sense. This lightweight visual development environment enables you to get a rapid, yet substantial introduction to web applications, after which you will surely want to learn more. Whether you want only to know the basics and produce a neat and workable website, or you aspire to greater things, this book will get you started on your journey, and we are confident you will enjoy the ride!

We are living in a world increasingly dominated by the Internet, with many possibilities evolving and vast numbers of people wanting to be part of this revolution. You may well have friends who have their own websites, talking about who they are and what they like. Wouldn't it be cool though, to have your own website that was **dynamic**, reacting to user input, displaying data, and giving your visitors a fun and interesting browsing experience? Of course it would, and these skills could start you off down the path to becoming a seasoned web developer, and getting your first job creating websites!

The **ASP.NET Web Matrix Project** is a great tool to use to start your path down this road. The pages you create using Web Matrix are built upon a Microsoft technology called **ASP.NET**. ASP.NET contains a powerful set of tools and functionality that developers can make use of to rapidly create the sorts of sites that really win when it comes to making functional and aesthetically pleasing sites. Web Matrix makes this process even easier, removing the need to type a lot of code by hand, enabling you to create impressive results in very little time.

## Who is This Book For?

This book will teach even a novice programmer how to construct ASP.NET websites quickly and easily, concentrating on the tools you're likely to use from day to day. You don't need to have done programming before, not even simple HTML, though a reasonable understanding of what HTML is would probably help you to get started. Along the way, this book will occasionally touch on deeper subjects, but if you work through all the examples in the book, we'll hold your hand along the way and explain what's actually going on, building your knowledge step by step.

# What Does This Book Cover?

This book will take you from very little knowledge to the point where you can construct data-driven websites, and give you an overview of some of the deeper areas of ASP.NET. Here's what you can expect to see as you work through the book:

## Section 1 – Getting Started

The first part of the book will help to get your environment set up correctly, and show you how to create simple pages in ASP.NET using Visual Basic .NET:

❑ **Chapter 1: Installing and Exploring Web Matrix** – this chapter guides you through all the steps required to get Web Matrix, the .NET Framework, and an MSDE database installed on your system.

❑ **Chapter 2: Writing Your First ASP.NET Web Page** – the first example in the book that teaches you how to construct web pages in Web Matrix, using a simple dice game as the example.

❑ **Chapter 3: Creating Web Pages** – start to learn more about web controls in this chapter, and how to create web pages using them.

❑ **Chapter 4: Writing Code** – in this chapter, we start to explain how Visual Basic .NET code works, and how we can write code in our pages that can be used for decision-making, looping through a set of instructions, and encapsulating functionality in a method.

❑ **Chapter 5: Storing Different Types of Data** – discover more about variables, and ultimately objects, in a chapter that discusses data types.

❑ **Chapter 6: Working with Collections of Data** – learn how to store collections of data in programming structures such as arrays, arraylists, and hashtables, before looking at namespaces and classes in a bit more detail.

❑ **Chapter 7: Debugging and Error Handling** – errors happen to all of us, so in this chapter, learn the difference between errors and exceptions, and how to cope when it doesn't all go quite to plan.

## Section 2 – Working With Databases

Most websites that have useful functionality built into them will probably rely on a database at some stage or another. These chapters in this section are designed to introduce you to the database management tools in Web Matrix, as well as teaching you how to programmatically access and manipulate data in your code:

❑ **Chapter 8: Working with Databases** – start by creating a database, learn how to connect to this database, and then add data to it. Also, we look at how to connect to the sample databases provided with MSDE.

❑ **Chapter 9: Displaying Data** – discover how simple it is to display data from a database using some of the built-in controls that come with ASP.NET and Web Matrix.

❑ **Chapter 10: Working with Data** – learn what the auto-generated code actually does, and gain a deeper understanding of .NET data management.

### Section 3 – Creating a Website

The third, and final, part of the book involves moving beyond the simple page-by-page model we use to this point, and looking at how to structure pages so that they flow together to form a cohesive unit that is a website. This section also looks at bigger issues involved in this process, such as remembering visitors to your sites and building and consuming web services.

❑ **Chapter 11: Linking to Pages and Files** – turning individual pages into a collection of related resources that form a website, also looking at smartening the appearance of sites using stylesheets.

❑ **Chapter 12: Reusable Content** – encapsulating functionality into user controls that can be reused across a whole site with relative ease, saving hours of development time.

❑ **Chapter 13: Case Study Part 1: Extending your Web Applications** – this chapter opens up our website to the world, and allows users to enter information into our database. Specifically, we'll implement a guest book that our visitors can sign after visiting the site.

❑ **Chapter 14: Case Study Part 2: Identifying your Users** – we move on to the second part of our application, which starts to add authentication to the site, forcing users to log in so that they can access certain functionality.

❑ **Chapter 15: Remembering your Visitors** – at this stage, we discuss remembering our visitors using tools such as cookies, which can store simple information about a visitor to a site. We also look at how users are remembered between pages using session and application state.

❑ **Chapter 16: Web Services** – discover more about web services, one of the buzzwords that many people talk about. Learn how simple it is to create and use web services using Web Matrix.

❑ **Chapter 17: Beyond Web Matrix** – a quick look at where you can go next having learned how to use Web Matrix to create simple pages and sites. This chapter previews Visual Studio .NET, and discusses other products available for larger-scale development.

## What You Need to Use This Book

The prerequisite system requirements for this book are intentionally very small so that someone with even the most basic system would be able to get to use the contents of the book with minimal hassle. This book requires that you have one of the following installed in order to run the examples in the book:

❑ Any version of Windows XP

❑ Windows 2000

You do not need to have a dedicated web server, such as Microsoft's Internet Information Services (IIS), installed to host your web applications since Web Matrix comes with a web server built into it. This is perfectly adequate for everything you will learn in this book but it would be a good upgrade if you want to use more advanced features later on.

## What's on the CD

Included with this book is Microsoft's ASP.NET Web Matrix Project CD which includes the following components:

- ❏ The .NET Framework
- ❏ Web Matrix
- ❏ The Web Matrix guided tour
- ❏ The MSDE database engine
- ❏ The Mobile Internet Toolkit
- ❏ Some additional resources that you may find useful

Full instructions on how to set up your system using this CD are contained in Chapter 1.

> We have to stress that the CD we have included with the book is a Microsoft copyrighted distribution. As such, we at Wrox Press have not been allowed to include our own materials such as a full code download or any other extra resources. You can however, still obtain the code from our website, as we detail later in this introduction.

## Style Conventions

We have used certain layout and font styles in this book that are designed to help you to differentiate between the different kinds of information. Here are examples of the styles that are used, with an explanation of what they mean.

As you'd expect, we present code in two different ways: code used inline with text, and code that is displayed on its own. When we need to mention keywords and other coding specifics within the text (for example, in discussion relating to an `If ... Else` construct or the `System.Web` namespace) we use the single-width font as shown in this sentence. If we want to show a more substantial block of code, then we display it like this:

```
<asp:TextBox id="txtNameBox" runat="server" />
<asp:Button id="btnSubmit" onclick="btnSubmit_Click"
                        runat="server" Text="Click Here!" />
```

Sometimes, you will see code in a mixture of gray and white backgrounds, like this:

```
private void Page_Load(object sender, System.EventArgs e)
{
    HeaderIconImageUrl = Request.ApplicationPath + "/Images/winbook.gif";
    HeaderMessage = "Informative Page";
}
```

In cases like this, we use the gray shading to draw attention to a particular section of the code – perhaps because it is new code, or it is particularly important to this part of the discussion.

*Advice, hints, and background information come in this type of font.*

> **Important pieces of information come in boxes like this.**

Bullets appear indented, with each new bullet marked as follows:

❑ **Important Words** are in a bold type font.

❑ Words that appear on the screen, or in menus like File or Window, are in a similar font to the one you would see on a Windows desktop.

❑ Keys that you press on the keyboard like *Ctrl* and *Enter*, are in italics.

# Customer Support and Feedback

We value feedback from our readers, and we want to know what you think about this book; what you liked, what you didn't like, and what you think we can do better next time. You can send us your comments, either by returning the reply card in the back of the book, or by e-mail to feedback@wrox.com. Please be sure to mention the book's ISBN and title in your message.

## How to Download the Source Code for the Book

When you visit the Wrox site, http://www.wrox.com/, simply locate the title through our search facility or by using one of the title lists. Then you simply need to click on Download Code on the book's detail page to obtain all the code for the book.

When you click to download the code for this book, you are presented with a page that has three options:

❑ If you are already a member of the Wrox Developer Community (in other words. if you have already registered on ASPToday, C#Today, or Wroxbase), you can log in with your usual username and password combination to download the code.

❑ If you are not already a member, you have the option of registering for free code downloads. By registering, you will be able to download several free articles from Wrox Press. It will also enable us to keep you informed about updates and new editions of this book.

❑ The third option is to bypass registration completely and simply download the code.

Registration for code download is *not* mandatory for this book, but if you *do* register for the code download, your details will not be passed to any third party. For more details, you can review our terms and conditions, which are linked from the download page.

When you reach the code download section, you will find that the files that are available for download from our site have been archived using WinZip. When you have saved the files to a folder on your hard drive, you will need to extract the files using a de-compression program such as WinZip or PKUnzip. When you extract the files, the code is extracted into chapter folders, so you need to make sure that your extraction software (WinZip, PKUnzip, and so on) is set to use folder names.

There is an important file included in the code download, ReadMe.htm, which includes more information on how to set up the samples in this book. We strongly recommend you read this file to better understand how the examples are structured.

## Errata

We've made every effort to make sure that there are no errors in the text or in the code. However, no one is perfect and mistakes do occur. If you find an error in one of our books, like a spelling mistake or a faulty piece of code, we would be very grateful for feedback. By sending in errata you may save another reader hours of frustration, and of course, you will be helping us provide even higher quality information. Simply e-mail the information to support@wrox.com, where your information will be checked and, if correct, posted to the errata page for that title, or used in subsequent editions of the book.

To find errata on the web site, go to http://www.wrox.com/, and simply locate the title through our search engine or title list. Click on the Errata link, which is below the cover graphic on the book's detail page.

## Technical Support

If you would like to make a direct query about a problem in the book, you need to e-mail support@wrox.com. A typical e-mail should include the following things:

❑ In the Subject field, tell us the **book title**, the **last four digits of the ISBN** (7922 for this book), and the **page number** of the problem.

❑ In the body of the message, tell use your **name**, **contact information**, and the **problem**.

We *won't* send you junk mail. We need these details to save your time and ours. When you send an e-mail message, it will go through the following chain of support:

1. **Customer Support** – Your message is delivered to one of our customer support staff – they're the first people to read it. They have files on most frequently asked questions and will answer anything general about the book or the website immediately.

2. **The Editorial Team** – Deeper queries are forwarded to the technical editor responsible for the book. They have experience with the programming language or particular product, and are able to answer detailed technical questions on the subject. Once an issue has been resolved, the editor can post the errata to the website.

3. **The Authors** – Finally, in the unlikely event that the editor cannot answer your problem, they will forward the request to the author. We do try to protect the author from any distractions to their writing; however, we are quite happy to forward specific requests to them. All Wrox authors help with the support on their books. They will mail the customer and the editor with their response, and again all readers should benefit.

> Note that the Wrox support process can only offer support to issues that are directly pertinent to the content of our published title. Support for questions that fall outside the scope of normal book support is provided via the community lists of our **http://p2p.wrox.com/** forum.

## *p2p.wrox.com*

For author and peer discussion, join the **P2P mailing lists**. Our unique system provides **programmer to programmer**™ contact on mailing lists, forums, and newsgroups, all *in addition* to our one-to-one e-mail support system. Wrox authors and editors and other industry experts are present on our mailing lists.

At p2p.wrox.com you will find a number of different lists that will help you, not only while you read this book, but also as you develop your own applications. Particularly appropriate to this book are the following lists in the .NET category:

- ❏ aspx
- ❏ aspx_beginners
- ❏ aspx_web_matrix
- ❏ dotnet_jobs
- ❏ dotnet_websites_discuss

To subscribe to a mailing list just follow these steps:

1. Go to http://p2p.wrox.com/

2. Choose the appropriate category from the left menu bar

3. Click on the mailing list you wish to join

4. Follow the instructions to subscribe and fill in your e-mail address and password

5. Reply to the confirmation e-mail you receive

6. Use the subscription manager to join more lists and set your e-mail preferences

# CHAPTER 1

# Installing and Exploring
# Web Matrix

So, you want to be a web developer eh? You want to write great looking Internet applications, but don't want to learn lots of arcane programming stuff? I can't say I blame you – most programming these days is far more complex than it needs to be. However, this doesn't have to be the case, so don't think it's beyond you – we're going to show you something that'll get you creating great applications in no time at all.

When Microsoft released ASP.NET in early 2002, Web development got much easier. The trouble was that it was still too hard for many people. Why? The breadth of what ASP.NET was able to do left some people floundering. Many developers who were used to an older way of creating dynamic web applications were overwhelmed by the scale of ASP.NET. But the problem wasn't with the new features; it was more a case of understanding how to make these new features work, both conceptually, and in practice. The development tool that Microsoft supply is designed for large-scale web application development, and such it is quite complex. It's also expensive – and both of these factors put many people off.

The solution to this particular problem is an easy-to-use tool, at the right price. That's where the Microsoft ASP.NET Web Matrix Project comes in. In this book we're going to teach you how to create great web applications using the easiest, and cheapest of tools. In this chapter we're going to look at:

❑ How and why Web Matrix came to life

❑ How to install the Microsoft .NET Framework, and associated products

❑ How to install the Microsoft Web Matrix development tool

❑ How to use the features available in Web Matrix

As we go through the book you'll see how easy web development can be when using the right tool.

# What is the Microsoft Web Matrix?

Microsoft Web Matrix is a web development tool designed for creating ASP.NET web pages. A simple description, but it doesn't really tell you much, such as what it does, why you should use it, and why it's available in the first place. You might not think those are important questions, but the answers give you some ideas as to why you'd want to use Web Matrix.

When .NET was released, the main development tool promoted was Visual Studio .NET (VS .NET). As Web developers, we've been used to a plethora of tools, but more often than not, when coding old-style ASP pages, we've used Notepad. It's small and quick, but doesn't have any features specifically designed for web development. VS .NET brought a really rich design-time environment, including database support, drag-and-drop design, and so on. However, VS .NET is an advanced development tool, with many features not required by many people creating ASP.NET applications.

The Web Matrix Project on the other hand, was designed with ASP.NET in mind. It's very small (it fits on a floppy disk), has great design features, and best of all, it's free!

## Web Matrix Features

Before we dive into the installation, let's take a quick look at the features of Web Matrix, to see why it's so compelling:

- ❑ It's small. This means it's quick to download, copy, or distribute to friends. It also means it doesn't take much memory or disk space.

- ❑ It has got great design features, such as a drag-and-drop page designer, templates for existing web pages, pre-supplied code, and so on. This makes it extremely easy to use.

- ❑ It doesn't require any other files. VS .NET uses a project-based system that creates extra files to manage a project. Web Matrix just uses a single file for each web page, and doesn't rely on any built-in features. This means that you can edit the pages in any other code editor if you need to.

- ❑ Community support. There's built-in support for links to the ASP.NET community, including the news groups and mailing lists.

Oh, and did I mention it's free? You can (and are encouraged to) freely distribute Web Matrix. Let's now run through the installation so you get to play with Web Matrix as quickly as possible.

# Installation

Installation of Web Matrix is simple, and takes place in several steps. Inserting the Web Matrix CD (included in the back of this book) will bring up a web page outlining the installation steps. If the web page doesn't appear, then just run the `startcd.exe` program from the CD directly – this will launch the start page.

## Installing Microsoft .NET

Before you can install Web Matrix you need to install the .NET Framework. If you've already got this installed then you can skip this step. The version on the Web Matrix CD is .NET Framework 1.0. From the main start page from the CD you'll see a set of steps, labeled 1 to 4. If you follow these in order you end up doing more work than is necessary, so skip straight to Step 4.

*The .NET Framework SDK, installed in Step 4, includes the .NET Framework, the MSDE database setup utility, the ASP.NET quickstart code samples, and the .NET Framework documentation. The only thing it doesn't include is Web Matrix, which we'll install from Step 2.*

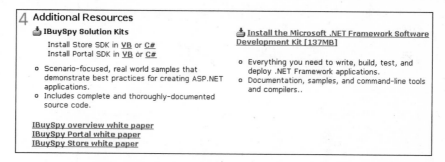

**1.** Pick the right hand link, to install the Microsoft .NET Framework Software Development Kit (SDK). This installs .NET version 1.0, plus all of the documentation:

**2.** Click **Open** to start the installation. You may receive this warning:

This just tells you that you haven't got a web server installed on the machine. Don't worry about this, as Web Matrix comes with its own web server, so you don't have to install a web server separately.

*If you have IIS installed on your system, you can use either the IIS web server, or the web matrix web server once you've installed Web Matrix – the Web Matrix installation doesn't overwrite anything, and the two co-exist nicely.*

So if you do see this message, just press Continue and you should see the following:

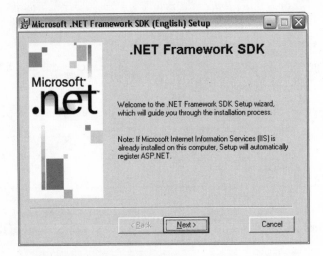

**3.** Press Next to start the installation wizard:

**4.** Select I accept the agreement, and press **Next** to continue:

**5.** Make sure that both optional checkboxes are ticked, and press **Next**:

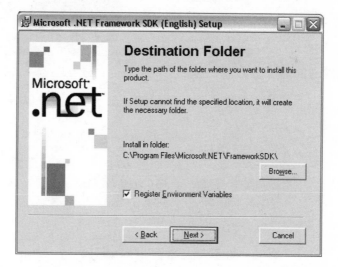

**6.** Leave the settings at their defaults, and press **Next**. This starts the SDK installation, and it's time to go and make a cup of coffee – watching the install screen is rather dull.

*Once this stage of the installation is finished, you can, and should, take time to install the service packs (which are updates designed to fix small bugs and potential security holes in the Framework). You can either install just the first service pack from the CD (as linked in Step 1), or you can go to the Microsoft Windows Update site (http://www.windowsupdate.com) and download the most recent service packs.*

## *Installing the Database Server Software*

Once the SDK installation has finished, you need to install the database server software – this will allow you to run the sample applications, as well as create your own databases.

**1.** Select the Microsoft .NET Framework SDK program group, and then select Samples and QuickStart Tutorials.

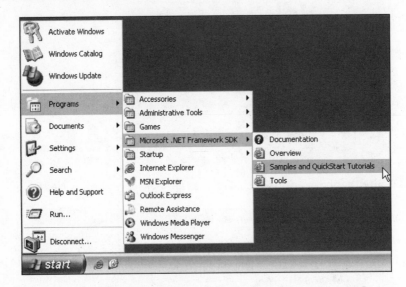

**2.** From the resulting page, select Step 1: Install the .NET Framework Samples Database:

**3.** You'll then be prompted with the following – select Open. This will install the database software.

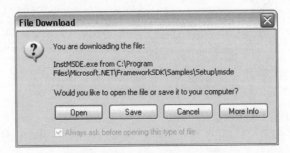

**4.** After rebooting your system, if you have IIS installed on your system, you can continue to Step 2 of the quickstart installation, and install the samples and tutorials. Included in this installation are four sample databases, one of which we'll be using later on, so we recommend that you then run Step 2 in the installation.

**Step 2: Set up the QuickStarts**
Because the QuickStarts demonstrate a wide variety of the .NET Framework technologies, some machine configuration is required. The link above configures your machine to run the QuickStarts. This includes importing four sample databases into the MSDE database server, creating several Internet Information Services (IIS) virtual directories, and compiling several samples. In order to complete these operations, you must be logged in using an account with Administrator privileges. For a complete list of tasks accomplished in this step, including manual instructions for configuring the QuickStarts, see the Configuration Details document.

## Installing the Sample Databases Manually

If you don't have IIS installed on your system, you can install it (on compatible operating systems) by following the instructions in Appendix A, then follow Step 2. For those of you who don't have the option of installing IIS (if you're running Windows XP Home Edition, or if you simply don't want to install IIS), you need to run some different code to install the database we'll use later in the book. You need to run a small installation script, available with the Chapter01 code download for this book (the details of how to download the code for this book are in the Introduction).

To install the databases using the installation script file in the code download for this chapter, open the Chapter01 folder, within the BegWebMatrix downloaded folder. Run the InstallDatabases.bat file, and the installation script will run and install the databases. When it's finished running, you will see the following screen:

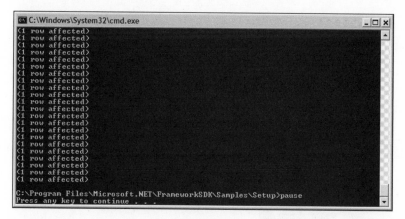

This script is also very useful if ever you need to restore the sample databases, for example, if you've inserted or deleted data from the sample databases and want to return them to their initial state. Whenever you want to do this, simply re-run this script, and the Northwind, Pubs, Grocer To Go, and Portal databases will be restored.

*After this installation, you will have a database configured to run with the instance name of (local)\NetSDK, and you will have access to four sample databases on that server. You'll find out more about what this actually means in Chapter 8.*

## Installing Web Matrix

At this stage you now have both .NET and database software installed. All that's left is Web Matrix. Now you can switch back to the screen from the CD (if it's closed just run `startcd.exe` from the root directory of the CD), and scroll to Section 2:

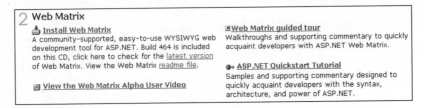

**1.** To install Web Matrix click the first link, to give the following:

**2.** Click Open to start the installation:

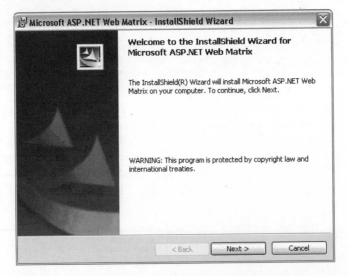

**3.** Click Next to continue:

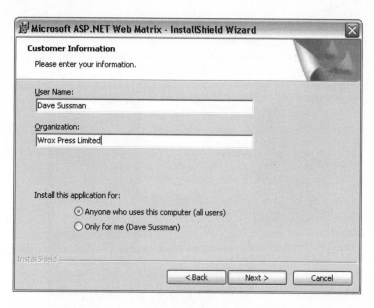

**4.** Enter your User Name and Organization (you can leave this blank if you like). By default the Web Matrix will be available for all users who use the computer, but you can make it available only to yourself. I'd recommend leaving the default here. Press Next to get to the features screen:

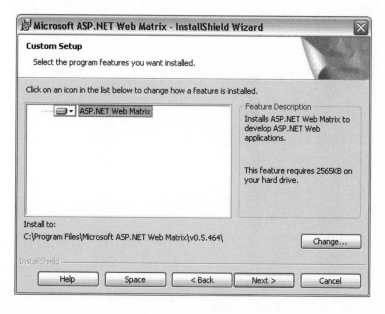

**5.** Since Web Matrix is very small and has all of its features included, there's not much to choose here. Just leave the settings as they are and press **Next** to perform the installation.

**6.** Once complete you can check to see if the installation was successful by running Web Matrix – there will be a new menu under the **Programs** menu from the **Start** button – it will be labeled **Microsoft ASP.NET Web Matrix**:

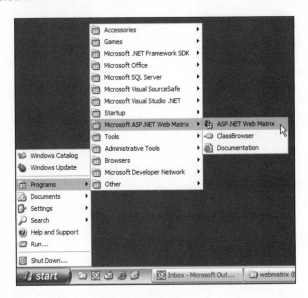

Upon starting Web Matrix you'll see the following screen:

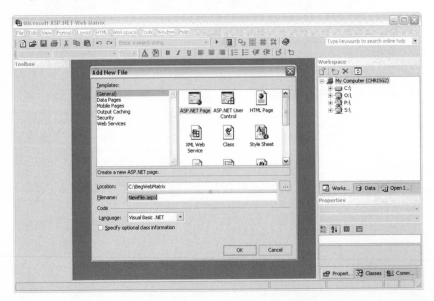

We'll look at these options a little later, but now you know it works, let's carry on looking at the installation options.

## Tours and Tutorials

As part of the set up routine from the Web Matrix CD there are three extra features. The first is a video, with some interviews with users of Web Matrix, telling you how great it is.

### The Web Matrix Guided Tour

The second is the guided tour – a set of HTML pages explaining how some of the features can be used.

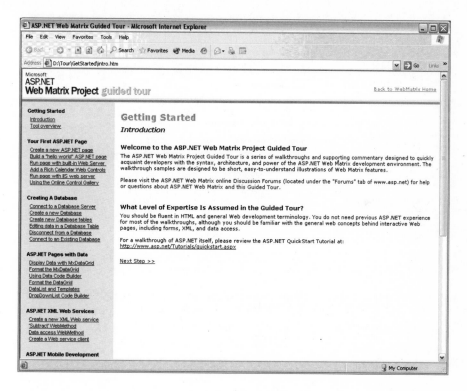

### ASP.NET Quickstart Tutorial

The third is the tutorial for ASP.NET itself.

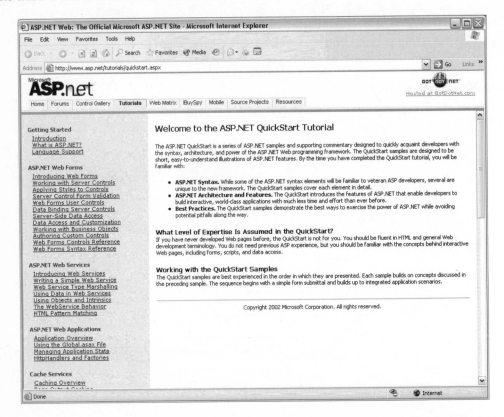

You don't need to explore any of these in detail yet, so let's carry on with the installation. However, once you've started using ASP.NET it's worth spending some time browsing through the ASP.NET QuickStart Tutorial. It's full of great examples of ASP.NET.

## Visit the Web Site

The home of ASP.NET is shown in the last step of the installation screen:

5 Visit www.asp.net and sign up for the forums

This site is maintained by the Microsoft team that develops ASP.NET, and should be on your Favorites list. Not only is it where new announcements are made, where articles are posted, and where controls are available, but it also provides a set of forums. These are invaluable for getting help with ASP.NET problems, and it's well worth joining.

# A Tour of Web Matrix

Now you've done all of the installation tasks, it's time to start looking into Web Matrix, to see exactly what features it has, and how to use them. This will be a quick tour around the interface so you know what each section is, and how it's used. The specifics of each area will be investigated in later chapters, as each becomes relevant.

## New Item Dialog

Let's start with the New Item dialog. This is what you see when you want to create a new ASP.NET file, and is the first thing you see when you run Web Matrix:

At the top we have two sections for templates – one for the type of template, and one for the template itself. Underneath that we have two text entry areas, where you can specify the location of the file, and its name. You should make sure you leave the file suffix (.aspx in this case) at the end of the file name, since Web Matrix doesn't automatically add one.

In the Code section at the bottom of the screen, there is a selection list to pick the language you want to use when writing code. We're going to be using Visual Basic .NET in this book (the other language you could use is C#). Finally there is a checkbox to allow you to specify advanced features for the new file. This is useful if you need to change the default class name and namespace for the file – we'll be keeping the defaults so you should leave this unchecked unless told to change it.

## *Templates*

Templates in Web Matrix act just like templates in other tools, such as Microsoft Word or Front Page. They provide a default for the style and content of the page. In some cases with Web Matrix the templates provide almost all you need to create great web pages. There are six template types, or groups:

- ❑ **(General)**. General templates for all types of ASP.NET pages. These don't have much in the way of content or code.

- ❑ **Data Pages**. Data pages, containing grids and lists. These have lots of code already in place, and provide a quick way to have pages that show tables of data from a database.

- ❑ **Mobile Pages**. For creating pages to be used on mobile devices, such as phones. The Mobile Internet Toolkit needs to be installed for this, which is Step 3 on the Web Matrix install page. We won't be looking at mobile devices in this book, but for more information have a look on the Wrox website – there are several books that cover this in detail.

- ❑ **Output Caching**. Pages that are cached in memory, and are therefore faster.

- ❑ **Security**. Login and logout pages, for creating secure websites.

- ❑ **Web Services**. Pages that can be called remotely by other applications. Web services are Internet applications that just provide functionality, and have no interface, allowing companies to use your code. For example, Amazon has a web service that allows you to programmatically access its database, search for files, access your wish list, and so on.

You'll see many of these in use as we go through the book, but feel free to have a play with them yourself.

To learn about the rest of the interface, let's show you the main areas of Web Matrix. To do that we need to create a new Web page, so select the **(General)** tab, and from the templates pick **ASP.NET Page**. You'll now need to specify the name and location for the file. You can leave the name of the file set to `NewFile.aspx` if you like, but change the directory for your file to `C:\BegWebMatrix` – you may need to create this directory if it doesn't already exist.

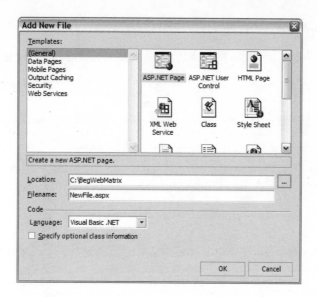

We recommend using a separate directory so that the web pages you create as you work through this book are kept separate from your other documents. In general, it's a good idea to create a separate directory for each set of files you are working on – this stops you getting them mixed up with each other. Once you've typed in the Location and Filename, press the OK button.

# The Main Window

You are now in the main window of Web Matrix, which has several areas:

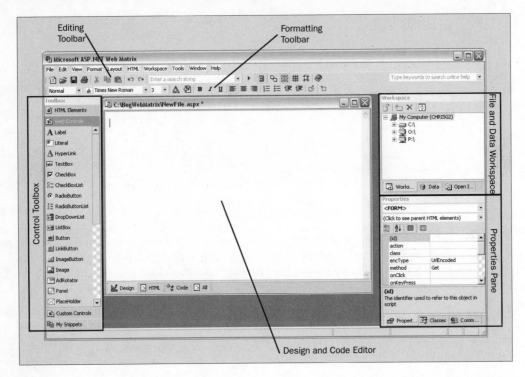

The file that you've just created is shown in the center – this is the **Design and Code Editor**. To the left, we have the **Control Toolbox**, which is where the web controls sit. Web controls are the way we provide content on our page – they can create buttons, areas for inputting text, and so on. We'll be covering them in more detail in Chapter 3.

To the right we have the **File and Data Workspace**, showing the files and directories and databases you are working with. Below that is the **Properties** pane, showing the properties for a selected item on the **Design** editor. At the top we have the **Editing** and **Formatting** toolbars, allowing you to change files, and modify the formatting and style of controls on your form.

Let's now have a look at these areas in turn.

# Design, HTML, and Code Pane

This area is the main work area, and shows you different views of your web page. By default you're shown the **Design** view, which gives you a visual view of your page. The HTML tab switches you to a view that shows the HTML equivalent of the design, and the **Code** view shows only the code associated with the page. The **All** tab shows all views together.

Let's have a go at using these tabs, so you get familiar with how they work.

1. If you haven't already got a file open (if you have, skip to Step 3), create a new ASP.NET file. To do this select New from the File menu, hit *Ctrl-N*, or use the New File toolbar button – that's the one that looks like this: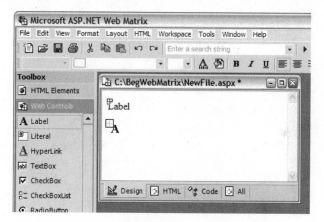

2. From the New File dialog, make sure the path is set to C:\BegWebMatrix (or any other path you wish to use), enter a name for the file, and press OK.

3. With the new file open, and the Design tab selected, pick a control from the Toolbox on the left. Start with a Label control, and drag it onto the Design surface and drop it there.

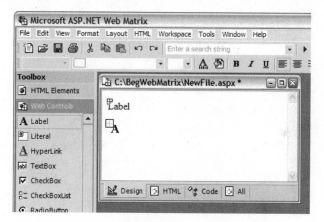

4. Do the same with a TextBox, and drop it next to the Label.

5. On the Design surface, place the cursor on the page to the right of the TextBox and press the *Return* key.

6. Now drag a DataGrid from the Toolbox and drop it under the Label and TextBox. Your page should now look like this:

**7.** Click the HTML, Code, and All tabs, and note how what's shown in the window changes. You're still dealing with the same file, it's just that the tabs give you a different view of that file. We'll be using these other tabs more as we go through the book.

## Properties and Formatting

At the bottom right of Web Matrix there's the Properties tab, which allows you to set the details on controls. Let's have a quick look at what you can do with these.

---

**Try It Out**  **Changing the Look**

**1.** Switch the main window back to Design view, and click on the Label.

**2.** In the Properties pane, you'll notice that there are two columns. The first column shows the name of the property, and the second shows the value. Scroll down to find the Text property, and change the text from Label to Enter your name:

**3.** From the formatting toolbar, click the bold button – this will turn the text for the label bold.

**4.** Now pick a different font and size from the drop-down list on the toolbar – I seem to have one called Poor Richard (who Richard is and why we should feel sorry for him is a mystery to me!). We look at fonts in more detail in Chapter 3.

**5.** Click on the TextBox and move to the Properties window.

**6.** Pick a color for the BorderColor property, change the BorderStyle to Dashed, and enter 5 for the BorderWidth.

**7.** Click on the DataGrid, and move to the Properties window.

**8.** At the bottom of the properties window you see two links in blue:

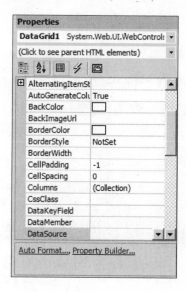

**9.** Click the Auto Format... link, to bring up the formatter. This is just like formatting tables in Word:

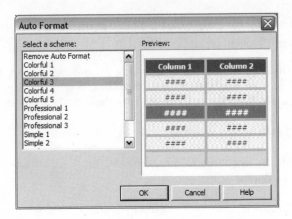

**10.** Pick a style of your choice, and click OK.

**11.** Your page should now look something like this:

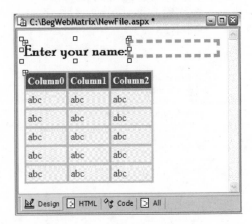

OK, it doesn't look particularly great, but you can see how the properties affect the controls. You can press *F5* to run this program in your browser. The first time you do this you'll see a message called Start Web Application – make sure that Use ASP.NET Web Matrix Server is selected and press Start. In the next chapter we'll create a more useful page and run it, so you'll get more practice of controls and properties. Let's now continue with our tour of the Web Matrix interface.

## Toolbars and Menus

The toolbars and menus are, for the most part, fairly obvious. However, a brief explanation never goes amiss, so let's start with the menu:

- ❏ **File:** Standard type of file menu, allowing addition of new files, saving files, printing, and so on.

- ❏ **Edit:** Cut, copy, paste, find, replace and so on.

- ❏ **View:** Allows switching between the different views (Design, HTML, Code, All), as well as some design view features (which are also shown on the design toolbar).

- ❏ **Format:** Mirrors some functionality of the formatting toolbar, allowing font changes, alignment, and so on.

- ❏ **Layout:** Allows alignment and sizing of controls.

- ❏ **HTML:** Allows insertion of standard HTML features, such as a hyperlink or a table. The issue of which controls to use is covered in Chapter 3.

- ❏ **Workspace:** Allows addition of new items, and connections to remote websites.

- ❏ **Tools:** Web Matrix tools, such as customization of the toolbox.

- ❏ **Window:** Cascade, Tile, and so on.

- ❏ **Help.** Links to the help file and URLs.

The two toolbars are equally sensible. The first is the editing toolbar:

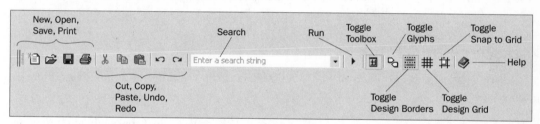

The second is the formatting toolbar:

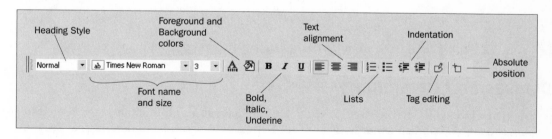

## Toolbox

You've already used the Toolbox, but it does warrant a little explanation. It works in much the same way as the Outlook Bar works in Microsoft Outlook, where there are different pop-up tab sections, and only one section is visible at once. There are five sections:

❑   HTML Elements, which contains the standard HTML controls

❑   Web Controls, which contains the ASP.NET Web Controls

❑   Custom Controls, for custom controls written by third parties

❑   Code Builders, for wizards that write code for you

❑   My Snippets, for snippets of code you want to keep and reuse

The Code Builders section is only viewable when you are viewing code via the Code tab or the All tab. You'll see examples of all of these in later chapters of the book. They all work in the same way though – you drag from the Toolbox onto your page. When in design view, the control appears on the design surface. When in code view, dragging a Code Builder starts a wizard that writes code, which is then inserted into the code at the position you dragged to (so, make sure you drag these onto an empty line). It's worth having a play with these, just so you are familiar with what they do. Don't worry about messing up your file, since you don't have to save it when you quit Web Matrix.

## Workspace and Data

The Workspaces area at the top right of Web Matrix deals with files and data. Here there are three tabs:

❑   Workspace, showing a view on your current disk (or FTP site if that's what you're using)

❑   Data, showing connections to databases, and the tables within the databases

❑   Open Items, showing a list of files currently open

Using the Workspace is covered in the next two chapters, and the Data tab is covered Chapter 8.

## Classes and Community

The two windows we haven't yet looked at are the Classes and Community tabs, which sit alongside the Properties window. The first of these shows all of the underlying classes that make up the .NET Framework. Some of these you may use as you get more experienced, some you may never use, and some just aren't relevant to ASP.NET. However, it's useful for exploring, and to understand what classes are available for use. Classes and code are covered in Chapters 4 to 6.

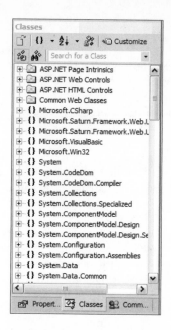

The Community window gives you links to the best places on the web for ASP.NET resources. Among these are the forums from http://www.asp.net/, where you can find a great many people available to help with any ASP.NET-related trouble you might be having, and also, some of the ASP.NET development team from Microsoft hang out there.

# Summary

This chapter has been all about beginnings. It's the start of a journey that will turn you into a web developer. Like many things in life, experience counts, so we need to gain that experience, and the only way to do that is actually do things. Yoda put it succinctly in a Star Wars film – "Try not. Do." So in this chapter we've "done". We've taken the first step towards our goal of learning how to create great web applications.

We started with installing the tools we needed – the Microsoft .NET Framework, a database, the Web Matrix development tool, and a whole bunch of documentation. This is exactly the same procedure that experienced web developers run through, so you're already on that journey – doing the things that need doing.

We then examined the Web Matrix itself, having a look at its features, and how you use them. We created a web page, dragged some controls on, and set some properties. Pretty easy stuff, but then most of what you'll be doing in the book starts with that easy stuff; how hard can it be? So, let's get on with it, and start creating some real web pages, that have real content, and allow the user to enter data and interact with them.

# CHAPTER 2

# Writing your First ASP.NET Web Page

In the previous chapter we installed both .NET and the Web Matrix, and we briefly examined the visual interface. Now it's time to start using that interface to create some web pages – after all, that's what you're really here for. So, what you are going to do is create your first web page, which will consist of some visual elements, and some code to make the page interactive.

Instead of starting off with the traditionally uninspiring "Hello World" example, we'll be creating a simple game to demonstrate how ASP.NET pages work. That way you can call it work when you play it! Remember, though, that playing Xbox or PS2 games doesn't count (even if you do say it's "User Interface Testing").

In particular we're going to:

❑   Create a new web page

❑   Use the Toolbox to drag controls onto this page

❑   See how to use the Properties window to define some details of these controls

❑   Add some code to make the game run

This will be your first look at creating a page, and you'll be amazed at how simple it is.

## The Snake Eyes Game

Snake eyes is a simple dice game, where you roll a pair of dice trying not to get two 1's (a combination known as, you guessed it, snake eyes!) If you throw any combination other than two 1's, then your total is increased by the value currently shown on the two dice and you roll again. You keep rolling, increasing your score, until two 1's come up, when you 'lose', and your score is set back to 0.

Knowing how the game works gives you an idea of what you need to do. It's always worth thinking about this before you dive in and start coding, as it's always easier to create pages when you've a good idea of what you need. In our page, there needs to be a way to represent the dice, and a way to simulate the roll. There also needs to be some way to keep score. As you build the game, you'll see how we use the controls and code to accomplish this.

## Creating the User Interface

The interface for this game is going to be quite simple. To represent our two dice, we'll be using ASP.NET Label controls, as it's easy to display numbers using these controls. In the next chapter we'll look at the Image control and show how to substitute the labels for pictures of the dice. We'll also need to add a button, to simulate the throwing of the dice. All in all, it's pretty simple.

### Try It Out — Creating the User Interface

1. Start the ASP.NET Web Matrix. If the Add New File dialog isn't showing, you need to display it using one of the following methods:

   - From the toolbar, by selecting the New File button (the one that looks like a sheet of notepaper)
   - From the menu, by selecting File then New
   - By selecting a directory in the Workspace, right-mouse clicking and selecting Add New Item...

2. From this dialog, make sure (General) is selected from the Templates list, and select ASP.NET Page from the list on the right.

**3.** Pick a suitable directory into which you're going to store the file. I've picked C:\BegWebMatrix, but you can choose any directory on your system.

**4.** Make sure the Language is Visual Basic .NET, change the file name to `Dice.aspx`, and press the OK button.

**5.** Click on the page and type the page title, which is Snake Eyes!:

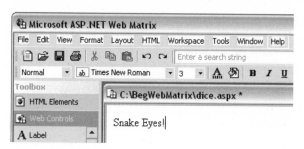

**6.** Since this is the title, we want it to stand out more, so, using the cursor, select the text. When the text is highlighted, select Heading 1 from the style list on the formatting toolbar:

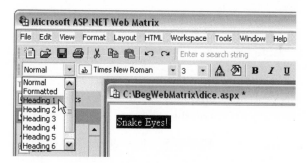

This formats the selected text, just like using the formatting in a word processor:

**7.** Now, place the cursor at the end of this line of text and press *Return*, then type the following:

> Keep going, but don't get two 1's...

**8.** Press *Return* again, then drag two Label controls onto the form from the Web Controls section of the Toolbox:

**9.** These are the labels that will represent the dice, so we want to format them to make them look a bit more like dice, and less like text. As in most other Microsoft products, you can select multiple items by holding down the *Ctrl* key and clicking on the items you wish to select. The second label is already selected, so holding down *Ctrl*, select the first label as well (just click it once with the left mouse button) – this will allow us to apply the same properties to both labels simultaneously.

**10.** Now go to the Properties window, and change the following (note that to access specific font properties, you need to expand the Font properties group within the Properties window by clicking on the + icon):

| Property | Value to use |
|---|---|
| BorderStyle | Solid |
| Font: Name | Verdana |
| Font: Size | X-Large |
| Height | 44px |
| Text | 0 |

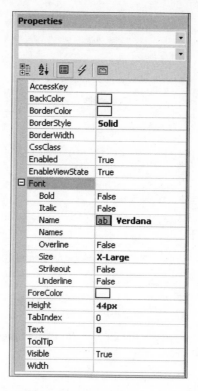

The labels should now look like this:

**11.** Now, back in the design view, click to the right of these labels, press *Return* to place the cursor on the next line below these labels. Add another Label control, changing the Text property to:

Ooops, you did it again :(

and the Visible property to False:

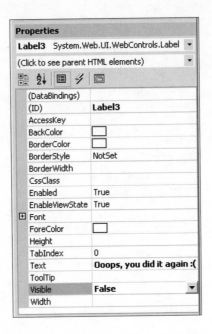

**12.** Back in the design view, place the cursor after this label, press *Return* again, and add a Button to the page, changing the Text property to:

Hit me baby one more time...

**13.** Finally, we need one more label, underneath the button. Press *Return* again and drag on another label, setting the following properties:

| Property | Value to use |
|---|---|
| Font:Name | Verdana |
| Font: Size | X-Large |
| ForeColor | Red |
| Text | 0 |

That's it for the design of this page, so let's have a look at exactly what Web Matrix has done for us.

## How It Works

In the previous chapter, we saw how the page designer has several tabs. The one we've been working with is the Design view, allowing us to use easy drag-and-drop features to add controls to a form. It also allows us to use toolbars to format text, in exactly the same way we'd use a word processor. All of these features are just an easy way of creating HTML, the language of the web page – after all, that's what our web browser is going to display. One of the great features of Web Matrix is that it's a visual design tool, so we get to see what the page looks like as we design it. We also have a Properties window that enables us to change properties on our controls, without having to learn what this really means in HTML.

Let's just have a quick look and see exactly what has been created, and then you'll really see how much easier the designer is to work with than hand-coding HTML. If you click the HTML view tab, what you see is the following code:

```
<html>
<head>
</head>
<body>
  <form runat="server">
    <h1>Snake Eyes!
    </h1>
    <p>
      Keep going, but don't get two 1's...
    </p>
    <p>
      <asp:Label id="Label1" runat="server" BorderStyle="Solid"
            Height="44px" Font-Names="Verdana"
            Font-Size="X-Large">0</asp:Label>
      <asp:Label id="Label2" runat="server" BorderStyle="Solid"
            Height="44px" Font-Names="Verdana"
            Font-Size="X-Large">0</asp:Label>
    </p>
    <p>
      <asp:Label id="Label3" runat="server">
        Ooops, you did it again :(</asp:Label>
    </p>
    <p>
      <asp:Button id="Button1" runat="server"
            Text="Hit me baby one more time...""></asp:Button>
    </p>
    <p>
      <asp:Label id="Label4" runat="server" Font-Names="Verdana"
            Font-Size="X-Large" ForeColor="Red">0</asp:Label>
    </p>
    <!-- Insert content here -->
  </form>
</body>
</html>
```

It won't look quite like this as I've made it a bit neater to make it easier to read on the page, but the *content* is the same. The important point is that the WYSIWYG (What You See Is What You Get) designer lets you see what the page will look like as you design it, while underneath it's creating all of this HTML for you. It's certainly much simpler to work in design view than to write all of this code by hand!

## *Adding the Code*

As it stands this page doesn't do anything; it's simply a visual interface with no interactive elements. Let's add some code to get this game going.

**Try It Out**       **Adding the Code**

1. Switch back to design view, and select the Button control.

2. Now double-click your mouse button, to switch to code view for this Button control.

3. Add the following highlighted lines of code (this code will run every time the button is clicked):

```
Sub Button1_Click(sender As Object, e As EventArgs)

    Label3.Visible = False
    Label1.Text = Int(Rnd() * 6) + 1
    Label2.Text = Int(Rnd() * 6) + 1
    If Label1.Text = "1" And Label2.Text = "1" Then
       Label4.Text = 0
       Label3.Visible = True
    Else
       Label4.Text = CInt(Label4.Text) + _
                   CInt(Label1.Text) + CInt(Label2.Text)
    End If

End Sub
```

4. Now save the file and press *F5* to run the page – you'll be shown the following dialog:

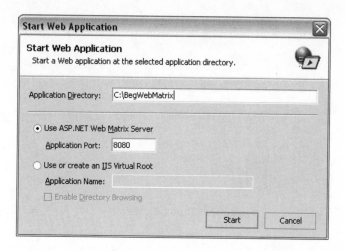

This gives you the choice of running the page using the **ASP.NET Web Matrix Web Server,** or via an already configured **Virtual Root.** Just leave it set to the first option, and press the **Start** button. The Web Matrix Web Server is started and the page runs:

**5.** Press the button a few times and see how the dice 'roll', and the score is increased:

Keep going until you get two 1's on the dice (this may take some time – I got up to over 700 before this happened to me!):

Notice how the score has been reset, and our hidden label has now appeared.

## How It Works

Let's look at how this code works. We'll be looking at code in more detail in Chapters 4, 5, and 6, so we won't go into a great deal of detail on the structure. However, it's really important to examine how we can set the properties in code – this way you can see how what you do to the code affects the properties you set in the **Property** window.

First off, let's see the code in its entirety:

```
Sub Button1_Click(sender As Object, e As EventArgs)

  Label3.Visible = False
  Label1.Text = Int(Rnd() * 6) + 1
  Label2.Text = Int(Rnd() * 6) + 1
  If Label1.Text = "1" And Label2.Text = "1" Then
    Label4.Text = 0
    Label3.Visible = True
  Else
    Label4.Text = CInt(Label4.Text) + _
                  CInt(Label1.Text) + CInt(Label2.Text)
  End If

End Sub
```

Notice that all of the code is within the Sub ... End Sub lines. This means that we have created a **subroutine**, sometimes known as a **procedure**. We'll look at these in detail in Chapter 4. Since this procedure was created by double-clicking the button, the code will only run when the button is clicked. Clicking the button when the page is running is called an **event**, and the procedure that runs when an event happens is called the **event procedure**. This means that we can have several buttons on page, each with its own bit of code (event procedure), and the procedures keep these bits of code separate. We're going to modify this game a little later and you'll see how this works.

OK, let's look at the code in detail, taking it line by line. The first thing we do is set the Visible property of Label3 to False, which means the label won't be shown on the page:

```
Label3.Visible = False
```

This is exactly the same as setting the Visible property in the **Properties** window – remember how we did that earlier when put the label on the page and changed its properties? "But hang on", I hear you say, "you already did then when you set the properties in design view – why do it again?" The difference is that when setting a value for a property at design time, that's the value the property will have unless it's changed in code. "Yeah, but why change it in code to the same value it's already got?" you argue. Well, later in the code we might be changing this property to True, thus making the label *visible*. This will happen when you lose a game. Once a game is lost you can start another one by simply pressing the button, and when starting a new game we *don't* want the label to be shown. So that's why we make it invisible – if we've lost a game and are starting a new one.

Next we need to roll the dice. We have two dice, represented by `Label1` and `Label2`, so we need to set the `Text` property on these labels to the values of the dice:

```
Label1.Text = Int(Rnd() * 6) + 1
Label2.Text = Int(Rnd() * 6) + 1
```

This looks a bit complex, but it's actually quite simple. Each line of code produces a random number between 1 and 6, and places the resulting values in the labels we are using to simulate the dice. The dice roll actually does the following:

- ❑ `Rnd()` produces a random number greater than or equal to 0, but less than 1.

- ❑ We multiply that by 6, so it is now greater than equal to 0, but less than 6.

- ❑ We use `Int` to convert it to an **integer**. This means that numbers with decimals, such as 4.32 become rounded to a whole number (in this particular example, we end up with 4).

- ❑ We add 1 to our result to bring it within the range 1 to 6.

Once we've got the two values for the dice we need to see if two 1's have been rolled, because that's what determines a lost game. The values of our dice are stored in the `Text` property of our two labels, so we examine this property to see if they are both equal to "1".

```
If Label1.Text = "1" And Label2.Text = "1" Then
```

If they are both 1, then the game is over. We reset the score to 0, and show the 'you lose' message in the third label control by setting its `Visible` property to `True`.

```
Label4.Text = 0
Label3.Visible = True
```

If it's *not* a losing throw, then we need to add the scores on the dice to the current score. To do this, we use a Visual Basic .NET function called `CInt`, which converts a string value into a number (converting a text representation of a number to a number the computer can work with *as* a number). Don't worry too much about this – Chapter 5 will explain all about this sort of thing. For the moment, all you need to know is that we are adding the dice values to the score:

```
Else
    Label4.Text = CInt(Label4.Text) + _
                  CInt(Label1.Text) + CInt(Label2.Text)
End If
```

`Label4` contains the current score, and `Label1` and `Label2` the values on the dice.

That's all there is to the code. It may look a little complex, and some of it may be confusing (especially if you haven't done any programming before), but be patient. Just revel in the fact that you've written your first ASP.NET web page. Go on. Sit back and feel smug. Feels good doesn't it? OK, you've still got lots to learn, but there's plenty of time.

# Remembering Information

Before we get into more about pages, let's do some more to this game, as there is at least one thing wrong with it. The problem is that when you lose a game, the score is immediately reset to 0, so you can't see what score you did get before the losing roll. What we need is a way to remember the score, and possibly a high score too. Let's give it a go.

| Try It Out | Saving the Scores |
|---|---|

1. Make sure you are in the design view for the web page (just hit the **Design** tab if not).

2. Select the **score** label, and from the **Edit** menu select **Copy**. You can also just press *Ctrl-C*, or use **Copy** from the menu that appears if you click the right mouse button on this label. We want our scores to all look the same, so rather than adding new labels and setting the font and color, we'll just copy the existing score label.

3. Add some text under the score label, saying:

    Last Score:

4. Now, from the **Edit** menu select **Paste** (or press *Ctrl-V*). This pastes a copy of the score label, and gives it a new name (`Label5`) and saves us having to do the formatting.

5. Now add more text underneath that:

    High Score:

6. Now paste another copy of the score label. This will be called `Label6`. Your page should now look like this:

We now need to add some more code to deal with these scores. Save the page before continuing (frequent saving is always a good idea with any product, but especially with a technology preview such as the Matrix!)

**7.** Switch to **Code** view by clicking on the **Code** tab, and modify the code adding in the following highlighted lines:

```
Label3.Visible = False
Label1.Text = Int(Rnd() * 6) + 1
Label2.Text = Int(Rnd() * 6) + 1
If Label1.Text = "1" And Label2.Text = "1" Then
  Label5.Text = Label4.Text
  If CInt(Label5.Text) > CInt(Label6.Text) Then
    Label6.Text = label5.Text
  End If
  Label4.Text = 0
  Label3.Visible = True
Else
  Label4.Text = CInt(Label4.Text) + _
          CInt(Label1.Text) + CInt(Label2.Text)
End If
```

**8.** Save the file and press *F5* again to rerun the program. This time you'll notice that we have two new labels. Keep playing for a while and watch how they work:

## How It Works

Let's see how this works. Remember that we have two new labels – Label5 is for recording the last score, and Label6 is for the high score.

The first thing we do if a game is over is to keep a copy of the current score. This is stored in Label4, so we copy that to Label5:

```
Label5.Text = Label4.Text
```

Now we want to see if this score is bigger than the current high score (which is 0, when the game starts). So, we use the CInt function again, to convert our scores into numbers, allowing us to compare them programmatically. Here we see if the current score (Label5) is greater than the high score (Label6). If it is, then we simply replace the high score with the current score.

```
If CInt(Label5.Text) > CInt(Label6.Text) Then
  Label6.Text = label5.Text
End If
```

You can see that, not only is creating a web page simple, but modifying it is too. It's easy to add controls to a page, and to change existing code. But what about adding new code? Remember how we said earlier that the code for the button is kept separate from any other code? Let's give this a go, just to see how it's done – we'll add another button that resets our high scores.

### Try It Out    Reset the High Score

1.  Make sure you are in the Design view for the page (just hit the Design tab if not).

2.  Add another button underneath the high score, and change its Text property to:

    Reset High Scores

3.  Double-click the button to view its code, and add the following:

```
Sub Button2_Click(sender As Object, e As EventArgs)

    Label6.Text = 0

End Sub
```

4.  Save the page and run it again. Play the game until you get a high score, and then reset it by clicking the new button. Notice that only the high score is reset, and nothing else happens.

### How It Works

Actually, how it works is something you really don't need to worry about too much at this stage. We'll be covering this in more detail in later chapters. For now, all you have to remember is that, if you have a button, and an event procedure for that button, then the code for each button is separate, and only run when that button is pushed. You'll see this technique used often in ASP.NET web pages, and there will be plenty of examples of this as we work through the book.

# Summary

Although this is a short chapter, you've actually covered a lot of ground. What you've learned is how to work with Web Matrix and how to build pages, using both the Design view and the Code view. In particular you've seen how to:

❑   Create a new ASP.NET web page

❑   Use the Toolbox to drag controls onto a page

❑   Use the Properties window to set properties on controls

❑   Add code to controls

❑   Run your page

Some of what you've seen might be simple, but that's the whole point – Web Matrix isn't hard to use! As we go through the book you'll find this lesson pays off as you realize you are comfortable with the way pages are designed. We're going to reinforce this lesson in the next chapter, when we look at creating user interfaces in more detail.

# CHAPTER 3

# Creating Web Pages

In the previous chapter you created your first web page, and you saw how easy it was to do. You might now be asking yourself, "Surely there must be more to it than this?" Well, Web Matrix makes it easy for us to create simple pages, like our dice game. You already know enough to *create* simple web pages, but wouldn't it be great to make them look great, and make it possible for users to interact with them? Sure it would, so that's what we'll be covering in this chapter.

In particular we'll be looking at the topics that bring web pages alive:

- ❑ How to design and lay out pages
- ❑ How we can get information from the user
- ❑ Creating web pages that react intelligently to the user

This may sound like a lot to learn, but it's all well within your capabilities. We'll start with a quick look at **HTML** and the **ASP.NET controls** so you understand how they work. Then, we'll move into talking about displaying content, capturing user input, and then processing user input.

## How it all Works

Before we dive into the meat of creating pages, a little explanation is required. It's important that you know how the whole process of the Web works, from the user requesting a page, through what happens in ASP.NET, to what the user gets back. It's fairly simple:

- ❑ The user **requests** a page. This can either be from typing it in the address bar of a browser, or by clicking a link on a page.
- ❑ The request is **sent** to the web server hosting that page.
- ❑ The web server does one of two things:
    - ❑ For a pure HTML page it sends the page straight back to the user.

❑ For dynamic pages (such as ASP.NET), the server **processes** the page. This means that ASP.NET will examine the page and see if there's anything it needs to do. This is defined as **server-side processing,** as it's happening on the server. The end result of the processing is HTML, which is sent back to the user.

❑ The user receives the HTML page, and the browser examines the HTML and shows the page with all of the formatting – this is called **rendering.**

The important point is that HTML is rendered by the browser, on the user's machine. All the server sends back is a stream of text.

## What is HTML?

The basis of all web documents is **HTML**, the **HyperText Markup Language**. HTML is a way of annotating text to define the look and feel of a page. For example, consider the following:

```
<h1>Some Poetry</h1>
<font face="Verdana" size="5">
Tiger, Tiger, <b>burning</b> bright <br />
It looks like your tail's alight
</font>
```

The HTML is the bits in angle brackets, < and >. These are called **HTML tags,** and they specify *how* the text within the elements formed by pairs of tags should be shown. The ones above are:

❑ <h1> </h1> – The text within this element is a heading. There are 6 standard headings levels, ranging from h1 to h6.

❑ <font> </font> – Defines what font should be used for the enclosed text.

❑ <b> </b> – The text should be shown in bold.

❑ <br /> – Output a new line.

There are two types of HTML elements – those that have start *and* end tags and enclose text (like the heading and bold ones), and those that have a *single tag* (like the new line). The new line one illustrates an interesting point about HTML – it ignores repeated whitespace (space and tab characters) and new lines in the text. You have to specifically add these if required.

HTML Elements can also have **attributes**, which these specify additional characteristics of the element. For example, in the font tag above we specified a specific font and size to use. The attributes consist of a name and value (often called a **name-value pair**). Here, we said that the browser should use the font called Verdana (in HTML the font name is called its face), and a size of 5.

When creating pages using the Web Matrix designer, the Toolbox has a tab called HTML Elements. Dragging these onto a page automatically creates HTML elements for you, and you can use the Properties window to set the attributes.

## Web Controls

One of the other tabs in the **Toolbox** is the **Web Controls** tab, which contains similar elements to the **HTML Elements** tab. You can drag these onto pages in just the same way as HTML elements, so what's the difference? Underneath, these web controls actually *produce* HTML, so in many cases, there seems to be little difference, but it's actually a little more important than that.

Web controls provide a more consistent and easily understood view of what you want on a page. For example, on the **HTML Elements** tab what are Div, Span, Anchor? What's the difference between TextBox and TextArea? If you don't know HTML this can be confusing. Web controls have been designed to avoid this confusion. For example, the TextBox and TextArea are essentially the same, the former being for single lines of text, and the latter being for multiple lines. Web controls just have a single control called TextBox, and you can set a property to define how many rows it allows.

Web controls are also **server based controls**, which means that they are designed to be processed on the server.

# Processing on the Server

So how does ASP.NET know what parts of a page it can process and what is HTML? There are two ways, although for the most part when using Web Matrix you're unaware of them. That's because Web Matrix lets you use the page designer, so the underlying code is hidden. As a result of this, you won't need to add these yourself, but it's worth knowing what they are so that when you use the **HTML** view you can understand what's what.

The first of these methods is by the addition of a specific attribute to an element. This is the runat attribute, which has a value of server. For example, consider the following HTML tag:

```
<input type="text">
```

The input element, unsurprisingly, allows input by the user; it shows up as a textbox in the browser. The trouble with this though, is that it is HTML, and therefore rendered by the browser. How then, can we access the contents of this input element when the server is processing the page? We can't unless we do this:

```
<input type="text" runat="server">
```

Now we've added the runat="server" attribute, the HTML element becomes a hybrid. It's still handled by the browser in the same way, but ASP.NET can also access it. When processed by ASP.NET the runat="server" attribute is stripped off, so the browser only sees the HTML parts.

For web controls, what you see in the HTML view doesn't look like HTML. For example, to allow text entry you use:

```
<asp:TextBox runat="server"></asp:TextBox>
```

This doesn't look like HTML, but because it's a server control, when ASP.NET processes the page, the TextBox actually outputs HTML. In fact, it outputs the following:

```
<input name="_ctl1" type="text" />
```

This is a standard HTML element that the browser knows how to display.

The second way of specifying server-side processing is to use the <% and %> tags. These are specific to ASP.NET and anything within them is handled by ASP.NET, and is never sent back to the browser. We won't be using these much in this book, but it's worth knowing about them so you don't wonder what they are if you see them.

## Should I use HTML or Server Controls?

When designing web pages, you have to make the decision as to whether you are going to use HTML elements or server controls. It seems a confusing choice, because they both provide much the same thing. In actuality, the choice is simple – only use server controls when you need to access the control from ASP.NET code.

For example, when just displaying text you don't even need HTML elements – you can just type the text straight in. You only need to add HTML when you want formatting. If you want to display text from ASP.NET code, then you need a server control, in this case, you could use the Label from the web controls. This is a server control that allows text display.

For text entry and buttons, you'll want to use server controls (TextBox and Button), so that you can use ASP.NET code to process the text. Using the HTML equivalents of these will mean you only get HTML, and they won't be available for use in your ASP.NET pages.

> For the remainder of the book we'll be using web controls unless otherwise noted.

## Page Layout

Before we can talk about layout you have to understand how what you type on a page in design view relates to what you see in your browser. Web pages work by displaying what you put on them, in the order it appears on the page. This is much like the way we read, where what you put on a page just flows from top to bottom, and left to right. However, there are certain HTML elements that don't flow in this way, and so, they cause the layout of a page to be disrupted. Another problem when laying out pages is lining controls up, such as getting textboxes to align vertically. For example, consider the following:

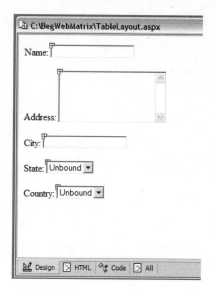

This is standard information to ask the user to supply, but it looks very untidy as the controls aren't lined up. No matter how well your website works, and how flash the design, it will never look professional if the controls are all jumbled like this.

Let's look at a way around this:

## Try It Out    Using HTML Tables for Layout

**1.** Create a new **ASP.NET Page** called `TableLayout.aspx`.

**2.** From the menu bar, select **HTML**, then **Insert Table...** to insert a table 5 rows deep and 2 columns wide. Don't use the `Table` element from the **HTML Elements** tab, as this doesn't offer you the chance to define the number of columns and rows.

**3.** Into the rows for the first column, type the text from the above form: **Name**, **Address**, and so on. Don't worry about the table resizing itself as it is just allowing room for the text you type. Your form should now look like the following:

**4.** For the second column, drag `TextBox` controls from the **Web Controls** toolbox into the first three rows, and `DropDownList` controls into the second two rows.

**5.** For the `TextBox` in the **Address** row, change the `TextMode` property to `MultiLine`, and the `Rows` property to 5:

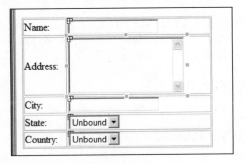

**6.** Save the file, and hit *F5* to run the page:

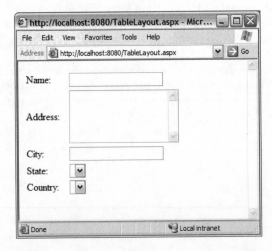

Already, this looks much better as the text entry fields line up neatly. One minor issue is that the label for Address is centered in the middle of the text – it would look better if it were at the top of the text area.

**7.** In Design view, click on the cell that contains the Address: text. From the Properties window change the vAlign property to Top. When you run the page again, the result of this change looks like this:

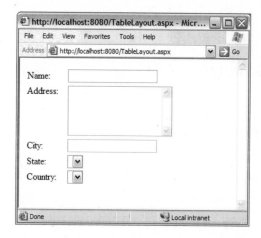

### How It Works

There's not a lot to explain here, since using an HTML table is similar to the way you'd use cells in a spreadsheet, or a ruler and graph paper to line things up. By default, the HTML table you've inserted doesn't show up because the border isn't shown, so the user doesn't see how the alignment is done.

For the Address: text, we changed the vAlign property of the table cell to Top, which indicates that we want any text displayed in the cell to be aligned to the top of the cell. This is only necessary because the cell spans more than one line, and by default, the alignment of text is to the middle of the cell.

# Lights – Improving the Look of the Page

So far in this chapter we've looked at how HTML works, and how controls and text can be laid out on a page to make it look neat and tidy. However, what we haven't looked at are some of the properties that can enhance the page and controls. For example, take the window title bar:

This looks rather messy, and unfriendly – wouldn't it better if we could change this to something more user-friendly?

Another point is that a textbox control will only allow one line of text by default, and the text for the labels is in a set font. This latter point may seem petty, but when you start thinking about readability, certain fonts are much more suitable than others. Let's take a look at how we can make pages look a little nicer.

**Try It Out**  **Formatting Page Elements**

**1.** Create a new ASP.NET Page called `Properties.aspx`.

**2.** Type some text onto the page – enough to make up a paragraph.

**3.** Drag a `Label` and `TextBox` onto the page:

**4.** Copy the text from the first paragraph and paste it underneath the first copy, but above the label and the texbox. Then, change the `Text` property of the label to `Address:`. Your form should look like this now:

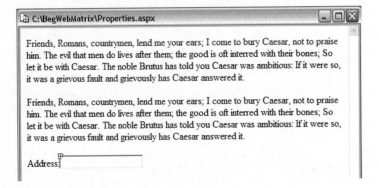

**5.** Select the text for the second paragraph, and from the formatting toolbar, change the font. Use the Verdana font (or Tahoma if Verdana isn't shown), and change the size to 2.

**6.** Select the `TextBox`, and in the **Properties** window change the `TextMode` property to `MultiLine`, and `Rows` to 5.

**7.** From the **View** menu select **Glyphs**.

**8.** Click to the right of the form glyph at the end of the page:

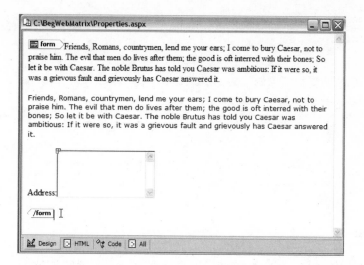

**9.** From the Properties window, change the `bgColor` property. Select a color of your choice – I used a pale yellow, which has a property value of #FFFFC0.

**10.** Switch to HTML view. At the top of the page you'll see:

**11.** Between the `<head>` and `</head>` elements, add the following:

```
<title>Setting Properties and Formatting</title>
```

**12.** Save the page and run it:

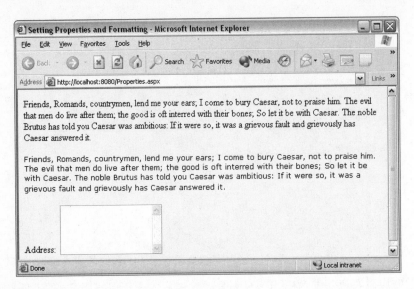

Notice how the page is no longer white, the top title bar contains some descriptive text, and that the second paragraph is easier to read than the first on the screen. You may have noticed the background color changing automatically if you switched to Design view after changing the bgColor property. Let's look at this in detail to see what we've done.

## How It Works

Let's first look at the font. The formatting is simple – just pick the font from the list, much as you would in a word processor. What's important is the font we chose, instead of the default Times New Roman. We used Verdana, which just happens to be much easier to read on screen than many other fonts – and that's an important point, as some fonts are much easier to read when printed, and some are easier to read on the screen. Since this is a web page, it is going to be viewed on screen, so it's best to pick a suitable font. Other fonts that are easy to read on screen are Geneva, Arial, and Helvetica.

One thing to note is what happens if the font you pick isn't on the user's machine. Remember that it is the browser that renders the text. If the user machine doesn't have the font you've requested, then it defaults to Times Roman. To get around this, you can specify multiple fonts; you just need to separate them by commas. For example, you can have something like this:

```
Verdana, Tahoma, Helvetica
```

It's also worth adding the default fonts that should be available to all browsers, on all platforms (remember, the user may not be using Windows). These fonts are:

```
serif, sans-serif, monospace, cursive
```

The second item to look at is the TextBox. In an earlier example we changed the look of this, but didn't explain what the effect was when we changed the properties. We changed the TextMode and Rows properties. TextMode can take one of three values: SingleLine, MultiLine, or Password, which have the following characteristics:

| TextMode | Characteristic |
|---|---|
| SingleLine | Textbox appears as a single line. Carriage returns are not accepted in the text. |
| MultiLine | Textbox has multiple lines. Carriage returns are accepted in the text. |
| Password | Textbox appears as a single line. Carriage returns are not accepted in the text, and entered text is shown as the * character so it can't be read. You'll find out more about this later in the book. |

The Rows property defines how many rows are shown when the textbox is in MultiLine mode. There is a corresponding Columns property, to set how wide (how many characters) the textbox will be. This is useful for not only address fields, but also for general text fields, such as when a lot of text is required.

Changing the background color of the page is probably the most confusing thing in this example. It's not the changing of the property, since you can just pick a color, but it's how you get to it. The problem is that everything we put on a page is within the form glyphs, which aren't normally shown. These identify the area of the page that ASP.NET has control over, but to change the color we need to access the properties of the page itself – or more accurately, the BODY element. This is the HTML element that contains the body of the page (as opposed to specific HTML parts such as the heading area). So, showing the glyphs allows us to select the BODY element, and thus to change the color.

To change the title shown on the title bar of the browser window, we have to use HTML view, since it's not possible to set this from design view in Web Matrix:

```
<head>
  <title>Setting Properties and formatting</title>
</head>
```

Here, we added a title element, and entered our heading text that should be displayed in the title bar of the browser.

# Using Images

We've now seen how to lay out pages and add some formatting to make them look better. Let's take this one step further by looking at the use of **images** within pages. The use of images generally falls into one of two categories – those used for products, such as a CD cover image on Amazon, and those used for styling, such as logos. While both kinds can bring a web page alive, it's easy to mistakenly abuse their use.

The most important thing to remember about images is that they can be big, and big means slower downloading time. It's easy to forget this when you are testing pages on your local machine, but once the page is on a public website, many people will access it through slow connections. Now, *big* doesn't necessarily mean big in terms of how much space it takes on a page, it can also mean its physical size on disk. Resizing an image in Web Matrix doesn't make the image physically smaller when it's sent to the browser. You can resize images by using a specialist graphics tool – I use Paint Shop Pro (see http://www.jasc.com/ for more details). This allows manipulation of the colors and file formats, has some great features, and is pretty cheap.

Let's look at modifying the dice game to add some images.

---

**Try It Out**      **Snake Eyes with Real Dice**

1.  Open up `Dice.aspx` (the one you created in the previous chapter) and create a sub-directory called `Images` (either from Windows Explorer or from the **Workspace** in Web Matrix – just right-click on a directory in the **Workspace** and select **Add New Folder...**).

2.  Copy `Dice.gif`, and the files `1.jpg` to `6.jpg` from the samples directory into the new `Images` directory.

3.  Drag an `Image` control onto the page, placing it at the top left corner, next to the title.

4.  In the **Properties** window enter the file name and path of an image in the `ImageUrl` property, `Images/Dice.gif`. You might need to resize it once it's on the page. To make sure we don't squash the image and make it either too narrow or too short, try setting the **Height** property to `100px`. The image will scale the width as appropriate, maintaining its aspect ratio.

5.  Drag two more `Image` controls onto the page, this time placing them underneath the `Label` controls that are currently used for the dice. You will need to press *Enter* to place a new line between the current labels and the **Ooops, you did it again :(** line. You don't need to set any properties for these. The page should now look like this:

**6.** Switch to **Code** view, and change the code. The lines you need to add are highlighted below:

```
Label3.Visible = False
Label1.Text = Int(Rnd() * 6) + 1
Label2.Text = Int(Rnd() * 6) + 1

Image2.ImageUrl = "Images/" & Label1.Text & ".gif"
Image3.ImageUrl = "Images/" & Label2.Text & ".gif"

If Label1.Text = "1" And Label2.Text = "1" Then
  Label5.Text = Label4.Text
...
```

**7.** Save the file and press *F5* to run it.

**8.** Click the button to roll the dice, and notice how you now get pictures of the dice too:

## How It Works

The first part of this is simple – we just used an Image control at the top of the page. The ImageURL property identifies where the image comes from. In our case we used Images/Dice.gif as the file name. Placing your images in a sub-directory is a good idea, as it keeps them separate from the rest of the files that make up a website.

The second part of this example is more complex. We started with two Image controls, but don't set the ImageURL properties – that's because we set them in code:

```
Image2.ImageUrl = "Images/" & Label1.Text & ".gif"
Image3.ImageUrl = "Images/" & Label2.Text & ".gif"
```

Although this looks complex, it's actually quite simple. You have to remember that `Label1` and `Label2` are the existing labels we use for the dice. Their `Text` properties contain the number that the dice 'rolled'. We want to show an image for that roll of the dice, so we need to convert the number of the roll into an image. We have six GIF images of dice, whose file name is just the number of the roll. So, `1.gif` is an image of a die rolled 1, `2.gif` shows a die rolled 2, and so on. To show the correct image we simply make up a string using the number rolled. In the screenshot, the first die rolled was a 4, as stored in the `Text` property of `Label1`. So the `ImageUrl` property of `Image2` becomes `Images/4.gif`.

This shows that you don't have to set all of the details for an image when you are designing the page. In other words, it is possible (and sometimes essential) to make certain display decisions at run time, based upon some external factors that cannot be known until our program is actually running.

## Who Turned out the Lights?

Another excellent use of setting properties at run time is when reacting to the user. In our dice game, we've reacted to the dice throws, and hidden or made visible label controls, and this is a really great technique. However, once you start doing it it's easy to get overwhelmed by trying to hide or unhide lots of controls. For example, if we consider adding high scores to the dice game, we might want to capture some user details, perhaps the name and e-mail address. Let's give this a go:

### Try It Out — Hiding Multiple Controls

1. Open `Dice.aspx`, and drag a `Panel` control onto the page, placing it right at the bottom. With this `Panel` control selected, click it again, and the border will go shaded – this means you can edit the contents.

2. Delete the word **Panel** that's showing, and add some text, two `TextBox` controls, and a `Button` control. Set the `Text` property of the `Button` control to **Submit High Score**. You form should now look like this:

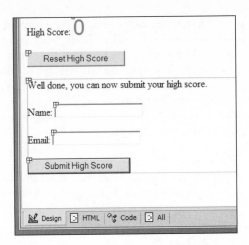

3. Select the `Panel`, by clicking outside on the main page, and then clicking on the `Panel` control again. This allows you to select the `Panel` itself, rather than the contents.

4. Change the **Layout** mode of the panel using **Absolute Position** from **Layout** on the menu bar, and drag the panel to the right of the **Reset High Score Button**. This just means the page is a bit easier to read since it's not so deep and won't scroll.

5. Set the **Visible** property for the **Panel** to **False**.

6. Double-click the **Submit High Score** button, and add the following line of code:

```
Sub Button3_Click(sender As Object, e As EventArgs)
    Panel1.Visible = False
End Sub
```

7. Change the **Button1_Click** code so it now looks like this – the new line is highlighted:

```
Sub Button1_Click(sender As Object, e As EventArgs)

    Label3.Visible = False
    Label1.Text = Int(Rnd() * 6) + 1
    Label2.Text = Int(Rnd() * 6) + 1

    Image2.ImageUrl = "images/" & Label1.Text & ".jpg"
    Image3.ImageUrl = "images/" & Label2.Text & ".jpg"

    If Label1.Text = "1" And Label2.Text = "1" Then
        Label5.Text = Label4.Text
        If CInt(Label5.Text) > CInt(Label16.Text) Then
            Label16.Text = label5.Text
            Panel1.Visible = True
        End If
```

```
      Label4.Text = 0
      Label3.Visible = True
   Else
      Label4.Text = CInt(Label4.Text) + CInt(Label1.Text) + CInt(Label2.Text)
   End If

End Sub
```

**8.** Save the file, and run it.

**9.** Notice that none of the controls in the panel have shown up.

**10.** Click the roll button until you lose, and see how the controls in the panel appear:

**11.** Click the **Submit High Scores** button, and the Panel disappears again.

**How It Works**

This works on exactly the same principle as showing and hiding Label controls. The big difference is that the Panel is a **container control** – it doesn't have any display of its own, it is simply used to contain other controls. This means that we can place controls within a panel, and show or hide them all together by setting the Visible property on just the panel control. In the page design we set the Visible property of the panel to False, so none of the controls it contains show up initially. Then, when a game is lost, the Visible property is set to True, so all of the controls are shown. If we hadn't contained these controls within a Panel, we'd have had to set the Visible property on each one individually.

Not only is a Panel useful for hiding collections of controls, but it's also useful for grouping and moving them together when using absolute positioning.

## Why does my Code Look Confusing?

One thing you may have noticed in the previous examples is that we haven't changed the name of any controls. We have Label1, Label2, Label3 and so on, but which is which? You can clearly see that as the number of controls increases, so does the confusion; it is difficult to keep track of which control is which.

To alleviate this we change the ID property of a control, giving it a meaningful name. For example, the labels used for the dice could be called Dice1 and Dice2, and the scores could be CurrentScore and HighScore. This makes our code much easier to read.

One thing we can also do is add something to the name to help us identify what type of control it is. For example, for the textboxes for the user name and e-mail address, we could change their ID values to Name and Email. The trouble is, how would we know what type of control this was is it a Label or a TextBox? Using txtName and txtEmail makes this clear; we've added txt to the beginning of the ID, using txt to stand for TextBox. Other common prefixes are:

- ❑  lbl for Label
- ❑  btn for Button
- ❑  lst for a list
- ❑  dg or grid for a DataGrid

You don't have to use prefixes, but they do make code easier to read, especially when you revisit that code after not looking at it for a while. If you decide to use these prefixes, it's worth being consistent, and using them throughout your code.

# Camera – Capturing User Information

In the previous section, we've looked at the "lights" – those things which make your web page nicer to look at and easier to use. Now it's time to move on to the section where we capture details. You've seen the `TextBox` control on a page, but it hasn't really been used to get details from the user. There are also other controls that we haven't looked at, such as those that supply lists of information, or allow selections from a small list.

## A Mailing List Page

Let's build a simple page to allow people to subscribe to a mailing list – we'll assume it's for the site for a band (which is what the sample download application uses). What we're aiming for is something like this:

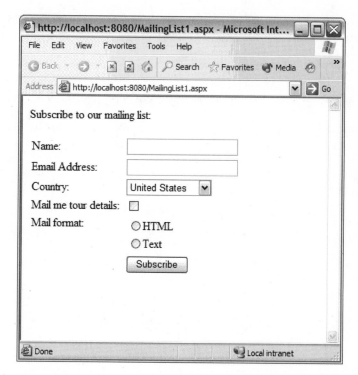

Here, we have fields for the name and e-mail address, a selection list for the country, a checkbox to see if the user wants tour details, and finally a selection of the format to use for e-mail messages. Let's give it a go.

**Try It Out**        **Getting the User Details**

**1.** Create a new **ASP.NET Page** called `MailingList.aspx`.

**2.** Add the text at the top of the page as shown above. Then add an HTML table (HTML | Insert Table... from the main menu bar), and make it 6 rows deep and 2 columns wide.

**3.** Add the text into the first column as shown above.

**4.** Add two `TextBox` controls (from the **Web Controls** menu) into the cells to the right of the **Name:** and **Email address:** prompts, and change their `ID` properties to `txtName` and `txtEmail`.

**5.** Add a `DropDownList` control into the third row and change the `ID` property to `cboCountry`.

**6.** Add a `CheckBox` to the fourth row, and change the `ID` property to `chkTour`.

**7.** Add a `RadioButtonList` to the fifth row and change the `ID` property to `radMail`.

**8.** Add a `Button` to the last row and second column and change the `Text` property to `Subscribe`.

**9.** Select the `DropDownList`, and click into the `Items` property in the **Properties** window. You'll see a button appear on the right:

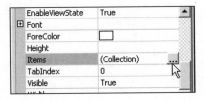

**10.** Click this button to launch the ListItem Collection Editor:

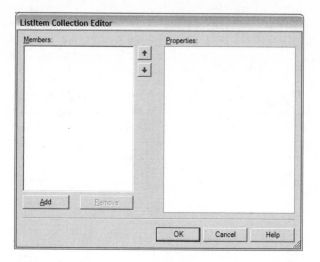

**11.** Click the Add button, and add details as follows for the United States, setting the Selected property to True:

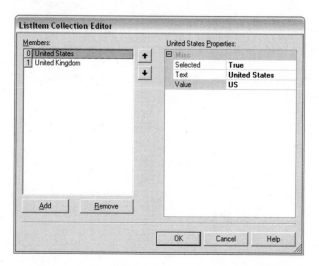

**12.** Click Add again, and add another country – I used United Kingdom for the Text value and UK for the Value, leaving the Selected property at False. Later in the book you'll see how to fill these from a database. (There are many more country codes that you can use, the full list of which can be found by searching Google.com for Internet country codes.) Press OK to close this window.

**13.** Click the `RadioButtonList` and follow the same procedure, selecting the `Items` property and clicking the button. In the editor, add two members HTML and Text, using the same values for both the Text and Value properties. Leave the Selected property set to False for both of them:

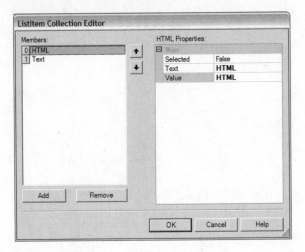

**14.** Press OK to close the window.

**15.** Finally for the design, add a Label underneath the table containing all of the above controls and delete its default text.

**16.** Double-click the button at the bottom of the table, and add the following code in the code window:

```
Sub Button1_Click(sender As Object, e As EventArgs)
   Dim Message As String

   Message = "Hello " & txtName.Text & "."

   If chkTour.Checked Then
     Message &= " We will send you details of the tour " & _
         "schedule for " & cboCountry.SelectedItem.Text
   End If

   If radMail.SelectedItem.Value = "HTML" Then
     Label1.Text = "Using HTML format for mail. Sending:<p />" & Message
   Else
     Label1.Text = "Using plain format for mail. Sending:<p />" & Message
   End If
End Sub
```

**17.** Save the file and run it.

**18.** Add a name, select a country, a preferred mail format, and press the Submit button:

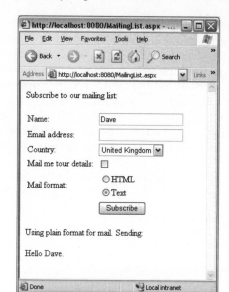

**19.** Now click the check box so a tick appears, select the HTML option, and press the Submit button again:

Notice how the message for the tour details e-mail now appears, and in that we have the country. Let's see how it works.

### How It Works

You've already seen textboxes in action, so let's concentrate on the other controls, starting with the country list. A `DropDownList` contains a collection of `ListItems`, for which there is a special editor. Each `ListItem` has two properties, `Text` and `Value`. The `Text` property is what's displayed on the page, with the `Value` property hidden from view but usable in code. This allows you to show easy-to-read strings of text, rather than odd codes. This may not seem much with only two values of `US` and `UK`, but consider a page that just shows the full list of codes – the official ISO country list has 239 countries in it, and you don't want to show all of these as 2 letter codes. So, the `DropDownList` allows us to show a nice country name, while still using the abstract country code underneath that refers to the country name.

To get access to the country that has been chosen we use the `SelectedItem` property, which returns the `ListItem` selected. We can then pick the `Text` from this, which gives us the country name:

```
cboCountry.SelectedItem.Text
```

If we wanted the code, we could have used the `Value` property:

```
cboCountry.SelectedItem.Value
```

This would give us either `UK` or `US`, depending upon which country the user has selected.

The `RadioButtonList` has the same feature, so we can just extract the `Value` property:

```
radMail.SelectedItem.Value
```

# Action! – Processing User Input

So far in this chapter we've seen the "lights" (making pages look good), and the "camera" (capturing information), so now it's time to take "action". This is where we are going to look at the controls that allow the user to submit information. There are several ways we can implement this behavior; buttons, links, and images. All three can act like buttons in their action, and give us the flexibility of making our interface look how we want it, rather than it being constrained by the controls.

While customizing your interface is worthwhile, there are traps that are easy to fall into. For example, we know what a `Button` is because it looks like a button. That may seem obvious, but having an image as a button can be very confusing for the user if they don't expect the image to be a button. This is called **affordance** – the design characteristics that convey the correct use of an object. We see it in real life all the time – knobs are round and turn, door handles like a lever give implicit indication of how they work, light switches go up and down, and so on. The same idea applies to our interface. Let's look at three different ways of getting user feedback.

## *Button Controls*

There are three types of button control, all providing the ability to send information back to the server. These are:

❏ Button – This is a standard button, and is useful for interfaces that want to look like standard forms.

❏ LinkButton – This is a link that behaves like a button (or a button that looks like a link, depending upon your perspective!). It's useful for situations where you need a button, but want it to look like text.

❏ ImageButton – This is a button that looks like an image, and is useful for interfaces that are more graphical in nature, or don't want the 3D look of buttons.

Which one you use depends on what look you are aiming for. For example, consider the previous mailing list example. What would happen if we use an ImageButton instead of a Button?

### Try It Out     The ImageButton Control

**1.** Open MailingList.aspx.

**2.** Select the Button and delete it.

**3.** Drag an ImageButton and drop it in place of the Button you've just deleted.

**4.** Copy the Register.gif image file from the samples directory, and put it in your Images directory.

**5.** Set the ImageURL property of the ImageButton to Images/Register.gif.

**6.** Double-click the ImageButton to view the code.

**7.** Copy the existing button code from the old Button1_Click procedure and place it in the new ImageButton1_Click procedure. You might want to tidy the code up by deleting the old Button1_Click procedure completely, although this isn't 100% necessary.

**8.** Save the file and run it:

Notice how instead of the button we have a nice looking image. Clicking this has the same result as a button, but we now have control over the appearance of our button.

## How It Works

There's not much to tell here – in action, the ImageButton is exactly the same as a Button, so you don't have to learn anything new. The only difference you might have noticed is that the code line starts with:

```
Sub ImageButton1_Click(sender As Object, e As ImageClickEventArgs)
```

instead of this for the Button:

```
Sub Button1_Click(sender As Object, e As EventArgs)
```

This is not something you need to understand just yet, but it's worth mentioning, as they do look different, even though they behave the same.

You can use the ImageButton in any place that you'd use a button. For example, consider this extract from the Wrox Press home page:

The buttons for Go and Find a Book are both `ImageButton` controls, as standard buttons wouldn't look as good in this context.

## The LinkButton Control

Let's now look at the `LinkButton` and see how that differs from the other button controls. We won't use the same example as before, since this doesn't improve the interface. For example, consider the register button as a link button:

Well, it looks OK, but it's not great. And it certainly doesn't look as good as the image. So, why, and when, should we use a `LinkButton`? One place where they are used with great effect is in tables full of data, where you want some data to be a button, or in a menu where you want to show text and not images.

Don't confuse the `LinkButton` with a standard HTML hyperlink. Although they look the same, they work very differently. The HTML hyperlink jumps to another page, whereas the `LinkButton` acts like a button and sends us back to the same page. This is explained in more detail in the section at the end of the chapter, where we look at events.

**Try It Out**     **The LinkButton Control**

**1.** Create a new ASP.NET Page called `LinkButton.aspx`.

**2.** From the HTML menu insert an HTML Table with 1 row and 3 columns. Change the `Height` to 20 then click OK.

**3.** Drag a `LinkButton` control into each of the table cells. Change the Text properties to Item 1, Item 2, and Item 3 respectively.

**4.** Add a `Label` control underneath the HTML table. The page should look like this:

**5.** Double-click each `LinkButton` control, switching back from Code view to Design view each time.

**6.** Now add the following highlighted lines of code:

```
Sub LinkButton1_Click(sender As Object, e As EventArgs)
   Label1.Text = "This is item 1"
End Sub

Sub LinkButton2_Click(sender As Object, e As EventArgs)
   Label1.Text = "Some stuff about item 2"
End Sub

Sub LinkButton3_Click(sender As Object, e As EventArgs)
   Label1.Text = "And now onto item 3"
End Sub
```

**7.** Save the file, run it and try clicking the links:

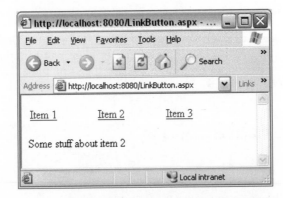

## How It Works

In action, the `LinkButton` works just the same as other buttons; the only difference is in its appearance, in that it just displays text. In reality, however, this control is different from the other button controls as it relies upon client-side scripting. Client-side scripting is code that runs on the client, within the browser. This allows you to run code without sending anything back to the server to be processed by ASP.NET. Some of the **validation controls** (more on those a little later), use client-side scripting to validate user input within the browser – this gives a much more responsive page.

### The LinkButton in Action

Two places where the `LinkButton` is used really effectively are in editable grids, and within the `Calendar` control. For example, take a look at the following screenshots:

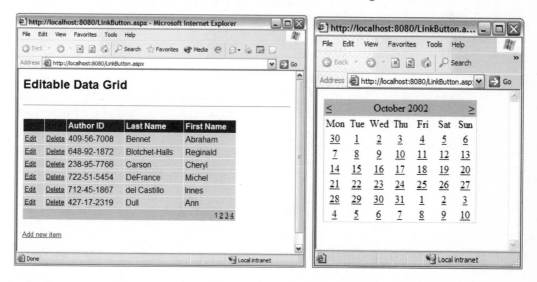

In the first image of the grid, the first two columns are `LinkButton` controls. This allows them to look similar to the data they are displayed with – ordinary buttons or images would draw the eye away from the data. In the second image, we see the `Calendar` control. This is a single control, but each of the days is a `LinkButton`, as are the two buttons at the top, < and >, that allow moving forward and backwards through the months.

# Trust No One

It may seem a bit of a paranoid heading, but it's a fact of life that some people will try to subvert your program, and attempt to hack into your system. There are many ways to prevent this sort of thing, but one that often gets overlooked is that of **protecting** your data. For example, you should always validate data that is supplied by the user. This not only ensures that the correct type of data is supplied, but also prevents certain forms of hacking.

ASP.NET has made validation fairly simple by the provision of a set of **validation controls**. These allow you to easily validate data, such as ensuring that data is filled in, or making it fit within certain criteria. Let's look at two of these to show how easy validation can be – we'll look at some of the others in Chapter 7, when we discuss how to prevent errors.

**Try It Out      Using the RequiredFieldValidator Control**

**1.** Create a new ASP.NET Page called `Validation.aspx`.

**2.** Add some text, two `TextBoxes` and a `Button` so that the page matches the following:

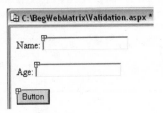

**3.** Drag a `RequiredFieldValidator` control and drop it to the right of the **Name:** textbox.

**4.** Drag a `RangeValidator` control and drop it to the right of the **Age:** textbox.

**5.** Drag a `ValidationSummary` control and drop it below the button:

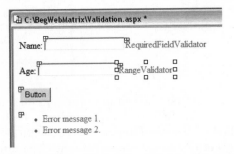

**6.** Select the `RequiredFieldValidator` and change the following properties:

| Property | Value |
|---|---|
| ControlToValidate | TextBox1 |
| ErrorMessage | You must enter your name |
| Text | Missing name |

**7.** Select the `RangeValidator` and change the following properties:

| Property | Value |
|----------|-------|
| ControlToValidate | TextBox2 |
| ErrorMessage | Age must be between 18 and 75 |
| Text | 18 – 75 |
| MaximumValue | 75 |
| MinimumValue | 18 |
| Type | Integer |

The page should now look like this:

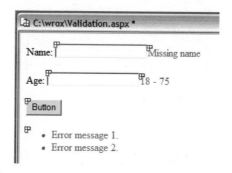

**8.** Save the page, run it, and press the button without entering any data:

**9.** Add a name, enter 4 for the **Age**, and press the button again:

**10.** Change the **Age** to 72 and press the button again:

Notice that there is now no error message, which means that the data is valid.

## How It Works

Let's first look at the `ValidationSummary` controls, since we didn't change any properties. When using validation controls you don't *have* to have a `ValidationSummary` control, but doing so allows you to display all of the error messages from invalid controls in a single location. When a page is invalid, the `ErrorMessage` property from each invalid control is displayed in the summary.

The `RequiredFieldValidator` ensures that a `TextBox` has a value entered, and an empty value causes the page to be invalid. The three properties we set were:

❏   `ControlToValidate` – The name of the `TextBox` control that has to be filled in

❏   `ErrorMessage` – The error message you want displayed in the validation summary

❏   `Text` – The text to display in the location where the validator is placed

If you don't have a validation summary, you can use the `Text` property to display the error message in line. Otherwise, it's a good idea to put a shortened message inline, or even just use a * to indicate the position of an error.

The `RangeValidator` uses the same properties as shown above, as well as:

❏   `MaximumValue` – Higher value to check against

❏   `MinimumValue` – Lower value to check against

❏   `Type` – The data type

In our example, we are checking ages, so we want to use whole numbers, and these are know as `Integers`. You'll find out more about data types in Chapter 5.

That's it for the properties, but what happens when the button is pressed? Well, ASP.NET takes care of this for us. It knows that there are validation controls on the page, and knows which textboxes they are linked to. If any of the content is invalid, the `ErrorMessage` for each invalid control is displayed in the summary, and the summary shown.

### Checking for Valid Content

One thing that you need to do is ensure that the content of the textboxes is valid before you do any processing. In our example above, we didn't have any code and the validation still took place. If we create code that should run when the button is clicked, then this will always run, whether or not there was valid content. What you have to do is check that the page is valid first, which is easy because there is a simple test:

```
Sub Button1_Click(sender As Object, e As EventArgs)

    If Page.IsValid Then
```

```
        ' The page is valid, so we can do stuff here
    End If

End Sub
```

The Page has an IsValid property, which is available to ASP.NET, and is True if the page content is valid. If the validation controls indicate invalid content, then the IsValid property is False.

# Server-Side Processing

One thing that's very important to understand is *when* sections of code actually run. It's easy to assume that code for buttons is all there is to it, but a little explanation will really help you to understand what's happening while users are interacting with your web page, and, more to the point, when.

## *Statelessness*

The first thing to understand is that every time you load a page, it's *distinct* from the previous time it was loaded. So, loading a page for the first time is different from loading the page that is a result of hitting a button, and different again from hitting that button once more. ASP.NET has no knowledge of the previous times the page has been loaded, so any code that ASP.NET runs doesn't know about the previous times it's been run. This is known as **stateless** – nothing is maintained in code between page loads.

So why is this important? Well, the answer is because you can't rely on anything that's previously happened in code. This means, for example, that if you perform some action as the page loads, then you might have to perform that same action again – each load of the page is distinct. Say you have a site that allows users to log in, and has a 'login' link on the page. Once logged in, you display a welcome message on a page. There are two separate pages here – the one before the user logged in, and the one after. They may have an order to the user, but to ASP.NET they are separate pages. This means you can't assume the page has any intrinsic knowledge of what's gone before. You'd have to check each time the page loads to see whether the user is logged in. For example, some code to do so might look like this:

```
Sub Page_Load()

  If User.IsLoggedIn Then
    lblWelcome.Text = "Welcome " & User.Name
  Else
    lblWelcome.Text = "Welcome stranger, please log in."
  End If

End Sub
```

### Server Controls and Statelessness

Statelessness only refers to standard HTML elements and to code; it doesn't refer to web controls. These have an in-built facility to retain their values each time a page is requested. You can easily see this in action by creating a new ASP.NET page. Drag an HTML `TextBox` from the **HTML Elements** tab of the **Toolbox** onto the page, followed by a `TextBox` and `Button` from the web controls. Run the page and enter some text in both textboxes. Press the button and notice how the text from the HTML element disappears, but that for the web control doesn't. This is because the HTML element is stateless, but the web control isn't.

So why is this good? Isn't it confusing to have code stateless, but web controls retain their state? Let's consider a page that is the checkout for a website allowing you to buy goods. The page has textboxes for the user name, address, credit card, and so on. The user has filled in all of their details and pressed the button. This sends the details back to the server, where the credit card is validated. However, the user mistyped their credit card number, the credit card validation fails, and the page is re-displayed. If you were using HTML elements, all of the entered text would disappear and you'd have to type it in again – very annoying indeed! With web controls though, the text is retained.

## Postback

Let's take this example further by assuming that there is a button on this page, to allow the user to login. When you hit a button, the information in any control is sent back to the server, and ASP.NET runs any code for that button. This is known as **postback** – the information is *posted back* to the server. Think of it in terms of a letter being posted to ASP.NET – it writes a new one back to you, and so on.

The postback causes the page to be sent to ASP.NET, which runs through any processing it needs to, and sends the resulting HTML back to the user. So, the process is the same as when the page is first loaded, and follows the same rules – there's no knowledge of any previous times the page has been loaded.

## When does my Code Run?

So, when does the code *actually* run? Let's take an example of a `DropDownList` control showing countries, which are stored in a database. If they are in the database, how do we get them into the list? The specifics of that are covered in detail in a later chapter, as part of the databases section of the book, but what's important for now is when we get them into the list. So far, you've seen code running when a button is pressed, but you can also have code running when the page loads – it's where we'd go off to the database, fetch the countries, and populate the list. However, this code would also be run when a button is pressed, because a button press means the page is reloaded. Would we want to fetch the countries list from the database again? No, because the `DropDownList` control will retain its values (remember, web controls retain their values – code doesn't). So filling the list would be a waste of time – we only want it filled the first time the page is loaded.

## Server-Side Events

The term "events" is what we call the actions that take place when something, or someone, interacts with our web page. For example, when a button is clicked, an event is generated (or **raised**, as it is sometimes called) – in this case, it is the `Click` event, indicating that the button has been clicked. This is represented by the following code:

```
Sub Button1_Click(sender As Object, e As EventArgs)
```

*The two arguments identify which control raised the event, and any extra information that the control is sending us. For a button, we don't get any extra information, but for more complex controls, such as grids and lists, we can find out which row has been selected. For more details on this you should consult the .NET Framework documentation.*

So far, we've just doubled-clicked on a button to get to this code, but you can also get to it through the Events section on the Properties window:

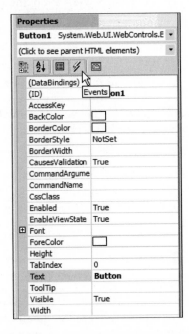

Clicking this icon will show the events for the selected control. In the following screenshot, we can see these for a `Button` control:

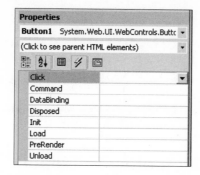

Double-clicking to the right of an event takes you to the code window for that event. If there is no code then it's created for you.

So, what about the page? We've said that code runs when the page is loaded. You'd think that clicking on a blank area of the page and then looking at the Events pane would show the events relating to the page itself, but it doesn't. This is because clicking on the page doesn't select the page itself. You have to click on the page, and then select Page from the list:

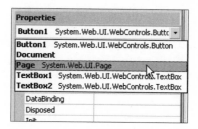

You can then click the Events button to see the events for a page:

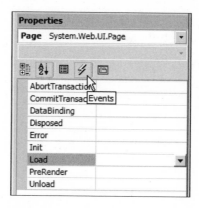

What you notice here is that there is a Load event, so you can double-click it, which will lead to this code:

```
Sub Page_Load(sender As Object, e As EventArgs)

End Sub
```

It's here that you enter any code to be run each and every time the page loads.

An alternative to the above method using the Properties and Events windows is just to switch to Code view, and to type in the above code by hand.

## Loading a page and Detecting Postback

So now you can see two distinct events; one for when a page loads, and one for when a button is pressed. If we only want code to run the first time a page is loaded, then we need a way of detecting that. This is where the IsPostBack property comes in. Let's give it a go.

### Try It Out          Using the IsPostBack Property

1. Create a new ASP.NET Page called Events.aspx.

2. Add a Button, and underneath it a Label, and underneath that another Label.

3. Double-click the button, and add the following to the code:

```
Sub Button1_Click(sender As Object, e As EventArgs)

    Label2.Text = "The button has been clicked"

End Sub
```

4. Now, at the bottom of the code window add the following code:

```
Sub Page_Load(sender As Object, e As EventArgs)

    Label1.Text = "The page has been loaded"
    Label2.Text = ""

End Sub
```

5. Save the file and run it:

In the resulting page, you can see how the text in the **Page_Load** event has been run.

**6.** Now press the button:

Notice that code in the **Page_Load** event has run, as well as the code we typed in for the button.

**7.** Close the browser, and switch back to Web Matrix.

**8.** Change the **Page_Load** event so that it contains the following code:

```
Sub Page_Load(sender As Object, e As EventArgs)

    If Page.IsPostBack Then
      Label1.Text = "The page has been loaded because of a button click"
    Else
      Label1.Text = "The page has been loaded for the first time"
    End If
    Label2.Text = ""

End Sub
```

**9.** Save the file and run it:

**10.** Now press the button:

Notice how two different sets of text are now displayed.

## How It Works

This works because of the `IsPostBack` property, which is `True` if the page is being re-displayed, in other words as a result of a button click. Remember how we mentioned earlier that pressing buttons generates a postback – the page is posted back to the server. For the first time a page is displayed `IsPostBack` is `False`. This allows us to test whether the page is being loaded for the first time, and take the appropriate action. We just displayed some text, but this is where you could decide whether or not to fetch data from a database.

# Summary

This has been a pretty involved chapter, but you've learned a huge amount. We've looked at lots of topics that not only make your web pages look great, but also make them work really well. We could quite easily have written an entire book on web page design (and many other people *have*), but that's not the real focus of this book. What we've concentrated on is getting your pages looking great, as quickly as possible.

We started with a discussion of HTML and web controls, how the two are related, and when and why you should use each. We then covered how to use HTML elements to lay out your pages so they look good, and how to improve that look by setting properties and using images as controls themselves. We followed that with a section on getting user input by using web controls. Once the user has entered the data, they need a way to send that back to the server, so we looked at how to use buttons to get that data back from the user.

Finally, we looked at some of the architecture involved in how pages work. It may seem rather complicated, but it's vital to understanding how web pages are processed, and the sort of things you need to do in ASP.NET code.

All in all, this is a large amount of what you need to know when creating functional and pretty websites. Now it's time to leave the design alone for a while, and delve into the world of code.

# CHAPTER 4

# Writing Code

Adding controls to pages and setting properties are only part of what's involved in creating an ASP.NET web site. The true power of ASP.NET comes from the code you write to make pages *dynamic*.

This chapter is all about doing some *real* work in **Visual Basic .NET** (or **VB.NET**, for short). You'll learn the most common elements of the Visual Basic .NET language, and then in the next two chapters you'll see how you can use the concepts learned in this chapter, coupled with methods of storing information temporarily, to make your code more powerful.

In this chapter you will learn:

- ❑ How to write **functions** and **procedures** that group a common set of tasks together
- ❑ How to make simple choices in an `If ... Then` statement, in other words, how to run a piece of code if certain conditions are met.
- ❑ How to use `Select ... Case` statements for multiple choices, running different blocks of code based on the value of an expression.
- ❑ How to perform repetitive tasks using `For ... Next` and `Do ... While` loops

We've got a lot to cover in this chapter, and we're going to be moving pretty quickly. You probably won't remember every single thing when you read it the first time, but you will grasp the main concepts – and you can always refer back to this chapter to get the details when you need them.

## Writing Code in Visual Basic .NET

Web Matrix supports code in two languages; Visual Basic .NET and C#. For this book, we've chosen to use Visual Basic .NET because Visual Basic .NET has a verbose and easy-to-read syntax that makes it a good choice for a beginner to programming.

Visual Basic .NET can also be used for more than simple web programming. The great news is that after you've read the next few chapters, you'll be a long way into learning Visual Basic .NET – a language that you can use for writing all sorts of programs.

The other great news is that you've already seen some Visual Basic .NET code in action, so it won't be completely new to you. In this chapter, we will expand on the outline knowledge that you gained in the first few chapters of this book, and you'll see how to write Visual Basic .NET code for yourself.

In order to prepare you for the contents of this chapter, we need to say a few words about **data types** and the types that we will be using in this chapter. By data type, we are referring to the type of data that can be stored by a variable or object. We'll be learning a lot more about these concepts in the next chapter, but to better understand the contents of this chapter, you will need to understand what the following two types of data are:

❑   A String is used to store textual data, information like a name, a word, or anything that is represented by a series of characters

❑   An Integer is a whole number, for example, 3, 68, or 254, which we can use for counting, or for arithmetic calculation

We can convert from one type to a different type for instance, we will occasionally want to write out a number into a sentence, so we will stop treating it as a number, and write it out as a String instead. Sometimes we want to take a number entered by a user in a text box (which means it will be a string value by default), and add it to another number, as we did in our dice game. In this case, we need to treat it as an Integer.

# Decision-Making

When a user clicks on a button in a web form, the code in the Button_OnClick event handler will be executed sequentially. When a web form is loaded for the first time, the code in the Page_Load event will be executed sequentially. The fact is that every line of code will execute sequentially from the first line to the last without branching. However, sometimes we need to do different things in different situations. We did this in Chapter 2 when we wrote our dice game – if the player rolled two ones, we ended the game and reset the score. Otherwise, we added the total of the two dice to the high score.

Let's take a more detailed look at how we can use Visual Basic .NET code to make decisions.

## Making Decisions with If...Then

The If ... Then statement is the most common decision-making approach. Using this statement simply says "if this **condition** is **true**, **then** do the following steps."

When you go to bed, you probably do the following:

**1.** Get ready for bed

**2.** Set your alarm clock

**3.** Go to Bed

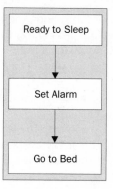

It's not quite that simple though. Depending on the day of the week, you might not need to bother setting the alarm clock. Therefore, your routine will be more like this:

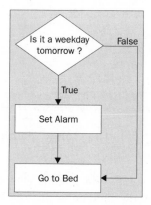

Nothing complicated there. Let's translate this concept into a computer program:

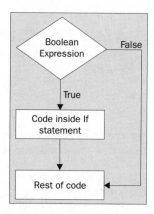

## Try It Out     The Basic If Statement

If you take a test at school, then chances are that there is a threshold mark to pass it. If a test score is above the pass mark, then that candidate will see the word "PASS" on the result slip. This is an example of a simple condition. We will translate this into a programming example that's quite easy to code. Let's get started.

**1.** Create a new file named `IfThen.aspx` in Web Matrix.

**2.** Start by entering the text **Your score:** into the designer, and add two more blank lines. Then drag a `TextBox` next to **Your score:**, and add a `Button` and `Label` control on each of the blank lines.

**3.** Your page should now look like this:

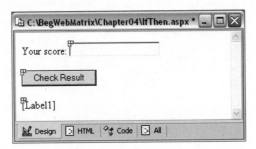

**4.** Change the `Text` property of the `Button` to `Check Result` and the `Text` property of the `Label` to be blank.

**5.** Now we can start writing some code. Double-click the **Check Result** button to add a `Button1_Click` event handler and enter the following code:

```
Sub Button1_Click(sender As Object, e As EventArgs)
   Label1.Text = ""

   ' Compare the entered score with a pass score, and set a
   ' congratulations statement to Label1.Text if it is True

   If CInt(TextBox1.Text) >= 50 Then
     Label1.Text = "Congratulations! You passed the test!"
   End If
End Sub
```

This will perform a comparison between the pass mark, 50 in this case, and whatever the user typed in, and then use this as a condition for the `If ... Then` statement.

**6.** And that's all there is to it. Run the page by pressing *F5*, or clicking the **Start** button, and try entering a sample test score to check the result. After you enter a value above the pass mark and click **Check Result**, the screen should look like the following:

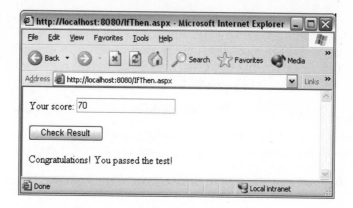

## How It Works

If you run the page, type in **70** in the textbox, and click the **Check Result** button, ASP.NET will call the code in the `Button1_Click` event handler. The first line in the handler is:

```
Sub Button1_Click(sender As Object, e As EventArgs)
    Label1.Text = ""
```

Hang on – we've already blanked the label's `Text` property in the **Properties** window, so what's this for? Be patient – this line of code is important, and we'll explain why in just a moment.

The next line of code after the two lines of comments beginning with a single quote ( ' ) is:

```
If CInt(TextBox1.Text) >= 50 Then
```

The part between the `If` and the `Then` is the **condition**. If this statement is true, then the code between the `Then` and the `End If` will run. This condition says, "The number that the user typed into the textbox is bigger than or equal to 50." This statement will be either true or false. In our case, we entered 70, so it's true – the code between the `Then` and the `End If` runs and the message is displayed:

```
    Label1.Text = "Congratulations! You passed the test!"
End If
```

If the condition is not true, then the program will skip the block of code and execute the statement after the `End If`. In our case, there is no code after the `End If` so nothing is seen by the user.

What about that line of code at the start?

```
    Label1.Text = ""
```

Once the code is run, the congratulations message is displayed in the label, and it will remain set until the next time the label is told to display a new message. The text of the label needs to be reset to blank each time the program is run otherwise the message will continue to be displayed no matter what value is entered into the textbox before the button is pressed. By setting it *back* to blank, it will then *only* be displayed again when a value is entered that passes the test.

## Doing Something Else

The decisions we make in life are not this simple all the time, and our programs won't be either. Often, we want to do one thing if the condition is true, and something else if it is false.

This is easy in Visual Basic .NET – we just add an Else section to our If ... Then block, like this:

```
Sub Button1_Click(sender As Object, e As EventArgs)

    ' Compare the entered score with a pass score, and set a
    ' congratulations statement to Label1.Text if it is True,
    ' otherwise, display a warning message

    If CInt(TextBox1.Text) >= 50 Then
        Label1.Text = "Congratulations! You passed the test!"
    Else
        Label1.Text = "Sorry, you have to try harder next time."
    End If
End Sub
```

Once the user clicks the button, the condition in the If ... Then statement will be evaluated. When the If condition is evaluated as True, the statements between Then and Else will be processed, and a congratulatory message will be displayed. Otherwise, the program will run the lines between Else and End If and a low score warning message will be displayed.

Now that we have added the Else statement, the value of the Label will be set every time the code is run, so we can remove the first line of the code that sets the value of the Label to blank.

## Even More Choices – Using ElseIf

Conditions in our If statements must always be *either* true *or* false – either it is Sunday or it isn't, the score is either above 50 or it isn't, and so on. However, many conditions are more complicated than this – there are cases where more than two possible courses of action are conceivable.

To make more complicated decisions using a computer, we need to break the decision down into smaller true or false conditions. When you first start programming, you might find this tricky – how can complicated problems be turned into lots of really simple ones? You'll soon learn, though, that the world is much simpler than you think it is!

## Try It Out    Multi-Choice If ... ElseIf Statements

Visual Basic .NET lets us add `ElseIf` in an `If ... Then` statement. In our exam results pass mark example, we can evaluate the result of a test as pass or fail by comparing it with a pass score. However, we want to display a special message to encourage those students who have achieved a very high mark (for example, 80 or above). This leaves us with three types of message:

❑ One for students who failed, scoring lower than 50

❑ One for students who passed with grades between 50 and 79

❑ One for students who passed with a score of 80 or more.

Let's see how to implement this in our code.

**1.** First of all, make a copy of the `IfThenElse.aspx` page we created from a modified version of `IfThen.aspx`. The easiest way to do this is by manipulating the files in Windows Explorer. Then, rename the page to `ElseIf.aspx`.

**2.** Next, open up `ElseIf.aspx` and make the following changes to the code:

```
Sub Button1_Click(sender As Object, e As EventArgs)

    ' Compare the entered score with a pass score, and set a
    ' message to Label1.Text according to the result of the condition

    If CInt(TextBox1.Text) >= 80 Then
      Label1.Text = "Well done!"
    ElseIf CInt(TextBox1.Text) >= 50 Then
      Label1.Text = "Congratulations! You passed the test!"
    Else
      Label1.Text = "Sorry, you have to try harder next time."
    End If
End Sub
```

**3.** Run the page by pressing *F5* or clicking the **Start** button, and try entering a numeric test score to check the behavior of code we have modified. After you have entered a high scoring mark and clicked **Check Result**, the page should look like this:

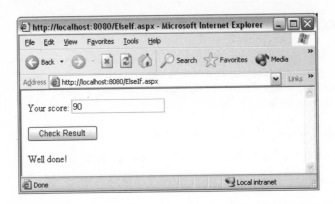

## How It Works

This example originally showed a pass message if the user entered a score greater than or equal to 50, or a fail message if the score was less than 50.

Now, besides these two messages, one more specific message will be shown if the candidate gets a very high mark. So, we can divide the marks into three categories: distinction, pass, and fail. First, we will check whether the mark belongs to the distinction score. The program will check whether the entered score is greater than or equal to 80, if this comparison is `True`, then `Label1`'s `Text` property will be set as `Well done!` immediately. This is due to the following code:

```
If CInt(TextBox1.Text) >= 80 Then
  Label1.Text = "Well done!"
```

If this condition is not true, then it may either belong to pass group or fail group. The next step is to know whether the mark is a pass (without distinction) or fail. If the entered score is smaller than 80 but greater than or equals to 50, it will be classified as pass as the second condition returns `True`:

```
ElseIf CInt(TextBox1.Text) >= 50 Then
  Label1.Text = "Congratulations! You passed the test!"
```

Finally, if the entered score returns `False` after evaluating with the all of the conditions above, then it will be treated as an `Else` case. So, the statement between `Else` and `End If` will be processed:

```
Else
  Label1.Text = "Sorry, you have to try harder next time."
End If
```

You can have as many `ElseIf` statements as you like, but remember that it *does* matter what order you put them in. The code goes through each one in turn, and will only execute the first one where the condition evaluates to true. For example:

```
If CInt(TextBox1.Text) >= 50 Then
  Label1.Text = "Congratulations! You passed the test!"
ElseIf CInt(TextBox1.Text) >= 80 Then
  ' THIS WILL NEVER RUN!
Else
  Label1.Text = "Sorry, you have to work hard next time."
End If
```

The `ElseIf` statement in this case will not run, because if the number tested is greater than 50 the `If` statement is exited after the first clause. Since only numbers less than 50 will be tested in the `ElseIf` condition, and no number can be both less than 50 *and* greater than 80, the statement will never evaluate to true, hence that part of the code will never be run.

## Testing Multiple Conditions

By now, we can get Visual Basic .NET to make some pretty clever choices. Even so, real life is often a lot more complicated. For example, if I feel hungry and I have sufficient money, I will order a pizza. There are two conditions in this example – *feeling hungry* and *having sufficient money*. Both of these conditions *must* be true for me to be able to order pizza, unless I really feel like having a pizza without actually being hungry, but that's another story!

### Try It Out          Testing Multiple Conditions

If the 13th day of a month is Friday, we will normally say something like, "Careful! Friday 13th is an unlucky day for some people!". Let's write a program to make sure we get a fair warning. We need to test for two conditions now – the day of the week being Friday, and the day of the month being the 13th.

**1.** Create a new **ASP.NET Page** called `MultipleConditions.aspx.` and enter some introductory text, such as **Please select a date:**, and then add a blank line after it.

**2.** Drag a `Calendar` control from the **Web Controls** tab in the **Toolbox** on the left onto the page and add one more blank line after this control. Place a `Label` control at the bottom of the page, which should now look like this:

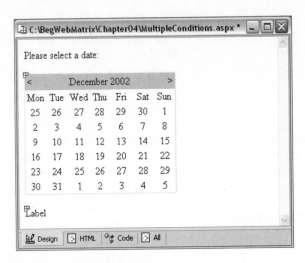

3. Change the `Text` property of the `Label` control to be blank in the **Properties** window.

4. We can write some code with this calendar control now. Double-click on the `Calendar` control to add the `Calendar1_SelectionChanged` event handler, and enter the following code:

```
Sub Calendar1_SelectionChanged(sender As Object, e As EventArgs)
   If Day (Calendar1.SelectedDate) = 13 And _
      Calendar1.SelectedDate.DayOfWeek = 5 Then
      Label1.Text = "Careful! Friday 13th is an unlucky day for some people!"
   Else
      Label1.Text = "It's just another day in life..."
   End If
End Sub
```

The first condition will test whether the selected date is the 13th day of the month, and the second condition is going to test whether the selected date is a Friday or not.

5. That's it, we're done. Press *F5* to run the example now, and try clicking on a date on the `Calendar` control. Depending on what day and date you click on, you will something like one of the two following screens:

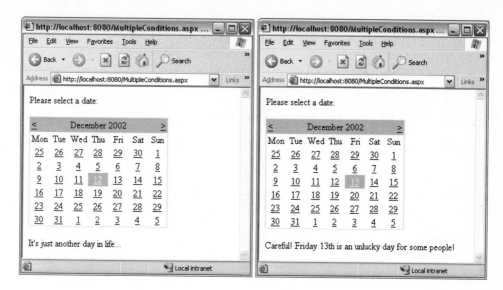

The highlighted date in the Calendar control indicates the selected date. You can try clicking on a Friday 13th to see the warning in the code, or you can choose another day that does not meet either or both criteria and see the relevant message displayed.

The Calendar control is a brand new rich control in ASP.NET, which we'll learn a bit more about in the next chapter. The SelectionChanged event handler is invoked if you click on any date on this control:

```
Sub Calendar1_SelectionChanged(sender As Object, e As EventArgs)
```

The first line of the event handler is:

```
If Day (Calendar1.SelectedDate) = 13 And _
   Calendar1.SelectedDate.DayOfWeek = 5 Then
```

Since this line is too long to fit on a printed page, I've used an **underscore** to split it over two lines. This is a good way to make your code more readable, especially when you're joining lots of conditions together. The underscore tells Visual Basic .NET to treat it as one line. You can type this line all on one line in your code if you prefer, since you are less likely to be constrained by physical page width!

In this statement, there are two conditions to be evaluated:

❑ Day(Calendar1.SelectedDate) = 13 – Check the selected date of its corresponding month

**107**

❑   `Calendar1.SelectedDate.DayOfWeek = 5` – Check the day of week of the selected date. 0 is a Sunday while 6 is a Saturday.

Sometimes you will want to combine conditions in other ways. The most common of these is using `Or` instead of `And`:

```
If Day(Calendar1.SelectedDate) = 13 Or _
   Calendar1.SelectedDate.DayOfWeek = 5 Then
   Label1.Text = "A bit dangerous, but you should be OK."
End If
```

Another useful trick is to say 'if one thing is true, and the other thing *isn't* true'. To test if something is *not* true, you just put `Not` in front of it:

```
If Not Day(Calendar1.SelectedDate) = 13 And _
   Calendar1.SelectedDate.DayOfWeek = 5 Then
   Label1.Text = "Hooray, it's a safe Friday, have a good weekend!"
End If
```

This is saying "If it's not the thirteenth, but it is a Friday, then display the following message."

However, this is where things start getting a bit complicated. It's hard to tell whether this means "if it's not the thirteenth, and it's not a Friday, then display the message"... does the `Not` apply to the whole condition, or just the first one?

To make things clearer, we can put things in brackets like this:

```
If (Not Day(Calendar1.SelectedDate) = 13) And _
   Calendar1.SelectedDate.DayOfWeek = 5 Then
   Label1.Text = "Hooray, it's a safe Friday, have a good weekend!"
End If
```

Now it's easy to see that the `Not` only applies to the first bit.

# Getting Selective with Select Case

The `If ... Then ... ElseIf ... Else ... End If` statement is a very simple and useful way to make decisions in your programs. Similarly, a `Select Case` statement runs different code blocks, based on the evaluation of an expression. Imagine that you have a program that does different things depending on the day of the week. You would have something like this:

```
If DateTime.Today.DateOfWeek.ToString() = "Sunday" Then
   'Do something on Sunday
ElseIf DateTime.Today.DateOfWeek.ToString() = "Monday" Then
   'Do something on Monday
```

```
ElseIf DateTime.Today.DateOfWeek.ToString() = "Tuesday" Then
   'Do something on Tuesday
ElseIf DateTime.Today.DateOfWeek.ToString() = "Wednesday" Then
   'Do something on Wednesday
ElseIf DateTime.Today.DateOfWeek.ToString() = "Thursday" Then
   'Do something on Thursday
ElseIf DateTime.Today.DateOfWeek.ToString() = "Friday" Then
   'Do something on Friday
ElseIf DateTime.Today.DateOfWeek.ToString() = "Saturday" Then
   'Do something on Saturday
End If
```

This will work perfectly, but it looks a bit of a mess. Why? You can answer this question by yourself after looking at the neater version using the `Select Case` statement, which would look like something like this:

```
Select Case DateTime.Today.DateOfWeek.ToString()
Case "Sunday":      'Do something on Sunday
Case "Monday":      'Do something on Monday
Case "Tuesday":     'Do something on Tuesday
Case "Wednesday":   'Do something on Wednesday
Case "Thursday":    'Do something on Thursday
Case "Friday":      'Do something on Friday
Case "Saturday":    'Do something on Saturday
End Select
```

When you've got lots of possible branches, the `Select Case` statement is far neater. It doesn't really let you do anything that you can't do with lots of `ElseIf`s, but it is often a much easier and tidier way to do things. Other conditions may exist in every `ElseIf`, while there is only one condition in a `Select Case` evaluation and different values of the condition evaluated will fire different blocks of code to execute.

> The condition in the **Case** statement must evaluate to **Integer** data type or to an enumeration data type, and the code will become more elegant and readable if you can use a **Case** statement appropriately.

## Try It Out    Select Case in Action

Let's take another look at test results. In this example, we'll let users select a score from a list, and then tell them what grade they got. Since there are lots of possible grades, this will look far neater using the `Select Case` statement than using an `If` block.

**1.** Create a new **ASP.NET Page** named `SelectCase.aspx` in Web Matrix.

**2.** Drag a `DropDownList` control and a `Label` control on a new line below it.

3. Erase the `Text` property of the `Label` control, and change the `AutoPostBack` property of `DropDownList` control to `True` in the **Properties** window.

4. Now we need to add some items to the list. If you click on the `Items` property of `DropDownList` control in the **Properties** pane, you will see a button with 3 dots in it. Click on this button and the **ListItem Collection Editor** will appear:

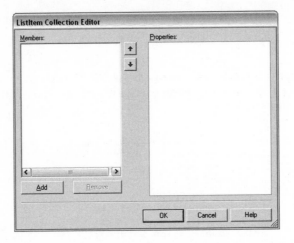

5. Click the **Add** Button and then enter - **Please select a range of score** - into the **Text** item on the right. Then, set the **Value** item the 0.

6. Now, we need to do a similar thing for the score ranges. Click the **Add** button to create another 5 items. Set the **Text** properties to 0 - 20, 21 - 40, 41 - 60, 61 - 80, and 81 - 100 with **Value** properties of 1, 2, 3, 4, and 5 respectively. The `Text` is used for displaying the text of an item, while `Value` is used for telling our program which item the user chose – we'll see this in action very soon.

7. Finally, mark the **Selected** property of the first item to **True**, so that users see the instructions when the page first loads:

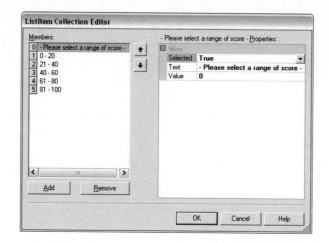

Finally, hit the **OK** button to accept the changes you have made in the dialog.

**8.** Now we move on to the code. Double-click the `DropDownList` control to add a `DropDownList1_SelectedIndexChanged` event handler to the code and modify it as follows:

```
Sub DropDownList1_SelectedIndexChanged(sender As Object, e As EventArgs)
    Select Case DropDownList1.SelectedItem.Value
      Case 0: Label1.Text = String.Empty   ' Reset the Label1.Text
      Case 1: Label1.Text = "You got Grade E!"
      Case 2: Label1.Text = "You got Grade D!"
      Case 3: Label1.Text = "You got Grade C!"
      Case 4: Label1.Text = "You got Grade B!"
      Case 5: Label1.Text = "You got Grade A!"
    End Select
End Sub
```

**9.** Run the page by using the usual methods and try selecting any item from the `DropDownList` control:

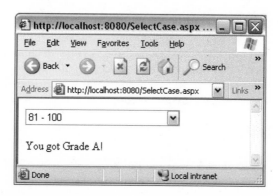

Depending on which range from the `DropDownList` control you chose, you will see an appropriate message.

## How It Works

Each item in the `DropDownList` has a `Text` and a `Value` property. The `Text` property is the visual text on screen and the `Value` property is associated with an item in the `DropDownList`, which is usually a numeric value corresponding to the friendlier (but lengthier) text being displayed. By selecting items in the `DropDownList`, the value of the selected item in the `DropDownList` changes too. Then, while testing the value of the selected item in the list, we know which item was selected, and thus the corresponding block of code will be executed. Moreover, like `Else` in the `If` statement, there is a `Case Else` condition that executes if a value fails to match with any of the `Case` conditions.

### What About that AutoPostBack Property?

When you make a client-side event for a server control, for example, change a selected item in `DropDownList` or click on a `Button`, it will submit the current document to itself – that's called **postback**. By raising a postback event, selected actions taken on the client would fire a request back to the server, and thus the corresponding server-side event handler will be executed.

# For My Next Trick – Loops

Other than helping us make decisions, computers can also save us from doing repetitive jobs. For example, if a student is late for school, they will probably be punished, for example, by writing "I will not be late for school" one hundred times for everyone to see.

Instead writing of these sentences themselves, the student may ask the computer for help by just telling the computer the sentence and number of times it has to be written. Then, they can just sit down, click a mouse button and let the computer do it for them; printing the meaningless sentence for a hundred times. The teacher didn't say anything about writing the sentence on the chalkboard!

## Try It Out          The For ... Next Loop

Imagine there are a boy and girl, the boy loves the girl very much and would like to marry her. However, in order to show he is sincere, the boy has to write "I love you!" one hundred times. What should he do? In his place, I would turn on my laptop and write a program immediately, as the computer will finish this great task in a couple of seconds without pain.

Let's see how to write this program to complete this task.

**1.** Create a new page in Web Matrix named `MarryMe.aspx` and start by placing an `ImageButton` control on the page.

**2.** Add a blank line under the `ImageButton` and place a `Label` control on the page.

**3.** Erase the `Text` property of the `Label` control and change the `ImageUrl` property of the `ImageButton` to `Images/Heart.gif`.

You can find the `Heart.gif` image in a subfolder named `Images` as part of the code download. In Chapter 11, we explain in more detail about linking to subfolders but for now, all you need to do is create an `Images` subfolder in the current directory you're working in, and place your image in there, specifying the appropriate file name, of course.

**4.** Let's write some code for this romantic program. Double-click on the `ImageButton` to add a `ImageButton1_Click` event handler and enter the following code:

```
Sub ImageButton1_Click(sender As Object, e As ImageClickEventArgs)
   Dim Counter as Integer
   For Counter = 1 To 100  ' Start looping 100 times
     Label1.Text &= Counter.ToString() & ": I  Love You! " & "<BR />"
   Next
End Sub
```

> The **&=** operator concatenates (sticks together) a **String** expression to a **String** variable and assigns the result to the variable. The **ToString()** method will convert the numeric value of an instance to its equivalent string representation.

**5.** That's it. Run the page and try clicking on the `ImageButton`. You should see something like the following:

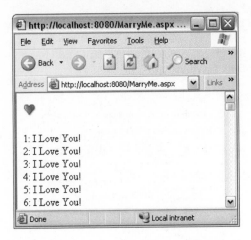

## How It Works

When you click on the ImageButton, ASP.NET calls the code in the ImageButton1_Click event handler. This is just like what a Button control does after the user clicks on it.

```
Sub ImageButton1_Click(sender As Object, e As ImageClickEventArgs)
```

The first line of code declares an Integer object called Counter:

```
Dim Counter as Integer
```

Visual Basic .NET will track the number of times the loop has been completed in the Counter variable as the program runs.

The loop starts iterating with the variable assigned to it (in this case Counter) with the initial value equal to the first number *before* the To in the For loop statement (in this case, 1), and continues until the Counter variable reaches the value of the number *after* the To (in this example, 100). With each iteration of the loop, the Counter variable is incremented by one, so in this case, the loop will run 100 times:

```
For Counter = 1 To 100  ' Start looping 100 times
   Label1.Text &=  Counter.ToString() & ": I  Love You! " & "<BR />"
Next
```

Each time it goes around, we append the value of Counter and the I Love You message to Label1.

In this example, the Counter increases in increments of 1, which is the default. We can change this if we want by using the Step keyword:

```
For Counter = 1 To 100 Step 5  ' Start looping 20 times
   Label1.Text &= Counter.ToString() & ": I Love You!" & "<BR />"
Next
```

# Doing the Do Loop

Sometimes, you don't know at the start exactly how many times you want to loop, so instead, you want to continue looping until a specific condition is met.

Say you need to walk up some stairs. You don't count the stairs before you start – you just keep walking until you get to the top. So instead of:

```
numberOfStairs = CountTheStairs()
For n = 1 To numberOfStairs
   Walk_up_a_stair
Next n
```

you might say:

```
Do
   Walk_up_a_stair
Loop Until you_reach_the_top
```

Let's see how to do this in code.

## Do ... Loop Until

In Chapter 2, we wrote the Snake Eyes dice game. It was quite a good game, except for one problem – it was a bit boring and repetitive to play!

Don't worry, though. Whenever there's something boring and repetitive to do, you can usually get a computer to do it. Let's write a program now that will play a whole game of Snake Eyes for us. We won't be looking at the pretty version of the game we made in the previous two chapters but we'll be looking at a stripped-down version, where the concept of snake eyes is still apparent, even if the visual appearance is different.

**Try It Out**      **Do ... Loop Until**

**1.** Create a new ASP.NET page called DoUntil.aspx. Add a Button control, then a blank line, and then a Label. Clear the label's Text property to blank, and the change the button's Text property to Play the whole game.

**2.** Now double-click the `Button`, and modify the handler so that it looks like the following:

```
Sub Button1_Click(sender As Object, e As EventArgs)
    Label1.Text = ""

    Dim dice1, dice2, score As Integer

    Do
        dice1 = Int(Rnd() * 6) + 1
        dice2 = Int(Rnd() * 6) + 1
        score = score + (dice1 + dice2)
        Label1.Text = Label1.Text & "Rolled a " & dice1 & _
            " and a " & dice2 & "<br/>"
    Loop Until dice1 = 1 And dice2 = 1
    score = score - 2
    Label1.Text = "You lost! Your total score would have been " & _
        score.ToString() & "<br/><br/>" & Label1.Text
End Sub
```

**3.** Done! Now press *F5* to run the page. When you click the `Button`, you'll get your score displayed, along with a log of every roll:

### How It Works

There's nothing really complicated here. Let's run through it line by line. First of all, we just make sure there isn't anything in the label from the last time the procedure ran. You have already seen this line from earlier in the chapter:

```
Label1.Text = ""
```

Next we declare some variables of type `Integer` – don't worry about this for now, we'll cover it properly in the next chapter. Just remember that we now have three numbers, `dice1`, `dice2`, and `score`:

```
Dim dice1, dice2, score As Integer
```

Now we come to the loop itself. Every time the loop runs, we want to roll both dice, add that to our score, and then append the dice values to the end of the label:

```
Do
   dice1 = Int(Rnd() * 6) + 1
   dice2 = Int(Rnd() * 6) + 1
   score = score + (dice1 + dice2)
   Label1.Text = Label1.Text & "Rolled a " & dice1 & _
      " and a " & dice2 & "<br/>"
Loop Until dice1 = 1 And dice2 = 1
```

We keep on doing it *until* our condition is reached, in other words, until both dice have a value of one.

If the player rolls two ones, we shouldn't add that to the score, but in the loop above we *always* add the values, so when the loop finishes, the score will be 2 higher than it should be. We simply take that away, and then put a summary of the game at the very beginning of the label:

```
Label1.Text = "You lost! Your total score would have been " & _
   score.ToString() & "<br/><br/>" & Label1.Text
```

You can see that we don't know at the start of the game how many times this loop will run – we just keep going until a particular condition is met. (In theory, this particular example could run forever – the computer/player would need to be very lucky though!)

## Do ... Loop While

In the example above, the computer keeps going until something suddenly becomes true – the case where both dice throw a one. Sometimes, you want a similar loop, but instead of looping *until* something *becomes* true, you want to loop *while* something *is* true. In this case, you just use While instead of Until.

It is usually possible to re-phrase Until conditions so that they will work in a While loop. For example, our loop above could be:

```
Do
   dice1 = Int(Rnd() * 6) + 1
   dice2 = Int(Rnd() * 6) + 1
   score = score + (dice1 + dice2)
   Label1.Text = Label1.Text & "Rolled a " & dice1 & _
      " and a " & dice2 & "<br/>"
Loop While dice1 <> 1 Or dice2 <> 1
```

but this is much harder to understand. You're saying "carry on while either one of the dice *isn't* 1". It's just far easier to say "carry on until both of them *are* 1".

There will be other circumstances where While is the clearer choice. You can choose whether to use Until or While – pick the one that you find easiest for the particular condition you're testing.

## Putting the Test Condition at the Start

If you put the While or Until condition at the end of the loop, then the loop will always execute at least once, even if the condition is definitely false. For example, this will run once:

```
Do
    ' This code will run once
Loop While 1=2
```

In our examples, we couldn't test the dice until we had rolled them – and the roll was inside the loop. However, sometimes we want to do the test *before* running for the first time. It's easy to do – you need to just move the condition statement:

```
Do While 1=2
    ' This code will not run at all
Loop
```

## Leaving a Loop

Sometimes, you'll want to get out of a loop before it's really finished. This often happens when you have an If statement inside a loop, and you find that really, there's no point in carrying on.

To exit a For loop, just type:

```
Exit For
```

Similarly for a Do loop:

```
Exit Do
```

You shouldn't need to do this too often, but occasionally it's a useful trick. For example, we might not want to let the computer's score get too high:

```
Do
    dice1 = Int(Rnd() * 6) + 1
    dice2 = Int(Rnd() * 6) + 1
If (score + dice1 + dice2) > 700 Then
    Exit Do
End If
```

```
    score = score + (dice1 + dice2)
    Label1.Text = Label1.Text & "Rolled a " & dice1 & _
      " and a " & dice2 & "<br/>"
  Loop Until dice1 = 1 And dice2 = 1
```

# Nesting

As we just covered making decisions and performing repetitive actions using loops, there are often cases where you will want to use one of these constructs inside another. This kind of coding technique is called **nesting** and is very useful. Let's take a look at an example of how it works right now.

---

**Try It Out**     **Nested Loops**

---

Here is an example using our snake eyes game. Make a copy of the DoUntil.aspx page and rename it Nesting.aspx. Modify the code in Nesting.aspx by adding a nested Do loop as follows:

```
Sub Button1_Click(sender As Object, e As EventArgs)
  Label1.Text = ""

  Dim dice1, dice2, score, counter As Integer

  For counter = 1 to 10
    score = 0

    Do
      dice1 = Int(Rnd() * 6) + 1
      dice2 = Int(Rnd() * 6) + 1
      score = score + (dice1 + dice2)
      Label1.Text = Label1.Text & "Rolled a " & dice1 & " and a " & _
        dice2 & "<br/>"
    Loop Until dice1 = 1 And dice2 = 1
    score = score - 2
    Label1.Text = "Game " & counter.ToString() & _
      ": Total score would have been " & score & "<br/><br/>" & Label1.Text
  Next counter
End Sub
```

When you run the page and press the button, the code will play the Snake Eyes game for you, not once, not twice, not three times, but ten times, as that is the value we have specified in the For clause with the counter variable. You should see something like the following:

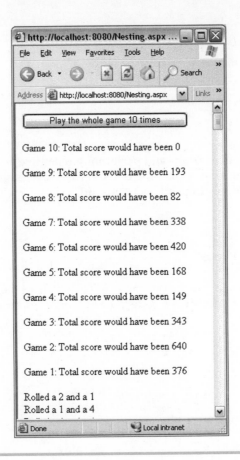

### How It Works

Each iteration of the For loop runs the complete Do loop within it once. Since the Do loop runs the Snake Eyes game and the For loop iterates 10 times (from 1 to 10), this example runs the Snake Eyes game 10 times.

We'll be covering functions and procedures next in this chapter, and at the end of that section, we will come back to nesting and see a quick reference on how it can be applied to these kinds of code blocks.

# Functions and Procedures

In Chapter 2, we saw that when you double-click a button in Web Matrix, you get a new **event handler,** and that this handler contains a block of code that *only* runs when a user clicks the button. It's often useful to create a block of code that is self-contained, and that *isn't* associated with a particular control. You can then run it whenever you want.

In Visual Basic .NET, a self-contained block of code that has a name and that you can call from other parts of your program, is called a **method**. There are two types of method in Visual Basic .NET:

❑ **Functions** – A method that does something, and then returns a result to the code that called the function.

Calling a function is like asking a question where you expect an answer or response. For example, if my boss said to me "Hey Colt, put the minutes for the last five meetings in this folder and *give it back to me*." I would need to go out, put all the minutes together properly, and then *return* the folder to my boss.

❑ **Procedures** – A method that does something, but doesn't return any result.

Calling a procedure is just like telling somebody to do something. For example, if my boss asks me to open a window, I simply open the window.

Both functions and procedures consist of any number of lines of code (called a **code block**, which is a term we have used before). This block is framed by a **signature** on the first line, which specifies the method's name and any values or parameters it expects to be handed, and the code inside will execute until reaching a line with the words of End Sub (for procedure) or End Function (for function). When the execution of this code block is complete, the code after the block will continue to execute as before.

> **A procedure just carries out a set of instructions, while a function will carry out some instructions, then return something to the caller when it's finished.**

For example, if you deposited an amount of money into a time deposit account, you would probably get the total balance (principal plus interest) at maturity. The calculation of such a total balance based on the interest rate would be:

```
Function FindTotalBalance(Principal As Double, InterestRate As Double) _
    As Double
    FindTotalBalance = Principal + (Principal * InterestRate)
End Function
```

So let's take a look at a function that's a bit more fun than a financial calculator (unless you're an accountant and like these kinds of functions!)

## Try It Out     Using Functions

Functions and procedures are very useful when there's something that you'll want to do over and over again, and in lots of different circumstances. One thing that you may want to do in your ASP.NET web pages is send e-mail messages. In this example, we'll do exactly that, and we'll end up with a function that you can use in any page where you want to send an e-mail, and return confirmation that the message was sent successfully.

> *This example requires the use of an SMTP server, which stands for Simple Mail Transfer Protocol. This is used by your ISP or network to send e-mail from the client on your machine to your selected recipient. To run this example, you need to know the name of the server you use to send your e-mail, which you can find out by asking your network administrator or by asking your internet service provider nicely! If you don't have access to such a sever, then unfortunately, you won't be able to try out the example here.*

**1.** Create a new ASP.NET Page in Web Matrix and call it `Function.aspx`.

**2.** First, we need to create our user interface. Start by entering **Your email address:**, and **Your message:** prompts onto two separate lines. Place a `TextBox` control next to each of the two prompts, and then add a `Button` and a `Label`, both on separate lines. Your page should now look like this:

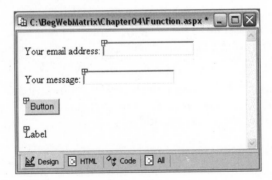

**3.** Change the `Button`'s `Text` property to `Send`.

**4.** The **Your message:** box is not wide enough or long enough to send a very interesting message. (On the bright side, it's not long enough to send a very boring one either!) We can fix this using the `TextMode` property that we saw in the previous chapter. Select the message `TextBox` and go to the **Properties** window. Now scroll down until you find the **TextMode** property, and choose **MultiLine**:

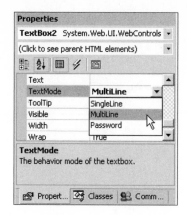

Another problem is that the visitor will see some text at the bottom of the page that just says Label. We can change that by erasing the Text property of the Label.

**5.** Now we can get down to writing some code. Double-click the Send button to add a Button1_Click event handler. Then, add the following code:

```
Sub Button1_Click(sender As Object, e As EventArgs)
    ' Call the SendMail function, and set Label1.Text to the
    ' recipient's e-mail address
    Label1.Text = SendMail("Feedback form", TextBox1.Text, TextBox2.Text)
End Sub
```

This line **calls** the SendMail() function. Label1.Text will be set to the value that the SendMail function returns when it is finished. We haven't written a SendMail() function yet, so if we run the page now the call won't work. Let's add the function now.

**6.** First of all, we need to **declare** the function. This is a way of saying that the function exists, and of describing a few things about it. This is very simple, so we just need to add the following to the existing code:

```
Function SendMail(Subject As String, FromAddress As String, _
    Message As String) As String

End Function
```

This tells ASP.NET that we are creating a function called SendMail() and that it has three **arguments** – Subject, FromAddress, and Message. In this case, every argument is a String, which basically means 'text'. Finally, with the final two words (As String), we tell ASP.NET that this function **returns** a String back to the code that called it.

**7.** Now we need to add the code that actually sends our e-mail. Web Matrix will write most of this for us. You just need to pick the Send Email code builder from the Code Builders tab in the ToolBox and drag it to the blank line between Function SendMail ... and End Function.

**8.** When you drop the code builder onto the code page, you should see the following dialog:

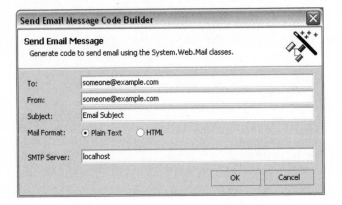

**9.** Put your own e-mail address in the **To** box, and the name or IP address of your SMTP server in the **SMTP Server** box. The SMTP server is the computer used to distribute mail that your computer sends. If you are not sure what yours is called, you can usually find out by looking at the account properties in your usual e-mail program (for example, Outlook Express). If you are part of a network, your administrator should be able to tell you. Chances are it will be something like `smtp.yourisp.com`. Don't worry about the other settings for now.

**10.** Click the **OK** button for this dialog box and the code is generated automatically. It looks like this:

```
Function SendMail(Subject As String, FromAddress As String, _
    Message As String) As String

    ' Build a MailMessage
    Dim mailMessage As System.Web.Mail.MailMessage = _
        New System.Web.Mail.MailMessage
```

```
mailMessage.From = "someone@example.com"
mailMessage.To = "someone@example.com"
mailMessage.Subject = "Email Subject"
mailMessage.BodyFormat = System.Web.Mail.MailFormat.Text

' TODO: Set the mailMessage.Body property

System.Web.Mail.SmtpMail.SmtpServer = "localhost"
System.Web.Mail.SmtpMail.Send(mailMessage)
```

```
End Function
```

Notice that we've kept the sample `From`, `To`, `Subject`, and `SmtpServer` properties set to the defaults for this example, but if you entered different details in the dialog box, then these values will be changed as appropriate in your generated code. You don't need to understand what all of the auto-generated code actually does, but as you work through this book, you'll start to work out what's actually going on here.

**11.** We just need to make a few changes so that this code works with our page as we want it to. Go ahead and make the highlighted changes to the code in the function:

```
' Build a MailMessage
Dim mailMessage As System.Web.Mail.MailMessage = _
   New System.Web.Mail.MailMessage
mailMessage.From = "someone@example.com"
mailMessage.To = "someone@example.com"
mailMessage.Subject = "Sending an e-mail from a web page"
mailMessage.BodyFormat = System.Web.Mail.MailFormat.Text

' TODO: Set the mailMessage.Body property
mailMessage.Body = Message

System.Web.Mail.SmtpMail.SmtpServer = "localhost"
System.Web.Mail.SmtpMail.Send(mailMessage)
```

**12.** A function needs to give something back to the line of code that called it. This function returns some text, and our program is going to use that text to set the value of `Label1.Text`. Add the following line to the end of the function, just before the `End Function` line:

```
SendMail = "Your message was sent to " & mailMessage.To
```

```
End Function
```

**13.** We're done! Run the page by pressing *F5* or clicking the start button, and try sending a message to yourself. After you click **Send**, it should look something like this:

Remember, you'll need to be online for this to work – ASP.NET needs to be able to connect to the SMTP server there and then, and both the web server *and* SMTP Virtual Server must running. This is because ASP.NET is hosting using a web server, in which the e-mail will be send via the SMTP server provided by your ISP, using the service provided by the SMTP Virtual Server in your computer – phew! OK, you can now just sit back and wait for the message to arrive!

## How It Works

When you click the **Send** button, ASP.NET automatically knows to call the code in the `Button1_Click` event handler. This only contains one line of code:

```
Sub Button1_Click(sender As Object, e As EventArgs)
   ' Call the SendMail function, and set Label1.Text to the
   ' recipient's e-mail address
   Label1.Text = SendMail("Feedback form", TextBox1.Text, TextBox2.Text)
End Sub
```

This is the function call. It tells ASP.NET to call the `SendMail()` function. If you look at the function declaration you'll see that the items between the brackets match up, for example, `"Feedback form"` is the `Subject`, `TextBox1.Text` contains the `FromAddress`, and `TextBox2.Text` contains the `Message`:

```
Label1.Text = SendMail("Feedback form", TextBox1.Text, TextBox2.Text)
```

> **This is very important for functions and procedures – the arguments in the call need to match the arguments in the declaration.**

Also, notice that we have `As String` at the end of each argument for the `SendMail()` function:

```
Function SendMail(Subject As String, FromAddress As String, _
    Message As String) As String
```

This means that the information that you send to the arguments in this function needs to be of data type `String` – a programming term for 'text'. We'll find out more about strings and other types of data in the next chapter. Other functions will require different types of information – not every function we write will require strings!

The final important thing is that the whole function has another `As String` at the end. This one means that the whole function returns a `String` – so it's a good thing that `Label1.Text` *is* a string! When the function is called, all of the code in it runs. Most of the code was written for us, and we don't need to fully understand how it works, although it seems quite readable. We've set some properties that describe whom the mail message will be sent to, what the subject of our message is, and so on. We also know that it works, which is the important thing! Let's focus on the very last line:

```
SendMail = "Your message was sent to " & mailMessage.To
```

This is where we set the value of the `SendMail()` function itself. Since a function will return a result to another part of the program in its function name, we have to ensure that the left of the equals sign has the *same* name as the function name. What's to the right of the equals here gets returned by the `SendMail()` function, which then gets passed back to `Label1.Text`. `Label1.Text` ends up being set to "Your message was sent to" and then the e-mail address of the recipient.

You can now copy and paste this whole function into other pages, and call it from wherever you want on the page.

## What About Procedures?

We've seen how to add functions, but we've not looked at how to add procedures. Don't worry though, procedures are even easier than functions – in fact you've already written some without even knowing it:

```
Sub Button1_Click(sender As Object, e As EventArgs)
    ' Call the SendMail function, and set Label1.Text to the
    ' recipient's e-mail address
    Label1.Text = SendMail("Feedback form", TextBox1.Text, TextBox2.Text)
End Sub
```

This is a procedure called `Button1_Click` (which is actually an event-handler procedure – we'll look at event handlers in just a moment). All procedures start with `Sub`, and end with `End Sub`. (`Sub` is short for **subroutine**, another word for a **procedure**.)

Like functions, procedures may have arguments. In the above example, we have an argument called `sender` and an argument called `e` – don't worry about what they mean, they are all system-generated arguments (which we'll look at in a moment), and the point is that they behave in exactly the same way as arguments in a function.

The other big differences are:

- Procedures have no `As Something` after the arguments, because they do not return anything
- Procedures do not have a final line where you set the procedure itself to a particular value, again, because there is no return value

This procedure is called automatically when you click `Button1`. You can also call a procedure any time you like just by adding a line of code with its name and some valid arguments.

For example, we could create a `Reset()` procedire that resets a form to its initial state (resetting values in controls), both when a page is first loaded, and if a button is clicked to reset the values manually. For example, if you had two textbox controls on a page, one to enter a name on a form, one to enter an age, and two buttons to either update a database, or to reset the form:

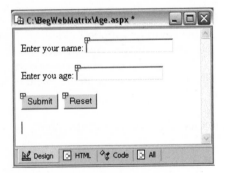

You can add code to the following sub to reset the form:

```
Sub Reset()

   Textbox1.Text = ""
   Textbox2.Text = "0"

End Sub
```

Then you can call this sub from a couple of places. Firstly in the `Page_Load` event, and secondly, when the `Reset` button is clicked:

```
Sub Page_Load(sender As Object, e As EventArgs)

   If Not Page.IsPostback
     Reset()
```

```
    End If

End Sub
...
Sub btnReset_Click(sender As Object, e As EventArgs)

   Reset()

End Sub
```

You can see this code in action in a file in the code download for this chapter, called `Age.aspx`, which also demonstrates some fun logic:

Since no-one knows how old Dave is, we've taken a guess!

## Why Bother with Functions and Procedures?

Why not just type all the code into a single method, instead of breaking it into different functions and procedures? Well, using functions and procedures is probably the single best way to make your code easier to read and write. They enable you to take a fairly complicated set of instructions, and group them together under one name.

Functions and procedures allow you to take a complex task and break it down into a series of sub-tasks. Each procedure or function performs a specific distinct function or job. This provides code that is easier to maintain because specific functions can be rewritten *without* affecting the rest of the code, as long as they have the same inputs and outputs as the original function or procedure. The code that calls the function or procedure does not need to change.

Using functions and procedures also makes a long, complicated task easier to read by calling various functions to perform the detailed work. Additionally, functions are **reusable** because they should perform one specific task that may be needed by other functions and code. Sending an e-mail is a function that is used in many different programs, for instance. This function can be used over and over again.

If you name your functions and procedures carefully, people can read the name and gain an understanding of what the function or procedure is designed to do. They don't need to look at the code itself and try to figure it out.

This also makes code easier to write, because you can start thinking about things without too much detail, and just have a series of method names – then you can start to implement each method as you add more detail to your program. This process is known as **step-wise refinement**. It's a great, easy way to write code, as we'll see later in the book.

The other important thing is that you can write a function or procedure once, and then reuse it over and over again. Later in the book, we'll see how to create special libraries of useful functions and procedures that you can use in any page you like. You can even share your library with other programmers, to save them the time of writing those methods themselves.

# Event Handlers

We have already seen event handlers in action, but here we are going to define it properly. An **event handler** is basically a kind of procedure, as it is asked to do something as a result of an event, and no result will be returned by it (although if the contents of the page change as a result of the event being fired, the user will see the page in their browser change). Say, for instance, the user enters the information for sending an e-mail and then clicks the Send button. This click event will fire the `OnClick` event handler and ask the web server to send it out. That is, the user asks the web server to do something, and the server just does it. This matches with the definition of procedure saying that a procedure is a type of method, which would perform some kind of action but without returning any value.

The two parameters, the sender and event arguments, are required for event handler. When we click on a button and fire the `OnClick` event handler, the code will look like this:

```
Sub Button1_Click(sender As Object, e As EventArgs)

End Sub
```

There are two arguments in this event handler. The first argument identifies the object that is raising this event, for instance, it maybe a `Button`, `TextBox`, or the `Page` itself. The second argument contains the event data or information related to the event handler. For example, when you click on an `ImageButton`, the X and Y coordinates of the point where the mouse was clicked are the information passed to the `ImageButton_OnClick` event handler, and can be retrieved and used in the event handler by referring to `e.X` and `e.Y`. Each argument has its data type and the compulsory parentheses are used to include the two arguments for that procedure.

# Nesting Revisited

Earlier in the chapter, we covered the concept of nesting. In that section, you had only seen loops before, so our discussion of nesting was limited. Now, though, you have also seen the concepts of functions and procedures, so let's look at how you can apply nesting to these kinds of code blocks. Some of these examples aren't strictly speaking nesting, but more like *combining* of different structures. The important thing to understand in each case is *how* each of these structures can be combined.

There are lots of ways to use nesting in Visual Basic .NET, so here is a quick reference:

❑   You can put decisions and loops inside procedures and functions:

```
Function myFunction() As Integer
  Do While condition
    ' This will work
  Loop
  If condition Then
    ' So will this
  End If
End Function
```

❑   You can call procedures and functions from inside loops and decisions:

```
Do While condition
  x = myFunction()
Loop
If condition Then
  myProcedure()
End If
```

❑   You can put loops inside decisions:

```
If Not sheLovesMe Then
  Dim n
  For n = 1 to 100
    Label1.Text = Label1.Text & "I love you! <br/>"
  Next n
End If
```

❑   You can put decisions inside loops:

```
Dim n
For n = 1 to 100
  Label1.Text = Label1.Text & "I love you! <br/>"
  If sheLovesMe Then
    Exit For
  End If
Next n
```

❑ You can have a loop within a loop, or a decision within a decision:

```
If testScore >= 50 Then
  Label1.Text = "Well done you passed"
  If testScore >= 80 Then
    Label1.Text = "... with a distinction - well done!"
  End If
End If
```

❑ But you cannot put one method definition (that is, a function or procedure) inside another:

```
Function myFunc() As Integer
  Sub myProcedure()
    ' THIS WON'T WORK
  End Sub
End Function
```

Although you can't *create* one method within another, you can *call* a function or procedure from within another function or procedure, so the following would be acceptable:

```
Function myFunc() As Integer
  myProcedure()
End Function
```

We saw this in action briefly when we looked at the age example during our discussion of procedures.

# Summary

In this chapter, you've learned a lot about the foundations and basic units of programming – making choices in code, branching, functions and procedures, and seeing how to lace all of these parts together into functional code. These techniques have been around since the very early days of programming, and you'll be using them in every program you write.

The topics we covered include:

❑ How we can define and use functions and procedures to group tasks together

❑ How to write If ... Then ... End If statements

❑ How to make more complex choices using Else and ElseIf

❑ How to make decisions that depend on more than one condition

❑ How to write more elegant and readable code for multiple decisions based on the value of one condition by using a Select ... Case Statement

❑ How to use a For loop to run parts of your program a certain number of times

❑   How to use Do loops, and the significance of the While and Until clauses

❑   How to nest one block of code inside another

In the next chapter, we'll learn about storing different types of data. You've already seen Dim statements here and there, and played around with numbers and text in this and the previous chapters, but now you'll learn exactly how to use the different data types available to you in your applications.

# CHAPTER 5

# Storing Different Types of Data

Pretty much every ASP.NET page you ever write will store information, or data, in your computer's memory. You'll almost always be getting information from a user and doing something with it, or getting data from somewhere else and showing it to the user. If you don't plan on using information in your programs, you don't need to write a dynamic web site and there is no point in using ASP.NET or Web Matrix – you might as well just type a document in Word and save it on to a web server!

In this chapter, you'll see how you can use your computer's memory to store information, and how you can make that information work for you. Specifically you will learn how to:

❑   Tell your computer *what* you'll be storing, by declaring **variables** of different **data types**

❑   Store, retrieve, and manipulate text when it is in memory

❑   Make your programs do math

❑   Get dates, keep them, and show them off

Technically speaking, a computer's memory *doesn't* contain information... it contains **data**. Data *becomes* information when you put it in a context where people can understand what it means. Your pages are useful if they present information, not just data – your users need to understand it, but to a computer, which really doesn't understand very much, it's all just data.

## Introducing Variables

**Variables** are basically values that can change, in other words, they can be **assigned** different values, hence their name. In ASP.NET pages, variables can only exist in memory from the time when the server receives a request for the page, until the time when the server has finished sending the page back to the web browser. This is not very long at all – often less than a second. You might think this means variables are not very useful. You'd be wrong. Even in this short time, variables can be extremely useful.

You'll be pleased to know that we've already met several different types of variables. In the previous chapter, we looked at looping structures that did some simple counting using variables that were `Integers`. We also used the `String` data type when passing in arguments to the e-mail function, which means that we used strings to communicate with the function. Strings and integers are two examples of **simple data types**.

## Declaring Variables

If you want to store some information in real life, you need something to write it on – such as a piece of notepaper, your hand, a wall, or whatever. Similarly, information in Visual Basic .NET is stored in variables, and before you can store any information you need a variable in which to store it.

Visual Basic .NET already knows how to make variables – you just need to ask for one. This is called **declaring a variable** because you are stating that a piece of memory is going to be used for a particular purpose. When you declare a variable, you also need to declare what **type** of data the variable will store. This is called the variable's **data type**. If you don't ask for the right sort of variable, you'll end up not being able to store the information you want.

The easiest way to declare a variable is using the `Dim` keyword, like this:

```
Dim emailAddress As String
```

The `Dim` keyword means, "I want a new variable", and is short for *dimension*. When you create a variable you can give it any name you want – but you should always try to use a name that describes what the variable is for. This makes it easier to understand your programs. I've called mine `emailAddress`, which is pretty clear. (I've written enough programs with variables called `eA` to know full names are a good idea.)

Next, we say what data type we want; in this case, we want a `String`. In programming, a **string** means a sequence of characters – effectively a piece of text, but doesn't have to contain *just* letters. Our `emailAddress` variable is used to hold text. Data types are very important because they define what sort of data variables can store, how they behave, and what they can do. We will look at several data types in this chapter, as well as the various operations that can be performed on the different types. In the following two *Try It Outs*, you'll see how – even if a data type can store the information you need, if it's the wrong choice then the variable can behave strangely.

**Try It Out**      **Using Variables**

In this example, we're going to create an ASP.NET page that can do some simple math. You'll soon see that – if you want simple math to *stay* simple – you need to choose the right data type to start with.

**1.** Start up Web Matrix, and create a new ASP.NET page called `Variables.aspx`.

**2.** Drag a `Label` control onto the page, then type + with a space on either side, drag on another `Label`, then type =, again with a space on either side, and finally add another `Label`. Next add a new line by pressing the *Enter* key, and drag a `Button` control onto the page. Your page should end up looking like this:

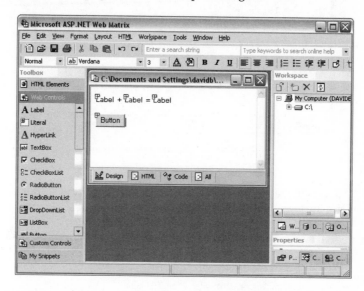

**3.** We won't bother with setting up properties this time – just double-click the button to wire up the event handler, and add the following code:

```
Sub Button1_Click(sender As Object, e As EventArgs)
    Dim myFirstNumber, mySecondNumber As Integer

    myFirstNumber = 7
    mySecondNumber = 8

    Label1.Text = myFirstNumber
    Label2.Text = mySecondNumber

    Label3.Text = myFirstNumber + mySecondNumber
End Sub
```

**4.** Now run the page using *F5* or the **Start** button and when it appears, click the button. You should see the following:

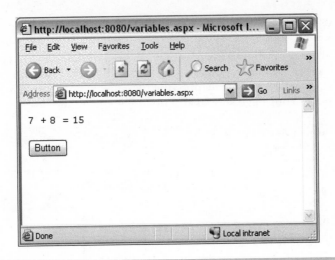

## How It Works

We'll be coming back to this example in a minute, but let's just have a look at what happened when we clicked the button.

First of all, we created two new variables for representing whole numbers, in other words of type Integer:

```
Dim myFirstNumber, mySecondNumber As Integer
```

In Visual Basic .NET, you can declare lots of variables of the same type in one line – you just separate the names by a comma. So, we have two variables for holding numbers, myFirstNumber and mySecondNumber. Next, we put some numbers into the variables:

```
myFirstNumber = 7
mySecondNumber = 8
```

myFirstNumber now has a value of 7, and mySecondNumber now has a value of 8. These numbers are stored in memory, and we can retrieve the values by the names we selected for our variables. The next two lines set our first two Label controls to display these values:

```
Label1.Text = myFirstNumber
Label2.Text = mySecondNumber
```

So, we've already got the "7 + 8 =" bit, next we need to actually do the math. Adding the two variables together is really easy – we just set Label3.Text to myFirstNumber plus mySecondNumber and this gives us a result of 15:

```
Label3.Text = myFirstNumber + mySecondNumber
```

This worked pretty well, but if we'd used the wrong data type, things would have behaved very differently, as we'll see!

## Try It Out      Your First Bug

1. Go back to your code, and change the declaration so that we create two `String` variables instead of two `Integer` variables:

```
Dim myFirstNumber, mySecondNumber As String
```

2. Now run the page again, and click the button again. The result is quite different:

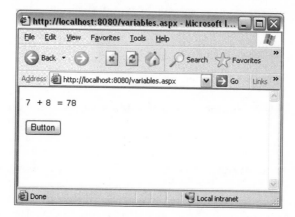

## How It Works

We have now ended up with 7 + 8 = 78 for some reason. While this isn't mathematically correct, it's not too hard to work out what's gone wrong. Instead of adding the numbers together, our program has *concatenated* the two numbers, writing a 7, and then an 8 to the page. In other words, the two numbers have been simply *stuck together* to give the final result of 78!

This is exactly the sort of the problem that can occur if you don't use the correct data type. Strings are designed for storing text, so you can't really do math with them – if you "add" two strings, Visual Basic .NET will simply join them together.

> If you don't declare variables with the correct data types, your program may produce unexpected and unwanted results at best, if not errors. Make sure you declare variables with the correct data types!

# *Where Can I Use My Variables?*

As we saw in the last chapter, the **Code** view in Web Matrix can contain functions and procedures: self-contained blocks of code. There is also the area of the code window that is outside any particular function or procedure. Variables can be declared inside any function or procedure, or in the area outside a function or procedure. However, the place where you declare variables affects the places where you can access them, *and* how long they retain their values.

In the last example we declared our variables inside the `Button1_Click` procedure, but that's not the only place we could do it. Let's say that we want to have two buttons on our form – one to add the numbers together, and one to subtract one from the other. Before we do that though, fix the bug by changing the `Dim` statement back to `As Integer`:

```
Dim myFirstNumber, mySecondNumber As Integer
```

Now that's fixed, the button does this, as we saw earlier:

1. Declares two `Integer` variables

2. Sets each variable to a number – one is set to seven, and the other to eight

3. Sets `Label1.Text` to `myFirstNumber`, and `Label2.Text` to `mySecondNumber`

4. Sets `Label3.Text` to `myFirstNumber` *added* to `mySecondNumber`

Next, go back to **Design** view, and change the existing button's `Text` property to `Add`, then drag a new one next to it and set its `Text` property to `Subtract`. The second button will do exactly the same as the **Add** button for the first of three steps listed above – only the fourth step is different because we want to subtract instead of add.

We could just retype most of our addition code into the subtract button's event handler. That way, we'd have two lots of code that do the same thing, which is a waste – and will become even more of a waste if we decide to add more buttons. So let's make a procedure to carry out the first three steps, and then we can call it from both of the buttons.

Go back to **Code** view, and add the following procedure:

```
Sub SetVarsToInitialValues()

End Sub
```

Now select everything from `Button1_Click`, except for the last line – the line where we do the addition. Either cut-and-paste or drag this code into the `SetVarsToInitialValues()` procedure. Now add a call to `SetVarsToInitialValues()` at the start of `Button1_Click`, so that your code should look like the following:

```
Sub SetVarsToInitialValues()
  Dim myFirstNumber, mySecondNumber As Integer

  myFirstNumber = 7
  mySecondNumber = 8

  Label1.Text = myFirstNumber
  Label2.Text = mySecondNumber
End Sub

Sub Button1_Click(sender As Object, e As EventArgs)
  SetVarsToInitialValues()
  Label3.Text = myFirstNumber + mySecondNumber
End Sub
```

Now try running the page. It won't work. You'll get a compilation error, which means that ASP.NET cannot work out what your code means. The problem line is:

```
Label3.Text = myFirstNumber + mySecondNumber
```

and the complaint is that we didn't declare myFirstNumber. Hold on, we *did* declare it, in the SetVarsToInitialValues() procedure! What is going on?

Our myFirstNumber is now declared *inside* the SetVarsToInitialValues() procedure, but we try to use it in the Button1_Click procedure. This won't work because if you declare a variable inside a procedure or function, it ceases to exist as soon as the procedure or function finishes. In fact, if you declare a variable inside a function (or procedure), you can *only* see it from inside that function. Variables declared within a procedure or function are limited to that procedure or function, unless you pass them into another procedure or function as an argument – as we saw in the previous chapter.

Fortunately, there's a really easy way to fix this particular problem – just move your declaration outside any procedures. If you do that, you can use the variables from anywhere in the page, so move the declaration from inside SetVarsToInitialValues() to the area outside any function or procedure:

```
Dim myFirstNumber, mySecondNumber As Integer

Sub SetVarsToInitialValues()
  myFirstNumber = 7
  mySecondNumber = 8

  Label1.Text = myFirstNumber
  Label2.Text = mySecondNumber
End Sub

Sub Button1_Click(sender As Object, e As EventArgs)
  Label3.Text = myFirstNumber + mySecondNumber
End Sub
```

The variables now exist from when the page gets requested right through to when it gets displayed, and *any* function or procedure in the page can use them.

> **The places where a variable is accessible are known as the variable's 'scope'.**

Let's clarify this a bit more. Take a look at the following table, which compares the behavior of variables declared inside a procedure or function with those declared outside:

| Variable declared | Is alive | Can be used by |
| --- | --- | --- |
| Inside a function or procedure | For as long as that function or procedure runs | The function or procedure where the variable is declared. Functions and procedures you call from within this one can receive the variable as an argument. |
| Outside any functions or procedures | From the time the page is requested, until all of the code has run | Any code in the page. |

# Dealing with Text – Strings

Now that we've covered the basics of creating and accessing variables, it's time to move on to some specific types of variable. We'll start by looking at strings, the data type used for holding text, in more detail. The web is all about strings. Pages are mainly text. Even the special tags used for displaying pictures or changing the format of a page are text, although the user doesn't get to see it (we'll see some examples of this later in the chapter).

In a website you will probably declare more strings than any other data type. You'll also use lots of strings that you don't declare – for example a control's `Text` property is a string, and we've already used them a lot. Since strings are so important, the designers of Visual Basic .NET made working with them easy.

## Defining a String

Whenever you place data into a string within your code, you must enclose it in quotation marks. This tells Visual Basic .NET which parts of your code are supposed to be names for variables, procedures, and so on, and which parts are **literals** – values that you actually type in when you are writing the program, such as numbers, dates, and text.

The following code:

```
Dim myName As String
myName = "David"
```

means "Create a string variable called `myName`, and set it to `David`." `myName` is a variable, and can change. `David` is a literal, a string that has its value defined in the program code.

Now look at this code:

```
Dim myName As String
myName = David
```

This means "Create a string variable called `myName`, and set it to the value of the variable called `David`." Since there are no quote marks, there is no way to tell that `David` is supposed to be a literal. If there is a string variable called `David` available, that's exactly what this will do, otherwise you will get a `Name 'David' is not declared` error message. Don't forget to open and close your strings with `"` and `"` marks. Sometimes, this even slips the mind of experienced programmers , and it's a frustratingly easy mistake to make!

If you want to put double-quotation marks `"` *inside* the string itself, you can. You just need to double them up, like this: `""`. So, a string assignment like this:

```
myString = "Hello, my name is ""Meryll Streep""."
```

will result in the string `Hello, my name is "Meryll Streep".`.

> *The pair of double-quotes used in this way to represent a double-quote within a string is known as an **escape character**. We need it because the double-quote is a **reserved character** in Visual Basic .NET, used to mark the start and finish of a string.*

## Joining Strings Together

We've already seen how to concatenate two strings using the + sign, even if it was accidentally on purpose! Most Visual Basic .NET programmers don't use + for joining strings because it's confusing to have two signs that do two different things (adding and joining). Instead, most programmers use the & sign:

```
myFullName = myFirstName & " " & myLastName
```

This does the same thing to strings as the + operator, but is less ambiguous. By the way, when joining strings together, always remember to add spaces if you need them, as shown in the above example by adding `" "` into the string. This is another of those "easy to do, easy to forget" programming necessities.

# Pulling Strings Apart

So much for joining strings together – we also often want to pull them apart. For example, we might want to get only the first three letters of a string, or we might want to break it down into smaller sections.

There are basically two ways to access parts of strings. The first is to get sections of the string by requesting specific characters based on their position within the string – for example, getting the first seven characters, or the last seven, or seven from the middle. The second is to split it into sections based on a particular character – for example, using the space character to split a string into individual words. Let's see an example of each.

---

**Try It Out**     **Pulling Strings Apart by Number**

In this example, we'll see how to get particular sub-sections of a string by expressing the positions of the range of characters that we are interested in.

1. Start a new page called `Strings.aspx`.

2. Drag a `TextBox` onto the page, then add a new line and type **start:** , and add another `TextBox` next to the prompt. Add another line, type **length:** , and add another `TextBox`. Finally on two separate lines, add a `Label` and a `Button`. You'll end up with this:

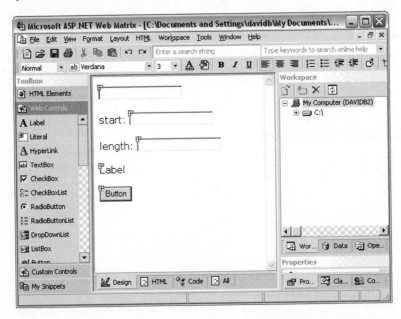

Set the TextMode property of the first TextBox to MultiLine, and make it a fair bit bigger than the default size. Set the Text property of the Button to Show Substring, and also clear the Text property of the Label control.

**3.** Now double-click the button, and add this code:

```
Sub Button1_Click(sender As Object, e As EventArgs)
   Dim fullString, subString As String
   Dim startPos, length As Integer

   startPos = CInt(TextBox2.Text)
   length = CInt(TextBox3.Text)

   fullString = TextBox1.Text
   subString = fullString.SubString(startPos, length)
   Label1.Text = subString
End Sub
```

**4.** Press *F5* to run the page, and then enter a sentence or two in the top textbox. Now enter a whole number into each of the other textboxes. The start number represents a position in the string where our substring will start. The length number represents how long our substring will be. You need to make sure that start plus length are not greater than the total length of the string in the box. When you click the button, you will see a subsection of the text you entered in the textbox:

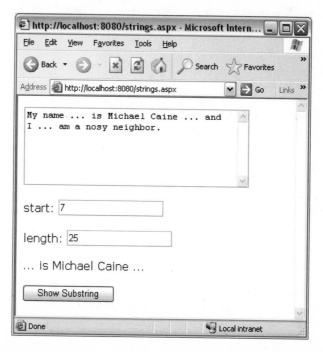

## How It Works

The number in the start box represents the starting point for the substring (with the very first character being zero). The second box represents the length that you want the substring to be. So the substring in the above screenshot starts at the 8th character position (because we're starting from zero), and carries on for 25 characters.

In the first couple of lines, we declare a pair of strings, and a pair of integers:

```
Dim fullString, subString As String
Dim startPos, length As Integer
```

In the next two, we assign the values in the second two textboxes to our integer variables:

```
startPos = CInt(TextBox2.Text)
length = CInt(TextBox3.Text)
```

As we saw in previous chapters, CInt() is a function that can convert a string to an integer – provided the string is actually a whole number within the acceptable range for an integer. (So if we enter something other than a whole number into one of these boxes, ASP.NET will detect the error, and throw an **exception**.)

*We'll look at how to cope with **exceptions** and other errors in Chapter 7.*

The next line assigns the value in TextBox1 to our fullString variable:

```
fullString = TextBox1.Text
```

This next line is where the magic happens. All strings have a built-in method that takes two integers as arguments, and returns the substring according to those values. We assign this to subString:

```
subString = fullString.SubString(startPos, length)
```

Finally, we assign the subString variable to the Label1.Text property:

```
Label1.Text = subString
End Sub
```

Often, it is not completely necessary to declare variables. To save space, we could have done all this on a single line – and not declared any variables at all:

```
Sub Button1_Click(sender As Object, e As EventArgs)
  Label1.Text = _
    TextBox1.Text.SubString (CInt(TextBox2.Text), CInt(TextBox3.Text))
End Sub
```

This works just as well, in fact it will be a little faster, but it's a bit long and unwieldy. This is sufficient reason alone for declaring variables – they can dramatically increase the readability of your code, which is an advantage when you're forced to review your own work months down the line!

**Splitting Strings**

Often we don't want to access a particular numeric position in a string – we want to break it down into separate units, based on what it contains. For example we might want to break a full name like "Dave Sussman" into separate first and last names. We can do this by breaking the string into different substrings, based on where the space appears. Let's see how to do that now:

**1.** Keep the same file open, add a space after the button, and then add another button. Set its Text property to Split.

**2.** Double-click this button, and add the following code:

```
Sub Button2_Click(sender As Object, e As EventArgs)
  Dim myString As String
  Dim myWords As String()
  myString = TextBox1.Text
  myWords = myString.Split(" ".toCharArray())

  ' Start bulleted list
  Label1.Text = "<ul>"

  Dim word As String
  For Each word in myWords
    Label1.Text = Label1.Text & "<li>" & word & "</li>"
  Next word

  ' End bulleted list
  Label1.Text = Label1.Text & "</ul>"
End Sub
```

**3.** Run the page, put some words in to the box, and click the Split button. You should see a bulleted list of every word you entered:

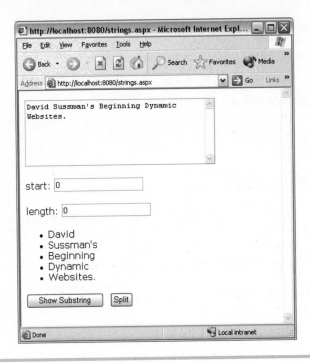

## How It Works

There's some new stuff going on here – and this example will take quite a bit of explanation. This is because we're using one language, Visual Basic .NET, to generate code for another language, HTML. The string that we end up passing to `Label1.Text` is actually something like:

```
<ul><li>Hello,</li><li>my</li><li>name</li><li>is</li><li>Meryll</li><li>Stre
ep.</li><li>Please</li><li>leave</li><li>a</li><li>message</li><li>after</li>
<li>the</li><li>beep!</li></ul>
```

but your web browser knows that the tags in the angle brackets represent bullets – so it displays a bulleted list. `ul` is short for "unordered list", and everything between `<ul>` and `</ul>` is therefore part of an unordered (meaning un-numbered) list. `li` is short for "list item", so everything between a `<li>` and `</li>` is a single item on that list.

This is HTML – if you look at the HTML tab for any page in Web Matrix, you will see a lot of stuff in angle brackets. Web Matrix makes it easy to avoid thinking about HTML, but if you're serious about web development you should definitely learn all about it.

This isn't the only new thing about this particular example, so let's take a proper look at the code. The first unusual line is this one:

```
Dim myWords As String()
```

When you have parentheses after the data type, this means that you want an **array**. An array is a single variable that contains many variables of the same type. We'll have a better look at arrays in the next chapter, but just remember that myWords is a single variable that can hold lots of strings. The next new line is this:

```
myWords = myString.Split(" ".toCharArray())
```

Strings have a Split() method that lets you split one string into a number of smaller strings, based on separator characters that you specify. To let you specify multiple separators, the Split() method takes an array of characters as an argument – that is, one variable made up of one *or more* individual Char (short for character) variables.

It just so happens that there's a very easy way to convert a string to an array of characters – the string has a ToCharArray() method, which will take a string of any length and convert it into an array of separate characters. For example, if you were to change the content of the string from " " to " /-\", the code would split words that were divided not only by spaces, but by slashes and dashes too.

We could split a string by any character or set of characters we wanted. The important thing is that these are individual characters – their order is not important in this case.

The last new thing in this example is a new kind of For loop. Remember, we now have an array of words – but we don't know how many words are in that array (because we don't know how many spaces there were in the string). We want to display every single word, so we want to loop through the array. The For Each loop is a very easy way to do this:

```
Dim word As String
For Each word in myWords
  Label1.Text = Label1.Text & "<li>" & word & "</li>"
Next word
```

In the above code, word is a String. Each time we go around the loop, the next item in myWords automatically gets assigned to word. We then add that word to our label, along with the additional tags needed for your browser to display a bullet.

*We will look properly at For Each loops in the next chapter.*

## Comparing Strings

We've played around with strings quite a bit now, but one of the most common things you'll want to do with strings is compare two or more of them to see if they're the same. There's a couple of ways we can do this – we could compare a string variable to a literal:

```
If emailAddress = "davidb@wrox.com" Then
   ' give the man a cigar
End If
```

or we could compare two string variables:

```
If emailAddress1 = emailAddress2 Then
   ' yep, this is the same person
End If
```

There is a complication here though. When you want to compare two strings to see if they match, the test is case-sensitive. This means that DavidB@Wrox.com does *not* equal davidb@wrox.com. In a lot of cases you would want them to be considered equal – after all, they will both work and end up sending e-mail to the same person because e-mail addresses themselves are *not* case-sensitive. The solution is to compare versions of the string that have been converted to all the same case. Let's have a go at that now.

**Try It Out      Changing Case**

1. Create a new page called StringCase.aspx, and drag on a pair of textboxes, a button, and two labels, and add some text, so that your page looks like this:

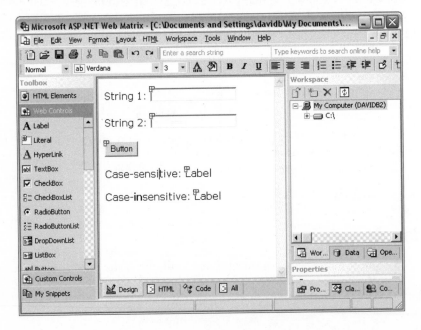

*Similar to Microsoft Word, you can use the formatting bar to make any of your text bold, italicised, or underlined, and so on.*

**2.** Double-click on the button, and add the following code:

```
Sub Button1_Click(sender As Object, e As EventArgs)
   Label1.Text = (TextBox1.Text = TextBox2.Text)
   Label2.Text = (TextBox1.Text.toUpper() = TextBox2.Text.toUpper())
End Sub
```

**3.** Run the page, and play around with different strings in each textbox. The top label will present the result of a normal (case-sensitive) comparison. The bottom one will present a case-insensitive one:

## How It Works

The first line tests to see if `TextBox1.Text` and `TextBox2.Text` are equal, in both value *and* case. If they are, this expression is true – and we assign `True` to `Label1.Text`.

On the second line, we use the `toUpper()` method to get an uppercase version of `TextBox1.Text` and `TextBox2.Text` – this means that whatever case people have typed into the textbox, we're comparing an uppercase version. For example, if I type davidb@wrox.com in one box, and DavidB@Wrox.com in the other then the first line will make `Label1.Text` display **False**, but the second line ends up comparing DAVIDB@WROX.COM and DAVIDB@WROX.COM, so we get **True** displayed in `Label2.Text`.

We can also use `toLower()` to convert a string to all lowercase, which works in a similar way.

# Strings on the Web

There are some problems with getting and displaying strings, which are *specific* to using strings on the Web. To really make use of strings, you need to understand how to get around these problems.

**1.** Go back to `Strings.aspx`, and add one last button next to the others, and set the `Text` property to `Copy`. Double-click it and add the following line of code:

```
Sub Button3_Click(sender As Object, e As EventArgs)
    Label1.Text = TextBox1.Text
End Sub
```

This just means that whatever's typed into the top textbox gets copied to the label.

**2.** Now run the page using the usual method of pressing *F5* or hitting the Start button to test the page out. Type in a few lines of text (and add some blank lines too). Now press the Copy button. It won't work quite as well as we hoped:

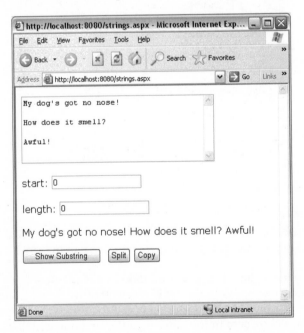

## How It Works

Although we entered text on different lines, we ended up with everything displayed on one line in the label. This is irritating, but there's a very simple reason for it – web browsers ignore the normal carriage return character. Web browsers use `<br/>` for adding a new line. If we want to present text on different lines, we need to replace each normal carriage return with a `<br/>` tag. We'll do that now, using the `Replace()` method.

## Try It Out      Using Replace()

1. Double-click the **Copy** button again in Web Matrix, and edit the code. You will need to change the line that we added before, modifying it to look like the following:

```
Sub Button3_Click(sender As Object, e As EventArgs)
    Label1.Text = TextBox1.Text.Replace(vbCrLf, "<br/>")
End Sub
```

2. Run the page again using the same joke as before and, as you will see, the results are much better:

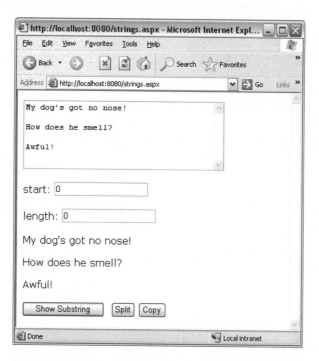

## How It Works

The key to this example is the `Replace()` method, which takes two strings as arguments – the first one is the string we want to remove, and the second one is the one we want to replace it with. It returns a copy of the string with the specified replacement:

```
Label1.Text = TextBox1.Text.Replace(vbCrLf, "<br/>")
```

In this case, we're replacing `vbCrLf` with `<br/>`. `vbCrLf` is the term Visual Basic .NET uses to refer to a 'normal' new line, and literally means "carriage return character followed by line feed character".

Of course, the `Replace()` method is useful in far more circumstances than replacing `vbCrLf` with `<br/>`, and can be used to replace any string with any other.

OK, now for another problem. HTML tags are based around angle brackets. If somebody types a < into our textbox, without a > afterwards, then the results can be messy, because the browser will attempt to interpret everything after the < bracket as HTML code. Try typing <a href=" or <!-- into the box for a particularly despicable result!

Fortunately, there is an easy way around this and you are about to see this in the next *Try It Out*.

## Try It Out    Using HtmlEncode()

The method we use to get round the problem we just spoke about is `HtmlEncode()`. This takes normal text, and makes sure that it's suitable for displaying in a web page. Let's give that a try now.

**1.** Re-open the code for the Copy button and modify it to read like this – make sure you get all the brackets right!

```
Sub Button3_Click(sender As Object, e As EventArgs)
    Label1.Text = Server.HtmlEncode(TextBox1.Text).Replace(vbCrLf, "<br/>")
End Sub
```

Enter your text into the box and whatever you type now should be accurately portrayed in the label below when you use the Copy button:

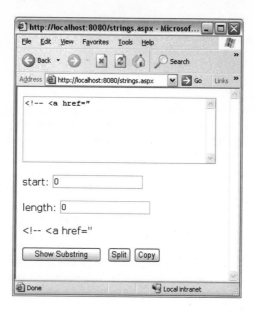

## How It Works

This line is starting to get a little bit complex now, and we could break it down into simpler units by declaring variables. I wanted to show you a more complex line of code, though, because you won't be able to avoid seeing them forever, like this:

```
Label1.Text = Server.HtmlEncode(TextBox1.Text).Replace(vbCrLf, "<br/>")
```

First of all, `TextBox1.Text` is HTML-encoded. This means that angle brackets – and other special characters – are replaced with special codes so that your web browser displays them, rather than thinking that they are special instructions, and then getting confused. This is the meaning of:

```
Server.HtmlEncode(TextBox1.Text)
```

This special function (which is actually provided by the `Server` object) returns a string. Instead of assigning the string directly to a variable, we perform another method on it – this time replacing `vbCrLf` – the special Visual Basic .NET code for a carriage return, which we saw earlier, with `"<br/>"`.

This in turn returns another string, so the whole expression to the right of the = sign is assigned to `Label1.Text`.

Instead of this line, we could have used:

```
Dim originalText, encodedText, replacedText As String
originalText = TextBox1.Text
encodedText = Server.HtmlEncode(TextBox1.Text)
Label1.Text = encodedText.Replace(vbCrLf, "<br/>")
```

This is longer, but clearer.

You can also keep adding more `Replace()` method calls onto the end, and have quite a bit of fun with them. Try finding a smiley face picture, and then adding the following line to the end of the procedure:

```
Label1.Text = Label1.Text.Replace(":-)", "<img src='mysmileyface.gif'>")
```

where `mysmileyface.gif` is the name of your smiley picture.

> As well as the **`Server.HtmlEncode()`** function, there is also
> **`Server.HtmlDecode()`**, which changes HTML-style text back into normal text.

That's all the discussion of strings we need for now, but you'll be seeing more ways to play with strings as we work through the book. Now let's turn our attention to an altogether different type of data – **numbers**.

# Dealing with Numbers

Computers have been used for numbers much longer than they've been used for strings, and as a result, there are lots of different ways of storing numbers in memory – all of which use memory in a different way. There are whole numbers (1, 2, 100, 543), which are known as **integers**, and numbers with decimal points (such as 1.2, 1.5343, 654.78), which are known as **floating-point numbers**.

When you ask Visual Basic .NET to create a number for you, it likes to know what sort of size number you'll be creating, so that it can allocate the right amount of memory. Although `Integer` is the general-purpose whole number, you can have them `Short` or `Long` if you want. And for fractions, you have `Decimal` for numbers with only a few figures after the decimal point, `Single` for numbers which need to be remembered more precisely, and `Double` for super-accurate numbers.

You might read in other programming books, or hear from other programmers, that you should use numbers as much as possible because they are more efficient than strings. They *are* more efficient, but they can also be a real pain. I only use numbers when I plan to use the data *as a* number – to perform mathematical calculations on it, for example. If you are capturing credit card details, telephone numbers, or anything else where you really just want a sequence of digits, strings are probably better.

I've never regretted choosing a string – but I've often tried to do things the 'efficient' way using numbers, and ended up wasting hours on extra bug fixes and validation routines. On the Web, the string is the king, in general of course!

Numbers do have their place though, and it's a very important one. They are useful for counting things, looping, and doing math. So let's find out about how to use them.

## Using Whole Numbers

Most of the time when you use whole numbers, you'll just use an integer without giving it a lot of thought. An `Integer` can store any whole number between 2,147,483,647 and -2,147,483,648. This is a large enough range for most purposes.

If you are using a *lot* of numbers, and they aren't all that big, you might want to try using a `Short` instead. This can hold a whole number between 32,767 and -32,768, and takes up about half the amount of memory.

If you need to store something really big, you could try a `Long` variable. This can store any whole number between 9,223,372,036,854,775,807 and –9,223,372,036,854,775,808 (about nine million, million, million; is there even a word for that amount?!). A `Long` variable takes up about twice as much space in memory as an `Integer`.

Despite the difference in size, what you can do with them remains the same whether it's a `Short`, `Integer`, or `Long` number.

## More Precise Number Types

If you want to go beyond whole numbers, then you can choose from three floating-point number types. These are:

❑  `Decimal` – Useful for financial calculations, and other general floating-point work

❑  `Single` – Can store a larger number than `Decimal` *or* can store a number of the same size, but to a greater degree of accuracy

❑  `Double` – Can store an even larger number than `Single` *or* can store a number of the same size, but to even more accurately

Understanding how floating-point numbers work can be quite hard  because they are limited by the simple size range (which means the potential number of zeroes both before *and* after the decimal point), and the level of accuracy. This rarely has practical implications, because very big numbers usually require less accuracy than very small ones. For most purposes understanding the mechanics is not very important. Just stick with `Decimal`, or `Single` if you're not worried about accuracy, and you are very, very unlikely to have any problems – unless you are trying to write a program to control a nuclear reactor or something.

## Declaring Numbers

Declaring number variables is easy – just follow the tried and tested formula of using `Dim`, like the following:

```
Dim mySavings As Decimal    'floating point number
Dim myOverDraft As Single   'bigger floating point number
Dim unitsSold As Long       'huge whole number
Dim pages As Short          'smaller whole number
```

You can assign values to them just as easily:

```
mySavings = 43.50
pages = 600
```

Note that numeric literals do not require quote marks. This is because Visual Basic .NET does not allow names to start with numbers, so anything that begins with a number must be a literal.

## Working with Numbers

Any programming language will let you do some pretty powerful stuff with numbers. For our purposes though, we don't need to think about trigonometry or calculating square roots. Let's see how to carry out basic math with Visual Basic .NET

Adding and subtracting is easy, you just use + and –:

```
mySavings = mySavings + myRoyalty
```

or something like:

```
myOverDraft = myOverdraft – myRoyalty
```

Unfortunately, the keyboard doesn't have a good multiply and divide sign, so the designers of programming languages need to improvise. The Visual Basic .NET designers chose * for multiplying (it is *quite* close to the multiplication sign) and / to divide (because it looks like the stroke of a written fraction).

Another arithmetic trick is to do integer division. You do this by using \ instead of /. It's much faster than normal division, and guarantees you a whole number as the answer (it just cuts of anything after the decimal point).

One very useful bit of math on the Web is checking credit card numbers. Every credit card number has a built-in checksum, or check number, which helps retailers to spot mistakes in the quoted credit card number. We can use this method to get a pretty good idea of whether a credit card number has been entered correctly – although it's far from foolproof. This will involve some string manipulation too, so watch carefully.

## Try It Out — Checking Credit Cards

This is probably the most powerful program you've written so far. Please stick with it. It will show you how to use many of the techniques we've learned so far in the book, and you'll be left with a function that will be very useful once you get into writing e-commerce sites.

**1.** Create a new ASP.NET page as usual and call it Numbers.aspx. Set up the page's interface to look like the following screenshot, by using some text, a TextBox, a Button, and a Label control:

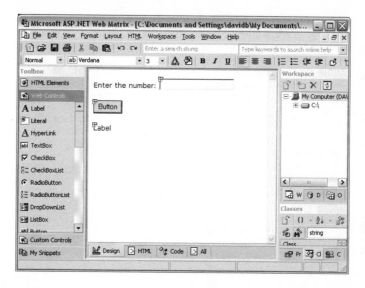

Clear the Label's Text property and change the Button's Text property to Check Card Number.

**2.** We're going to use some stepwise refinement to make this program easier to read and more useful. Double-click on the the button, and add the following code to the handler:

```
Sub Button1_Click(sender As Object, e As EventArgs)
   If ValidateCard(TextBox1.Text) Then
     Label1.Text = "That'll do nicely sir!"
   Else
     Label1.Text = "There's nothing for you here!"
   End If
End Sub
```

As you can see, this code is pretty easy to understand – any programmer can look at the procedure, and quickly see that this button validates the card number. You can easily see the message that comes back if the user gets the number wrong, and you can make it more polite if you want. Unfortunately, Visual Basic .NET doesn't already know how to validate credit cards, so we need to write that function ourselves.

**159**

**3.** In the space above the `Button1_Click` procedure, add the `ValidateCard()` function:

```
Function ValidateCard(cardNumber As String) As Boolean

  ' Reverse order
  Dim reverseNumber As String
  Dim ch As Char

  For Each ch in cardNumber
    reverseNumber = ch & reverseNumber
  Next

  ' Double every other number
  Dim doubledAlternates As String
  Dim thisDigit, index As Integer

  For index = 1 to reverseNumber.Length
    thisDigit = CInt(reverseNumber.SubString(index - 1, 1))
    If index mod 2 = 0 Then
      thisDigit = thisDigit * 2
    End If
    doubledAlternates = doubledAlternates & thisDigit
  Next

  ' Add every single figure together
  Dim sum As Integer
  For index = 1 to doubledAlternates.Length
    sum = sum + CInt(doubledAlternates.SubString(index - 1, 1))
  Next

  ' If sum is divisible by ten, and not zero, then you're through
  ValidateCard = sum <> 0 AND sum mod 10 = 0

End Function
```

**4.** Press *F5* to run the program, and try typing different numbers into the `TextBox`. It does have to be a number – you can't have spaces, or the function won't work. For nearly every number you try, you should be told that the storeowner doesn't really want to serve you. Now find a credit or debit card, and type the number from that in. The result should be much more positive. (If you're worried about typing your card number here, you don't need to be. If you're still worried, find somebody else's card and use that!)

## How It Works

Let's go through and look at exactly what happens when you click the button on the page. First of all, ASP.NET automatically calls the `Button1_Click` procedure, which consists of a simple `If ... Then ... Else` block:

```
If ValidateCard(TextBox1.Text) Then
   Label1.Text = "That'll do nicely sir!"
Else
   Label1.Text = "There's nothing for you here!"
End If
```

The condition for this If ... Then ... Else block is actually a function call. To understand how this works, let's look at the function's definition:

```
Function ValidateCard(cardNumber As String) As Boolean
```

You can see from this that the ValidateCard() function returns a **Boolean**. A Boolean is the simplest variable in programming; it has only two possible values – true or false. If a function returns a Boolean, then it can be used as the condition in a decision-making statement. What we're saying is "if the card is valid then be nice, otherwise be rude". Of course, the computer needs to know *how* to check if the card is valid, which is exactly what we do in the body of the ValidateCard() function.

Looking at the argument defined in our Function definition, even though the argument is a credit card *number*, I've chosen to use a string to store our number. This is because a credit card number is not really a number as we understand it. You never add two credit card numbers together, or subtract one from another, or divide a credit card number by two. A credit card number is really a sequence of digits, and a string is the best way to represent a sequence of digits. We're going to find this is especially true now, because we're going to be treating the credit card number as a sequence of *individual* digits, and not as a single, big number.

Credit card numbers are created to follow a special (and quite complicated) formula. This function is going to check that cardNumber obeys this formula. The first stage is to reverse the number. The following For Each loop goes through cardNumber character by character from start to finish, and adds each character it meets to the *beginning* of another string. The result is that a cardNumber value of 1234567 becomes a reverseNumber value of 7654321:

```
' Reverse order
Dim reverseNumber As String
Dim ch As Char

For Each ch in cardNumber
   reverseNumber = ch & reverseNumber
Next
```

The next step is to work through each digit, doubling the second, fourth, sixth, eight, and so on. Every alternate digit is doubled in size, so 7654321 becomes 71258341:

```
' Double every other number
Dim doubledAlternates As String
Dim thisDigit, index As Integer
```

```
For index = 1 to reverseNumber.Length
  thisDigit = CInt(reverseNumber.SubString(index - 1, 1))
  If index mod 2 = 0 Then
    thisDigit = thisDigit * 2
  End If
  doubledAlternates = doubledAlternates & thisDigit
Next
```

There are two things here that we haven't seen before. The first is the Length property of a String variable. This simply tells us how long the string is ('7654321' is 7 characters long). Using this means that the For loop will go around once for each character in the string. The reason for doing this, instead of using For Each again, is that we need to know exactly what position in the string we have reached at any time.

> Remember that string indexes are zero-based. In other words, a 7-character string consists of character positions 0-6. Our loop counts from 1-7, so we need to subtract 1 from the loop's index to get to the correct position in the string. Alternatively, we could have looped from 0 to reverseNumber.Length – 1 and not subtracted 1 within the loop. The final effect would be the same.

The second thing we have that's new is the mod operator. This is a math operator that works out the remainder you'd get if you divided one number by another. You can find out if something is an even number because if you mod it by two you will get no remainder – so we use it to find out if we are on an even-positioned character (in other words, the second, fourth, sixth, and so on)

We end up with another string called doubleAlternates – which if we started with 1234567 will be 71258341. The next step is to add every digit in *this* string together. This is a much simpler step:

```
' Add every single figure together
Dim sum As Integer
For index = 1 to doubledAlternates.Length
  sum = sum + CInt(doubledAlternates.SubString(index - 1, 1))
Next
```

We keep doing an integer add of the current digit to the running sum total. So in our little example we'll have 7 + 1 + 2 + 5 + 8 + 3 +4 + 1, which gives a sum of 31.

Credit card numbers are designed in such a way that, by the end of this process, you'll have a number that ends in zero (but isn't zero itself). Here's the line that checks whether this is the case:

```
' If sum is divisible by ten, and not zero, then you're through
ValidateCard = sum <> 0 AND sum mod 10 = 0
```

As you know, when you assign a value to a variable, the data type of the variable on the left of the equals sign needs to be compatible with the data type of the expression on the right. `ValidateCard` was defined `As Boolean`, so the type on the left is a Boolean – a true/false value. The expression on the right needs to boil down to a Boolean too – and it does. It's saying "if sum *isn't* zero, *and* if sum *does* divide by 10 without a remainder" then `ValidateCard` should be true. If not, `ValidateCard` should be false.

*This is a very useful and quick way of checking for mistakes in credit card numbers. However, it does not guarantee that the credit card number is genuine. With a bit of thought, anybody could make up a number that obeyed these rules. If you are accepting credit card payments, you need to be much more certain than this that the card number is genuine. You can do this by using a credit card processing company, which can check that the card really does exist, that it has funds available, and even that the name and address match those given by the user.*

Once this has been worked out, the `Button1_Click` procedure will display either the polite or rude message – in our example it will be a rude one. Sorry to do that to you – but I'm not going to tell you my credit card number just so that you can see a polite message.

The Boolean type was a new concept in the above example so let's have a proper look at the Boolean data type.

# Booleans – True or False?

A Boolean is a data type that can store one of two states – whether you choose to call it true/false, yes/no, on/off, 1/0, or whatever. Visual Basic .NET calls the two values `True` and `False`.

If you're new to programming, you might not think it's very useful to store something so simple in memory. After all, the chances of wanting to store one of just two fixed possibilities is pretty remote, right? Wrong. Booleans are used whenever you use a computer to make a decision. For example when you compare two values to see if they are equal, you state "value1 = value2" and are told that the statement is either `True` or `False`. Also, it takes up less memory space for a simple true/false evaluation.

This is how the `If` statement works. `If` expects you to give it a `True` or `False` value. Give an `If` statement a `True` condition and whatever follows the condition will run. Give the `If` statement a `False` condition, however, and whatever follows the `Else` will run:

```
If myBooleanValue Then
   ' This runs if myBooleanValue = True
Else
   ' This runs if myBooleanValue = False
End If
```

You have seen this kind of construct in code many times before, but now you should understand *how* the code knows what to do and where to go.

Declaring a variable as a Boolean is just like declaring any other variable:

```
Dim myBooleanValue As Boolean
```

Often, you will want to perform the steps from the If ... Then statement a while *after* you've decided whether you are going to perform them. Saving the Boolean lets you do this. It enables you to remember a decision, and then act on that decision later.

Booleans are also great at acting as little switches. Let's say you needed to know whether a vital operation has already taken place or not. All you would have to do is create a Boolean and set it to True to indicate that it has taken place, and False if it hasn't:

```
AlreadyDoneThis = True
```

You can also use Booleans as arguments, which is often a very useful way of providing 'optional extras' to your functions:

```
Function validateCard(rejectCardIfWrong As Boolean) As Boolean
```

That's all you really need to know about Booleans for now – simple aren't they?! They are very useful though, and before long you'll be using them all over the place.

# It's a Date (and Time)

You'll often want to work with **dates** in your pages. You'll want people to enter dates into your forms, and you'll want to display dates back to users later. Dates and times are an essential part of many business transactions, and as more business is done over the web, dates in ASP.NET can only become more important.

The key to dates is the Date type. It can store a precise moment in time (right down to minutes and seconds) – and it gives you nearly 8,000 years before you need to worry about another millennium bug.

## Entering a Date and Time

You declare a Date in exactly the same way as any other variable – you just use As Date. It's also pretty easy to define a date value in your code. Remember how we use the quotation marks, " ", to define strings so that Visual Basic .NET doesn't think our strings are variable or method names? Similar problems occur if we just put a date into our code – Visual Basic .NET won't know what to do with it. Or at least, it will know exactly what to do with it – but it will be wrong! Try creating a new page called DateTest.aspx, and adding a Label and a Button on separate lines. Double-click on the Button and add the following:

```
Sub Button1_Click(sender As Object, e As EventArgs)
   Label1.Text = 3/6/2003
End Sub
```

Then press *F5* to run the page. Click the button, and you should see the label display the value we just entered:

```
0.000249625561657514
```

but this isn't really what we wanted. We put in a date, but we've got 3 divided by 6, divided by 2003 – Visual Basic .NET has interpreted our date as a piece of arithmetic, because all it sees are numbers and division operators. The way to tell Visual Basic .NET that the whole thing is a date is to enclose it in # characters, like this:

```
Label1.Text = #3/6/2003#
```

Visual Basic .NET will interpret this date as March 6, 2003. This will seem perfectly sensible to you if you're in America, but if you aren't then you might have expected June 3 instead. Well, Visual Basic .NET is American and when you define a date in # marks, it should always be in m/d/yyyy format. As a programmer, you just need to get used to it.

As well as entering a date this way, it's pretty easy to convert a string to a date, and this feature means you can express your date in lots of different ways. Here's an example:

```
Label1.Text = CDate("3/6/2003")
```

CDate() is a good way to convert text that your users enter into dates, but it's quite unreliable; if the user enters 3/6/2003, it's not easy to tell whether they mean March or June. How the computer decides will depend on its regional settings (you can find your regional settings in Start | Settings | Control Panel | Regional Options). If you write your ASP.NET pages on your own computer, and then copy them to a server with different regional settings then the decisions will change. My favorite way around this is to always use a shortened word for the month – such as Jun:

```
Label1.Text = CDate("3 Jun 2003")
```

Another way to get dates from a user is to use a Calendar control. We'll have a look at this useful control in a minute, but first let's see how to display dates to the user.

## Displaying Dates

The way Visual Basic .NET stores dates in memory is very different from the way a human writes them down. When you want to show a date to a human, you have lots of choice about how to display it. You can display the date in words, or as a shortened version with numbers. You can also choose to display the part of the date that signifies the time of day, rather than the day, month, and year.

**Different Date Formats**

**1.** Start a new page called `Dates.aspx`. Drag on four `Label` controls and a `Button`, with carriage returns between each one.

**2.** Double-click the button and add the following code:

```
Sub Button1_Click(sender As Object, e As EventArgs)
   Dim myDate As Date
   myDate = Now()
   Label1.Text = myDate.ToLongTimeString()
   Label2.Text = myDate.ToLongDateString()
   Label3.Text = myDate.ToShortTimeString()
   Label4.Text = myDate.ToShortDateString()
End Sub
```

**3.** Press *F5* to run the page. My screen looks like this, but yours may well be different:

## How It Works

First of all we create a new `Date` variable. Then we set it to the current date and time using the `Now()` function (which simply returns a `Date` variable for the current time and date).

The next four lines display the date in different ways – and the exact detail of how they display will depend on the 'regional' settings of the server that hosts the ASP.NET page. We can't be completely sure of exactly how our dates will display. You could type in exactly the same code as I did, but get quite a different date format.

## The Calendar Control

One reliable method of getting dates from the user is the `Calendar` control. This is a web control that displays a calendar, and lets the user pick a particular day. (It actually lets them choose whole months or weeks too, but let's take things one step at a time.)

**1.** Create a new page called `Cal.aspx`, and drag a `Calendar`, a `Button`, and a `Label` onto it, each on a separate line.

**2.** Double-click the button and add the following code:

```
Sub Button1_Click(sender As Object, e As EventArgs)
    Label1.Text = Calendar1.SelectedDate.ToLongDateString()
End Sub
```

**3.** Run the page and have a play selecting dates and clicking the button:

### How It Works

When you click the button, we're getting the currently selected date, and displaying it in long date format using `Label1`.

By default, the `Calendar` loads up to display today's date. If you want to make it jump to a different date, you need to set its `TodaysDate` property. If you wanted to show people a calendar for July 2005, then you would add the following code:

```
Sub Page_Load(sender As Object, e As EventArgs)
   Calendar1.TodaysDate = #7/15/2005#
End Sub
```

Have a go at adding this to the `Page.Load` event handler, or set the property on the control when you're in **Design** view.

Of course a calendar has far more properties and methods than the ones we've seen here, but we've covered some of the useful ones. We can play with the other properties using the **Properties** window in Web Matrix – we get a lot of control over the appearance and behavior of our calendar controls.

# Using Constants

Variables are values that can change. We give them a name, and then we can read to and write from the value that they hold. Literals are values that we directly type into our program code, like `"Hello"`, `12.3`, or `#1/3/2003#`. Of course, these values can't change while the program is running – they can only change if a programmer edits the code.

**Constants** are named values that cannot change during the running of a program. They are declared in a similar way to variables, but they use the word `Const` instead of `Dim` – and they must *always* be assigned a value when they are declared. Here's an example:

```
Const pi As Single = 3.14159265358979
```

It's clear why this would be useful. If we need to use the value of *pi* several times in our program, we can now refer to it by a short name – `pi`. Skillful use of constants can also make code easier to understand. Although most programmers would know that `3.14159265358979` is an approximation of *pi*, and is unlikely to mean anything else, a number like 7 could mean lots of things. Days in the week? Colors in the rainbow? Dwarves? Without analyzing the code, it would be impossible to tell. Using constants, it becomes much easier:

```
Const numberOfDwarves = 7
```

From then on, we can use the constant instead of the number itself. Of course, in this case the name is longer than the value so we lose some initial coding time, but it's usually worth the extra effort.

The real value of constants, though, is that they make code much easier to maintain. If disaster strikes and we're left with only six dwarves, or we decide that our approximation of pi needs to be more accurate, we only need to make the change once – in the constant declaration. Everywhere that uses the constant will be updated automatically.

These are the main reasons for using constants. They are simple and there isn't really much of consequence to say about them, but they are very useful.

# Converting Between Types

In a few of our examples now we've had to convert values from being strings to being integer values so that we can perform some math calculation on them. To do this, we've used the `CInt()` function, which is a quick 'n easy VB.NET-specific method for grabbing a string value and converting it to an integer. In a similar way, we can use `CStr()` and `CBool()` to convert to a string, or to a boolean value, and so on. The functions you'll probably use most often include:

| Function | Result | Acceptable Inputs |
|---|---|---|
| CBool | Converts to a Boolean value | A string of `True` or `False`, or a numeric input of either zero (which converts to False), or any number other than zero (which converts to True) |
| CDate | Converts to a date/time value | A string that is correctly formatted as a date or a time, for example, December 31, 2002, or 7:23:05 PM |
| CInt | Converts to an integer | Any numerical value, including ones with decimals. The resulting Integer will be rounded to the nearest whole number. |
| CStr | Converts to a string | Pretty much anything! |

When we convert from one type to another, we must take care to convert from and to values that are compatible. To demonstrate this, we've included a simple example for you to play with!

| Try It Out | Converting Between Types |
|---|---|

This example will give you a neat page that you can experiment with to better understand how type conversions work.

**1.** Create a new page and call it `Conversions.aspx`.

**2.** In the designer, type Original input: onto the page, then drag a `TextBox` control onto the page, give it an ID of `txtValueToConvert`. Then drag a `Button` control onto the page, set its ID property to `btnConvert`, and its `Text` property to Convert!

**3.** Type the following text, pressing Return after each line:

**169**

> Convert to Integer produces:
> Convert to Date/Time produces:
> Convert to Boolean produces:

**4.** At the end of each line of text, drag a `Label` control onto the page, and name them `lblToInt`, `lblToDateTime`, and `lblToBoolean` respectively. Clear their `Text` properties and you should have the following:

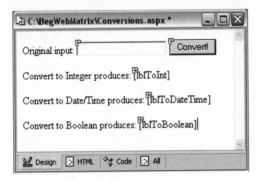

**5.** Double-click the `Convert` button to switch to **Code** view, and enter the following code:

```vb
Sub btnConvert_Click(sender As Object, e As EventArgs)

   Try
      lblToInt.Text = CInt(txtValueToConvert.Text)

   Catch
      lblToInt.Text = "Could not convert to Integer"

   End Try

   Try
      lblToDateTime.Text = CDate(txtValueToConvert.Text)

   Catch
      lblToDateTime.Text = "Could not convert to Date/Time"

   End Try

   Try
      lblToBoolean.Text = CBool(txtValueToConvert.Text)

   Catch
      lblToBoolean.Text = "Could not convert to Boolean"

   End Try

End Sub
```

**6.** Run the page, and try entering different types of values:

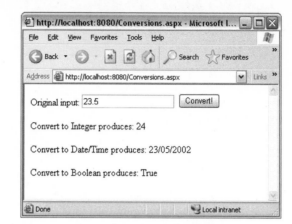

## How It Works

When we enter a value in a textbox on a page, we are entering a string of text into the text property of the textbox control. All of our conversions will therefore be converting from a `String`, to the type of our choice.

You'll notice in the code that we entered that there are a couple of new constructs in our code that we've not yet met. The `Try ... Catch ... End Try` blocks in our code are there to handle exceptions. If we try to convert to a different type that doesn't meet the acceptable conversion criteria, we will cause an exception to be raised. An exception, as we'll see in Chapter 7, is an unexpected error. The `Try ... Catch` statements handle this exception, by presenting the user with a simple error message, instead of an ASP.NET error page, allowing execution of the page to continue as normal.

So, there are two things to consider. Firstly, what happened when we typed in 23.5 into our example, as shown above, and secondly, what happens if we can't convert to a specific type? Let's start with the first question.

- ❑ The string 23.5 is successfully converted to an `Integer`, and is rounded up to 24 (the nearest whole number)

- ❑ 23.5 is interpreted on my system (which is set to UK locale) to be the 23rd of May, 2002.

- ❑ 23.5 can be interpreted as a number that isn't zero, so it equates to `True` when converted to boolean

If you're in the US, or use US date and time settings, you would see an error message for the conversion to a date, because 23 isn't a month. In fact, let's look at the answer to the second question – what happens if you enter a value that can't be converted to the type you require?

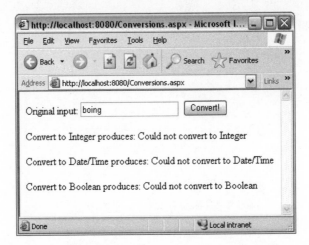

We've entered text that is obviously a word. It's not a number, so it can't be converted to an `Integer`, it's not a date or a time, and it doesn't say `True` or `False`, so we can't convert it to a `Boolean`. Notice how we see text that states that there's been an error, but we don't get an error page. This is one of the great features of VB.NET that we'll look at in Chapter 7.

Before we move on, it's worth considering one more thing, which is that we are displaying our results in the `Text` property of a `Label` control, so we're actually doing an implicit conversion to type `String` in our code! This is a clear example of how versatile a `String` can be.

In addition to these built-in functions, we could also use the `CType()` function, which takes two arguments. The first is the value you want to convert, and the second is the type to which you want to convert, for example:

```
Dim IntegerAnswer as Integer
IntegerAnswer = 42

Dim StringAnswer as String
StringAnswer = CType(IntegerAnswer, String)
```

This function can take any `Dimable` type as the second argument, so we could use `String`, `DateTime`, `Integer`, and so on.

# From Variables to Objects

In this chapter, we've learned a lot about variables, but a term you will probably hear more frequently as a .NET developer is **object**. If you've heard much about programming before, you've probably heard about objects. You might even have heard that Visual Basic .NET is 'object oriented'. Being 'object oriented' may sound a bit daunting, but using objects is easy – you've already done quite a lot of it.

Very simply, an object is a *thing*. You can't necessarily see it, but you know its there. People sometimes say "In Visual Basic .NET every *thing* is an object." Here's what they mean. A textbox is a *thing*, and so in Visual Basic .NET it is an object. A piece of text is a *thing*, and so in Visual Basic .NET is an object. A number is a *thing*, and so in Visual Basic .NET is an object. Every *thing* in VB.NET is an object of one sort or another.

Look at this line of code:

```
Dim numberOfChildrenInClass As Integer = 34
```

Variables, like this one, allow us to give names in our code to *things* that we need to make use of. In other words, variables are *names* that we attach to objects. When we create an integer variable like this, we're creating a name for an integer object. If we create a variable called `numberOfChildrenInClass`, and assign it a value of 34, what we're doing is creating an integer object with the integer value of 34, and giving it the name `numberOfChildrenInClass`. When we use the variable, we call it by name in order to get at the value that the integer object holds. For these simple objects, our variables only hold a value, for example, an integer, a string, a date, and so on.

Likewise, when we work with a textbox control, we are actually using a textbox object, and referring to it by its name. The ID property is the name for our textbox, so in a lot of our examples, we have textbox objects called Textbox1, Textbox2, etc. as these are the system-generated names when a new textbox object **instance** is created. It is important for code maintenance that these name are made meaningful, otherwise in a few weeks anyone, including yourself, will have difficulty understanding how the code works.

> *The technical definition that we'll explore in the next chapter is that we're using an* **instance** *of the TextBox* **class**. *Creating a new object that we can use in our code means that we are creating a new instance of the object, the definition (or template) for the object is held in a class. Creating an instance of an object is a process known as* **instantiation**.

The `TextBox` object is a bit more complicated than a simple `Integer` or `String` object, as an instance of a `TextBox` object will contain all of the properties we assign to the `TextBox` (so, the `ID` property, the `Text` property, and many more will all be stored in our instance of the object).

That's as far into object land as we're likely to go for now, but we'll be using some interesting objects in the next chapter, as well as learning more about classes and namespaces, which will help you to better understand what's actually going on when we use objects.

# Summary

We've seen a lot of new concepts in this chapter, and there's been a lot to take in. I've deliberately moved through things very quickly to get you familiar with the most important issues of declaring and using variables. We've seen how to declare variables using the `Dim` keyword, use them to store information, and then make powerful changes to that information.

Specifically we've seen:

- ❑ How to declare a variable using `Dim`

- ❑ What parts of a page can see a variable, why some can't, and how to control it

- ❑ Ways of manipulating strings of text in our code

- ❑ Different ways of storing numbers

- ❑ Why it's useful to have your program remember true/false values, and how to do it using Booleans

- ❑ Date variables, how to obtain correct dates, and how to use them in your pages

- ❑ How to obtain dates reliably using the `Calendar` control.

We also touched on arrays, which are special variables that can hold lots of other variables of the same type, but we'll be learning much more about this in the next chapter. We'll also learn more about converting objects from one type to another, something we briefly discussed in this chapter when we used `CInt` and `CDate`.

Perhaps even more importantly, we've see how to store data for longer than the split second between a page being requested and the request being completed.

The things you've seen in this chapter will be useful every day of your programming life. As you program more and more, you'll realize just how powerful these simple data types are.

# CHAPTER 6

# Working with Collections of Data

In the previous chapter, we learned all about simple objects with simple data types, and we saw how the type of object we use in any situation is very important. In this chapter, we'll learn more about *how* to work with different types of objects that are used to store collections of data.

Our collections of data will be short groups of values, and we can display these values in controls that work with collections on our web pages.

In this chapter, you'll learn how to:

- ❑ Store a simple list of values and display them on a page
- ❑ Sort that list of values, and add more values to the list
- ❑ Work with different types of collections of values that have different functionality
- ❑ Use the .NET Framework to store collections of classes within **namespaces**

So, let's start by looking at what collections are, and how we can use them.

## Storing Collections of Data in Code

Storing single values in our code is all very well, but sometimes we might want to store *more* than one related value in our code and collect these values together. For example, we could store a list of the colors of the rainbow; red, orange, yellow, green, blue, indigo, and violet, and refer to these values in our code.

You may recall from Chapter 3 that we looked at creating a collection of values using the **ListItem Collection Editor** builder in Web Matrix. (This is in the *Try It Out* section entitled *Getting the User Details*.)

There are several different types of collections in .NET that we can use for storing values. These are **arrays**, **array lists**, and **hashtables**, so let's take a look at each of them in turn.

# Arrays

A simple list **array** is used to store a series of items, and each item is referenced by a number. Let's take a look at a simple array of string values. The following array is called `ColorList` and, as you can expect, contains the colors of the rainbow:

| Item | Value (String data type) |
|------|--------------------------|
| 0    | Red                      |
| 1    | Orange                   |
| 2    | Yellow                   |
| 3    | Green                    |
| 4    | Blue                     |
| 5    | Indigo                   |
| 6    | Violet                   |

In this array, we are storing the seven colors of the rainbow, and giving each of them an individual index number. Indexes in Visual Basic .NET *start from 0*, so although there are seven items, our numbering only goes up to 6.

So, we can store information in an array, but what can we do with it? Well, somewhere, over the rainbow, there's an answer – let's take a look at an example of arrays in action. Buckle your seatbelt, Dorothy, 'cause Kansas is going bye-bye!

**Try It Out**　　**Working with Arrays**

In this example, we'll take our simple colorful array and incorporate it into a simple page.

**1.** Create a new ASP.NET page and call it `Arrays.aspx`.

**2.** Start by typing in something like the following text onto the page: Select a color from the list:.

**3.** Next, drag a `DropDownList` control onto the page, and change its `ID` property to `ddlColorList`.

**4.** Drag a `Button` control onto the page next to the `DropDownList` control, and change its `ID` property to `btnSelectColor`. Also, change its `Text` property to `Click here!`.

**5.** Place the cursor to the right of the button, then press *Return* to start a new line. Add a `Label` control to the page, clear its `Text` property, and set its `ID` to `lblOutputMessage`. You should now see the following in **Design** view:

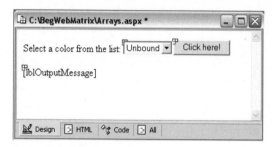

**6.** Now switch to the **Code** view. Firstly, we need to enter some code that creates and fills the array, fills the drop-down list with the colors:

```
' Create an empty array with seven elements
Dim ColorList(6) as String

Sub Page_Load
  ' Add the colors to the array
  ColorList(0) = "Red"
  ColorList(1) = "Orange"
  ColorList(2) = "Yellow"
  ColorList(3) = "Green"
  ColorList(4) = "Blue"
  ColorList(5) = "Indigo"
  ColorList(6) = "Violet"

  If Not Page.IsPostback
    Dim ColorName as String

    ' Display the colors in our drop-down list
    For Each ColorName in ColorList
      ddlColorList.Items.Add(ColorName)
    Next
  End If
End Sub
```

**7.** Then, go back to the **Design** view and double-click on the button to have the `Click` event handler wired up by Web Matrix for us. You will need to add the following code so that the page can react to that event:

```
Sub btnSelectColor_Click(sender As Object, e As EventArgs)
   ' Display the confirmation message on the page
   lblOutputMessage.Text = "You selected " & ddlColorList.SelectedItem.Value
   lblOutputMessage.ForeColor = _
      System.Drawing.Color.FromName(ddlColorList.SelectedItem.Text)
End Sub
```

**8.** Run the page, select a color, and click the button. You should see something like the
following:

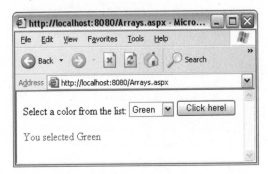

## How It Works

This example produces some quite simple results, but as we were putting it together, we've used
quite a few useful tools along the way. Let's take a look at what we've done in a bit more detail.

The first thing we do in our code is to create our blank array:

```
' Create an empty array with seven elements
Dim ColorList(6) as String
```

We have to do this outside all of the methods on our page because we need to be able to access
the array from all of them. The *scope* of our array is crucial for our application to work, as we
discussed in the previous chapter. We also specify the data type of all of the elements in the
array in this statement. An array can only store items of the same type.

Once we have our blank array, we need to fill it with our list of colors. We want our drop-down
list to have the list of colors in it when the page is loaded, so we add some code to the
Page_Load event-handler, which runs each time the page is loaded.

```
Sub Page_Load
   ' Add the colors to the array
   ColorList(0) = "Red"
   ColorList(1) = "Orange"
   ColorList(2) = "Yellow"
   ColorList(3) = "Green"
```

```
ColorList(4) = "Blue"
ColorList(5) = "Indigo"
ColorList(6) = "Violet"
```

When the page is loaded, we populate our array with our colors, as we saw earlier. Now we need to fill the list with these values, but we *only* want to do this the *first* time a page is loaded, so we use a condition we first met in Chapter 3 to determine if the page is being posted back to the server or not:

```
If Not Page.IsPostback
```

So, let's now add the colors to the listbox:

```
  Dim ColorName as String

    ' Display the colors in our drop-down list
    For Each ColorName in ColorList
      ddlColorList.Items.Add(ColorName)
    Next
  End If
End Sub
```

We create a temporary variable, called `ColorName`, to store an individual value from the array. We then use a `For Each` loop to work through the colors in our array, one by one, by working with *each* value in the array in turn. The first value in the array is `Red`, so the first item added to the drop-down list is `Red`. The next one is `Orange`, and so on, and so on.

The final part of our code writes our message to the screen when the button is clicked:

```
Sub btnSelectColor_Click(sender As Object, e As EventArgs)
   ' Display the confirmation message on the page
   lblOutputMessage.Text = "You selected " & ddlColorList.SelectedItem.Value
   lblOutputMessage.ForeColor = _
     System.Drawing.Color.FromName(ddlColorList.SelectedItem.Text)
End Sub
```

We start by displaying the message itself, taking the currently selected color from the drop-down box, and adding that to the end of a fixed message. The message is displayed as the `Text` property of the `Label` control. The last part of our code changes the color of the message:

```
   lblOutputMessage.ForeColor = _
     System.Drawing.Color.FromName(ddlColorList.SelectedItem.Text)
End Sub
```

In this final step, we are setting the `ForeColor` property of our label to the currently selected color from the drop-down box. It's a little more complicated than that though. The drop-down box has a list of string values. The `ForeColor` property requires an object of type `Color` in order to set the color of the text. We need to have some way to generate the right kind of object so that we can set the color. This is where the `FromName()` method comes in.

Later in this chapter, we'll learn more about the System.Drawing part of this method call. All we need to understand for now is that .NET has a Color **class**, stored within the System.Drawing **namespace**.

> We introduced two important new words in that last paragraph – class and namespace. As we'll learn later in the chapter, classes and namespaces are a core part of .NET, and an essential concept to understand if you want to be a proficient ASP.NET developer.

The Color class contains a FromName() method. This method takes a string of a color, and creates an object of type Color from this name. The name we pass in is the currently selected item from our drop-down list, generating a Color object representing this color. This means we can change the color of our text.

So, we've used a simple array on a drop-down list on a page. Arrays are a great way of storing a list of values of a specific type. We could store an array of integers, an array of dates, and so on. Arrays are just a way of collecting together a set of related values of a certain type.

## Taking it Further – Arrays

A cool feature of arrays is that they can be **sorted**. If we wanted to turn our rainbow inside out, we could do so by reversing the order of the colors in our list, or we could even sort our colors alphabetically. All we need to do is add a single line of code to our example.

If you want to try this out, try adding the following line to your example to sort your array in reverse order:

```
' Add the colors to the array
ColorList(0) = "Red"
ColorList(1) = "Orange"
ColorList(2) = "Yellow"
ColorList(3) = "Green"
ColorList(4) = "Blue"
ColorList(5) = "Indigo"
ColorList(6) = "Violet"
Array.Reverse(ColorList)
```

Alternatively, add the following to sort the array alphabetically:

```
...
ColorList(6) = "Violet"
Array.Sort(ColorList)
```

If you tried these two modifications out, you would end up with the following screens – after saving and restarting the page of course:

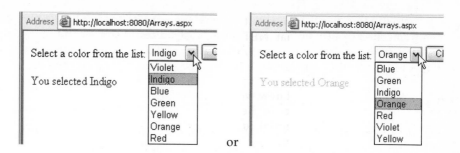

On the left screenshot, the order of the array has been reversed. On the right-hand image, the array has been sorted alphabetically.

What if we want to insert a value between two existing elements? Well, it is possible to extend the boundary of our arrays by using the Visual Basic .NET ReDim statement. This will allow us to create a new array that is larger but empty, or we can preserve the existing content, and add more elements to our current list. Let's take a quick look.

If we want to add another color to our list of colors, we can either amend the original code to create an array that stores 8 colors, or we can change the size of our array dynamically later on in our code, using something like the following:

```
Dim ColorList(6) as String

Sub Page_Load
  ColorList(0) = "Red"
  ...
  ColorList(6) = "Violet"

  ReDim Preserve ColorList(7)
  ColorList(7) = "Magenta"
```

This will add Magenta to our list of colors for the benefit of those who feel there's not enough pink in the rainbow:

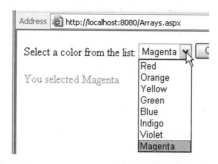

Arrays aren't actually that flexible though. It would be great if we didn't have to resize our arrays when we needed to add more elements, and instead could simply add more and more elements whenever we needed them. It would also be great if we could insert elements into the array. For operations like this, we need a different type of collection. Enter the `ArrayList`!

# Array Lists

An `ArrayList` is a special kind of array that has some advantages over the simple array. With an `ArrayList`, we can store a collection of elements, and add or remove items from that collection, all without any real difficulty. So, it's easier to use, and it can do more than an array – so why use arrays in the first place? The answer is that simplicity comes at a cost, because the performance of an application can suffer a bit if you use an `ArrayList` (this is because it requires more processing power than a simple array, which can have significant performance implications on larger-scale web applications). If you're only using a fixed list of values, such as the seven colors in the rainbow, an array is perfectly adequate.

Let's look at how `ArrayLists` work by expanding our previous example.

---

**Try It Out**       **Using ArrayLists**

---

For this example, make a copy of your `Arrays.aspx` page in the state we finished with it in the previous *Try It Out*. The reason I say this is because you may have played with some of the code in the previous section to see the effects of reversing and sorting arrays. Rename the copy to `ArrayLists.aspx`.

**1.** Firstly, in the Design view, position your cursor after the drop-down list control (before the button), and then press *Return* twice to add a couple of new lines. Type the following text to prompt the user: Then select a font style from the list:.

**2.** Add another drop-down box at the end of this text and set its ID property to `ddlFontList`. Your design view should now look like this:

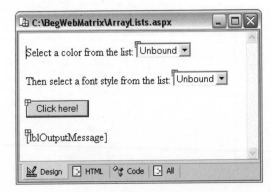

**3.** There are several small pieces of code that we need to add to our example to add `ArrayList` functionality, so take care to add all of the following four sections of highlighted code:

```
Dim ColorList(6) as String
Dim FontList as new ArrayList()

Sub Page_Load
...
  ColorList(6) = "Violet"

  FontList.Add("Times New Roman")
  FontList.Add("Arial")
  FontList.Add("Verdana")
  FontList.Add("Comic Sans MS")

  If Not Page.IsPostback
    Dim ColorName as String

    For Each ColorName in ColorList
      ddlColorList.Items.Add(ColorName)
    Next

    ddlFontList.DataSource = FontList
    ddlFontList.DataBind()
  End If
End Sub

Sub btnSelectColor_Click(sender As Object, e As EventArgs)
  lblOutputMessage.Text = "You selected " & _
    ddlColorList.SelectedItem.Value & " text written in " & _
    ddlFontList.SelectedItem.Value
  lblOutputMessage.ForeColor = _
    System.Drawing.Color.FromName(ddlColorList.SelectedItem.Text)
  lblOutputMessage.Font.Name = _
    ddlFontList.SelectedItem.Text
End Sub
```

**4.** After adding all that lot, it's time to see it in action! Run the example, select a color and a font, then click the button:

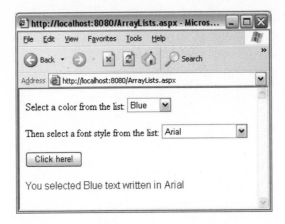

## How It Works

Let's look at the new sections of code that we added. The first line simply created a new `ArrayList` object, ready to hold some information:

```
Dim FontList as new ArrayList()
```

We don't have to specify how many items our list will contain – we simply declare that we're creating a new `ArrayList`. We include the `new` keyword to specify that we are creating a new instance of the `ArrayList` object.

So, in our `Page_Load` event, we add values to our `ArrayList`:

```
FontList.Add("Times New Roman")
FontList.Add("Arial")
FontList.Add("Verdana")
FontList.Add("Comic Sans MS")
```

The syntax we use when adding values to an `ArrayList` is slightly different from that of an array. We add items to an `ArrayList` by using its `Add()` method, without specifying a position in the list.

We also used a slightly different method to add these items to the second drop-down list, a process known as **data binding**:

```
ddlFontList.DataSource = FontList
ddlFontList.DataBind()
```

Data binding, as we'll see in Chapters 8 through to 10, is the process of adding all the items in a collection to a web control that can display a collection. Binding to an array is a very simple process – we set the data source for our control to the collection we want to bind to, then we call the `DataBind()` method to initiate the binding process. It's a little easier than iterating through the collection, as we did before, but it has the same effect. Our second drop-down list box will now contain a list of fonts.

Finally, we alter our output message to integrate a font into the output:

```
lblOutputMessage.Text = "You selected " & _
    ddlColorList.SelectedItem.Value & " text written in " & _
    ddlFontList.SelectedItem.Value
```

The actual text of the message is changed slightly to include the two different values. Then we set the color as before:

```
lblOutputMessage.ForeColor = _
    System.Drawing.Color.FromName(ddlColorList.SelectedItem.Text)
```

Finally, we change the font of our output text to the font specified in the font list.

```
lblOutputMessage.Font.Name = _
    ddlFontList.SelectedItem.Text
```

## Taking it Further – ArrayLists

We said earlier that `ArrayLists` make the process of adding and removing elements very simple. Let's take a look at how we could extend our example to incorporate this.

---

**Try It Out**     **Adding New Items to an Existing ArrayList**

**1.** Head back to the **Design** view and add another line to the bottom of our page. Add the text: Enter a new font for the list:.

**2.** Add a `TextBox` to the page, and set its ID to `txtAddFont`. Then add a `Button`, set its `Text` property to `Add New Font` and set its ID to `btnAddFont`. You should have the following layout in **Design** view:

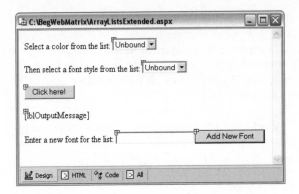

**3.** Double-click the **Add New Font** button, and add the following code:

```
Sub btnAddFont_Click(sender As Object, e As EventArgs)
  FontList.Add(txtAddFont.Text)

  ddlFontList.DataSource = FontList
  ddlFontList.DataBind()
End Sub
```

**4.** Run the page once more, and add a new font to the page by entering the name of a font installed on your system, and clicking the **Add New Font** button. Once you've done this, try outputting the message in this new font:

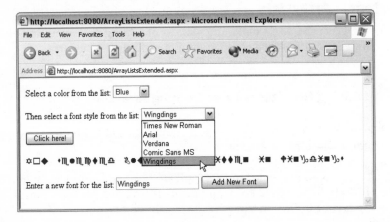

## How It Works

Well, it certainly works, but Wingdings is hardly a readable font! Still, you can choose any font on your system, so if you like to display symbols instead of text for that Matrix look, that's perfectly acceptable.

The new code we added was fairly simple – let's take a look:

```
Sub btnAddFont_Click(sender As Object, e As EventArgs)
  FontList.Add(txtAddFont.Text)

  ddlFontList.DataSource = FontList
  ddlFontList.DataBind()

End Sub
```

We add the new font by using the `Text` property of the textbox we've just added. We then have to re-bind our list of fonts to our drop-down list. The new font is added to the end of the existing list.

Our example has a couple of limitations, for example, if you try to add a font that doesn't exist, you will not be able to change the text to the new font style (there isn't a font called "boing" on my web server machine, but the font name boing would still be added to the list if I were to try to add a font called this. Selecting it from the font list will leave the text written in the default font (Times New Roman).

The other limitation is that adding another new font to the list will remove the previously added font. We didn't store the new font anywhere, so if you want to remember all of the fonts added, you need to add more code.

One of the advantages of `ArrayLists` is that we can insert values into any point in the list. If we wanted to specify the location that our new font would occupy in the list, we could have used the following syntax:

```
FontList.Insert(1,txtAddFont.Text)
```

This would insert our new font, in our case, Wingdings, as the second item in the list (since the items are ordered starting from zero, as with every array). We can remove items from the list quite easily too:

```
FontList.Remove("Verdana")
```

This syntax can be used to remove a named item. Alternatively, we can remove by the current index number of the items:

```
FontList.RemoveAt(0)
```

This will remove the first item in the list, in our case, Times New Roman. Whenever we add, insert, or remove items, the index numbers of the items adjust accordingly.

Let's move on now to look at another type of collection, the `Hashtable`.

## Hashtables

`Hashtables` are a great way of associating values with keys that can identify them. For example, when we used the `ArrayList`, we could refer to the index number of each value, but we needed to figure out the number corresponding to the item we required. With a `Hashtable`, we have a way of replacing the index number system with a key that we specify for each item, which relates to a corresponding value.

It all sounds a bit confusing, so let's take a look at an example:

| Key | Value |
|-----|-------|
| UK | United Kingdom |
| US | United States |
| AR | Argentina |
| IN | India |
| AU | Australia |

In this simple list of keys and values, we can relate the name of a country to its two-digit country code, so rather than having to type out the whole of "United Kingdom", we can use the key value "UK" if we prefer. Let's take a look at the `Hashtable` in action by extending our example.

### Try It Out          Keys, Values, and Hashtables

So far, the text we've used has been quite uninspiring. We're going to extend the example to include something more interesting to read.

**1.** Open up `ArrayLists.aspx` once again. We won't be adding fonts in this example, so we will base this example on the earlier `ArrayLists` example. Save the file as `Hashtables.aspx`.

**2.** We can now start modifying our example. In the **Design** view, we will need to delete the final line on the page, from our previous example. This is the one we used previously to add a font to the drop-down list. Then, add another line on the form, with the text as above. You'll also need to add in a drop-down list (with an ID of `ddlQuoteList`), so that your design-time view looks as follows:

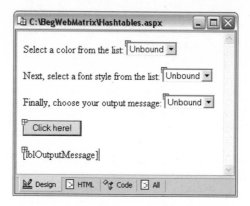

**3.** Head back into code view, and add the following highlighted lines of code. Make sure that the text of the "Joke" is all on one line in your code – we've had to spread it over two lines because of the limitations of page width! Again, we've omitted a full listing to save space:

```
Dim ColorList(6) as String
Dim FontList as new ArrayList()
Dim QuoteList as new Hashtable()

Sub Page_Load

   ...
   FontList.Add("Comic Sans MS")

   QuoteList.Add ("Quotation", _
    "English? Who needs that? I'm never going to England. ")
   QuoteList.Add ("Joke", _
    "There's a pizza place near where I live that sells only slices... in the
back you can see a guy tossing a triangle in the air...")
   QuoteList.Add ("Wisdom", _
    "There is a difference between knowing the path and walking the path.")
   QuoteList.Add ("Saying", _
    "A rolling stone gathers no moss.")

   If Not Page.IsPostback
     ...

     ddlFontList.DataSource = FontList
     ddlFontList.DataBind()

     ddlQuoteList.DataSource = QuoteList.Keys
     ddlQuoteList.DataBind()
   End If
End Sub

Sub btnSelectColor_Click(sender As Object, e As EventArgs)
```

**191**

```
    lblOutputMessage.Text = QuoteList(ddlQuoteList.SelectedItem.Text)
    lblOutputMessage.ForeColor = _
      System.Drawing.Color.FromName(ddlColorList.SelectedItem.Text)
    lblOutputMessage.Font.Name = ddlFontList.SelectedItem.Text

End Sub
```

*Remember to delete the* Click *event handler for the* btnAddFont *button, and its*
*contents, as that button no longer exists.*

**4.** Run the page, enter some values, and select the message you'd like to see. Then click
the button. You should see the following:

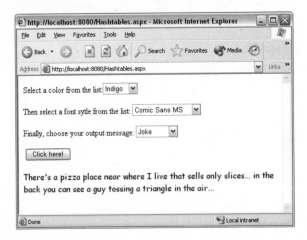

### How It Works

We now have the option to display four different types of messages. Personally, I'm rather fond
of Steven Wright jokes, but you can feel free to display quotes from the Simpsons, wise quotes
from The Matrix, strange proverbs, or whatever you feel like.

Let's see how the code worked. Firstly, we declared a new Hashtable object:

```
Dim QuoteList as new Hashtable()
```

Then we have to fill our newly-created Hashtable with data:

```
QuoteList.Add ("Quotation", _
  "English? Who needs that? I'm never going to England. ")
QuoteList.Add ("Joke", _
  "There's a pizza place near where I live that sells only slices... in the
back you can see a guy tossing a triangle in the air...")
QuoteList.Add ("Wisdom", _
  "There is a difference between knowing the path and walking the path.")
```

```
QuoteList.Add ("Saying", _
  "A rolling stone gathers no moss.")
```

Notice that the Add() method takes two arguments, the **key**, and the **value**. It's important to remember, as mentioned above, that because of page limitations, the joke value appears to break over two lines but you need to make sure that the value is all on one line in your code.

Next, we use code to bind our Hashtable values to the type of quote drop-down list, which looks similar to that used to bind the list of fonts to the font list drop-down box:

```
ddlQuoteList.DataSource = QuoteList.Keys
ddlQuoteList.DataBind()
```

The main difference from our previous binding statement is that we are specifying that we want to bind the Keys in the Hashtable to the list of values in the drop-down list, so we will display only the shortened values in the box. The keys are still associated with their values, though.

Finally, we change the output message to display the selected quote:

```
lblOutputMessage.Text = QuoteList(ddlQuoteList.SelectedItem.Text)
```

We can then apply the correct font and color to the quote as appropriate.

```
lblOutputMessage.ForeColor = _
    System.Drawing.Color.FromName(ddlColorList.SelectedItem.Text)
lblOutputMessage.Font.Name = ddlFontList.SelectedItem.Text
```

## Taking it Further – The SortedList Collection

A slightly different type of collection is the SortedList collection. This collection is very similar to the Hashtable we've just used, except that the keys are sorted alphabetically automatically, regardless of the order in which they're entered, for example:

| Hashtable sorting | SortedList sorting |
| --- | --- |
| Quotation | Joke |
| Joke | Quotation |
| Wisdom | Saying |
| Saying | Wisdom |

All we'd have to do to change to a SortedList collection is to change the line that creates the Hashtable:

```
Dim QuoteList as new SortedList()
```

This would produce the following:

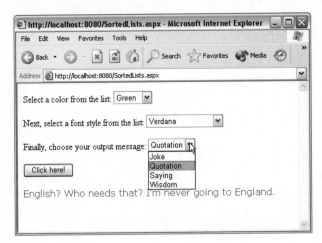

Notice that the list of types of quotes are now sorted alphabetically, even though we didn't change the order in which they were added to the collection in our code.

In our examples, we've worked exclusively with the drop-down list control to display our collections, but there are many other controls we can use for this purpose, including the `ListBox`, and the `DataGrid` controls. We'll be looking at these controls in more detail when we look at working with data stored in a database starting in Chapter 8.

# Classes and Namespaces

In this chapter, we've been looking at different types of collections. Now, we're going behind the scenes of collections, and we'll be introducing some new terminology that will expand your understanding of what's *actually* going on.

The array is a special sort of collection that is slightly different from the other types of collection we've been looking at. Arrays are created as instances of the `System.Array` **class**. The other collections are members of the `System.Collections` **namespace**, and are created as instances of the `System.Collections.ArrayList`, `System.Collections.Hashtable`, and `System.Collections.SortedList` classes. Classes and namespaces are a core part of .NET.

> **Every class that is part of the .NET Framework is part of a namespace that groups classes of similar types – there are over 60 namespaces grouping the thousands of classes that are part of the .NET Framework.**

As you saw in the previous paragraph, we used a period (.) character as a separator for namespaces and classes. The last item in the list is the item that we are considering, for example:

❑ System.Array refers to the Array class, which is part of the System namespace.

❑ System.Collections is a namespace and refers to the System.Collections namespace.

❑ System.Collections.ArrayList refers to the ArrayList class that is part of the System.Collections namespace.

Naturally there is a possibility for confusion, but once you understand the principle, you will quickly learn to identify classes from namespaces. There are far fewer namespaces than classes, and you will gradually get used to them. So, let's explain a bit more about how namespaces and classes work.

The .NET Framework is at the core of every piece of code you write. Classes describe functionality, and when we create a new instance of a class, we have a new **object**. So, the controls we use on a page are described in general classes, which are a bit like templates. When we actually start to use a control, we use a new **instance**, or copy, of that template, and we can then work with that copy as an object with the specific functionality (methods, properties, and so on) of the class it was originally based on.

So, when we create a new ArrayList object, for example, we are creating it from the ArrayList class that describes what every ArrayList object can do. There are several thousand classes in .NET, and looking through a long, long list of classes could get confusing, so to categorize all of these classes, they are grouped together into **namespaces**.

Let's look at some of the namespaces we've already worked with:

| Namespace | Description |
|---|---|
| System | Contains core functionality for .NET, including the Array class, and also includes classes describing the basic data types we met in the previous chapter, such as String, Integer, Boolean, and so on. |
| System.Collections | Contains the classes that store collections of data, including the ArrayList, Hashtable, and SortedList classes. |
| System.Drawing | Contains classes for graphical drawing. We met this namespace briefly when we used the Font class earlier in this chapter. |
| System.Web.UI.WebControls | Contains the classes for all of the web controls we've used, including the Button, the TextBox, and the Label controls. |

If you have the .NET documentation installed, or if you search MSDN online for the reference information on the .NET Framework (via the following URL: http://msdn.microsoft.com), you can see the full list of namespaces available to all .NET programmers:

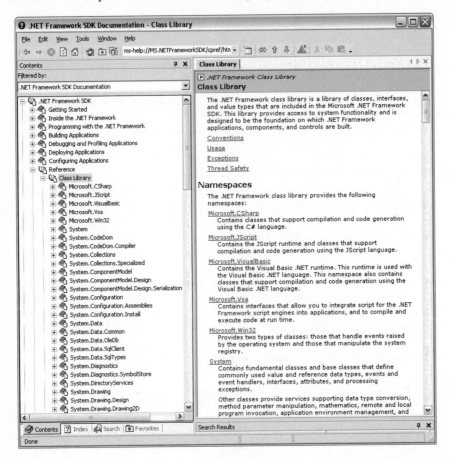

When we meet the chapters on database access (Chapter 8 onwards), we'll learn more about classes contained within the `System.Data` namespace. We'll also meet many other classes as we progress through the book.

*We can even create our own classes, each with their own methods, properties, and so on, which is a topic a bit beyond the scope of this book. For more information, you can refer to* Beginning ASP.NET 1.0 with Visual Basic .NET, *Wrox Press, ISBN: 1-86100-733-7.*

# Summary

In this chapter, we've looked at collecting related information together into a structure that we can use to populate certain types of ASP.NET controls with information. While it would eventually become tedious to enter a great deal of information in this way, it is a useful technique when working with short lists or collections of data.

We have covered:

- ❑ Using arrays to store simple collections of data
- ❑ ArrayLists, and the advantages they have over the simple array, including the ability to dynamically insert, add, and remove items from the collection
- ❑ Storing key-value pairs of data using a Hashtable and a SortedList
- ❑ What namespaces and classes are, and how the .NET Framework stores classes hierarchically in the .NET Framework

In the next chapter, we'll look at how to deal with problems that arise when errors occur in our applications.

# CHAPTER 7

# Debugging and Error Handling

"Errors happen, deal with it", as one of the early ASP.NET specifications stated. A bit abrupt, but it's true. We are, after all, only human. We make mistakes, and things go wrong. There's nothing wrong with admitting that. The important thing is not to panic, and to learn what to do. The best thing to do is not make the errors in the first place, but then that's not always so easy. Besides, errors aren't always your fault – pre-supplied software, users, and events beyond our control can cause plenty of trouble too.

In this chapter we're not only going to look at how to handle problems when they occur, but also how to code so that errors can be avoided, or at the very least, handled gracefully. So what we're going to look at is:

- ❑ What compile errors are, and how to correct them
- ❑ How to handle errors when the web page is running
- ❑ How to prevent errors
- ❑ How to find out what's going on in your code
- ❑ How to debug your code

Some of this may seem a bit like 'real programming', but hey, that's what you are now – a real programmer. You can collect your badge after class.

## Errors and Exceptions

Before we start with the practicalities of dealing with errors, we need to understand a couple of terms. We tend to use the word "error" for most things that go wrong, but there's a difference between things that we know can go wrong, and the unexpected. There are three general types of errors:

❑   **Syntactic errors** – these are found in code that violates the grammar rules of the programming language, and are detected and reported by the compiler.

❑   **Semantic errors** – these occur in code that follows the rules and compiles, but doesn't work as intended.

❑   **Input errors** – these occur when our program gets bad information that it doesn't know how to handle.

You might think that if we know something can go wrong then we can prevent it, but that's not always the case. For example, take user input. We can't control what the user is going to type, so we have to check their input to make sure it's in a format we're able to accept.

The flip side of this is dealing with the unexpected – **exceptions**. For example, when dealing with disk files, we might write our program so that it assumes it has permissions to read them, but what if it doesn't? That's an exceptional situation, but it's one we need to allow for. Likewise, when dealing with databases we expect the database to be available, but what if it isn't? What if the system administrator has mistakenly kicked the plug and switched off a whole rack of machines (don't laugh, it happened to me once!). That's an exceptional situation, but one that's certainly conceivable.

So there are two sides to this story – an error is a generic term that describes something going wrong. An exception, a term to describe the unexpected, is what .NET calls an unexpected event. If something goes wrong in the code, an exception is raised – think of this like giving a lecture, and one of the students raising their hand to ask a question. In the case of .NET, the system raises its hand to say "Something has gone wrong". We can use special code to watch out for these exceptions, and thus take some appropriate action, interrupting the flow of the 'lecture' to deal with the interruption, before hopefully resuming where we left off. This is called catching an exception, and we'll look at that later.

When programming, we never assume that anything is going to work, so we build in defenses to prevent errors and exceptions that would crash our page.

# Compilation Errors

The first thing to look at is errors that happen during compilation. Since ASP.NET pages are compiled when they are run, this can be fairly alarming when you first see it, but don't worry. If we go by my experience, most of these will just be typing errors!

**Try It Out**     **A Compilation Error**

**1.**   Create a new ASP.NET Page, called `CompileError.aspx`.

**2.**   Add a `Label` and a `Button` to the page.

**3.** Double-click the button to get to the code window, and type the following in:

```
Label1.Test = "Some Text"
```

Type it in exactly as it is here – there's a deliberate error.

**4.** Save the page and run it:

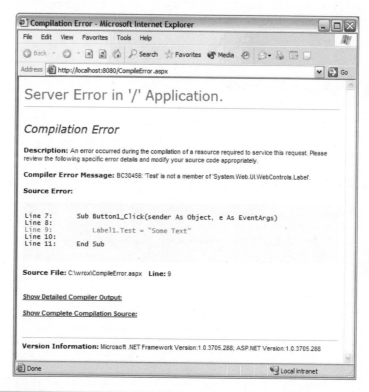

Well, it's somewhat obvious what's wrong from the error message:

'Test' is not a member of 'System.Web.UI.WebControls.Label'.

We simply mistyped the property name, using `Test` instead of `Text`. However, what's important is seeing what happens and understanding the error. On the above screen you can see the source code is shown with the line containing the error highlighted. There are two links on the page that allow us to see more detailed information – you can click them if you like, but for most errors you'll find the default details give enough information. We're not going to look at these here, but the .NET documentation has more details on them.

Fixing the error is simply a matter of correcting the typing mistake and trying again.

# Errors at Run Time

Run-time errors can occur after the program has been compiled, and while the code is running. For these situations you have to build in defenses, to try and prevent things from going wrong. Sometimes though, you have to find out what's going on yourself. So, let's revisit a web page we created early in the book (the `MailingList` example from Chapter 3), and look at an error that we left in.

## Try It Out     Finding an Exception

1. Open `MailingList.aspx`. (`MailingList_part2.aspx` in the code download.)

2. Press *F5* to run the program.

3. Without filling in any fields or changing any defaults, press the **Register** button:

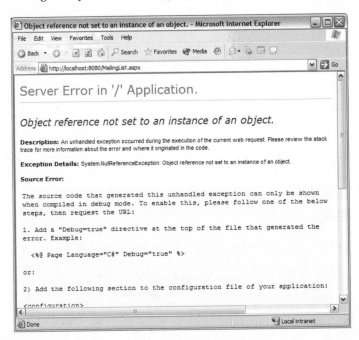

Aha, an exception, but not a helpful message. This is because debugging is turned off.

**4.** In Web Matrix, switch to the **All** view, and add the following to the top line:

```
Debug="true"
```

It should now look like this:

```
<%@ Page Language="VB" Debug="true" %>
```

**5.** Save the page, run it, and press the button again:

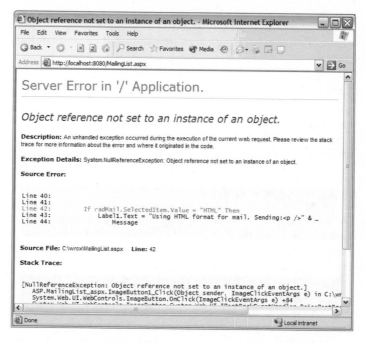

Much better – now we can see the line that the error occurred on.

## How It Works

This is fairly simple – by default debugging is turned off. This means that you can't see the line numbers or the code where exceptions happen. The reason for this is security – once you have deployed a page you wouldn't want any errors to show source code – this could give hackers information about your system that you wouldn't want them to have. So, here's an important note:

> **Always turn off debugging before you deploy your web pages.**

Turning debugging on allows ASP.NET to keep track of line numbers and code details, and from that it can show you where the error was. Of course, showing you where the error was is great, but the error message can often be confusing. Take our error above as an example. What is an 'Object reference', and why should it be set to an 'instance of an object' anyway? Although this sounds like programmer gobbledygook, it does make sense. What you have to remember is that everything in .NET is an object, but objects don't always exist.

To explain what we mean by this let's look at a simple analogy. Consider a catalogue of products – let's pick ice cream. Each item in the catalogue is an object, but it doesn't exist in your space (that is, your house, room, or other area) – it's just a description of what could exist. Until you purchase that item and have it sitting in front of you, it's just an object. Once you have that large tub of double choc–chip it becomes a real-life thing – an instance. The same goes for our code – not everything exists when we think it does. Let's look at the error line in detail, to see what this means:

```
If radMail.SelectedItem.Value = "HTML" Then
```

radMail is the radio button list, and we know that exists since it's on the page. But what about SelectedItem? Surely this exists – it defines which radio button from the list has been selected. Aha – we haven't selected anything, so there's no **instance** – it doesn't exist.

## Preventing Invalid User Input

So now we can see where the error occurred, what can we do to prevent it? One option would be to trap the exception, and handle it gracefully, perhaps by displaying a nice message to the user. However, this isn't the best solution on this occasion. The problem occurs because the radio button list for the mail format (HTML or Text) doesn't have a default – neither one is set. The solution here is to just set one of these to be selected, so that if the user does just press the button, then it doesn't matter. You can set the default by selecting the RadioButtonList on the design surface, and viewing the ListItem Collection Editor for the Items property. This shows the list items, and on each item there is a Selected property – this is the default state of the radio button. Select either one of the items in the left-hand pane and change the Selected property in the right-hand pane to True.

So we've prevented an error by ensuring that the interface doesn't allow an invalid selection. But what about the text entry fields, for name and e-mail address? Well we can do the same thing here, by protecting the interface, to ensure that the name and e-mail address are filled in, and that the e-mail address looks like a valid one. You've already seen some validation in earlier chapters, where we used the RequiredFieldValidator to ensure that fields were filled in. We won't cover that again here – instead we'll look at making sure that the e-mail address is valid.

**Try It Out**     **Validating E-mail Addresses**

**1.** Drag a `RegularExpressionValidator` onto the page, and drop it next to the e-mail textbox. You may need to make your layout table a bit wider to accommodate this.

**2.** Set the `ControlToValidate` property to txtEmail.

**3.** Set the `ErrorMessage` property to Invalid Email Address.

**4.** Click into the `ValidationExpression` property and click the builder button. From the **Regular Expression Editor** window select **Internet E-mail Address**:

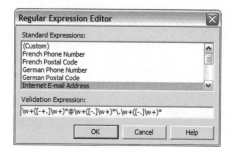

**5.** Press OK, save the file and run it.

**6.** Enter some text in the e-mail address field – make sure it *isn't* a valid e-mail address:

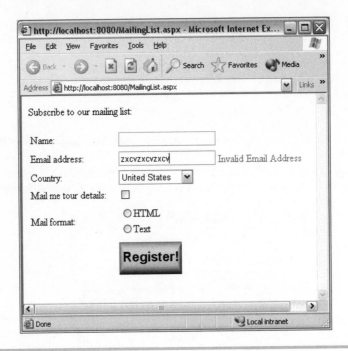

## How It Works

The RegularExpressionValidator works in the same way as the RequiredFieldValidator, in that when a button is pressed, it validates the content of a control. However, instead of just checking that the field has been filled in, it compares the text to a regular expression. A regular expression is a special string that defines how patterns in strings can be matched. In our case it defines how an e-mail address should look, and is checking for something@something.something. So, it's not a great check, but it is better than nothing. The only way to do proper validation of e-mail addresses is to use some code, and actually contact the mail server that the user uses, checking for the e-mail alias. That's all a bit beyond the scope of this book.

As you may have seen in the Regular Expression Editor dialog, you can have expressions to check for phone numbers, zip codes, and so on.

### Other Validation Controls

There are several other validation controls that are worth mentioning:

- ❑ CompareValidator, which compares the contents of two fields. This is useful, for example, in registration pages, where you ask for a password, and a confirmation of that password. The CompareValidator ensures that both fields are the same.

- ❑ RangeValidator, which compares a control with a set of values. This could be used if you had pages asking for an age, or a quantity.

❑   CustomValidator, which allows you to call a custom function to perform validation. This is useful if you have specific validation rules, such as for an ISBN number.

# Defensive Coding

Of course, ensuring that the user interface doesn't allow users to make errors is only one part of the process. There are plenty of times when this just isn't possible, so we have to add preventative measures in our code. This all revolves around the understanding that exceptions can happen, but that you can contain them in a safe way. To do this in code we use Try ... Catch statements, to allow us to Try some piece of code, and Catch any exceptions that occur. The general syntax is like this:

```
Try
      'code to try goes here
Catch ex As Exception
      'code to run when an Exception occurs
End Try
```

What you do when an Exception occurs really depends upon what the exception is. For example, an error connecting to a database might be fatal since you can't continue with the program. On the other hand, trying to access a file that you don't have permission for might not be fatal – you could display an error message to the user and continue. Let's have a look at the first of these, and see how the Try ... Catch works.

## Try It Out        Adding Try ... Catch

**1.**   Create a new ASP.NET File called TryCatch.aspx.

**2.**   Switch to the All view, and add the following between the Register and Script parts:

```
<%@ Page Language="VB" %>
<%@ Import Namespace="System.Data" %>
<%@ Import Namespace="System.Data.Sqlclient" %>
<script runat="server">
```

**3.**   Switch back to Design view, and add a Button, a DataGrid, and a Label to the page.

**4.**   Double-click the button to get to the code view. Add the following code:

```
Sub Button1_Click(sender As Object, e As EventArgs)
   Dim conn As New _
     SqlConnection("Server=foo;Database=pubs;Trusted_Connection=true")
   Dim cmd As New SqlCommand("select * from authors", conn)

   Try
    Conn.Open()
```

```
      DataGrid1.DataSource = cmd.ExecuteReader(CommandBehavior.CloseConnection)
      DataGrid1.DataBind()
   Catch ex As Exception
     Label1.Text = "Could not connect to the database - " & _
                   "please try again later."
   End Try
End Sub
```

**5.** Save the page and run it. Click the button:

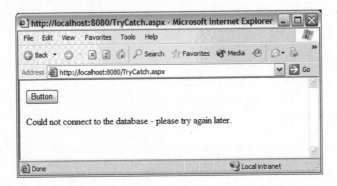

## How It Works

The workings of this are fairly simple. First we define a connection to a database, and a command to run on that database. However, the details of the database server are incorrect – it's pointing to a server called `foo`, which doesn't exist. This will cause the connection to fail.

```
Dim conn As New _
    SqlConnection("Server=foo;Database=pubs;Trusted_Connection=true")

Dim cmd As New SqlCommand("select * from authors", conn)
```

Now we come to the `Try` block – this is where the code is placed in which something may go wrong.

```
   Try
```

The code it contains opens a connection to the database, fetches some data, and displays it in a grid.

```
   Conn.Open()

   DataGrid1.DataSource = cmd.ExecuteReader(CommandBehavior.CloseConnection)
   DataGrid1.DataBind()
```

Now we have the `Catch` block. With this line we are saying that if an exception occurs, we don't want automatic messages shown. Instead, we want to handle the exception ourselves. So we define a variable (ex) of type `Exception`, and when an exception is raised, ex will contain the details of any problems that have occurred:

```
Catch ex As Exception
```

Now we add the code that will run if something goes wrong. Here we set the text of a label to some nice message, rather than displaying a nasty error message.

```
Label1.Text = "Could not connect to the database - " & _
              "please try again later."
End Try
```

## Exceptions

It's worth looking at this topic a little more, since it's very important to understand how exceptions work and can be handled. The example above shows the simplest form – just trapping an exception and displaying some text. However, it's not a very clever piece of code, since we are only displaying some generic text. What happens if the connection to the database succeeds, but some other error occurs? We'd still get the same error message, and this could be very confusing to the user.

What we need is a way of breaking down exceptions into narrow bands, and luckily this has already been done for us. There are many types of exception, including:

❑   `Exception`, which identifies a generic, default exception.

❑   `SqlException`, which is for SQL Server exceptions.

❑   `NullReferenceException`, which is when an object is not set. You saw this happen in the second example in this chapter.

❑   `DivideByZeroException`, for arithmetic errors where a number is divided by 0.

There are many others, and you'll need to look in the documentation for a complete list.

The use of these becomes much clearer when you look at another form of `Try ... Catch`:

```
Try
   'code to try goes here

Catch SQLex As SqlException

   'code to run when a SQL Server exception occurs

Catch ex As Exception
```

```
    'code to run when an Exception occurs

End Try
```

Here you can see we've got two `Catch` blocks – one to run if a SQL Server exception is raised, and one for any other type of exception. The `SqlException` has a narrower focus (only SQL Server or MSDE will raise this), so we handle this type of exception first. If we put the general exception first, then the general exception handler would always catch the exception, whatever type it was. So now we have code that caters for two types of exceptions. However, it's still not perfect, because there could be a number of types of SQL Server exception – for example, insufficient permissions for accessing a particular table in a database. In this case, you wouldn't want to display the message we've displayed – you'd probably want to tell the user to contact the web site administrator.

To find out the details of an `Exception` we can examine its properties and methods:

- ❑ `Message` – the descriptive text of the exception
- ❑ `Number` – the unique exception number
- ❑ `Errors` – a collection of `SqlError` objects giving detailed information about the exception
- ❑ `ToString()` – displays all details of the exception

There are a few others, but those listed above are the important ones. We could use the `Number` property to make our exception handling code more intelligent:

```
Try
  conn.Open()

  DataGrid1.DataSource = cmd.ExecuteReader(CommandBehavior.CloseConnection)
  DataGrid1.DataBind()

Catch SQLex As SQLException
  If SQLex.Number = 17 Then
    Label1.text = "Could not connect to the database - " & _
                  "please try again later."
  Else
    Label1.Text = "SQL Error: " & SQLex.Message
  End If

Catch ex As Exception
  Label1.Text = "Fatal error: " & ex.Message
End Try
```

Here we check for the number of the error – 17 indicates a connection problem, so we show a connection error message. This technique isolates us from one message being used for potentially more than one fault. Of course the big question is how did I know that the error number 17 means a connection problem? Well, I cheated. I just displayed the error number and the message, and then took the number that had already been displayed and used it in the code. The number isn't documented, so it makes it hard to find out, and hard to understand for someone not familiar with it. I use it here to illustrate an important point – you should avoid hard-coded numbers like this in your code. Not only does it make code harder to maintain, but also it ties you down to a specific error number. What happens if Microsoft changes the error number in future releases?

A much better way of tackling this problem would be to wrap distinct parts of the code in `Try` ... `Catch` statements:

```
Try
   conn.Open()
Catch ex As Exception
   Label1.text = "Could not connect to the database - " & _
                "please try again later."
End Try


Try
   DataGrid1.DataSource = cmd.ExecuteReader(CommandBehavior.CloseConnection)
   DataGrid1.DataBind()

Catch SQLex As SQLException
   Label1.text = "Error fetching data."

Catch ex As Exception
   Label1.Text = "Fatal error: " & ex.Message
End Try
```

This code allows us to isolate the process of connecting to the data source from other data-access code. We can now have an explicit message for each exception.

# Finding Out What's Going On

Exceptions and defensive programming are all very well, but there are plenty of times during development that you'll have trouble finding out exactly what's going on in your code. Sometimes it's difficult to understand the flow of your program, and where things are happening. There are two ways to attack this problem. The first is by tracing your code, so you can add information to the page to let you see the page, plus some trace information. The second is by debugging your code, which is where you step through the code line by line as it is executing.

# Tracing

Tracing in ASP.NET is extremely clever, and allows you to put statements throughout your code, which can then appear in a specific location at the bottom of the page. This allows the page to look correct, but still contain trace information. Let's give it a go.

**1.** Using the `TryCatch.aspx` example from above, switch to **All** view.

**2.** Change the top line so it looks like this:

```
<%@ Page Language="VB" Debug="true" Trace="true" %>
```

**3.** Save the page and run it:

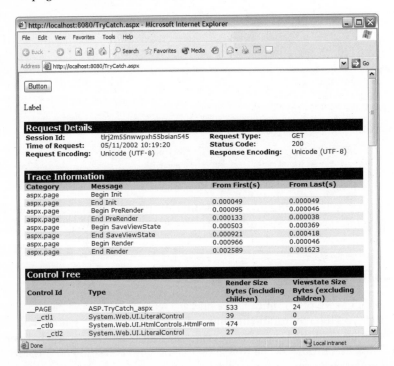

Even without doing anything you'll see that a lot of information has been added to the end of the page. You don't need to worry about most of this at the moment – the important section is the **Trace Information** section. You see some default messages from ASP.NET, but you can also write into this section.

## Try It Out    Writing to the Trace Log

**1.** Switch to **Code** view, and add the following line as the first line of code in the
`Button1_Click` event:

```
Sub Button1_Click(sender As Object, e As EventArgs)
   Trace.Write ("Click", "Start")
```

**2.** On the line between the `Try` and the `conn.Open()`, add the following:

```
Try
  Trace.Write("Opening connection")
  Conn.Open()
```

**3.** On the line after the `Catch`, add the following:

```
Catch ex As Exception
  Trace.Warn(ex.Message)
```

**4.** Save the program, run it, and press the button:

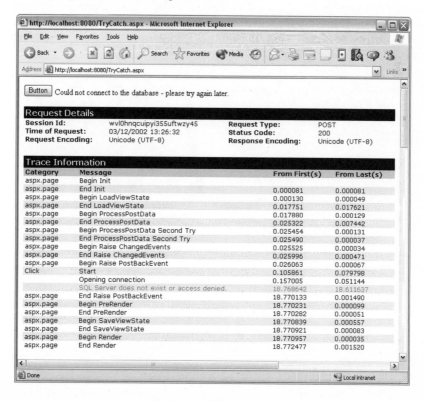

Notice that there are more details in the Trace Information section than before.

## How It Works

The first point is the addition of the trace directive at the top of the page:

```
Trace="true"
```

This tells ASP.NET to output trace information. You can set this to false, and the trace information doesn't show. This means that you can switch tracing on and off without removing any of the trace statements from the code, which is a great time-saving technique.

Next are the lines that write your own information to the trace output. These are all variations on the same theme:

```
Trace.Write ("Click", "Start")
Trace.Write("Opening connection")
Trace.Warn(ex.Message)
```

The first of these has two arguments. You can see from the output that the first argument appears as the Category, and the second as the Message. When only one argument is used (as in the other cases), no Category is shown. The final example uses Warn instead of Write, in which case the output appears in red. This makes it easier to see (except in a black and white book of course!).

# Missing Pages

One of the classic problems that occur far too often is that of missing pages – that dreaded 404 error message:

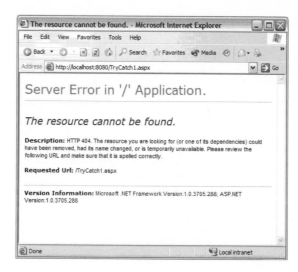

There are many reasons for this happening, but the three most common are:

❑  You've mistyped a URL in your code.

❑  You've re-written your site, and people still have links or bookmarks to old pages.

❑  People mistyped a URL in the browser.

The first is easily fixed, and should never really be a problem in a live site. The second reason in this list is a problem that can be tackled. If you are rewriting a site to the extent that the links will change or pages will be removed permanently, you should always ensure you have pages that redirect from the old structure to the new structure. There's really not a lot we can do if users end up mistyping URLs though – if you could remotely control people's typing you'd be a millionaire by now. However, it would be better to show a nice page, rather than the generic error page shown above.

In ASP.NET this can easily be handled, but it doesn't work if you are using the Web Matrix Web Server. That's because the Web Matrix Server is designed for the development environment. What you need is Microsoft Internet Information Server (IIS), which is available on Windows 2000 (all versions) and Windows XP Professional. It's not installed by default on either Windows 2000 Professional or Windows XP Professional, but it is included on the installation CDs for these two operating systems as an optional add-on component. (It is installed by default on Windows 2000 Server and higher). If you haven't got IIS, or just plain don't want to install it, then don't completely skip this section. It's worth reading through so that you know what's possible, and how to do this when you need to. If you do want to install IIS, then the instructions are in Appendix A.

The example below requires an IIS Application to be created. If you're unfamiliar with configuring IIS, then take a look at the instructions in the Appendix. We configured a new Virtual Root called Wrox pointing at the directory C:\Wrox, where we have our sample code.

## Try It Out    A Custom 'Missing Page' Page

1. Create a new file, picking the Web.Config template from the (General) tab, and put it in the Wrox application root (in our example C:\Wrox).

2. Scroll down until you find the customErrors comment section that looks like this:

```
<!--

The <customErrors> section enables configuration of what to do if/when an
unhandled error occurs during the execution of a request. Specifically, it
enables developers to configure html error pages to be displayed in place of
a error stack trace:

<customErrors mode="RemoteOnly" defaultRedirect="GenericErrorPage.htm">
  <error statusCode="403" redirect="NoAccess.htm"/>
  <error statusCode="404" redirect="FileNotFound.htm"/>
<customErrors>

-->
```

3. The lines at the top and bottom of the above code indicate that the lines of code between the <!-- and --> are commented out. These commented-out lines exist to show you an example of the structure, leaving the implementation to you. We need to add some code here, so add the following below the comment block:

```
<customErrors mode="On">
  <error statusCode="404" redirect="FileNotFound.aspx"/>
</customErrors>
```

4. Create a new ASP.NET File called FileNotFound.aspx.

5. Add some text about a missing page:

**6.** Save the page.

**7.** Open your browser and type http://localhost/wrox/whatever.aspx in the address bar. Notice how instead of the unfriendly message, we now have our own nice message.

## How It Works

The way this works is quite simple. The `customErrors` section in the configuration file allows us to define what happens under certain error conditions. By turning this `On` we are telling ASP.NET not to display the standard error details, but to perform a custom action. In our case we have the following:

```
<customErrors mode="On">
  <error statusCode="404" redirect="FileNotFound.aspx"/>
</customErrors>
```

The `error` tag allows us to indicate a particular error code, and the file that should be shown if that error code occurs. Code `404` is the standard "page not found" error. So, if IIS doesn't find a page it returns this `404` error code, and ASP.NET shows our file instead.

The great thing about this is that you don't have to add any special coding to handle this. You just create your error pages, and change the configuration – ASP.NET handles everything else.

# Debugging at Run Time

The second method of finding out what's going on in your code is to debug it. This allows you to step through the code line by line, and even examine the contents of variables. Many people consider debugging to be an arcane art, but it's actually really simple – you just have to know how to do it – and since it's so simple, let's dive right in.

The example overleaf again requires that an IIS Application is created, called `Wrox`.

## Try It Out — Debugging a program

**1.** Create a new ASP.NET Page called `debugging.aspx`.

**2.** Add a `Button` and a `Label` to the page.

**3.** Double-click the button to show the **Code** view.

**4.** Add the following code:

```
Sub Button1_Click(sender As Object, e As EventArgs)
   Dim i As Integer
   Dim j As Integer
   Dim Sum As Integer

   i = 3
   j = 4
   Sum = i + j

   Label1.Text = Sum
End Sub
```

**5.** Switch to **All** view, and add the debugging attribute to the top of the page:

```
<%@ Page Language="VB" Debug="true" %>
```

**6.** Save the page and navigate to it from your browser. Press the button to prove it works OK.

**7.** From Windows Explorer, navigate to `C:\Program Files\Microsoft.NET\FrameworkSDK\GuiDebug`. If you've installed Visual Studio.NET instead of just the .NET Framework, then substitute `Microsoft Visual Studio.NET` for `Microsoft.NET` in the path.

**8.** Double-click `DbgCLR.exe` to launch the debugger.

**9.** From the **Tools** menu select **Debug Process....**

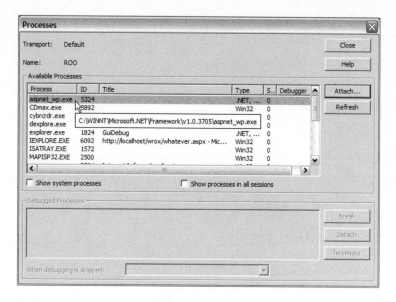

**10.** Click Attach…, and then click Close.

**11.** From the File menu select Open and File.

**12.** Navigate to C:\wrox and open debugging.aspx.

**13.** Click on the gray border at the left, next to the i = 3 line of code you entered:

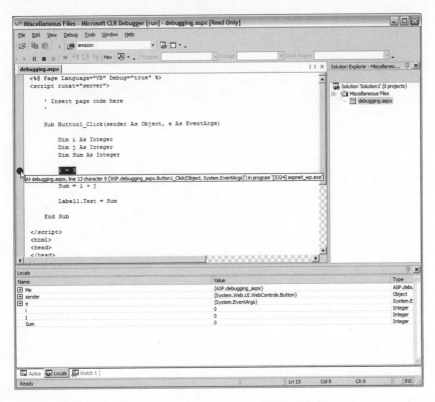

This sets a breakpoint on that line. A breakpoint is a line where the processing of the code will halt temporarily in the debugger.

**14.** Switch back to your browser, and click the button again. Notice how you are switched to the debugger, with the line highlighted. Also notice the **Locals** window at the bottom, showing the values of our three variables.

**15.** Press *F11* three times, watching how the current line changes, as do the values of our variables.

**16.** Press *F5* to continue. The page will now complete execution, and the browser will be re-displayed.

It's worth having a look at the **Debug** menu while debugging to see what other things you can do – there are tools in here that will enable you to step over a function rather than into it, clear breakpoints and so on. We just used the **Step Into** command to step through our code, and there is no complex code here. But, if you've got functions and branches (If ... Then statements), then the debugger follows each line as it executes. This gives you a great way of understanding the flow of your program, and combined with the ability to see what values your variables contain, it's invaluable in tracking down problems.

# Help, I'm Lost!

So far in this chapter we've looked at debugging and tracing, and the sort of things you can do when you've got problems. However, one of the problems that comes from working with .NET is the breadth of what it provides. It's never easy to find things, and knowing where things are takes time. For example, let's consider you're writing an application that requires some math functions. You're hoping that Microsoft has included this sort of thing, but you don't know where these functions might be found if they've been included. You have two options:

❑   Use the Web Matrix Class Browser

❑   Use the documentation

We don't need to teach you how to use the documentation, as it's got great search features. Let's concentrate on the Class Browser, and then after that we'll tell you why you might need the documentation after all.

## Try It Out     Using the Class Browser

1.  In Web Matrix, click on the **Classes** tab in the bottom right of the screen.

2.  In the text entry area above the list of classes, enter **Math** and press return. Notice how only one entry is found – that's the `Math` class.

3.  Double-click this to show the details for the class. Expand the **Methods** to see what it provides:

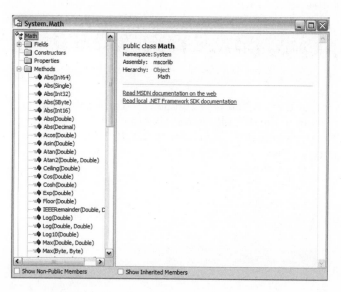

Where this comes in really useful is finding out the **Namespace** of a class. Namespaces are logical separations, allowing classes to be grouped together. The `Math` class is in the `System` namespace, so you don't have to do anything to use it. You could just do something like:

```
Label1.Text = Math.Cos(Angle)
```

There are, however, plenty of other classes that you can't use directly without telling ASP.NET that you're going to use them. For example, consider the case of accessing databases. You want to use some of the data classes, and you code your page. When running the page however, you get:

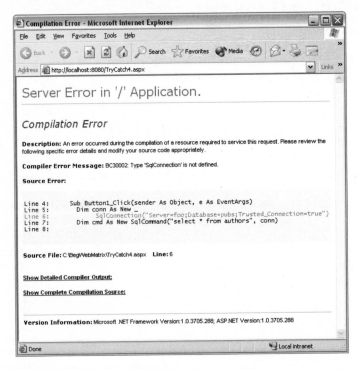

Hmm, why can't it find the `SqlConnection` object? You know it exists. The reason is that `SqlConnection` is not in the default namespaces that ASP.NET automatically searches, so ASP.NET doesn't know where it is – you have to tell ASP.NET where to find it. However, you don't know where it is either, so you resort to the class browser:

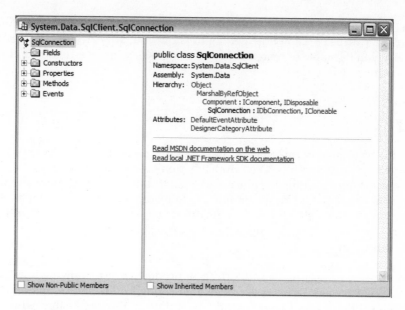

Aha. You can now see it's in the `System.Data.SqlClient` namespace, so you can add the reference accordingly:

```
<%@ Import Namespace="System.Data.SqlClient" %>
```

This is a special page directive, that you can add in the All tab. All it does is tell ASP.NET where to look for classes it can't find. You'll see this in action in Chapter 10.

An alternative to using `Import` is just using the full namespace for a type. For example:

```
Dim conn As New System.Data.SqlClient.SqlConnection(" ... ")
```

Here we put the full namespace in front of the type. It has just the same effect, but when declaring lots of types it becomes much harder to read. Using the `Import` statement is the preferred option.

## Where the Class Browser Falls Down

The class browser is great, but what if you don't know the class name? How do you then search for things? This is where you have to resort to the documentation, not that there's anything wrong with that. In fact, .NET is one product where the documentation is essential, since there are so many classes, and so many properties and methods.

The documentation contains a complete reference of all namespaces, classes, methods, and properties, as well as sections on building applications, data access, debugging, and so on. There's also a whole host of samples with lots of code for you to examine.

The search features in the documentation also allow you to search for anything, not just a class name. It's really worth spending time getting to know your way around the documentation, as there's no way you'll be able to remember everything. Knowing where to go to find it is, I think, more important.

# Summary

As I said at the beginning of this chapter, mistakes will happen, especially if you are a beginner. Remember learning to ride a bike? You probably don't remember falling off, but I bet you did. Luckily mistakes while learning to code are less painful (and there are none of those complaints from your Mom about grazed knees, or muddy clothes again). However, not all mistakes will be yours, so the process includes coping with other people as well. This may be code supplied by another person, or just user input – either way you should make sure you can handle whatever is thrown at you.

This means not only protecting your interface and code, but also knowing how to track down problems. A long time ago I once spent three days trying to track down an obscure bug in someone else's code. It's very easy to spend lots of time on things like this, which is bad for two reasons. Firstly it's very frustrating, especially as a learner. Hitting a problem sometimes seems like a high brick wall, and you wonder if you'll ever get over it, or can even be bothered to. Secondly, when working to a schedule, you can easily slip because of simple mistakes.

So in this chapter we've looked at some of the areas where problems can be caused, and shown how to get around them. Now it's time to get on with more exciting coding, by looking at the data features of Web Matrix.

# CHAPTER 8

# Working with Databases

In this chapter, we start to look at how we can use a database to power our web pages. Web Matrix provides a great environment for working with data in a SQL Server or MSDE database. It's nearly all just "point and click", and you don't really need to know a great deal about how the database works. But, even though they say that a little knowledge is a dangerous thing, we'll show you a bit of what's going on under the hood as well in this chapter.

We start by looking at the tools built into Web Matrix for working with data, and then see how we connect to our database server, build a new database, and add some data. We'll build one of the tables that are used in the Cornflakes at Midnight website you'll see later in the book.

The tasks for this chapter are:

- ❑ Take a look at the Data Explorer in Web Matrix
- ❑ Connect to an existing database and show some data
- ❑ Create a new database for our Cornflakes at Midnight website
- ❑ Add a table to the database, and put some data in it
- ❑ Use some database code, known as a Stored Procedure, to extract that data

So, let's get on with it right away by looking at the Data Explorer window in Web Matrix.

## The Data Explorer

In the top right of the Web Matrix window is a section with three tabs named Workspace, Data, and Open Items. You won't be surprised to know that the Data tab is where we're heading, so click on it now and you should see something like the following:

At the moment, the window is empty, except for a row of icons across the top. We'll see what all these do later on. Before we do, we need to make sure that you have everything set up ready to go.

## Which Database Engine can I use?

The Data Explorer in Web Matrix can be used to work with either:

❑ The full installation of Microsoft SQL Server from version 7.0 upwards, and any of the editions such as the *Developer Edition*, *Personal Edition*, and so on.

❑ The Microsoft Data Engine (MSDE). This is a cut-down version of SQL Server, designed for desktop use rather than as an enterprise-level database.

You can always tell if the full version of SQL Server installed (if, for some reason, you don't remember installing it), by looking for the entry named Microsoft SQL Server in your Start menu. It's not so easy to tell if MSDE is installed. If you followed the setup instructions in Chapter 1 for installing .NET, Web Matrix, and the sample files then all should be well. If you intend to use MSDE, and you haven't followed the steps described in Chapter 1, then you need to head back and follow the steps described in the section titled *Installing the Database Server Software* in Chapter 1.

## Connecting to a Database

OK, so we know that you've got a database server ready to work with, so it's time to see what we can do with the Web Matrix Data Explorer. The *Try It Out* that follows shows you how easy it is to connect to a database and view the contents. It uses one of the sample databases provided with SQL Server and MSDE (the pubs database), which can be installed on MSDE by following the steps described in the installation instructions in Chapter 1.

**Try It Out**     **Connecting to a Database**

**1.** Open Web Matrix if it's not already running, and create a new page called DBConnection.aspx.

**2.** Go to the **Data Explorer** window at the top right of the screen (click the **Data** tab) and then click the left-hand **New Connection** icon – the one that shows a database (the yellow cylindrical blob) with a wire and plug coming out of it. This opens the **Connect to Database** dialog:

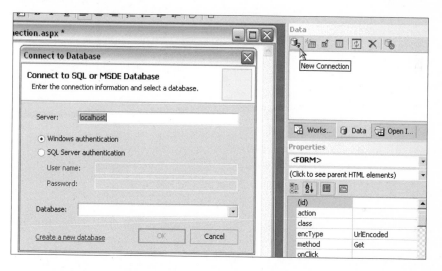

**3.** Now you need to tell Web Matrix what database server to use. The default entry in the **Server** text box is **localhost** (as you can see in the screenshot above), which will connect to a local SQL Server database engine. If you are using the default named instance of MSDE, which was installed with the .NET Framework samples, you must change this entry to (local)\NetSDK. This is the instance name of the MSDE server on this (local) machine, as explained in Chapter 1 when you first installed MSDE.

**4.** If you are using MSDE, leave the option buttons in the center of the dialog set to the default of **Windows authentication**. This should also work if you are using SQL Server, providing that it runs under a system account.

*If you have problems connecting when using SQL Server (not MSDE), select SQL Server authentication and enter the user name and password for the **sa** (system administrator) account, or another account that has full administrative privileges for the database. However, the **sa** account should only ever be used for testing and trouble-shooting, and must **never** be used in the release version of any application.*

**5.** Next, you must select the database you want to use. Later we'll create a new database, but for the time being we'll connect to an existing one. Click the down arrow of the **Database:** listbox, and, after a few seconds of furious disk activity, you will see a list of all the databases on the server you specified. Select the entry for **pubs** (the sample "publishers" database provided with SQL Server and MSDE):

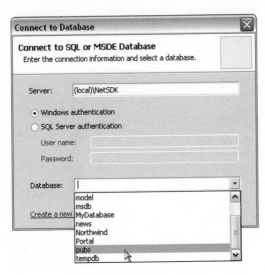

**6.** Click **OK**, and you'll see that now the **Data Explorer** window shows the contents of the database. The top entry in the window is the database name preceded by the name of the server – in the following screenshot you can see that this is (local)\netsdk.pubs. Underneath this are collapsible lists showing the **Tables** and **Stored Procedures** within the **pubs** database. Double-click one of the table names, and the **Edit Table** window opens to show the contents of that table:

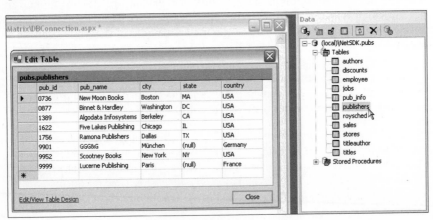

7. Close this window, and go back to the Data Explorer window. Expand the Stored Procedures group, and double-click on one of the entries in the list of stored procedures. The Edit Stored Procedure window opens, showing the stored procedure:

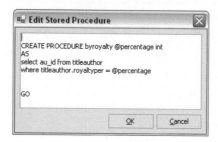

8. Another way to open either the Edit Table or Edit Stored Procedure dialog is to use the Edit icon on the toolbar within the Data Explorer window (the third one from the left). Select a table or stored procedure in the lists in the Data Explorer window and click this icon:

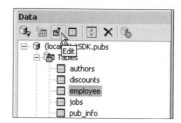

## Stored Procedures and SQL Statements Explained

There are two main ways of working directly with databases using the tools available to that database. The first one is to use **SQL statements**. SQL (Structured Query Language) statements can be used for administrating our database. For example, we can select, add, delete, and sort information in the database, as well as administering database security, and much more. They are a way of administering the database by hand. Web Matrix has some great features that we'll learn about in this chapter that automate a lot of database processes, such as creating new databases, and adding tables, which would otherwise be a bit tricky to do by hand-coding SQL statements. An example of a simple SQL statement that will return a list of publishers from the Pubs database, similar to the list we saw in the example, is as follows:

```
SELECT * From Publishers
```

We'll learn more about SQL statements later in the chapter, as they will also help when it comes to working with databases in our websites.

The second method of working with a database is to use **stored procedures**. Stored procedures are a set of database instructions, rather like a mini-program, that are executed by the database to perform some specific task or tasks more efficiently than directly executing SQL statements. If you look at the code in the previous *Try It Out*, you can see that stored procedures use SQL statements to perform operations on the database (in our case, a SELECT statement). However, these statements are stored within the database, which means that the database can compile and optimize the statements to get the best performance.

Stored procedures also provide better security than using SQL statements directly. They "hide" the table and column names, because you only have to know the stored procedure name and what **parameters** it requires. Parameters are used to pass values into the stored procedure, and sometimes to receive values from it as well.

## Connecting to More Than One Database

The Data Explorer window can connect to more than one database at a time. This is useful if the data you need to build your pages is not all in the same database. If you want to try this, go back to Step 2 and select a different database, repeating the process until you have all the connections you want. If you have both SQL Server and MSDE installed on the same machine, you can use this dialog to connect to databases from both simply by changing the local server name at the top of the dialog. You can also connect to SQL Server databases on other machines on your network by entering the name of the server instead of localhost. In this screenshot you can see that we've connected to three databases:

The first is the Northwind sample database in a local SQL Server database server. The second is the pubs database in the local instance of MSDE, and the third is the pubs database in a SQL Server database server that is running on a machine named delboy.

# Displaying Data from a Database

Now that you know how to connect to a database, and what the **Data Explorer** window can do, we'll see how easy Web Matrix makes it to display some data. In the next chapter, we'll be looking at this topic in depth, but you'll be surprised just how quickly you can build a web page that extracts data from a database and builds an attractive display in a browser.

**Try It Out**     **Displaying Data from a Database**

**1.** Connect to the pubs database as demonstrated in the previous *Try It Out*.

**2.** Open the list of tables in the database, select the Publishers table by left-clicking on it, then left-click and drag it onto an empty ASP.NET page:

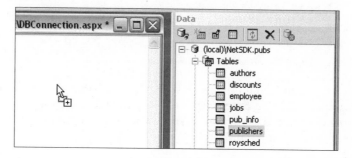

**3.** Web Matrix automatically adds two controls to the page for you – at the top is a SqlDataSourceControl, and below it a DataGrid. These two controls work together to display the data in the table you selected. We'll look at these two controls (and others) in more detail in the next chapter:

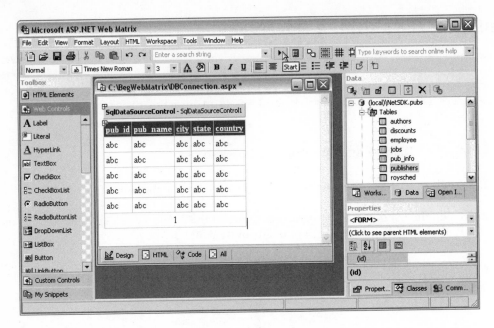

4. Now click the Start icon on the main Web Matrix toolbar to run the page. The page is then displayed, and you can see the values in the table shown within a grid – all with one simple drag-and-drop action! If you want to see that code that has been generated, just open the All tab in WebMatrix:

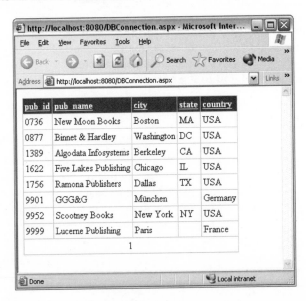

*The MxDataGrid control that is used in this page is a clever little beast. Notice that the column headings are hyperlinks, and that clicking one automatically sorts the rows on the values in that column. The grid also automatically divides the output into "pages" containing ten rows, and displays a list of the pages as hyperlinks at the bottom of the grid. Our table only has eight rows, and so there is only one page. Repeat this* Try It Out *with the* titles *table in the* pubs *database to see paging in action.*

**5.** Before you finish this *Try It Out*, you can disconnect from the pubs database, as we aren't going to be using it again for a while. You don't actually *need* to do this, but it does help to reduce clutter in the **Data** window and free up a connection for other users if you are using a remote database. Select the top entry in the list in the **Data Explorer** window (the server and database name), and the icon on far right of the toolbar becomes available. Click this to close the connection to the database, and the **Data Explorer** window is cleared as well:

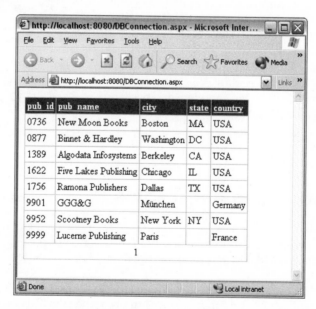

> Take care not to click the **Delete** icon (to the left of the **Disconnect** button) when you only want to disconnect from a database. A confirmation dialog is displayed to warn you that the complete database will be deleted, but it's easy to click **OK** without actually reading the warning!

## Other Icons in the Toolbar

There are four icons on the toolbar in the **Data Explorer** window that we haven't used yet. We've looked at the first and the third icons so far, for creating connections, and editing information. We'll be using some of the other icons later on, but let's take a look at what they do now:

The second icon displayed in the Data Explorer is used to create a new table or stored procedure in the currently selected database. We'll use this to create a new table in the next *Try It Out*:

The fourth icon allows us to query the contents of one or more tables in the database. You'll see this towards the end of the chapter:

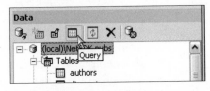

The fifth icon simply refreshes the lists in the Data Explorer window. To use it you must first select the entry named Tables (to refresh the list of tables), or Stored Procedures (you guessed it – to refresh the list of stored procedures!):

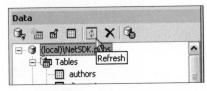

The sixth icon deletes whatever is currently selected in the lists in the Data Explorer window. You can select a table or a stored procedure, or the complete database (by clicking on the entry for the server and database name):

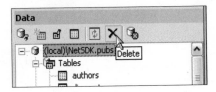

# Creating Databases and Tables

The Data Explorer we have just looked at can be used to create a new database, and to create tables and stored procedures within a database. In this section of the chapter, we'll see how it is done. Then, later on, we will add some data to the new table we create.

The Cornflakes at Midnight example site you'll see in the latter part of this book uses a database to store several sets of information that are used to drive the site. This includes a list of discs that the band has released (though, according to our publishers, it's more like they *escape* rather than being released!):

## Storing the Details of the Discs

Obviously, we could just write the list of discs, and all their individual details, as text and HTML content directly in the source code of the page, but it makes a lot more sense to store them in a database, and then extract the details each time we want to build the page. This way, updates to the list are easy; we just have to update the database and the page will automatically show the current details.

The database is named simply **CAM** (Cornflakes at Midnight), and we're using the instance of MSDE that is installed with the .NET Framework SDK samples to host it.

> *We'll be using a fair bit of database terminology in this chapter. We'll be talking about tables, rows, and columns. Each table consists of a number of columns. Each column describes what data can be stored in a table. Tables then store data in rows, each row stores data corresponding to an item. In our* Try It Out *example, we saw a web page that displayed a table of data. The column headings (*pub_id, pub_name, city, *and so on) are the columns in the* Publishers *table. The rows of data correspond to the rows in the* Publishers *table. This example is a very direct representation of the contents of the database table.*

The details we store about each disc are:

❏ A numeric identifier that is different for each disc, and which acts as the **primary key** for the rows in the table. A primary key is simply a column containing values that are unique for all the rows in the table, and so can be used to uniquely identify a specific row within the table. Our database can create the value for this column in our table automatically when new rows are added, in which case we refer to it as an IDENTITY column in MSDE or SQL Server terms (in Access and some other databases, it is called an AutoNumber column). This column in our database of type Int (integer) and is named DiscID.

❏ The title of the disc, which is a string of up to 50 characters. The column type in SQL Server and MSDE for this type of data is VarChar (variable length character string), and the column name is Title.

❏ The date that the disc was released. This is a DateTime column in SQL Server and MSDE, and is named ReleaseDate.

❏ The sleeve notes for the disc. This is also a string of characters, but this time we use a special type of column in SQL Server and MSDE called a Text column. This allows us to store large volumes of text in the column, without having to worry about the exceeding the maximum length for a VarChar column (2,048 characters). This column is named Notes.

❏ The name of the publisher (the record label) that released the disk. This is also string of characters, but we know it will be less than 50 characters in total so we use a column of type VarChar that allows for up to 50 characters. The column name is Label.

❏ The URL of the disc cover (packaging) image, as located on our web server. We use this to display the disc cover in our pages by inserting it as the value of the src attribute of a hyperlink element. Although the URL in our example site does not contain many characters, we allow for up to 255 in the VarChar column we use. This column in named CoverImageURL.

## Creating a New Database

Before we can build the table for our list of discs, we must create a new empty database into which we can place all the tables and stored procedures we create for our site. Providing that you carried out the previous *Try It Out* successfully, we know that your database server is configured and working properly, and so we can get straight on and create the new database.

**Try It Out**    **Creating a New Database**

**1.** Click the New Connection icon at the top left of the Data Explorer window, as we did at the start of the first *Try It Out* in this chapter, to open the Connect To Database dialog. Type in the location of the Server you are using, in our case this is the local instance of MSDE named NetSDK that is installed by the .NET Framework samples.

**2.** We want to create a new database on the server this time, rather than connecting to an existing database, so click the **Create a new database** link at the bottom of the dialog, as shown below:

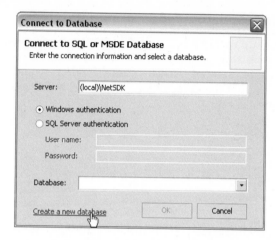

**3.** The Enter Information dialog should now open, asking for the name of the new database. Since we're working on the database for the Cornflakes at Midnight example site, name the database CAM, then click OK.

*Note that if you have already installed the database from the book samples, you won't be able to create another database with the same name, so you can either skip this example, or continue with this example and create a new database with a different name, for example CAM2 or TEST.*

**4.** Web Matrix creates the database on the server we specified, and shows it in the **Data Explorer** window. The two lists, **Tables** and **Stored Procedures** are shown, but they are, of course, both empty, as we haven't created any in the new database yet:

That's all we have to do to create a new empty database. What we need to do now is to put some tables and data into it, so leave the connection to the new database open, ready for the next *Try It Out*.

## Creating a New Table

Tables provide the structure within which our data is stored in a database. They consist, as you've seen in earlier screenshots and descriptions, of one or more columns, and each column defines the type of data that is stored in that column. Modern databases like MSDE and SQL Server provide lots of different data types that we can use, but in most cases, we're only concerned with three basic types:

❑ Text (character strings)

❑ Numbers

❑ Dates

### Database Data Types

The basic data types can be divided into many different subtypes. Without getting too involved in the many types and their specialist uses, it's important to understand which columns to choose for different tasks. The table below summarizes the common choices for our three basic data types.

While the multitude of data types may seem confusing (and there are other more specialist types available as well), the table will make it much easier to understand the differences between them and choose the most appropriate for your needs:

| Type of data | Data Type Name | Description |
| --- | --- | --- |
| Text (character) data | Char<br><br>NChar | Text strings up to 2,048 characters long, though the default setting in the **Data Explorer** is 50 characters. If the value placed in the column is less than the specified length, the remainder is padded (filled) with spaces. When extracted from the database, the returned value has these trailing spaces appended, so that the String is always the length specified for the column size. The Char data type stores the characters in ANSI code (8-bit) form. The NChar data type stores characters as Unicode (16-bit) form. |

| Type of data | Data Type Name | Description |
|---|---|---|
| | VarChar<br>NVarChar | Text strings up to 2,048 characters long, though the default setting in the **Data Explorer** is 50 characters. In this case, however, the value is not padded with spaces to fill the column. This saves space in the database, and gives faster performance when reading or writing the data. When extracted from the database, the returned value is a String that is the same length as the value stored in the column. The VarChar data type stores the characters in ASNI code (8-bit) form. The NVarChar data type stores characters as Unicode (16-bit) form. |
| | Text<br>NText | The values are stored in a separate section of the database as **pages**, each of which can contain 8,080 characters (around 8KB). Although the number of pages for the column must be specified when the table is created, pages are only used as required, and do not take up space if the value is less than the maximum specified for the column. The Text data type stores the characters in ASNI code (8-bit) form. The NText data type stores characters as Unicode (16-bit) form. |
| Numbers | Int<br>SmallInt<br>TinyInt<br>BigInt | An Int column stores whole numbers from around minus 2 billion to plus 2 billion (which usually proves to a large enough range for everyday purposes!). For smaller ranges of numbers, use SmallInt (-32,768 to +32,767) or TinyInt (0 to 255). For larger numbers, BigInt can store numbers one billion times larger that Int, but the requirement for this is quite rare. |
| | Bit | The values zero or one (0 or 1), useful for data that is effectively Boolean (things like True/False or Yes/No). |
| | Float<br>Real | Numbers with fractional parts, in other words not whole numbers. The way that they are stored means that they cannot be guaranteed to be absolutely accurate, but it allows them to hold huge values (for example, with 308 trailing zeros) or very small values (up to 308 decimal places) in only a few bytes of actual database disk space. |

*Table continued on following page*

| Type of data | Data Type Name | Description |
|---|---|---|
| | Decimal | Numbers with fractional parts, but stored in a way that means there is no loss of accuracy. Values with up to 38 trailing zeros can be stored this way. The trade off is the use of more database disk space. |
| | Money<br>SmallMoney | Monetary values, accurate to one ten-thousandth of the monetary unit (in US dollar terms, up to one-hundredth of a cent). The SmallMoney type can hold values from around minus 200,000 to plus 200,000, while the Money type can hold values close to plus or minus ten thousand billion. |
| Dates and Times | DateTime | A date and time between 1st Jan 1753 and 31st Dec 9999 |
| | SmallDateTime | A date and time between 1st Jan 1900 and 6th Jun 2079 |

So, with a new database in place, we can now build the table that will hold the details of our discs. We'll work through the process in this next *Try It Out* using the database we just created. If you named your database something other than CAM, the process is still just the same. The only difference is that the name of the database shown at the top of the **Data Explorer** window is different.

**Try It Out**      **Creating a New Table**

1. In the **Data Explorer** window, select the entry **Tables** in the database you created in the previous *Try It Out* and click the **New Item** icon on the toolbar:

2. The **Create New Table** dialog opens. Type the name of the table, **Discs**, in the **Table Name** textbox near the top of the dialog. The left-hand list shows the columns defined for the table. When the dialog first opens it is empty, so click the **New** button below it, and you'll see a new column created with the name **Column1**:

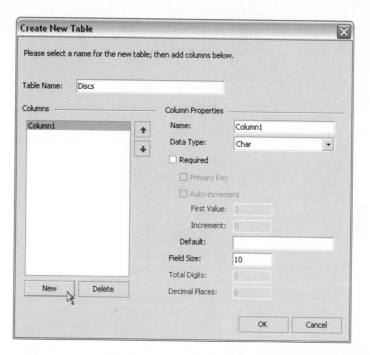

**3.** We talked about the columns we want in this table earlier in the chapter. The first column, the one we just created, needs to be our **DiscID** column. It is the **primary key** for the table, and will be an `Integer` value that is automatically incremented by the database as we add new rows to the table. So, the first step is to change the column name in the **Name** textbox from the default of **Column1** to **DiscID**, and choose the correct data type for the column from the **Data Type** drop-down list – it should be **Int** (which gives us an `Integer`-type column):

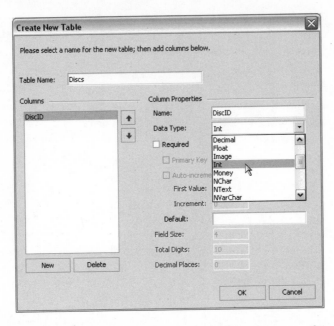

*Don't be tempted to click the **OK** button when creating columns — there is no need to. The **OK** button closes the dialog and updates the definition of the table in the database. While we keep it open, we can define all the columns we need and then have the table created in one go in the database itself. Of course, you can always open the table for editing again if you do close the dialog, which we'll show you how to do later. The only thing that changes if you do this is that you can no longer change the **name** of the table in this dialog*

The Column Properties section of the dialog, where we have just set the Data Type, contains several other controls for the specific settings of each column. Some are disabled, depending on the data type chosen and a few other factors, but for our new DiscID column, you will see that several of these controls become available after we set the data type to Int.

**4.** We want to specify that this column is the primary key of our table, which means that we must check at least the first two checkboxes: Required (it must always contain a value), and Primary Key (which is only available after checking Required because the primary key column in a row cannot be empty). As we want our DiscID column to be populated with values automatically, we also check Auto-increment. The default First Value and Increment are fine, and can be left as they are:

**5.** Now we can add the second column. Click the New button again, and change the name of the new column to Title. In the Data Type drop-down list select VarChar. You'll see that the Field Size is then set to 50 by default, which is just what we want for our Title column:

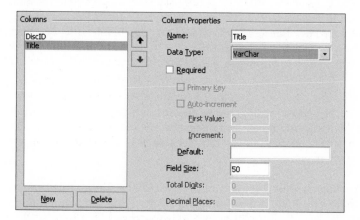

**6.** The next column we need is the release date for the disc. Click the New button, change the column name to ReleaseDate, and select the data type DateTime. We'll demonstrate the use of a default value for this column, so enter (getdate()) in the Default textbox:

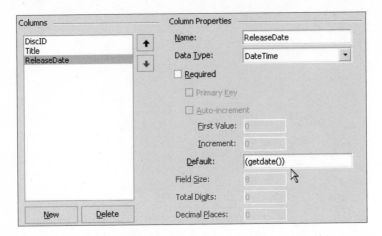

*The **Default** value we specify will be used to set the value of this column when a new row is inserted into the table, if no value is specified for that column. We can still set the value when we create the new row if we want to, or change it later (after inserting the new row). The value we used in the dialog shown above, **getdate()**, is the name of a function built into the SQL Server and MSDE that returns the current date, so new rows will have this value for the **ReleaseDate** column. Enclosing the name of the function within brackets indicates that we are using the return value of a function as the default value, rather than entering a specific value to be used every time as a default.*

**7.** The next column we need is the one for the sleeve notes for the disc. This is of type Text. Click the New button, change the column name to Notes, and select the data type Text in the drop-down list. You'll see that the Field Size is set to 16 automatically, and cannot be changed. Remember that because this is a Text column, the value means "16 pages", not "16 characters".

**8.** After the Notes column comes another VarChar column, this time named Label. Create this as before by clicking the New button, changing the column name to Label, and selecting the data type VarChar in the drop-down list. The default value of 50 (characters) for the Field Size is fine for this column.

**9.** The final column is the one that holds the URL of the disk cover image. This is also a VarChar column, but this time of size 255 characters. Click the New button again, change the column name to CoverImageURL, and select the data type VarChar in the drop-down list. Change the default value 50 in the Field Size text box to 255:

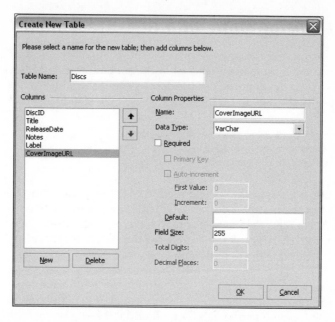

*If you decide to change the order of the columns after creating them, or at a later date, you can do so using the up and down arrows next to the list of column names in the left-hand side of the Edit Table Design dialog.*

**10.** Now that we've defined all the columns we want for our new Discs table, click the OK button at the bottom of the dialog to create the new table within the database. The Create New Table dialog closes, and the new table can be seen in the Tables list in the Data Explorer window:

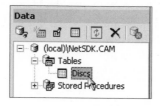

## How It Works

Let's take a quick look at the structure we've created:

# Editing and Retrieving Data from a Table

OK, so we've built a new database, and added the new table named Discs to it, but the table is still empty – there is no data in it. The next step is therefore to think about how we can fill it with data.

# Inserting and Editing Data with SQL Statements

The examples that come with the code samples for this chapter include a simple **SQL script** that can be used to create the sample Cornflakes at Midnight database and fill it with some sample data. This script contains the definition of the database and the tables, and a series of **SQL statements** that specify the data to fill the tables. These SQL statements look something like this:

```
INSERT INTO Discs (Title, ReleaseDate, Notes, Label, CoverImageURL)
VALUES ('No Inspiration', '10-10-2002', 'The debut album', 'Wrox Records',
        'http://oursite.com/covers/noinsp.gif')
```

This script inserts the values in the second section of the statement into the columns of the table named Discs listed in the first part of the statement. Since the DiscID is an `IDENTITY` column that automatically generates the values for new rows, we can't insert values for this column. However, even though there is a default value for the ReleaseDate column, we can still insert values for this and over-ride the default value.

However, it's unlikely that we'll already have suitable scripts available for new databases and tables we build, and typing SQL statements is laborious. It is really only useful when we want to create copies of a database and install it on other database servers, such as the installation script for the example CAM database.

# Inserting and Editing Data with an ASP.NET Page

Another alternative is to build an application or web page that accepts values typed into textboxes, or selected in other controls, and inserts them into the database tables automatically. Web Matrix includes an example of this type of ASP.NET page, called the Editable Data Grid type. This type of page can be found in the Data Pages section of the Add New File dialog that appears when you start Web Matrix, when you select File | New from the main menu bar, or when you hit the New File icon on the toolbar:

If you create a new file based on this template and run it, you'll see how data can be inserted into a table from an ASP.NET page. Simply click the **Add new item** link at the bottom of the page, and fill in some values for the columns. Then, click the **Update** link on the left-hand side of the column and the data is saved into the database (you may have to use the numbered links in the footer of the table to go through the pages to find the new row afterwards):

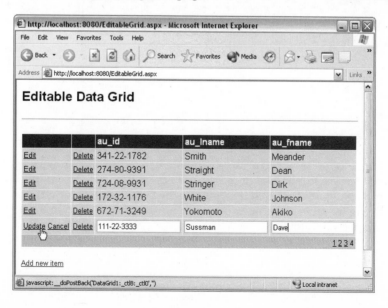

This page displays values from, and updates values in the authors table within the sample pubs database (the database we used in the first *Try It Out* in this chapter. So it's clear that we can easily build pages that can insert new rows and update existing rows in our database.

## Inserting and Editing Data with Data Explorer

Now, we'll look at the features that come as part of Web Matrix that are used for inserting and editing data in a database. The Data Explorer allows us to do both of these things quite easily – in fact, we've already seen the dialog we use to perform these tasks earlier in the chapter.

### Try It Out    Inserting and Editing Data in a Table

1.  Make sure you are connected to the CAM database you created earlier in this chapter. If not, connect to it using the New Connection icon in the Data Explorer window as described in the first *Try It Out*.

2.  In the Tables entry in the Data Explorer window, find the table named Discs that we created previously. Either double-click on it, or select it and then click the Edit icon on the toolbar, to open the Edit Table dialog for the Discs table:

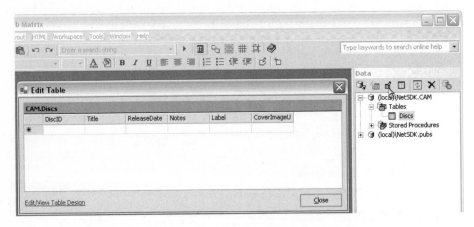

3.  The table has no rows in it at the moment, but a new empty row is displayed (the asterisk * at the left-hand end indicates a new row). Click in the title column of this new row, and you'll see that the value of the DiscID column is automatically set to -1 (providing that this is the first row you've inserted into the table), and the other columns are set to (null):

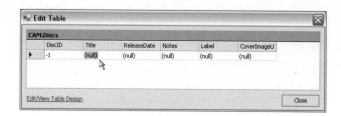

**4.** Type some values into the Title, Notes, Label, and CoverImageURL columns. Another new empty row is created automatically as soon as you start typing, and the row you are editing now has the "pencil" symbol to indicate that it's been changed but not yet saved to the database.

**5.** Now press the *Tab* key to move to the next row, or click on one of the cells in the next row, and you'll see the row you just completed updated so that the DiscID has its "proper" value. The "pencil" symbol also disappears to indicate that the row has been saved to the database. However, there is one problem in this release of Web Matrix (which will be fixed in future releases). The default value for the ReleaseDate column is not set, and is left as (null):

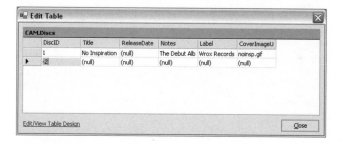

**6.** However, the Edit Table dialog can also be used to modify values in existing rows of a table. Click on the ReleaseDate column in the first row, and enter a date. Depending on where you are in the world, and what International Settings you have set in Windows Control Panel, you may have to enter it in the form *mm-dd-yyyy*, *dd-mm-yyyy*, *dd/mm/yyyy*, or possibly some other format. You can also get away with *yyyy-mm-dd* or *yyyy/mm/dd* in most cases, again depending on your international settings. We used 10/10/2002 for our example here, as you'll see shortly.

**7.** Add another row (or more) to the table, and experiment editing the values of columns in existing rows until you are happy with the way that this dialog works. To **delete** a column, click on the gray cell at the left-hand end so that the entire row is highlighted and press the *Delete* key. We added a couple of rows to our table, and then deleted the second row. You can see in the screenshot that the row with DiscID value 2 has been deleted, because the second row has the value 3 for this column. The values of a primary key IDENTITY row can't be changed once the row has been inserted into the table, and even if you delete a row, the values for this column are not re-used:

8.  At the bottom of the **Edit Table** dialog is a link **Edit/View Table Design**. You won't be surprised to know that it opens the table design dialog that we used to create the table in a previous *Try It Out*. However, this time the dialog has the title **View Table Design**, rather than **Edit Table Design**. Since the table contains data, we can't edit the actual structure (the table name, column names, or other column properties); they are all disabled in the dialog:

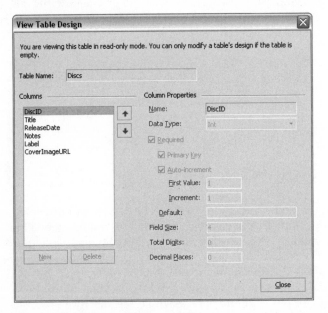

*The reason for this behavior is because, as we just said, the table contains data. The structure can only be changed when the table is empty. To change the structure of the table, you have to delete all the existing rows first. However, this dialog does provide a useful way to see what the table design looks like when we are working with it – for example when building ASP.NET pages that use the data.*

9.  OK, now we're done, so you can now click the **Close** buttons to close the **View Table Design** and **Edit Table** dialogs.

## *Viewing Data in the Query Dialog*

Now that we have some data in our new table, we can look at ways that we can extract it again. In the next two chapters, we'll be playing with some more controls for listing data that come as part of Web Matrix, or are built into the .NET Framework. However, while we're looking at the Data Explorer window in this chapter, we'll see how we can use it to look at data in an existing table, and even search for specific rows in a table. We do all this using the Query dialog.

| Try It Out | Viewing Data in the Query Dialog |
| --- | --- |

**1.** Connect to the database we built earlier in this chapter, and select the Discs table in the Data Explorer window. Then click the Query icon in that window to open the Test Query dialog. You can see that the top section of this dialog contains a SQL statement already built which uses the table we selected:

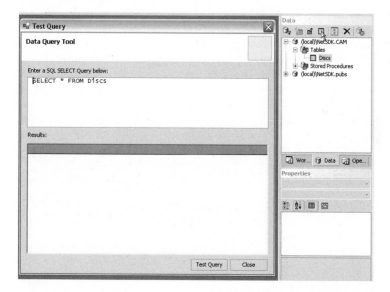

**2.** The default SQL query, SELECT * FROM Discs, extracts all the columns for all the rows in the table. To see the results, just click the Test Query button at the bottom of the dialog:

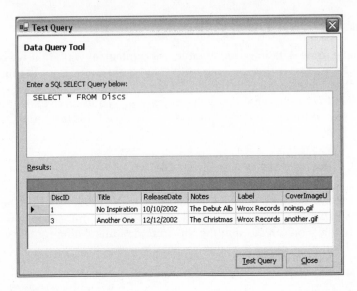

3. By editing this query, we can select specific rows, which is useful if there are a lot of rows in the table. It also allows us to test SQL SELECT statements directly against our table to make sure that they work like we expect. Add WHERE DiscID=3 to the end of the existing query, as shown in the next screenshot, which specifies that we only want rows with the value 3 for the DiscID column to be returned by the query. Then click the Test Query button to select and display the single matching row:

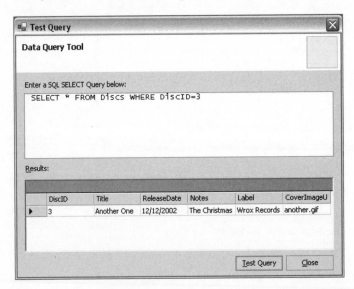

4. You can also select rows based on other column values, not just the DiscID primary key (IDENTITY) column. For example, change the SQL statement to read:

```
SELECT * FROM Discs WHERE Title LIKE '%no%'
```

and then click **Test Query**. This returns only rows that have the string no somewhere in the Title column. In SQL, the percent character % is a **wild-card** that means "any characters". Note that this particular query will return both albums, because the string occurs in both of them: "**No** Inspiration" and "A**no**ther One".

**5.** A SQL SELECT statement can also be used to return specific columns, rather than all of them. We just have to replace the asterisk (which means "all columns") with a list the columns we want, separated with a comma. Change the SQL statement to that shown in the next screenshot to select just the row with **DiscID** value 3, and return just the column named Title. Then click the **Test Query** button to see the results:

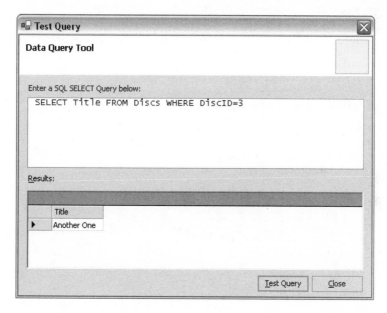

**6.** After you've finished experimenting, close the **Query** dialog and go back to the **Data Explorer** window.

## How It Works

SQL statements such as the simple SELECT statement can be executed against any table in a database. In our example, we are simply viewing some rows in the database, but we can use this query tool to execute INSERT or UPDATE statements to add or amend data if we want to. For a more thorough discussion of SQL syntax, you may want to refer to **Beginning SQL Programming**, *Wrox Press, ISBN: 1-86100-180-0*, or you can visit some useful online sites, including http://www.sqlcourse.com, or http://www.w3schools.com/sql/.

# Creating and Using Stored Procedures

To finish off this chapter, we'll plug together a few of the things we've seen so far and show you how we can build and work with stored procedures. We'll create a fairly simple one, and then see the results by modifying one of the standard pages that Web Matrix can create. There is no built-in way of executing a stored procedure to view the results directly, but we can use the Query dialog we just looked at to test the SQL statement in our stored procedure.

Stored procedures can be very simple, or very complex, or, as is usually the case, somewhere between these two extremes. They can contain any number of separate SQL statements, which are executed sequentially or according to rules and constructs within the stored procedure. In some ways, it's just like writing code for an ASP.NET page, because we can use IF statements and various other selection statements within a stored procedure.

However, our stored procedure is going to be simple, with only one statement. Let's get on and build it now.

---

**Try It Out**      **Creating a Stored Procedure**

**1.** Make sure you are connected to the CAM database and in the Data Explorer window, select the Stored Procedures entry and click the New Item icon. This opens the Create Stored Procedure dialog, with some default text already in place:

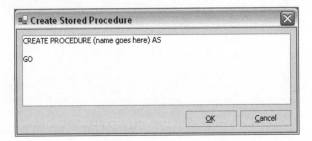

**2.** Add the following text to the dialog box:

```
CREATE PROCEDURE AllDiscsByDate AS
SELECT Title, ReleaseDate, Notes, Label, CoverImageURL
FROM Discs
ORDER BY ReleaseDate DESC
GO
```

**3.** Click OK to save the new stored procedure into the database, and return to the Data Explorer window. If you want to edit the stored procedure at a later time, simply double-click on the entry in this window, or select it and click the Edit icon:

**4.** The next step is to test our new stored procedure. An easy way to do this is to use one of the ASP.NET pages that Web Matrix can create automatically. Close the page you have open, and click the New File icon on the main toolbar, or select New from the File menu. In the New File dialog that appears, open the Data Pages list, and select the Simple Stored Procedure item:

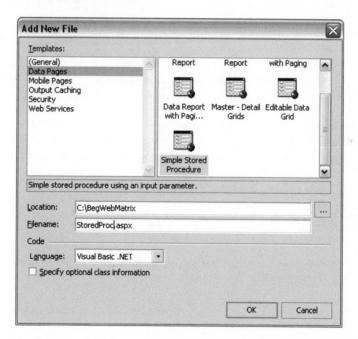

**5.** Click OK and the Simple Stored Procedure example page opens in Design view. It contains a DataGrid control (like the one we saw in use earlier in this chapter), and uses ASP.NET code to fill it with data from a stored procedure. We're going to hijack this example to run our own new stored procedure:

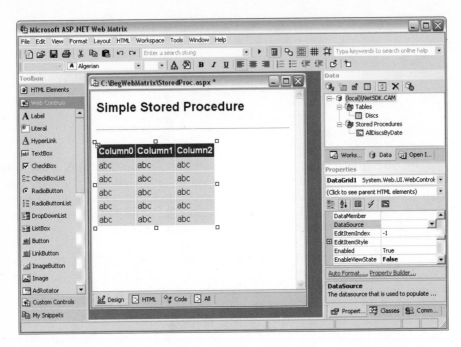

**6.** Click the **Code** tab at the bottom of the main Web Matrix editing window to see the code in this page. There isn't much, and we only need to make a three minor changes. These changes are highlighted in the code listing below, and described afterwards:

```
Sub Page_Load(Sender As Object, E As EventArgs)

    ' TODO: Update the ConnectionString for your application
    Dim ConnectionString As String = _
        "server=(local)\netsdk;database=cam;trusted_connection=true"

    ' TODO: Update name of Stored Procedure for your application
    Dim CommandText As String = "AllDiscsByDate"

    Dim myConnection As New SqlConnection(ConnectionString)
    Dim myCommand As New SqlCommand(CommandText, myConnection)
    Dim workParam As New SqlParameter()

    myCommand.CommandType = CommandType.StoredProcedure

    ' TODO: Set the input parameter, if necessary, for your application
    ' myCommand.Parameters.Add("@OrderId", SqlDbType.Int).Value = 11077

    myConnection.Open()

    DataGrid1.DataSource =
            myCommand.ExecuteReader(CommandBehavior.CloseConnection)
    DataGrid1.DataBind()

End Sub
```

**7.** Finally, click the Save button on the main Web Matrix toolbar to save the updated code, and then click the Run button to display the page in your browser. You'll see the results returned by the new stored procedure displayed in the DataGrid control:

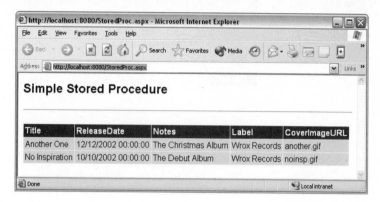

## How It Works

The name of the new stored procedure is AllDisksByDate, and you can see that it contains a single SQL statement rather like the ones we used in the previous *Try It Out*. This time though, we have specified all of the columns except for the DiscID. We probably won't want to display this column – we don't need to display information about how our data is stored to users, after all. We've also added the clause ORDER BY ReleaseDate DESC. This specifies that the rows should be sorted into reverse date order when they are returned:

```
CREATE PROCEDURE AllDiscsByDate AS
SELECT Title, ReleaseDate, Notes, Label, CoverImageURL
FROM Discs
ORDER BY ReleaseDate DESC
GO
```

When writing a SQL statement like this to be used as part of a stored procedure, you can do so in the Query window and run it to make sure that it is correct, and that it returns the data you want. Open the Query window by selecting the Tables entry in the list in the Data Explorer window and clicking the Query icon. Type in the SQL statement and click the Test Query button. Once it is working properly, highlight the SQL statement, press *Ctrl-C* (copy), close the Query dialog, open the Stored Procedure dialog, and paste it into the stored procedure with *Ctrl-V*. Also, remember to replace (name goes here) with a name for your new procedure.

In the page code, we added/amended three parts:

```
Dim ConnectionString As String = _
    "server=(local)\netsdk;database=cam;trusted_connection=true"
```

The auto-generated connection string in the first section of the code refers to the Northwind sample database, but we need it to refer to the database we created in this chapter instead, so we changed it so that is says the same as the code in the listing above (you need to omit the `netsdk` part if you are using SQL Server rather than the NetSDK instance of MSDE).

```
Dim CommandText As String = "AllDiscsByDate"
```

We changed the name of the stored procedure in the second section from `CustOrdersDetail` to `AllDisksByDate`, as shown in the listing above. Finally, we commented out a line of auto-generated code:

```
' myCommand.Parameters.Add("@OrderId", SqlDbType.Int).Value = 11077
```

We added an apostrophe before the line starting `myParametrers.Add` to comment it out, though we could have deleted the entire line. This line of code sets the value of a parameter for the stored procedure. Parameters are used to pass in values to the stored procedure, but since our new stored procedure does not use any parameters, we can omit this line.

# Summary

In this chapter we've introduced you to most of the ways that Web Matrix provides us with support for working with databases when we build ASP.NET pages. The Data Explorer window allows you to connect to a database server, create databases and tables and fill them with data, and modify existing tables and data.

We used the Data Explorer window to build the database for our Cornflakes at Midnight website, and to add a table that holds details of our discs. We also populated this table with a couple of rows, and showed you how we can query this data and display it. This included building a stored procedure that extracts the data in a specific format, and we then ran this stored procedure by adapting one of the existing example pages that Web Matrix can create for us.

The topics we covered are:

❑ Taking a look at the Data Explorer in Web Matrix

❑ Connecting to an existing database and showing some data

❑ Creating a new database for our Cornflakes at Midnight website

❑ Adding a table to the database and putting some data in it

❑ Creating a stored procedure and using it to extract the data

In the next chapter, we'll continue the data theme, but we'll be looking at more practical tasks. We'll use the database we've created to build some ASP.NET pages from scratch that can display the data, using the controls that are part of the .NET Framework, or which are supplied with Web Matrix

# CHAPTER 9

# Displaying Data

In the previous chapter, we showed you how easy it is to work with a database using the **Data Explorer** window, and other features of Web Matrix. We created a database, added a table, filled it with data, and then displayed this data on a page. We looked at how we can display data by simply dragging a table from the **Data Explorer** window onto a page, and by creating and using a stored procedure.

In this chapter, we need to look in a bit more depth at what is happening in these examples of displaying data. We didn't discuss the way in which they worked, or how you can build your own custom pages that take advantage of the same techniques. These are the tasks we'll be completing in this chapter.

In this chapter, you'll learn:

❑   How the visual drag-and-drop controls we use in Web Matrix actually connect to a database table to extract and display data

❑   How we can modify the appearance and content of the **MxDataGrid** control

❑   How to populate web controls with data using server-side data binding

❑   What list control templates are, and an example of how we can use them

We start with a look at the way Web Matrix displays pages with data on them.

## Displaying Data from a Table

We saw how easily we can create a page that displays the contents of a database table in the previous chapter. By simply dragging a table from the **Data Explorer** window and dropping it into an ASP.NET page, Web Matrix builds the page and all the code required automatically. The result is repeated in the next screenshot:

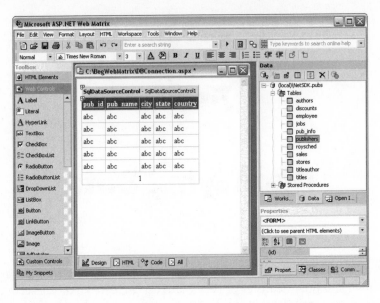

The part to focus on at the moment is the **gray box** labeled SqlDataSourceControl at the top of the page, above the grid control. While we are all familiar with what a "black box" is (especially if you are what the airlines like to call "a frequent flyer"!), few of us know exactly what's inside it. Likewise with our "gray box" – it's identified in the page as being a SqlDataSourceControl, but what's going on inside it?

Obviously, it is something to do with extracting the data from the database. The following screenshot shows the ASP.NET page running in the browser, and it displays all the data from the table that we dragged onto the ASP.NET page in the first place (the publishers table from the pubs database):

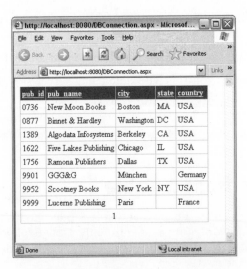

# Inside the SqlDataSourceControl "Gray Box"

So, let's look inside the SqlDataSourceControl and see in a bit more detail what it does. This will help you to understand how Web Matrix builds ASP.NET pages that can work with data in a database. The SqlDataSourceControl is listed in the Web Controls section of the Toolbox, and we can add one to our ASP.NET page simply by dragging it onto the page, just like any other control from the Toolbox.

## Try It Out — Exploring the SqlDataSourceControl

1.  Open a new blank ASP.NET page in Web Matrix and call it
    `SqlDataSourceControl.aspx`. Find the `SqlDataSourceControl` from the Web
    Controls section of the Toolbox and drag it onto the empty page:

2.  The now familiar gray box appears on the page. Click on it to make sure it's selected,
    and look in the Properties window at the bottom right of the screen. You can see the
    kind of things that this control expects us to provide values for. The properties are
    mostly concerned with **commands**, and whether they are **auto-generated**:

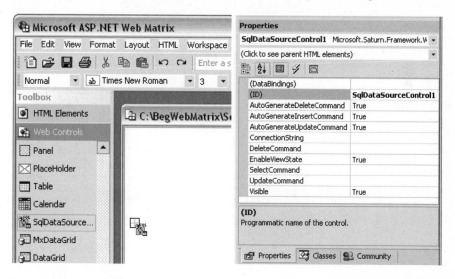

We could approach our exploration of this control by explaining all the properties, one by one, until you finally drifted off to sleep! However, instead, click on the SqlDataSoureControl again and press *Delete* to remove it from the page. We're going to work with this control in a slightly different way.

3.  Open a connection to the CAM database in the Data Explorer window, as shown in the
    previous chapter, by clicking the New Connection icon, entering the name of the
    database server to connect to, and selecting the database in the drop-down list:

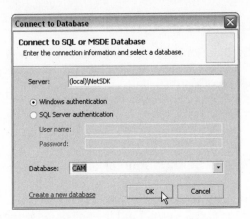

**4.** Select the Discs table, and drag it onto the ASP.NET page. Web Matrix places a SqlDataSourceControl and a DataGrid onto the page automatically:

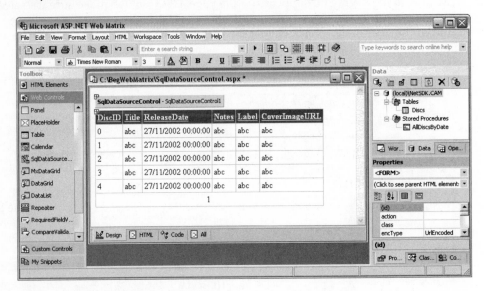

**5.** Click the Start button on the main Web Matrix toolbar, and the browser displays the contents of the Discs table:

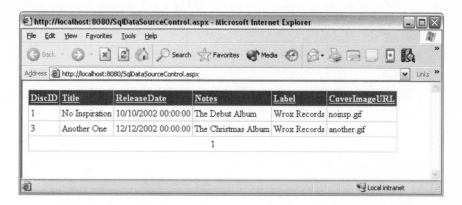

**6.** Now close your browser, and click on the **SqlDataSourceControl**. Look at the **Properties** window. This time many of the values have been filled in automatically:

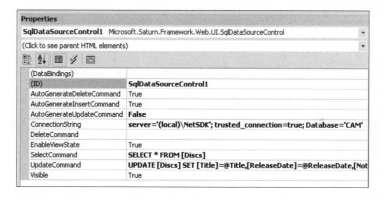

**7.** To see the effects of these property settings, we'll modify the one containing the SQL statement that selects the row for display. In the **Properties** window, change the value of the **SelectCommand** property to SELECT * FROM [Discs] WHERE DiscID=3:

**8.** Now click the **Start** button on the main Web Matrix toolbar and you'll see the results appear in the browser. There is just the single row that we specified in the SQL statement used for the **SelectCommand**:

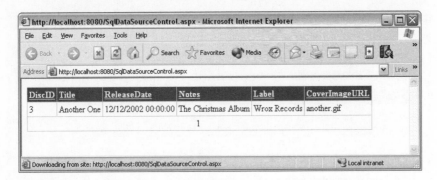

9. Close the browser, but leave the current page open in Web Matrix. Select the SqlDataSourceControl on the page, go to the **Properties** window, and change the value of the SelectCommand back to its original value by removing **WHERE DiscID=3**, so that it will display all the rows again. We're going to use this page again in the next *Try It Out*.

## How It Works

By dragging the table onto the page, we caused Web Matrix to create a `SqlDataSourceControl` with some interesting properties.

Web Matrix has created two SQL statements, as seen in the **SelectCommand** and **UpdateCommand** properties. Since it has created the value for the **UpdateCommand** property, it has also set the **AutoGenerateUpdateCommand** property value to **False** to tell the control not to create an **UpdateCommand** property itself. We'll talk about what these terms mean in more detail later on.

In the meantime, you should recognize the **SelectCommand** value. This is the same SQL statement that we used in the **Query** window of the **Data Explorer** in the previous chapter to extract a list of the rows in our table (the square brackets around the table name are there only to prevent an error should the table name contain a space). The `SqlDataSourceControl` uses this SQL statement to extract the rows for the grid control in our ASP.NET page.

Web Matrix has also figured out the **connection string** that's required to connect to our database, and placed it in the **ConnectionString** property. Again, we'll discuss connection strings in a little more detail later in this chapter.

The `SqlDataSourceControl` uses the SQL statements we specify (or which Web Matrix creates for us) to access the data in the database. The techniques it uses are actually very similar to those of ADO.NET, upon which all of this stuff depends. (In fact, you'll see this at the start of the next chapter, where we learn more about what ADO.NET is, and how it's used to access data programmatically.) The `SqlDataSourceControl` is like a wrapper around one of the basic ADO.NET objects – the `DataAdapter` – which we use to interact with a database when writing code outside Web Matrix.

We'll be looking at the `DataAdapter` and other ADO.NET objects later. In the meantime, we'll summarize the way that the properties of the `SqlDataSourceControl` are used in Web Matrix.

### The SqlDataSourceControl Properties

We've seen that the `SqlDataSourceControl` exposes three **command properties**, and that at least two of them can be specified as SQL statements:

- ❏ The SQL statement in the **UpdateCommand** property (although we didn't demonstrate it) is an UPDATE statement, used to *change* the values of rows in the database table.

- ❏ The SQL SELECT statement in the **SelectCommand** property, as we saw in our example, is used to extract the data from our database table.

- ❏ The same logic applies to the **DeleteCommand**, with can contain a SQL DELETE statement. This will be used to delete rows from the table that the control is linked to.

However, there is one type of SQL statement for which a matching property is not provided – the SQL INSERT statement – so this control can't be used to insert new rows into a database table.

### Auto-Generated Commands

The other three properties that we mentioned, but did not expand on earlier, are the three **AutoGenerate** properties. The value of each one is a `Boolean` (**True** or **False**) value.

If it is set to **True**, the control will automatically generate SQL commands for deleting, updating, and inserting data. It does this using an ADO.NET object known as a `CommandBuilder` to create suitable SQL statements based on the value of the **SelectCommand** property of the `SqlDataSourceControl`.

> *This means that we always have to provide a value for the **SelectCommand** of our `SqlDataSourceControl`, though the others (**DeleteCommand** and **UpdateCommand**) are optional. They are only used when we come to update or delete a row, and not for just displaying data.*

However, if we decide to create our own SQL statement for the **UpdateCommand** and/or **DeleteCommand** properties (perhaps because we want to perform some specific checks on the values in the existing rows), we set the **AutoGenerate** property for that command to **False**. You can see that this is what Web Matrix does when it creates the `SqlDataSourceControl` – it fills in the **UpdateCommand** property and sets the **AutoGenerateUpdateCommand** property to **False**:

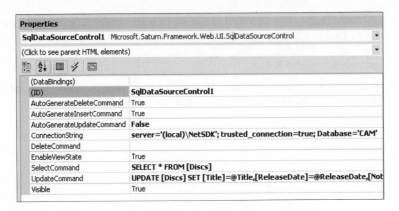

Having said all this, the process of performing updates to a database using a
SqlDataSourceControl is not straightforward. It's likely to be an improved process in future
releases of Web Matrix, but for now we suggest you use the techniques we describe in the next
chapter for updating data. However, it is useful to appreciate the meaning and purpose of these
properties, as they are just about identical to those you'll meet when we look at updating a data
source through a DataAdapter object in the next chapter.

### Connection Strings

Obviously, the controls and code in our ASP.NET pages have to know where to get the data
that they're supposed to be working with. This is done using a connection string, which
specifies where to get the data from (the name of the server, the security protocols involved, the
database to be used, and so on).

When we created a connection in the Data Explorer window using the New Connection icon, we
set a lot of these properties. The settings used in the New Connection dialog determine the
values used in the connection string. Let's take a look at an example:

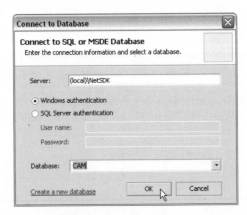

The settings shown above are the settings we used in the previous examples, and these settings
generated the following connection string in our code:

```
server='(local)\netsdk';trusted_connection=true;Database='CAM'
```

*A "trusted connection" is one that uses the account under which the ASP.NET page is running to access the database, and so this account must have access to the database. If you have IIS installed on your system, the default used for this is called **ASPNET**. The .NET SDK samples installation routine adds this account to the sample databases in MSDE, though you may have to add it yourself if you are using a different database. If, however, you don't have IIS installed, the currently logged-in user's account is used instead.*

If we specify a different server, for example a machine named dingley (yes, it's a Dell machine!), and that the connection should be made using a specific user name and password, the connection string we get contains these new values. The settings in the next screenshot demonstrate this:

The connection string we get this time contains the user ID and password, rather than the special instruction, trusted_connection=true, that we got when we specified Windows authentication in the previous example:

```
server='dingley'; user id='sa'; password='secretone'; Database='CAM'
```

*This means that the account specified will be used to access the database, rather than the account that is used for a trusted connection. The account used for trusted connections is always a local account (it is only valid on the local machine), so when connecting to a database server on another machine you must specify an account that is valid on the target machine. You also have to make sure that the specified account has permission to access the database and its tables and stored procedures. In SQL Server, this is done using **Enterprise Manager**.*

So, while Web Matrix can create the correct connection string for us automatically, it's worth understanding how you can edit it if required. When we come to write our own code that connects to a database and accesses data, rather than just using the controls provided with Web Matrix, we often have to specify the connection string ourselves. This is particularly the case if we use a database other than SQL Server or MSDE.

# About the MxDataGrid Control

So far in this chapter, we've talked about the `SqlDataSourceControl`, and how it connects to the database and extracts the data. However, the presentation of this data is what we're after. The presentation is the responsibility of the other control that Web Matrix automatically adds to the page when we drag a table from the **Data Explorer** window onto an ASP.NET page – the `MxDataGrid` control. In the screenshot we showed at the start of the chapter, you can see it lurking below the `SqlDataSourceControl`:

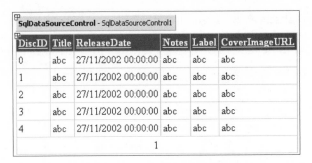

If you select this control in the page and look at the **Properties** dialog, you can see how the `MxDataGrid` is "connected to" the `SqlDataSourceControl`. The `MxDataGrid` control has a property named `DataSourceControlID`, and this is set to the ID of the `SqlDataSourceControl` on the page, in this case, **SqlDataSourceControl1**:

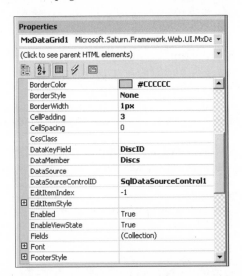

Between them, these two controls do all the work required to extract the data and present it as a grid on the page. To prove this, when the page we ended up with at the end of the previous *Try It Out* is open in Web Matrix, click the **Code** tab at the bottom of the editor window to switch to **Code** view. Other than the default line ' **Insert page code here**, the code section is empty.

In the next *Try It Out*, we'll explore how we can work with the MxDataGrid control, and modify the output it generates. Along the way, you'll see how it works – and this will come in extremely useful when we come to look at how we can work with the more generic ASP.NET list controls in the next chapter.

**Try It Out          Using the MxDataGrid Control**

**1.** Create a new ASP.NET page called MxDataGrid.aspx, connect to the **CAM** database, and drag the **Discs** table onto the page. This adds the SqlDataSourceControl and MxDataGrid controls, and sets their properties automatically.

**2.** Click on the MxDataGrid control in the page, and go to the **Properties** window. Find the property entry named **Fields** and select it. A button with an ellipsis (three dots) on it appears:

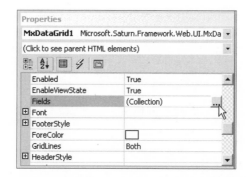

**3.** Click this button and the **MxDataGridField Collection Editor** dialog appears (which, for brevity, we'll refer to as the field editor dialog from now on!). This dialog is used to specify the fields that the grid control will display, and how it will present them. You can see that there are six **BoundField** items shown in the left-hand list (numbered from zero to five). As you select each one, the right-hand list shows the properties of each one, and the current values. You can see that Web Matrix has set several of these properties when it created the control:

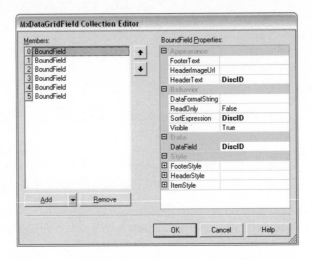

**4.** Select the DiscID column in the left-hand list and click the <u>R</u>emove button at the foot of this list:

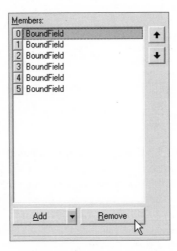

**5.** The first column (shown as column zero) is now our Title column, and this is fine as it is with the default settings. However, we can make the next column, which contains the release date of the disc, look much better by editing its properties. Select this column in the left-hand list, and change the following properties: change the HeaderText from ReleaseDate to Released, and enter the text {0:MMM yyyy} for the DataFormatString property:

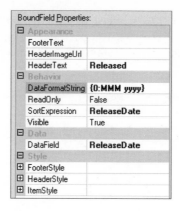

6. The next two columns, Notes and Label, are fine with default values that Web Matrix applies when it creates the control. However, we could do with trying to sort out the final column that contains the URL of our cover image. It would be nice if it were a hyperlink rather than just text. So, select the last column (column 4) and click the Remove button at the foot of this list. Then click the drop-down button next to the Add button to see a list of column types that we can use in our grid control:

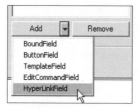

7. Select the HyperlinkField, and the field editor dialog shows this column at the end of the list. Specify the HeaderText as Cover, and type in the field name within the source data, CoverImageURL, for the values of the DataNavigateField and DataTextField properties:

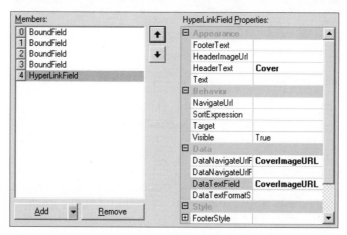

**8.** Click <u>O</u>K to save the new field collection settings, and you'll see the grid in the ASP.NET page updated to these settings. The column headings have changed as we specified, and the content of the Released and Cover columns has also been updated to the new format:

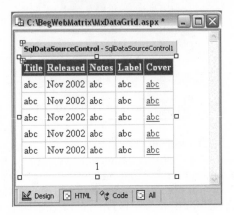

**9.** Now click the Start button to run the page in your browser. Again, you can see the effects of the changes we made to the properties of the columns. You can also see that most of the column headings are hyperlinks, and clicking on one sorts the rows on the value of that column. The Cover column header is not a hyperlink, however, because we didn't enter any value for the SortExpression property of this column, but the important point to notice that the *values* in the Cover column are now hyperlinks:

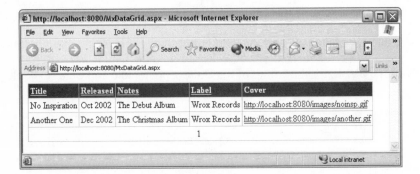

**10.** One thing we didn't do when changing the column properties was to modify the visual appearance and style of the columns and their content. However, there are plenty of properties that you can play with in the field editor dialog for each individual column, and in the main Properties window (where the settings affect all the columns). The next screenshot shows the same grid after we changed some of these settings for the Title, Label, and Cover columns (in the field editor dialog) and the grid as a whole (the HeaderStyle, ItemStyle, and AlternatingItemStyle). Have a go yourself, and experiment with these settings:

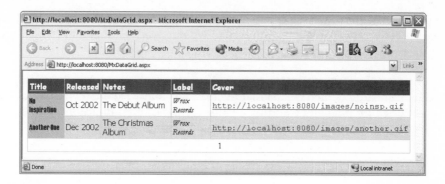

## How It Works

In the MxDataGridField Collection Editor dialog, we saw that the six columns in the database had been bound to the `MxDataGrid`. Let's look at how this collection editor works.

The HeaderText property defines what will be shown as the column heading in the grid, and the DataField is the name of the field (data column) in the source data from which the column will extract the values for display. Columns can be set to be read-only using the ReadOnly property, though this only has any effect when we use the control to edit data in the rows. However, the Visible property can be used to show or hide columns if required.

The SortExpression is used to enable the rows in the grid to be sorted, by clicking on the column heading in the browser. It is the name of the column that the rows should be sorted by when the heading for this column is clicked (you can enter more than one column name, separated by commas, to sort the rows based on the values in these columns). The remaining properties (in collapsible explorer-style lists in the Style section) specify the visual appearance and style of the column, and you can experiment with these if you want to see how the appearance of the grid is achieved. We'll be looking at these properties in more detail with the generic ASP.NET list controls in the next chapter (the `MxDataGrid` is based on the standard `DataGrid` control, and most of the properties are the same for both).

We didn't need to display the DiscID column in our page. We could just have hidden it by setting the Visible property to False, but instead we removed it altogether (which saves ASP.NET the processing required to create it and then not display it).

We then formatted the ReleaseDate column to be more customized. We first changed the text to be used in the header, which means that the grid will show Released instead of ReleaseDate at the top of this column. Then by adding a value for the DataFormatString property, we controlled how the value in the column is presented (formatted):

    {0:MMM yyyy}

This property accepts the standard .NET format strings where the curly brackets contain two values separated by a colon. The first value is always zero, indicating that the first value it encounters in the data source is the one that will be formatted.

The second value, after the colon, is the format string made up of a set of standard characters that have special meaning. MMM means the month in three-letter abbreviated form, and yyyy means the year as four digits, so we'll get something like Oct 2002 displayed in the grid. There are many other formats we can use, such as C for currency, or F2 for a number fixed to two decimal places. We look at formatting strings in a little more detail later on in this chapter.

Our next step was to change the CoverImageUrl field to be a hyperlink. We deleted the original column details, and added a new column of a different type, as a hyperlink. As we saw in the example, the HyperlinkField column has a different set of properties from a BoundField column. When displayed, it creates a normal hyperlink element in the column, and uses the property values to set the attributes and content of the element. The DataNavigateUrlField specifies the field in the source data that will provide the information on what to display when the link is clicked, and the DataTextField specifies the field in the source data that will provide the text of the element (the blue underlined text). We'll learn more about linking to files and pages in Chapter 11.

# Server-Side Data Binding

So, we can display data from a database table, and exert very fine control over the way it is presented, but what's actually going on here? How does the data get from the table into the page? While you don't need to know all about this to use the controls, in the same way as you don't need to be a mechanic to drive a car, where we're going from here on in will require at least a basic appreciation of the topic. Maybe compare it to driving across a very large desert, where it would be quite useful to learn how to get sand out of a carburettor before you set off.

All the list controls we use in ASP.NET provide a feature called **data binding**. The idea is that we just tell a control what the data source is, and it fetches the data and builds up the appropriate section of the page containing that data. If you think about it, that's what the SqlDataSourceControl and MxDataGrid controls are doing in the examples we've seen so far in this chapter. The data is taken from the database, and used to fill the control on the server, then the resulting page is sent to the browser. We saw this in action briefly in Chapter 6 when working with collections. In this chapter, and the next chapter, we'll take this a bit further, and bind data from the database to different types of controls.

## Data-Binding to .NET Server Controls

The way that we accomplish data binding varies, depending on the control we're applying it to. The different types of list control that are part of the .NET Framework have different capabilities, and so, apply different requirements to the process of setting up this binding. In the next chapter, we'll look in more depth at the different types of list controls that are provided with .NET, and see these differences.

Data binding is not limited to list controls either. We can bind a data source to almost any control, or even to the page itself. Again, we'll see more of this in the next chapter. What we want to look at here is a topic that is fundamental to the data binding process in many scenarios, and which requires a broad appreciation of data binding techniques. This topic is the use of **templates**.

## Using a Template to Display Data

If you studied the list of column types that are available in the MxDataGrid control's field editor dialog while working through the previous *Try It Out*, you'll have seen the option for a using TemplateField column:

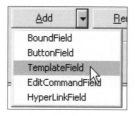

We didn't use this column type in our example, instead choosing a HyperlinkColumn so that we could display the value from the source data in that column as a hyperlink. What actually happens in this case is that the control automatically generates a normal HTML <a> element (the element used to create links), and the values we specify for the column's properties translate into the values used to make the link work.

So, we set the DataNavigateField and DataTextField properties to the name of the column, which means that the *value* of the column in each row is used to generate the <a> element for that row. Since the same value is used in both fields, the displayed text will match the link to the file. If you view the source of the page in the browser (by using the View | Source menu option from the browser menu bar), you'll see that we end up with the following code for the Cover column in the first row (we've added some line breaks to make it easier to see):

```
...
<td>
  <a href="http://oursite.com/covers/thisone.gif">
    http://oursite.com/covers/thisone.gif
  </a>
</td>
...
```

This is obviously an extremely useful technique for generating customized output. What about if we want to display the image itself in this column though, rather than a hyperlink that points to it? In this case, we would need to generate an <img>, which is an HTML image element, so we'd need Microsoft to build in an ImageColumn option, and what if we wanted to include an image and some text, or a pair of radio buttons, or a drop-down list? We could have so many column types that choosing one would take longer than building the rest of the website.

## Using a TemplateField Column in the MxDataGrid Control

This is where the concept of a TemplateField column comes in. Basically, it's a column where you specify exactly what you want to be generated for that column as the output from the control is being created and sent to the browser. Web Matrix includes the tools we need to create these templates for most of the list controls in ASP.NET. We'll see how it works with the MxDataGrid control here, and then look at how the technique is applied to other list controls in the next chapter.

At the end of the previous *Try It Out* we had produced a page that lists the rows in the Discs table of our CAM database. The last column in the MxDataGrid we use to present the data is a HyperLinkField column, which displays the value of the CoverImageUrl as a hyperlink. In the next *Try It Out* we'll do better than this. We'll display the actual cover image in our page, and make it a hyperlink that opens a page from some fictitious online retailer that allows visitors to buy the disc.

### Try It Out        Displaying an Image in the MxDataGrid Control

**1.** At the moment, the last column in the MxDataGrid is a HyperLinkField column, which displays the value of the CoverImageUrl as a hyperlink. Open the field editor dialog by selecting the MxDataGrid in the page and clicking the "three dots" (ellipsis) button in the Fields property in the Properties window of the grid, just as we did in the previous *Try It Out*:

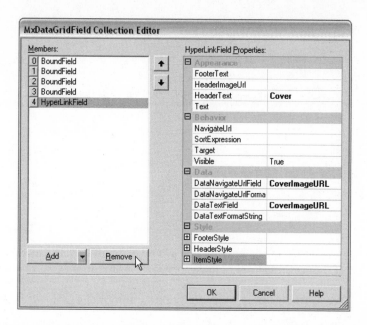

**2.** Select the last column and click the R̲emove button to remove it from the grid, as shown in the previous screenshot. Then click the drop-down list arrow next to the A̲dd button, and select TemplateField to add a TemplateField to the grid:

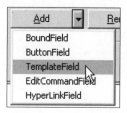

**3.** The TemplateField appears in the list of columns for the grid. Select it in the left-hand list, and change the HeaderText property to Cover. Notice that, unlike the other column types we've used previously, there are no properties such as DataField or DataTextField that we can use to tell the grid where the data for this column comes from:

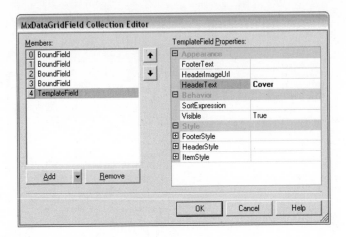

A TemplateField column demands that we provide all the information about the output that the control should create for that column ourselves, within a **template**. With the MxDataGrid, there is no fancy UI that we can use to generate this template, and we have to (shock, horror!) actually *type it* into the HTML window ourselves.

**4.** Click the <u>O</u>K button to save the new grid configuration and close the field editor dialog. Then click the HTML tab at the foot of the main Web Matrix editor window to see the HTML that Web Matrix has created for us. You can see the definitions of the SqlDataSourceControl and the MxDataGrid. If you scroll the page to the right, you'll also see all the attributes that have been added to each one, which represent the properties we set:

**5.** The definition of the `MxDataGrid` control includes a series of **BoundField** elements. These are the columns that Web Matrix defined for the grid, and they include attributes that define the various properties we set for these columns. At the end of the list of columns in the `MxDataGrid` definition is the new **TemplateField** column we added. You can see that this is empty, and so, we'll get no content generated for this column as it stands:

```
<wmx:TemplateField HeaderText="Cover"></wmx:TemplateField>
```

*You can try running the page to see the result. The **Cover** column appears, because there is a **TemplateField** declared for it, but it is empty; and, while you can see this column in **Design** view, you can't drag and drop controls from the **Toolbar** into it.*

**6.** We want to add an image that is also a hyperlink to the **Cover** column. So, in HTML view, type in the highlighted code shown below, between the opening and closing `<wmx:TemplateField>` elements:

> **You must type the complete `<asp:Hyperlink>` element definition, including all the attributes, on one line, and not broken up with line breaks as we've had to do to get it on the page, and make it easier to read:**

```
<wmx:TemplateField HeaderText="Cover">
  <ItemTemplate>
    <asp:Hyperlink
      ImageUrl='<% #DataBinder.Eval(Container.DataItem, "CoverImageURL") %>'
      NavigateUrl='<% #DataBinder.Eval(Container.DataItem, "DiscID",
                      "http://somesite.com/buy.aspx?code={0}") %>'
      ToolTip='<% #DataBinder.Eval(Container.DataItem, "Title",
                  "Buy {0} Online Now!") %>'
      runat="server" />
  </ItemTemplate>
</wmx:TemplateField>
```

**7.** We also want our new column to come at the left of the grid, so open the field editor dialog again (from the ellipsis button in the **Fields** property of the **Design** view), and use the arrows next to the list of columns to move it to the top of the list:

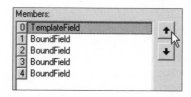

8. Click <u>O</u>K to close the field editor dialog, and run the page. You might not get the images displayed, depending on the path to them you entered into the CoverImageURL column of the Discs table when you created it in the previous chapter. If this is wrong, you'll just get the "missing image" symbol. Either edit the values in the Discs table, or copy the images from the sample code into the folder that the CoverImageURL values point to:

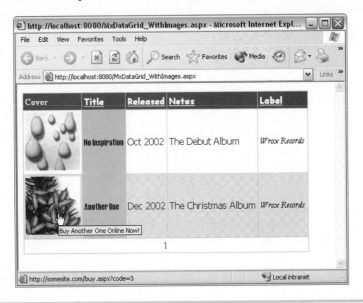

## How It Works

In our earlier examples of displaying data, we've relied on **bound column** controls to generate the output for a column. All we do is tell the column where the data comes from, what heading text we want for the column, and perhaps some formatting and styling details as well. It looks after extracting the appropriate values, and building the output for that column in the page.

However, many of the ASP.NET controls can accept a column definition that is made up of one or more **templates**. The MxDataGrid is just one of these, and we'll see more examples later in the book. Using a **templated column** effectively says to the control "leave it to me, I will create the content I want". We have to define the template and all its content. In the case of the MxDataGrid, we did this by manually typing it in. With some other list controls, there are UI dialogs that can help out.

The ASP.NET Hyperlink control that we used in this example is an interesting control that we'll look at in Chapter 11 in more detail. To see what effect it has, look at the generated page. Notice (in the status bar of the browser) that each image is also a hyperlink, and that it points to our fictitious site. Furthermore, it actually points to a specific page on that site – and it includes a query string that contains the DiscID value of the row containing the hyperlink. So, the hyperlink could open the page showing this specific disc, and you can also see that the pop-up tool-tip displayed when the mouse is over the image contains the disc title.

## *The Six Types of Template*

There are six different kinds of template that we can include in a templated column of a list control. Not all list controls support all of these types of templates, but the `MxDataGrid` supports them all – as do the standard ASP.NET `DataGrid`, `DataList`, and `Repeater` controls we'll meet in the next chapter:

❑ A `HeaderTemplate` is used to specify the content that we want the list control to display as the heading row, before any data rows.

❑ A `FooterTemplate` is used to specify the content that we want the list control to display as the footer row, after all the data rows.

❑ An `ItemTemplate` is used to specify the content that we want the list control to display for each row in the list when just displaying the contents.

❑ An `AlternatingItemTemplate` is used to specify the content that we want the list control to display for each alternate row. If this template is not declared, the content of the `ItemTemplate` is used for every row.

❑ A `SelectedItemTemplate` is used to specify the content that we want the list control to display for the row that is currently selected. A row can be selected by setting the `SelectedItem` property of the list control to the index of the row (starting from zero).

❑ An `EditItemTemplate` is used to specify the content that we want the list control to display for the row that is currently being edited. A row can be displayed in "edit mode" by setting the `EditItemIndex` property of the list control to the index of the row (starting from zero).

To create the content for the **TemplateField** column in our example, we only defined an `ItemTemplate`. This is the content we used:

```
<wmx:TemplateField HeaderText="Cover">
  <ItemTemplate>
    <asp:Hyperlink
      ImageUrl='<% #DataBinder.Eval(Container.DataItem, "CoverImageURL") %>'
      NavigateUrl='<% #DataBinder.Eval(Container.DataItem, "DiscID",
                        "http://somesite.com/buy.aspx?code={0}") %>'
      ToolTip='<% #DataBinder.Eval(Container.DataItem, "Title",
                  "Buy {0} Online Now!") %>'
      runat="server" />
  </ItemTemplate>
</wmx:TemplateField>
```

You can see that the content of the template is an `<asp:Hyperlink>` control, which we'll examine in more detail in Chapter 11. What makes it look complicated is that we want the attributes of the control (the `ImageUrl`, `NavigateUrl`, and `ToolTip`) to reflect some of the values that are in the **current row** of the data. Remember that this template is processed (used) for each row in turn, as the list control creates the output to send to the browser. So, we need a way to get at the values in the columns of the current data row that was extracted from our database.

## Accessing Row Values in a Template

To get at the contents of the current row in our template, we use the `Eval()` method that is exposed by the `DataBinder` object – the thing that actually carries out the binding of the data to the list control:

```
DataBinder.Eval(Container.DataItem, "column-name" [, "format-string"])
```

The third parameter, *format-string*, is optional. If it is not provided, the simple string representation of the value is used. However, if we do provide it, we can exert a great deal of control over the appearance and content that is placed into the output for this column and row.

## Setting the ImageUrl Attribute Value

To set the `ImageUrl` attribute value of our `<asp:Hyperlink>` element, we don't need to do any formatting, so we just use:

```
ImageUrl='<% #DataBinder.Eval(Container.DataItem, "CoverImageURL") %>'
```

Notice the special data-binding statement delimiters `<% # ... %>`. We wrap the statement between `<%` and `%>` to tell ASP.NET that this is server-side code that it should execute (the language it uses is defined in the `Page` directive at the top of the page). Then, to indicate that it's a data-binding statement, we precede it with the hash character, `#`. As the data-binding statement includes double-quotes, we use single quotes to enclose the whole thing and indicate that we want whatever it evaluates to be used as the `ImageUrl` property.

We could alternatively have used a simpler syntax for this attribute, because we don't need to format the values and we're working in Visual Basic .NET:

```
ImageUrl='<% Container.DataItem("CoverImageURL") %>'
```

*This is in fact marginally faster and more efficient at run time than using the Eval() method, but is only any good where we are using Visual Basic .NET, and where we don't need to format the value. For these reasons, most data binding statements use the Eval() method.*

## Formatting the Values

The simplest format strings are like those we used to format the **ReleaseDate** column of our grid earlier in this chapter. To display the value as "short-month and year", we used `{0:MMM yyyy}`. This simply means "Format the first value you come to (the column value) using the string after the colon, which represents the month as three letters and the year as four numbers."

So, if we were using the template to display the release date, we would write something like this:

```
<% #DataBinder.Eval(Container.DataItem, "ReleaseDate", "{0:MMM yyyy}") %>'
```

Other common format strings are {0:C} (currency), {0:D} (standard date), and {0:P} (percentage). A full list, and descriptions of their use, can be found in the local .NET SDK at ms-help://MS.NETFrameworkSDK/cpguidenf/html/cpconformattingtypes.htm, or online at http://msdn.microsoft.com/library/en-us/cpguide/html/cpconformattingtypes.asp.

## Setting the NavigateUrl and ToolTip Attribute Values

Now we know how we can format the values in a data row, but the format string we use can also include literal characters. In other words, we can specify the text that we want to appear in the page, and then insert the column value within that text.

This is what our example does for the NavigateUrl of the hyperlink. We want it to include the URL of the site that sells our discs, the name of the page that displays them, and a query string that specifies which disc the user selected (by clicking on the cover). The following string:

```
"http://somesite.com/buy.aspx?code={0}"
```

tells ASP.NET to use the string value http://somesite.com/buy.aspx?code=, and add onto the end the value from the column – but from which column? We don't want the value from the current column (the URL of the cover image), we want to value from the DiscID column. No problem, we just specify this column in the Eval statement:

```
NavigateUrl='<% #DataBinder.Eval(Container.DataItem, "DiscID",
                "http://somesite.com/buy.aspx?code={0}") %>'
```

*This must be on one line in Visual Basic .NET. If you have to wrap the contents of the Eval statement, as shown above, you must use the underscore line continuation character, like the following:*

```
NavigateUrl='<% #DataBinder.Eval(Container.DataItem, "DiscID", _
                "http://somesite.com/buy.aspx?code={0}") %>'
```

The result, as you saw in the status bar of the browser at the end of the previous *Try It Out* is something like http://somesite.com/buy.aspx?code=3. Likewise, we create the value for the ToolTip property using a format string. This time, the value comes from the Title column (the disc title), and we insert it into the middle of the literal characters in the format string:

```
ToolTip='<% #DataBinder.Eval(Container.DataItem, "Title",
            "Buy {0} Online Now!") %>'
```

If you look at the code that the page we used in the previous *Try It Out* creates in your browser (by viewing the source in your browser using the View | Source menu), you'll see the content that is generated by our TemplateField column and the hyperlink we defined within it:

```
<a title="Buy Another One Online Now!"
   href="http://somesite.com/buy.aspx?code=3">
   <img title="Buy Another One Online Now!"
     src="http://localhost/covers/nextone.gif" border="0" />
</a>
```

# Using a Template to Edit Data

To show you how we can use one of the other types of column in a grid control, and how we can use another of the types of template that we mentioned earlier in the preceding section of this chapter, we'll finish this chapter with a short *Try It Out* that demonstrates both. We aren't in a position to be able to actually update the database contents yet, but we can see how we build the parts of the interface (the web page) that allow the user to enter new values for the columns in a table.

We'll add an EditItemTemplate to the Cover column of our MxDataGrid control, and see how the display for that row changes when we put that row into "edit mode".

---

**Try It Out**     **Adding an EditItemTemplate to a Grid Control**

**1.** Open the field editor dialog again, by clicking on the ellipsis in the Fields property when the MxDataGrid control is selected on the page. Click the drop-down button next to the <u>A</u>dd button, and add an EditCommandField column to the grid:

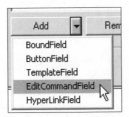

**2.** In the list of properties in the right-hand section of the dialog, select PushButton for the ButtonType property (the default is LinkButton), and type in the text captions that will appear on the buttons as the values of the CancelText, EditText, and UpdateText properties, as follows:

**3.** We want this new column to be the first one in the grid (on the left when displayed), so use the arrow button next to the list of **Members** to move it to the top of the list:

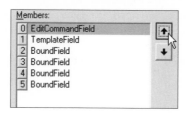

**4.** Click <u>OK</u> to save the new grid design and close the field editor dialog. In the ASP.NET page in **Design** view, you can see the new column displayed:

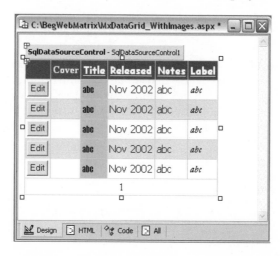

**5.** Now we need to tell the grid what to do when this button is clicked. In an EditCommandColumn, the Edit button raises the **EditCommand** event when it is clicked. The first step is to open the list of event properties by selecting the grid control in the page and clicking the **Events** icon at the top of the **Properties** dialog:

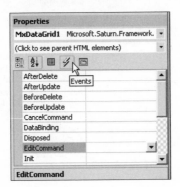

**6.** Then, find the **EditCommand** event and double-click on the **EditCommand** text itself. This switches the main Web Matrix editor window to **Code** view, and automatically inserts the outline of the event handler we need to write. We only have to add one line of code, which will tell the grid control that the row that was clicked should be the one that is shown in "edit mode". We get the index of the current row from the `ItemIndex` property of the `Item` object that is exposed by the arguments to the event handler, and we just have to assign this index value to the `EditItemIndex` property of the grid control:

```
Sub MxDataGrid1_EditCommand(
    source As Object, e As MxDataGridCommandEventArgs)
      MxDataGrid1.EditItemIndex = e.Item.Itemindex
End Sub
```

*The first line of code above, generated by Web Matrix automatically, is actually on one single line with no line breaks – we just can't physically fit it all on the page!*

**7.** Now we have to add an appropriate template to the **TemplateField** column that displays the image of the cover. We need an **EditItemTemplate**, and you can see this as the highlighted section of the next listing. Switch to **HTML** view in Web Matrix, and add these lines to your **TemplateField** column definition:

```
<wmx:TemplateField HeaderText="Cover">
  <ItemTemplate>
    <asp:Hyperlink ... />
  </ItemTemplate>
    <EditItemTemplate>
      <asp:TextBox
        Text='<% #DataBinder.Eval(Container.DataItem, "CoverImageURL") %>'
        runat="server" />
    </EditItemTemplate>
</wmx:TemplateField>
```

*As with the <asp:Hyperlink> element in the <ItemTemplate>, the complete <asp:TextBox> element is on one single line, with no line breaks.*

**8.** Click the **Save** icon on the main Web Matrix toolbar to save the page, and click the **Start** button to view it in your browser. You'll see the new column with an **Edit** button in each row:

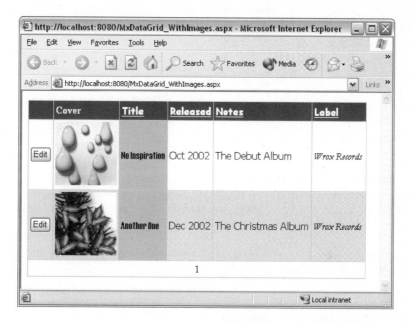

**9.** Click the **Edit** button in the first row. The page is posted back to the server and the new page contains two different buttons, **Update** and **Cancel**, and all the values in the row are now presented in textboxes. You can edit any of them:

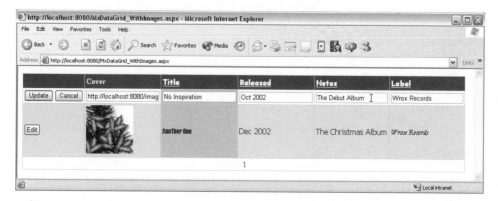

Click the Cancel button, and the row goes back to the way it was. Or click the Edit button in a different row. The first row goes back to "normal", but the other row is now shown in "edit mode".

## How It Works

You've just seen how easy it is to build editing into the interface when we use the ASP.NET MxDataGrid control. We haven't seen how to save these changes yet – the Update button won't work – but we'll add this feature in the next section.

All we had to do in this example was add a column that contains the buttons to switch the grid into "edit" mode, and link up the buttons in this column to an event handler that sets the EditItemIndex of the grid control. Then we added an EditItemTemplate to the templated column that specifies what we want the column to contain when that row is in "edit mode".

We specified that, instead of the <asp:Hyperlink> that displays the cover image, the column should display the value in a textbox. However, we don't have to use a textbox here. If we have a list of possible values, we can use an <asp:DropDownList> or <asp:ListBox>. Or, if there are only a small number of possible values for the column, we might use a set of radio buttons. The great thing about using a TemplateField column is that we are free to include whatever controls we need to generate the output we want in the page.

OK, that looks clever... but it's not very useful yet. Let's see how to make the Update button work. It's easy to do, but the inner workings are fairly complex.

## Try It Out        Updating the Database

1. Return to the Design view, and select the MxDataGrid. Now click the lightening bolt icon in the Properties pane, and double-click the BeforeUpdate event. Web Matrix will create a new event handler procedure for you, and assign it to MxDataGrid.BeforeUpdate event.

2. Add the following code (remember that I've had to break lines in two to fit on the page):

```
Sub MxDataGrid1_BeforeUpdate(source As Object, _
                                    e As MxDataGridUpdateEventArgs)
    e.NewValues.Add("@Title", _
                        CType(e.Item.Cells(2).Controls(0), TextBox).Text)
    e.NewValues.Add("@ReleaseDate", _
                        CType(e.Item.Cells(3).Controls(0), TextBox).Text)
    e.NewValues.Add("@Notes", _
                        CType(e.Item.Cells(4).Controls(0), TextBox).Text)
    e.NewValues.Add("@Label", _
                        CType(e.Item.Cells(5).Controls(0), TextBox).Text)
    e.NewValues.Add("@CoverImageURL", _
                        CType(e.Item.Cells(1).Controls(1), TextBox).Text)
```

```
e.NewValues.Add("@DiscID", _
    MxDataGrid1.DataSource.DataSource.Tables(0).Rows(e.Item.DataSetIndex)(0))

End Sub
```

**3.** Now try running the page. You'll be able to make a change to a record and save it.

## How It Works

We really didn't need to do very much to get that working. This is because Web Matrix and ASP.NET are doing the hard work for us. Even so, to understand the code we really do need to understand what's going on.

The key to this update is the `UpdateCommand` property of the `SqlDataSourceControl`. It's a SQL string used to update the database – and it was generated automatically when we dragged the table onto the page:

```
UPDATE [Discs] SET [Title]=@Title, [ReleaseDate]=@ReleaseDate,
[Notes]=@Notes, [Label]=@Label, [CoverImageURL]=@CoverImageURL WHERE
[DiscID]=@DiscID
```

SQL is pretty close to English, and this really doesn't take a lot of explanation. The `Update [Discs]` part means, "Update the table called Discs." The `SET` keyword indicates that what follows a series of column name and value pairs. The `WHERE` clause indicates that we don't want to update every record in the table – only the ones that conform to the `WHERE` clause. This works just like the `WHERE` clause in a `SELECT` statement. In our case we only want to update *one* record – the record that the user has edited. We can identify this uniquely using the `DiscID` for the chosen record.

So, Web Matrix and ASP.NET have done that work for us. All we need to do is assign values to every variable in the SQL string, and that's what our code does. Let's take a closer look at it now. We'll start with the first line we typed:

```
e.NewValues.Add("@Title", _
                CType(e.Item.Cells(2).Controls(0), TextBox).Text)
```

This is all based around the `e` object. In Chapter 4 we learned a bit about what `e` is for in an event handler. In this particular case we're using it to assign values to our SQL variables. The two important properties of `e` are `NewValues` and `Item`. `NewValues` is a collection of name-value pairs we use to assign values to variable names. `Item` contains details about our `MxDataGrid`, so we use it to read the values from the `TextBox` controls in the grid. The part of the line that says:

```
CType(e.Item.Cells(2).Controls(0), TextBox).Text
```

Simply boils down to finding out what the `Textbox` in the `Title` column contains. Let's break this segment down to see how it works. `e.Item.Cells(2).Controls(0)` means "return the content of the first control in the third cell in the active row." Remember, arrays are zero-based so `Cells(2)` means "the third cell". This cell only contains one control, the `TextBox`, so we access it.

As we saw in Chapter 5, `CType` is a function that will try to convert the value passed in as the first argument into the type passed in as the second argument. So here the `CType` function converts the control into a fully-functional `TextBox` object. We then return the `Text` property of the `TextBox`, which of course contains the value the user typed.

`ReleaseDate`, `Notes`, and `Label` work in the same way – taking the first control in the relevant cell, and assigning it to the `@ReleaseDate`, `@Notes`, or `@Label` variables.

> *Although I'm calling these variables, it's only SQL that sees them that way. VB.NET sees them as normal strings, which is why we enclose them in quote marks – something we don't do with VB.NET variable names.*

The `CoverImageURL` column works slightly differently because it's not a regular text value. Instead of specifying `Controls(0)`, we specify `Controls(1)`. This is because the `TextBox` is not the first control held in this particular cell:

```
e.NewValues.Add("@CoverImageURL",
                CType(e.Item.Cells(1).Controls(1), TextBox).Text)
```

It's not easy to tell when there are 'hidden controls', and some trial-and-error changes may be required in cases where you have templated edit columns like this one.

The `DiscID` column is quite different again. Remember that this value is not editable, but we need it to uniquely identify the row that we're editing. The difference in how we use it here is because it is not displayed in our `MxDataGrid`, but it is present in the underlying data source – the `SqlDataSourceControl`. Here's the code:

```
e.NewValues.Add("@DiscID", MxDataGrid1.DataSource.DataSource.
                Tables(0).Rows(e.Item.DataSetIndex)("DiscID"))
```

The expression first of all accesses the `MxDataGrid DataSource` property, which is the `SqlDataSourceControl` itself. We then access *this* control's `DataSource` property, which is a `DataSet` – something we'll hear more about in the next chapter. We then access the first (and only) `Table` in the `DataSet`. So we're gradually zooming in on the part of the `DataSet` that we're interested in – we've got to the correct table, but haven't yet identified what row we want, or what column. This is what `Rows(e.Item.DataSetIndex)("DiscID")` does. `Rows` is a collection of `DataRow` objects – each `DataRow` is a single complete row in the table. The expression in the first set of brackets defines what row we want, and the expression in the second set of brackets defines the column. `e.Item.DataSetIndex` gives us the row number of the selected row in the underlying `DataSet`. We then request a specific column by name. The end result is that the `"@DiscID"` and the value for that particular `DiscID` are paired up in `NewValues`.

The `SqlDataSource` will use these pairs to execute its `UpdateCommand`. There's a lot going on under the hood here, but the practicalities of making it work are elegant and quite easy.

## Default Behavior with No Templates

One point you may have noticed in the previous example is that all the other columns in the row that we switched into "edit mode" also showed textboxes. We didn't configure this, or create any templates for these columns. However, because they are BoundField columns (which are linked, or bound, to the other columns in our table), they automatically display a default-sized textbox when the row is in "edit mode", unless we set the ReadOnly property of the column to True. The default is False.

Meanwhile, the appearance of the columns (including read-only ones) can also change when the row is in "edit mode". It depends on the setting of the EditItemStyle property of the grid control.

## Taking it Further – Using a SelectedItemTemplate

We can do much the same by adding a button that switches the row into "selected mode". We would use the more general ButtonField in this case (rather than an EditCommandField), which displays a button in each row of that the column to create a column that contains a LinkButton or a PushButton. The caption for the button goes into the Text property, but we also have to be sure to set the CommandName property as well – in general we use the same as the Text value, but with no spaces:

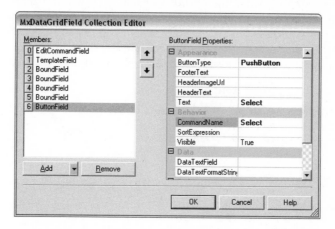

Then, we would link this button up to an event handler for the `ItemCommand` event that sets the `SelectedIndex` property of the grid control (rather than the `EditItemIndex`) to the index of the row containing the button that was clicked.

One point to watch when using a **ButtonField** column is that the `ItemCommand` event is actually called by **all** the controls in a grid that cause a postback. So any **Edit, Update,** and **Cancel** buttons that also exist in the grid will cause the `ItemCommand` event to execute as well as their "own" event. This means that, if we have both types of column (a **ButtonField** and an **EditCommandField**), we have to include some code in the `ItemCommand` event to check which button was clicked. We look for the `CommandName` property value that we specified for the button when we added the **ButtonField** column to the grid, so our `ItemCommand` event handler would look like this:

```
Sub MxDataGrid1_ItemCommand( _
   source As Object, e As MxDataGridCommandEventArgs)

   ' see if it was button with CommandName "Select" that was clicked
   If e.CommandName = "Select" Then

      ' set SelectedIndex of grid to index of item that was clicked
      ' obtained from properties of second parameter to event handler
      MxDataGrid1.SelectedIndex = e.Item.ItemIndex
   End If
End Sub
```

Plus, when we have both types of column (so that the grid can be switched into "selected mode" and "edit mode") we should add a line of code to each event handler that sets the "other" grid property to $-1$. In other words, in the `EditCommand` event handler, which runs when an **Edit** button is clicked, we would set the `SelectedIndex` property of the grid to $-1$ so that no rows are selected. Likewise in the `ItemCommand` event handler, which runs when the "select" button is clicked, we would set the `EditItemIndex` to $-1$ so that there are no rows in "edit mode".

```
Sub MxDataGrid1_EditCommand( _
   source As Object, e As MxDataGridCommandEventArgs)
   MxDataGrid1.SelectedIndex = -1
   MxDataGrid1.EditItemIndex = e.Item.Itemindex
End Sub

Sub MxDataGrid1_ItemCommand( _
   source As Object, e As MxDataGridCommandEventArgs)
   If e.CommandName = "Select" Then
      MxDataGrid1.EditItemIndex = -1
      MxDataGrid1.SelectedIndex = e.Item.ItemIndex
   End If
End Sub
```

You'll also find that the columns in a "selected row" generated by a **BoundField** column, like all the other columns of our example grid, automatically highlight the values in that column of the selected row, and can even change the background color of the column. The actual highlight effects depend on the settings of the **SelectedItemStyle** property of the grid control.

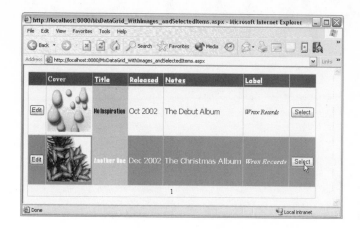

# Summary

In this chapter, we've concentrated on how you can build pages that display data extracted from a database. Web Matrix makes this easy, where a single table is involved, with its custom `SqlDataSourceControl` and `MxDataGrid` controls. As we've seen a couple of times now, it's just a simple drag-and-drop operation, perhaps with a few property setting changes to tidy it up and get exactly what you want displayed on the page.

We looked at how to display the data from the sample Cornflakes at Midnight database, and how we can modify the display to make it more attractive and intuitive, by choosing useful column headings for the grid, and changing the way the values are displayed. These changes included both the format of the text, and displaying hyperlinks and images within the rows of the grid.

The core technology behind all the presentation magic is server-side data binding, and we talked a little about what this actually is. We also saw it in action in all of these examples, and hopefully you can understand how cool it is to be able to work with data so simply.

Data binding also led us on to the idea of list control templates, and we looked at a simple example with the **MxDataControl**. You'll see plenty more examples of templates in the next chapter.

The list of topics we covered is:

❑ How Web Matrix actually connects to a database table and extracts the data

❑ How we can modify the appearance and content of the `MxDataGrid` control

❑ What server-side data binding is, and how we take advantage of it

❑ What list control templates are, and an example of how we can use them

In the next chapter, we'll continue our exploration of list controls and data binding, learning more about the code we use to work with databases.

# CHAPTER 10

# Working with Data

In the two previous chapters, we've been looking at how Web Matrix can be used to create pages that display data from a database table, and even (briefly) at how we can build pages designed to allow data to be edited and updated. We examined the SqlDataSourceControl and the MxDataGrid control that Web Matrix uses to provide a complete environment for displaying data without requiring you to write any code.

In this chapter, we will move to the next stage of accessing data, where we no longer depend on the clever built-in controls that are part of the Web Matrix installation. Instead, we'll be using the controls that are an integral part of the .NET Framework. To use these controls, we need to be able to access data in a fundamentally different way – by writing some code. However, as you'll see, Web Matrix contains tools that can relieve us of the bulk of the effort required.

So, in this chapter, we'll look at:

❑   How ASP.NET exposes data that we can use with a range of standard .NET controls

❑   How we create code routines that can access a database and return data

❑   How we select individual columns and return specific sets of rows from a database

❑   How we can use some of the generic .NET Framework data controls to display data

Let's get started and think about how accessing data using code is different from using controls and drag-and-drop wizards.

## Accessing Data Using Code

OK, so it's now time to face reality. Perhaps you want to sit down while we break the bad news to you. The pages we've used to display data in this chapter take advantage of two special controls that are not actually part of the standard .NET Framework. The SqlDataSourceControl and MxDataGrid controls are special additions to the range of standard controls, and are designed to make it easy to work with data when building pages with Web Matrix.

What this means is that the pages we've created in the previous chapter won't work unless these controls are installed into the .NET Framework class library on the server. Installing Web Matrix does this, and many hosting companies that support ASP.NET will also install them on their servers. However, it's useful (if not vital) to know how we can create the same kinds of pages without depending on these extremely useful controls. To do this, we have to write some code.

## Getting Back to Basics

You'll recall that we noted in the previous chapter how the page we built that used the `SqlDataSourceControl` and `MxDataGrid` controls contained no server-side code – the Code window in the editor was empty. This is because the two controls automatically react to events that happen in the page, and extract and display the data using their own internal routines. Simply setting the `DataSourceControlID` property of the `MxDataGrid` control to the ID of the `SqlDataSourceControl` links them together so that no code is required to make it all work.

Behind the scenes, these two controls use the basic controls and objects that are part of the standard .NET Framework class library. The `SqlDataSourceControl` uses the ADO.NET `DataAdapter` class to access the data and create a `DataSet`, while the `MxDataGrid` control is like a clever version of the standard ASP.NET Web Forms `DataGrid` control.

With only a little extra effort, we can use these standard controls from the .NET Framework instead. It also provides us with more flexibility, the ability to tailor our code more closely towards specific requirements as we work with more complex data. It also gives us independence from the special controls provided with Web Matrix. On top of this, the same techniques are used with a whole range of standard Web Forms list controls, not just the `DataGrid`. There are list controls that provide more freedom to control the layout of the content, list controls that require far less processing overhead than the `MxDataGrid`, and controls that are specialized to provide things like HTML `<select>` lists, lists of radio buttons, and lists of checkboxes.

Interestingly, we can still use the `SqlDataSourceControl` with the other .NET Framework list controls if we wish, though there is little real advantage in doing so. All the standard list controls we'll be looking at in this chapter can use server-side data binding to a data source, through code that we write (or which, to some extent, Web Matrix writes for us).

# The ADO.NET Data Access Objects

All our data access tasks in ASP.NET depend on the objects (classes) that are exposed by the .NET Framework as part of the class library. Part of this class library consists of the objects that make up **ADO.NET**. Predominantly, these come from the three **namespaces**:

❑   `System.Data`

❑   `System.Data.SqlClient`

❑   `System.Data.OleDb`

*A namespace in programming terms is simply the scope within which a name or variable is valid. In terms of the .NET Framework class library, a namespace is a "package" that contains a series of classes that implement the objects we use in our code. So, adding a reference to the `System.Data` namespace to our page, for example, makes all the classes within that namespace available without us having to include the `System.Data` prefix each time we want to use one of these classes. For more information on namespaces and classes, see Chapter 6.*

When we create a page in Web Matrix (or in a text editor) that uses ADO.NET, we have to **import** the appropriate classes into the page so that the objects they expose are available to our code.

If we are using SQL Server or MSDE as the data source, we just need the `System.Data` and `System.Data.SqlClient` namespaces:

```
<%@Import Namespace="System.Data" %>
<%@Import Namespace="System.Data.SqlClient" %>
```

We use the `SqlClient` namespace in all the data access examples in this book, because Web Matrix is designed to work with SQL Server or MSDE databases, as we've seen in our examples so far. However, if you are using some other database, for example, a Microsoft Access database, you will probably use a combination of the `System.Data` and `System.Data.OleDb` namespaces:

```
<%@Import Namespace="System.Data" %>
<%@Import Namespace="System.Data.OleDb" %>
```

*You can also obtain a separate set of classes that allow you to work with databases that have an **ODBC driver** from the Microsoft Universal Data site at http://msdn.microsoft.com/downloads/default.asp?URL=/downloads/sample.asp? url=/MSDN-FILES/027/001/668/msdncompositedoc.xml. ODBC is a generic data connection technology that is supported by many non-Microsoft databases. This data provider, and a provider for accessing Oracle database, are both included in the .NET Framework version 1.1, released early 2003, meaning you don't have to download these providers in order to access these data sources – you simply reference the appropriate namespace in your code. For more information, see* Beginning ASP.NET Databases with VB.NET, *Wrox Press, ISBN: 1-86100-619-5.*

Whichever set of namespaces you use, they will provide a series of classes that include five common objects. These are:

❑ The `Connection` object, which provides the connection between the data source (in our examples, this is a database) and the ADO.NET objects we use. In our examples, because we are using MSDE as our database, we will use the `SqlConnection` object from the `System.Data.SqlClient` namespace. (The `OleDbConnection` object from the `System.Data.OleDb` namespace is the equivalent for non-SQL Server data sources that connect via OLEDB).

❑ The Command object, which uses the Connection object to execute commands against the data source. These commands can be in the form of SQL statements or stored procedures. We'll be using the the SqlCommand object from the System.Data.SqlClient namespace.

❑ The DataReader object, which is used to access the results of executing a command that returns data, such as a SELECT statement. We'll be using the SqlDataReader object from the System.Data.SqlClient namespace.

❑ The DataAdapter object, which uses Connection and Command objects to extract data from a database and push it into a DataSet, or push changed rows held in a DataSet back into the database. We'll be using the SqlDataAdapter object from the System.Data.SqlClient namespace.

❑ The DataSet object is a repository in which we can store data in the form of tables containing rows and columns. It can store more than one table, and even the relationships between the tables. There is only one version of the DataSet, as it comes from the System.Data namespace.

While Web Matrix hides from us some of the details of how these objects are used, and how they work, it is useful to be aware of what they actually do. In particular, you need to appreciate the difference between a DataReader and a DataSet.

## The Command and DataReader Objects

When we execute a SQL SELECT statement or a stored procedure against a database that returns a set of rows, the database engine accesses the stored data, and builds up a **rowset** containing the rows that will be returned. To get at these rows from our ASP.NET page, we can use a DataReader. We call the ExecuteReader() method of the Command object to execute our SQL statement or stored procedure. When the command has completed, this method returns a DataReader object that is "pointing to" the results, and we can tell the DataReader to fetch the rows from the database and expose them to the code in our page.

The important point to take away from this is that a DataReader does not actually **contain** any data. It just provides a way for us to access the results set stored in our database. It means that we have to have a connection to the database all the time we are extracting the data.

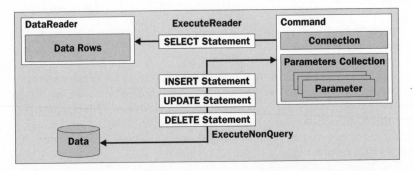

When we want to update data in the database, and not return any rows, we just use the Command object directly – we don't need a DataReader. The Command object executes a SQL statement or stored procedure against the database and returns a value that indicates what happened. Usually, this is a count of the number of rows that were affected. The Command object's ExecuteNonQuery() method is used in this case.

A DataReader is suitable for use when we are displaying data using data binding, as we did in the examples in the previous chapter. We'll show you how in this chapter. Just bear in mind that we can also access the data exposed by a DataReader directly, without using data binding, if we wish.

## The DataAdapter and DataSet Objects

The DataSet object is the direct opposite of a DataReader, and provides an opportunity to work with data in a completely different way. The DataSet can **store** data in the form of tables, just as they are stored in a database. We can extract data from a database, put it into a DataSet, and then disconnect the DataSet from the database. In some circumstances, such as where we want to access the same data repeatedly, the DataSet can improve performance of the page.

To connect a DataSet to a database, and extract data, we use a DataAdapter object. The DataAdapter uses a Connection object and a Command object to connect to the database, in a similar way to the DataReader we just looked at. When we call the Fill() method of the DataAdapter, the Command object executes a SQL SELECT statement or a stored procedure that fetches the data, and then the DataAdapter pushes the data into the DataSet to create a table.

However, a DataAdapter can also be used to push changes to the data stored in the DataSet back into the database. This involves using three more Command objects to execute the SQL statements or stored procedures that perform the updates. The three we need are an Update command, an Insert command, and a Delete command.

The schematic diagram shows the four Command objects (three for updating and the one that we use to extract data). If we are only extracting data, we don't need the UpdateCommand, InsertCommand, or DeleteCommand:

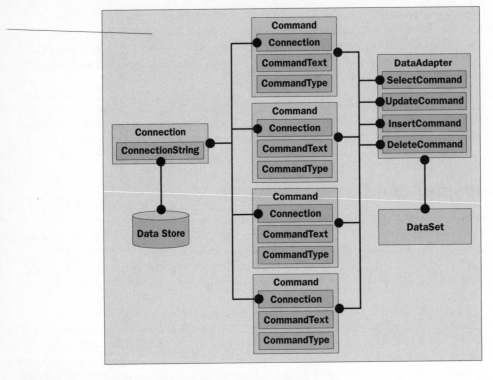

## The DataAdapter and SqlDataSourceControl

Looking at the DataAdapter object in the schematic, and remembering what we discussed with regard to the SqlDataSourceControl object at the start of the previous chapter, you can probably now see how the latter depends on the former. The SqlDataSourceControl object provides us with a way to connect to a database and extract data without having to worry about the various objects that are used "under the hood":

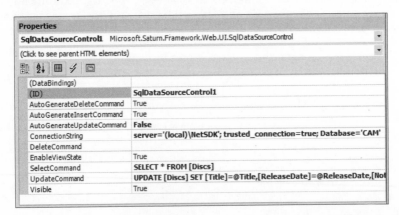

The `SqlDataSourceControl` object *can* be used to provide data for the generic ASP.NET list controls, though in reality there is little real benefit in this. We prefer to use the combinations of a `Command` and `DataReader`, or a `DataAdapter` and `DataSet` to achieve the flexibility we want, and reduce the overhead associated with the `SqlDataSourceControl`. The good news, as we hinted earlier, is that there are tools built into Web Matrix that can help us to create the code we need to use these objects. By good fortune (or perhaps just excellent forward planning!), this is the topic of the next section of this chapter.

# Accessing Data with Code Builders

Web Matrix provides a set of four useful Wizards named **code builders**. These can create sections of code automatically, based on a few options that we specify in the Wizard dialogs. The resulting code is a method (a function) that we can use in our page.

The four code builders are:

❑ **SELECT Data Method** – Creates a function that uses a SQL `SELECT` statement to access a database table and returns the data as either a `DataReader` or a `DataSet`.

❑ **INSERT Data Method** – Creates a function that uses a SQL `INSERT` statement to insert new rows into a database table and returns the number of rows that were inserted (one or zero).

❑ **DELETE Data Method** – Creates a function that uses a SQL `DELETE` statement to delete one or more rows from a database table and returns the number of rows that were deleted.

❑ **UPDATE Data Method** – Creates a function that uses a SQL `UPDATE` statement to update one or more rows in a database table and returns the number of rows that were updated.

The code builders are available on the **Toolbox** when you have an ASP.NET page open in **Code** view in the Web Matrix editor window. To start a code builder, you simply drag it from the **Toolbox** onto the page.

## *Displaying Data in a DataGrid Control*

We'll use the **SELECT Data Method** code builder in our next example to create a method that returns a `DataReader`, and then use this to populate an ASP.NET `DataGrid` control.

| Try It Out | Using the SELECT Data Method to Populate a DataGrid |
|------------|-----------------------------------------------------|

**1.** Starting with a blank new ASP.NET page called `SelectDataMethod.aspx`, click the **Code** tab at the bottom of the editor window to switch to **Code** view. Find the **SELECT Data Method** in the **Code Builders** section of the **Toolbox**, click on it, and drag it onto the page:

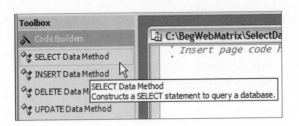

**2.** The **SELECT Data Method** Wizard starts up, and the first thing you see is the **Connect to Database** dialog. This is the same dialog as we used in the previous chapters to create a connection to a database in the **Data** window. Enter the name of your database server – probably `(local)\NetSDK` – and select the CAM database in the drop-down list at the bottom of the dialog:

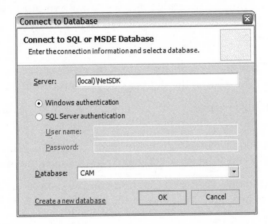

**3.** Next comes the **Query Builder** dialog. Here, you specify which table from the database to use, which columns should be returned from the method, and, optionally, any criteria that will select individual rows (this is used in the WHERE clause of the SQL statement that the **Query Builder** creates). We only have one table, named **Discs**, in our database, and this is selected by default. Select the asterisk (all columns) entry in the top list, and leave the <u>W</u>HERE clause section empty so that we get all the rows returned:

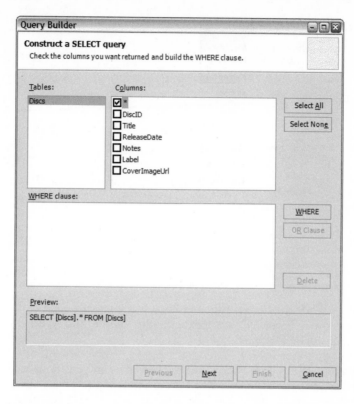

4. Click the Next button, and the Query Builder now allows you to test the query that you have created. We haven't specified any WHERE clause, so when you click the Test Query button you'll get all the rows from the database table:

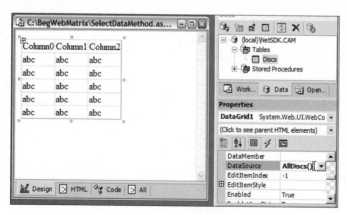

5. Click Next again to go to the last page of the Wizard.

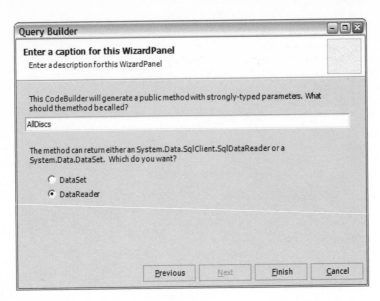

Here, you specify the name of the method, and select the type of data access object you want it to return. Enter AllDiscs for the method name, and select the **DataReader** option, then click **F**inish:

**6.** The Code window in Web Matrix now contains the complete data-access method. You can see that it is a Function named AllDiscs, and that it returns a DataReader object:

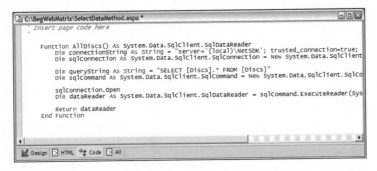

Not all of the code is visible in this window. The code that Web Matrix creates (with line breaks added so that it fits on the page) is:

```
Function AllDiscs() As System.Data.SqlClient.SqlDataReader
  Dim connectionString As String = _
    "server='(local)\netsdk'; trusted_connection=true; Database='CAM'"
  Dim sqlConnection As System.Data.SqlClient.SqlConnection =
    New System.Data.SqlClient.SqlConnection(connectionString)
  Dim queryString As String = "SELECT [Discs].* FROM [Discs]"
  Dim sqlCommand As System.Data.SqlClient.SqlCommand = _
```

```
    New System.Data.SqlClient.SqlCommand(queryString, sqlConnection)

  sqlConnection.Open
  Dim dataReader As System.Data.SqlClient.SqlDataReader = _
    sqlCommand.ExecuteReader(System.Data.CommandBehavior.CloseConnection)

    Return dataReader
End Function
```

This function, named AllDiscs(), accepts no parameters, and returns a DataReader that references all the rows in the Discs table from our example database. It does this by creating a Connection object, using this to create a Command object, and then calling the ExecuteReader() method of the Command object to get back a DataReader. Notice that Web Matrix references them using the full namespace name and class name each time, instead of Importing the namespaces that contain the data-access objects into the page.

**7.** Now we can use this function to extract the data we want, and bind it to a list control that will display it. Switch to **Design** view in the main Web Matrix editor window, and find the DataGrid control in the **Web Controls** section of the **Toolbox**. Select it, and drag it onto the page.

**8.** This adds the DataGrid to the page, with a default set of property values. You can see in the following screenshot that the ID is set to **DataGrid1**. Find the DataSource property in the **Properties** window, and type in the name of the function we just created, AllDiscs():

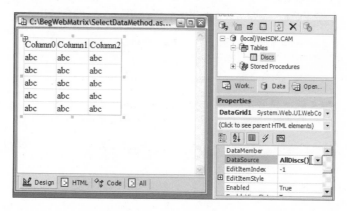

**9.** Setting the DataSource property connects the AllDiscs() function to the DataGrid, but this is not enough to display the data in the page. Unlike the MxDataGrid we used in the previous chapters, we have to tell the generic ASP.NET list controls when they should carry out the data-binding process to display the data. We do this by calling their DataBind() method, and the usual place to call this method is during the Page_Load event. Go to the drop-down list right at the top of the **Properties** window, which displays the ID of the currently selected item, and select the **Page** object:

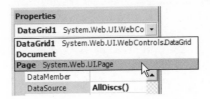

10. Now click the Events icon just below it to display the events that are available for the Page itself:

11. We want to handle the Load event for the Page object, so double-click on the entry for the Load event. This switches the editor window to Code view, and inserts an empty event handler for the Page_Load event. Add the following highlighted line of code to it, which calls the DataBind() method of our DataGrid control:

```
Sub Page_Load(sender As Object, e As EventArgs)
   DataGrid1.DataBind()
End Sub
```

12. Click the Start icon in the main Web Matrix toolbar to run the page. You'll see the contents of the Discs table displayed in the page by the DataGrid control:

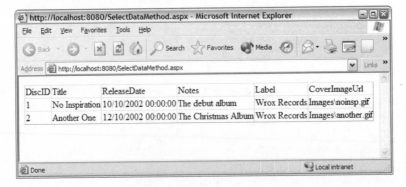

**13.** The output doesn't look as attractive as that we got from our `MxDataGrid` control. This is because Web Matrix automatically sets some default values for the style and formatting of the `MxDataGrid` control when we dragged a table from the **Data Explorer** onto our page in the examples in the previous chapter. However, we can easily change the appearance of the `DataGrid` control using the built-in **Auto Format** Wizard that is provided with Web Matrix. With the `DataGrid` selected in **Design** view, click the **Auto Format...** link at the foot of the **Properties** window:

**14.** The **Auto Format** dialog opens. In it, you can select from several pre-defined styles for the grid, and also preview each one. Here, we've selected the **Colorful 1** style:

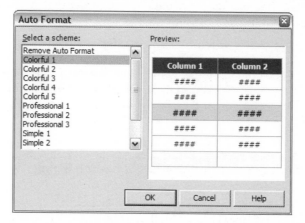

**15.** Click OK in the Auto Format dialog, and you'll see the DataGrid control in the page updated to the new style. Then click the Start button to run the page again. The output from the grid control is presented in the selected style:

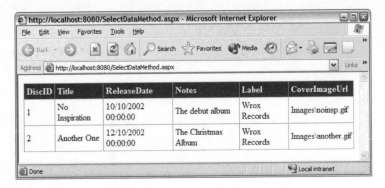

# Selecting the Rows to Display

The previous example demonstrates how easy it is to use one of the "generic" list controls from the .NET Framework class library. We used a DataGrid control, but the principles are much the same for other list controls. We also took advantage of the WebMatrix SELECT Data Method code builder to create the data access code for us.

However, there are some more advanced topics that we need to look at, and we'll do this next. We'll use the same techniques as those you've just seen, but build a page with some important differences:

❑  We'll allow the user to enter a criterion (search string) and display only the rows that contain this value in a specified column.

❑  We'll use a DataSet as the source data object, rather than a DataReader as we did in the previous example.

❑  We'll display only a few specific columns, rather than all of them as we've done before.

We'll use the example pubs database that comes with the .NET SDK in this example. The titles table in this database contains 18 rows, so there are plenty of different things in the title column of each row that we can search for, and each row has some columns that we do not want to display in our page.

**Try It Out**     **Selecting Rows that Contain a Search String**

**1.**  Start with a new blank ASP.NET page, call it SelectingRows.aspx, switch to Code view, and drag the SELECT Data Method code builder from the Code Builders section of the Toolbox onto the page. In the Connect to Database dialog, specify your database server and select the Pubs database.

**2.** Click <u>O</u>K, and in the Query Builder dialog select the titles table from the list of tables in the pubs database. The columns in this table are shown in the C<u>o</u>lumns list. Instead of checking \* and displaying all the columns as we did in the previous example, select just the title, price, notes, and pubdate columns:

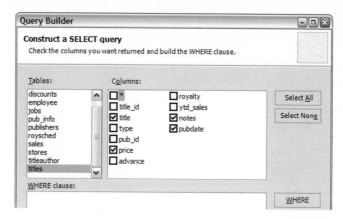

**3.** Now we want to add a WHERE clause that will limit the rows that are returned by our new data-access method to a specific subset. Click the <u>WHERE</u> button in the Query Builder dialog to open the WHERE Clause Builder dialog. Select the title column in the <u>C</u>olumn list, select like in the O<u>p</u>erator drop-down list, and change the <u>F</u>ilter to @search:

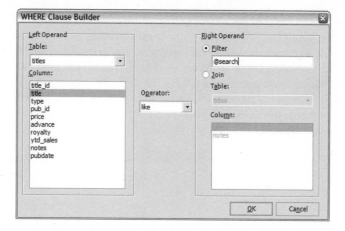

**4.** Click <u>O</u>K to return to the Query Builder dialog. The combination of settings we specified creates a WHERE clause that will select only rows where the value in the titles column is the same as the value we provide for the @search parameter when we call the new data access method we're building. The LIKE operator in SQL is used to compare two String values. You can see the <u>WHERE</u> clause in the Query Builder dialog, together with the complete SQL statement that will be used in the method:

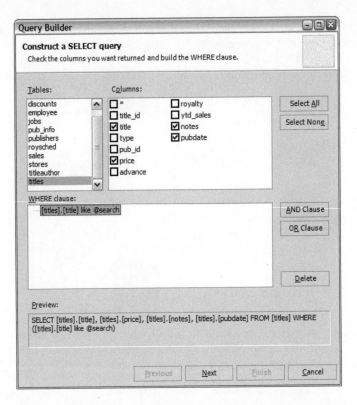

5.  Click **Next** to go to the next page of the **Query Builder**, and click the **Test Query** button. Since there is a parameter required for the method, the **Preview** window opens (it didn't in the previous *Try It Out* because there was no parameter specified for the method). The **Preview** window displays the SQL statement, and prompts for the value to use for the @search parameter. Enter %computer%, which will select only rows where the title column contains the string computer (remember that the percent character is a wildcard in SQL):

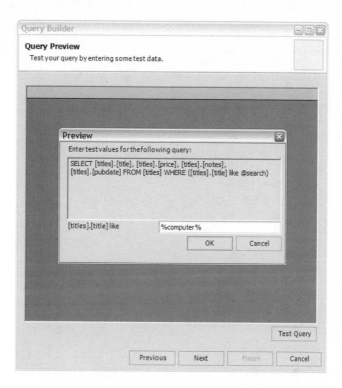

6. Click OK in the Preview dialog, and Query Builder displays the matching rows. You can see that it found five matches:

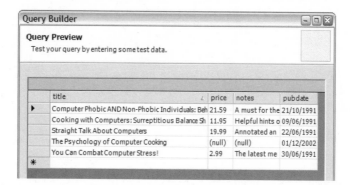

7. Click Next in the Query Builder, and now we have to specify the name of the method and the kind of data-access object we want returned. Enter FindByTitle for the name, and select the DataSet option. Then, click Finish to create the new method in the page:

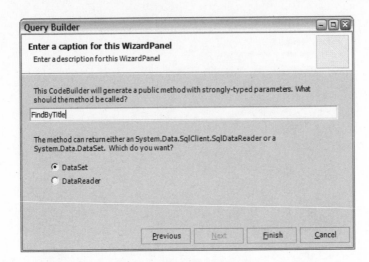

**8.** Now you can see the code that the wizard created in the page:

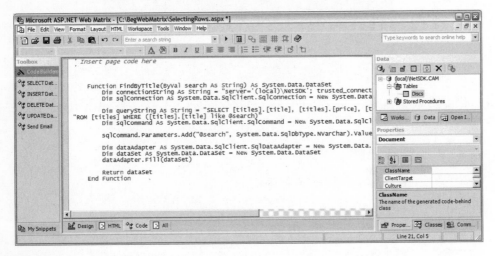

## How It Works

The code that has been created is similar to that created by the **SELECT Data Method** code builder in the previous *Try It Out*, but with some important differences. We've listed it below, adding line breaks to make it easier to see. This time, the function expects us to provide the value for a parameter named `search`, and it returns a `DataSet` rather than a `DataReader`:

```
Function FindByTitle(ByVal search As String) As System.Data.DataSet
    Dim connectionString As String = _
        "server='(local)\netsdk'; trusted_connection=true; Database='pubs'"
```

```
   Dim sqlConnection As System.Data.SqlClient.SqlConnection = _
     New System.Data.SqlClient.SqlConnection(connectionString)

   Dim queryString As String = "SELECT [titles].[title], [titles].[price]," _
     & "[titles].[notes], [titles].[pubdate] " _
     & "FROM [titles] WHERE ([titles].[title] like @search)"
   Dim sqlCommand As System.Data.SqlClient.SqlCommand = _
     New System.Data.SqlClient.SqlCommand(queryString, sqlConnection)

   sqlCommand.Parameters.Add( _
     "@search", System.Data.SqlDbType.NVarChar).Value = search

   Dim dataAdapter As System.Data.SqlClient.SqlDataAdapter = _
     New System.Data.SqlClient.SqlDataAdapter(sqlCommand)
   Dim dataSet As System.Data.DataSet = New System.Data.DataSet
   dataAdapter.Fill(dataSet)

   Return dataSet
 End Function
```

Inside the function, you can see that a `Connection` object is created:

```
Dim connectionString As String = _
  "server='(local)\netsdk'; trusted_connection=true; Database='pubs'"
Dim sqlConnection As System.Data.SqlClient.SqlConnection = _
  New System.Data.SqlClient.SqlConnection(connectionString)
```

Then, using this and the SQL statement that the Wizard generated, a `Command` object is created:

```
Dim queryString As String = "SELECT [titles].[title], [titles].[price]," _
  & "[titles].[notes], [titles].[pubdate] " _
  & "FROM [titles] WHERE ([titles].[title] like @search)"
Dim sqlCommand As System.Data.SqlClient.SqlCommand = _
  New System.Data.SqlClient.SqlCommand(queryString, sqlConnection)
```

Next, the code adds a parameter named `@search` to the `Command` object, using the value that is provided in the `search` parameter to the method:

```
sqlCommand.Parameters.Add( _
  "@search", System.Data.SqlDbType.NVarChar).Value = search
```

Then, a `DataAdapter` object is created using this `Command` object. When we create a `DataAdapter` in code, as in the `FindByTitle()` method shown above, the `Command` object specified in the constructor (the parameter `sqlCommand` in our case) is used to set the `SelectCommand` property of the `DataAdapter`.

```
   Dim dataAdapter As System.Data.SqlClient.SqlDataAdapter = _
     New System.Data.SqlClient.SqlDataAdapter(sqlCommand)
```

Finally, the code calls the `Fill()` method of the `DataAdapter` to pull the values from the database and push them into a new `DataSet` object, after which the `DataSet` is returned from the method.

```
Dim dataSet As System.Data.DataSet = New System.Data.DataSet
dataAdapter.Fill(dataSet)
```

Notice that the method uses **type-safe parameters**. What this means is that, when the function is called, the data type of the values that are passed as parameters (in our case there is only one – the `search` parameter) must be correct. As long as they are correct, they will automatically match the data type of the column in the database table. This helps to prevent errors where you might call the method with the wrong types of values in the parameters.

We'll use this method in our next *Try It Out*, so leave the page open in Web Matrix for the moment.

## Displaying Selected Rows in a DataGrid

OK, so we've got a method that will return a `DataSet` containing specific rows, depending on the value we provide for the parameter of the method. This parameter is a string value that equates to the value of the title column in the titles table in the pubs example database.

What do we do with it now? It's like being all dressed up with nowhere to go. So we had better get on and build a page that uses this method. We'll provide the user with a textbox where they can enter a value for the parameter, and a button to start the process. We'll then use our new method to select just the matching rows, and display them in a `DataGrid` control.

**Try It Out      Using the FindByTitle() Method in an ASP.NET Page**

1. With the page we created in the previous *Try It Out* open, switch to Design view. Type Find: and a space at the top left of the page, then drag a `TextBox` control from the Toolbox onto the page. Type a space and then drag a `Button` control onto the page. Go to the Properties window and change the `Text` property of the `Button` control to Go. Then, back on the page, press *Return* to start a new "line" and drag a `DataGrid` control onto the page:

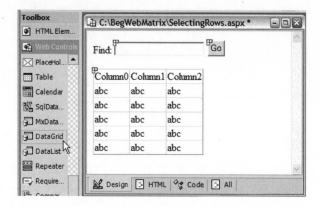

**2.** Now we need to write some code that will run when the **Go** button is clicked. Double-click the button to switch the editor window to **Code** view, and the outline of the event handler for the `Click` event of the `Button` control is inserted:

```
Sub Button1_Click(sender As Object, e As EventArgs)

End Sub
```

**3.** When the button is clicked we want to set the `DataSource` property of the `DataGrid` control. In the previous *Try It Out*, we set this in the **Properties** window of the `DataGrid` control, but we can't do that here because we need to set the value of the `search` parameter. Our code extracts this value from the textbox, by accessing its `Text` property, and places it in a `String` variable named `sTitle`. Then, we can set the `DataSource` property of the `DataGrid` control to the result of executing the `FindByTitle()` method with this value as the parameter:

```
Sub Button1_Click(sender As Object, e As EventArgs)
    Dim sTitle As String = TextBox1.Text
    DataGrid1.DataSource = FindByTitle(sTitle)
    DataGrid1.DataBind()
End Sub
```

Notice that we also have to call the `DataBind()` method of the `DataGrid` to tell it to generate the output that creates the display in the page.

**4.** Click the **Start** button on the main Web Matrix toolbar to run the page. When first opened, it only displays the textbox and the **Go** button. This is because the `Click` event for the `Button` control has not been raised, and so, the `DataGrid` has no `DataSource` property set, and the `DataBind()` method has not been called. Enter the value %computer% into the textbox and click the **Go** button. Now the page displays the matching rows:

**319**

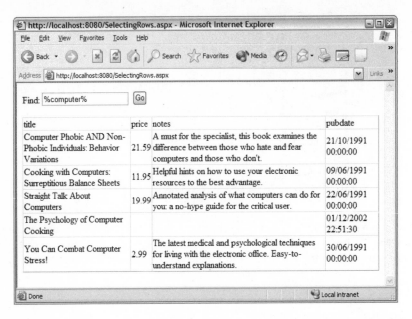

**5.** Well, that was easy enough, but the result isn't very pretty. We could just apply one of the **Auto Format** designs, like we did in the previous *Try It Out*, but instead, we'll use another of the tools provided by Web Matrix. In **Design** view, select the `DataGrid` control on the page and click the **Property Builder...** link at the bottom of the **Properties** dialog:

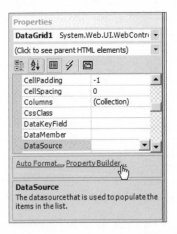

**6.** In the DataGrid1 Properties dialog that opens, select the **Format** entry on the left-hand side of the dialog. The **Objects** section in the center of the dialog displays a list of things that we can provide format details for. Select the **Header** entry, and set the values for some of the options in the right-hand section of the dialog. Here, we've specified the foreground and background colors of the text in the header row of the grid, and the font name and size. We've also specified a bold font:

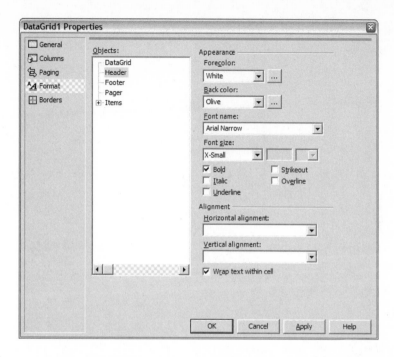

7. Now select the Normal Items entry within the Items entry, and set some values for this. We have just specified the font name, Arial Narrow, and size, X-Small, in this case. Then, select the Alternating Items entry and set any values you want for alternating rows. We changed the background color to Silver but left the others blank. Any values we don't provide are inherited from the Normal Items entry.

8. Select the Borders entry in the left-hand side of the dialog and specify the values you want for the borders of the grid. Here, we've specified the cell padding (to separate the row and column contents a little), turned on grid lines, and specified the border color and width:

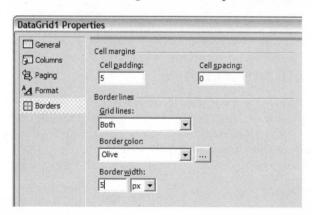

9.  Click OK to close the DataGrid1 Properties dialog, and the grid in the page shows the effects of the property settings you just applied:

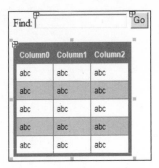

10. Click the Start icon to run the page and view the results. A lot neater!

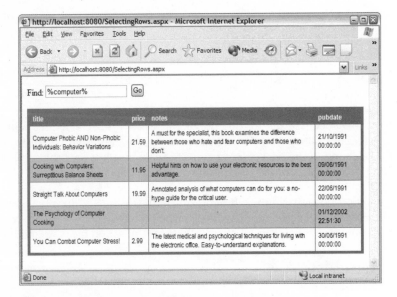

## Using the Other Code Builders

The other code builders are slightly different from the SELECT data method because, while SELECT is primarily concerned with returning information to the program, DELETE, INSERT, and UPDATE are mainly concerned with transferring data from the program to the database. Here's a quick rundown of how each one works. You've already seen how to use SELECT, and you should feel fairly at home with the others. Give them a try – they are fast, easy, and very useful!

## INSERT Data Method

The wizard will ask you to connect to the database in the normal way. It will then ask you to choose which table you want to insert a record into, and whether any of the fields have default values. If the database itself defines default values, then the wizard will detect this… so adding an INSERT method for the CAM database will bring up the following dialog:

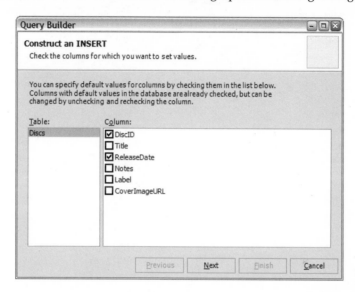

As you can see, DiscID and ReleaseDate are already selected as having default values. You can add others if you wish. Once you click **Next**, you'll be asked for a name for the method.

The method you end up with will have arguments that let you specify values for all of the columns that don't have default values, so if we are building an INSERT method from the example above we will get the following method definition:

```
Function MyInsertMethod(ByVal title As String, ByVal notes As String,
        ByVal label As String, ByVal coverImageURL As String) As Integer
```

The return value will be an integer that tells you how many rows were added. Usually this will be 1. Checking the value in the code that calls the function is a useful way to check nothing unexpected happened.

## DELETE Data Method

Once again, you need to specify the database connection. Then you have a dialog that lets you choose a table. You also need to build a WHERE clause that specifies exactly what records you want to delete. Let's say we want to build a function that deletes any album made before the specified date. Once we've connected to the database, we'll see the following dialog:

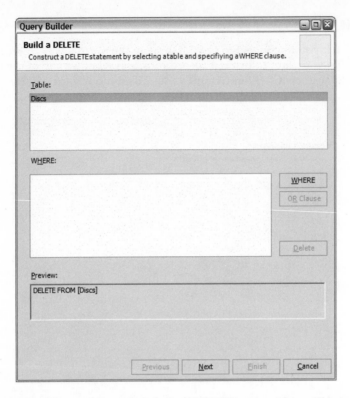

First of all we select the Discs table, and click the WHERE button. This will bring up the following:

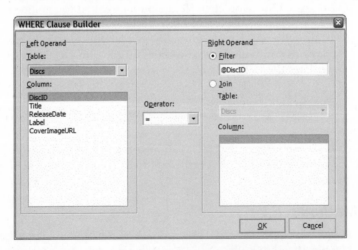

where we can select the Column that will act as the condition, and the filter we will use. Select `ReleaseDate` in the Column list, < in the Operator dropdown, and leave the Right Operand section as it is (filtering on a SQL variable called `@DiscID`). Click OK.

It is very important to specify **WHERE** clauses when deleting or updating a
database... if you do not, every single row in the table will be deleted
or changed!

Now, if you click **Next**, you'll be given the chance to test the query by clicking the **Test Query**
button and entering a date. After clicking **Next** again, you can name the function and finish.

You'll now have a function that takes a date as a parameter, deletes all albums released before
that date, and then returns the number of albums deleted – a useful way of making sure that
the correct number of records was removed. (If no records match the WHERE clause in a DELETE
statement, no error is raised... so it's often useful to check that this value isn't a zero.)

## UPDATE Data Method

This is more complicated than the previous code builders because you need to specify the data to
place in the database, and a WHERE condition. But we've seen both these on their own, so it's
really not too bad. Connect as usual, then specify the columns that you want to update. Let's say
we want to add a note to every disc produced before 1990 that there will soon be a remastered CD
version with bonus tracks that are even worse than the songs on the album itself.

First of all, we select the **Notes** column and click **OK** on the dialog that pops up:

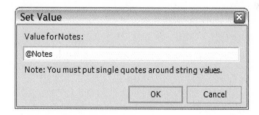

Next we need to specify the WHERE clause, so click the **WHERE** button and choose `ReleaseDate`
from the **Columns** list, < from the **Operator** list, leave the **Right Operand** filter criterion set to the
default value of `@ReleaseDate` allowing us to specify a date in the program code).

Now click **Next**, skip the test, and click **Finish**. You'll get a function that takes a value for **Notes**
as a parameter, and once again returns the number of affected rows. If you chose not to select a
value for `ReleaseDate`, but left it variable, then you'll get a parameter to specify that too.

This is the most complex of the data method code builders. It's worth taking a look at the code
and trying to understand broadly what's going on. Even though it uses some objects you aren't
familiar with, the general ideas are the same as the code you've already seen – declaring objects,
setting properties, and calling methods.

Let's take a quick look at it now (there are a lot of long lines which I've had to break).

```
Function MyUpdateMethod(ByVal releaseDate As Date, _
                                ByVal notes As String) As Integer
```

First of all there's the method declaration. Next we define a `connectionString`, and use it to create a `SqlConnection` object – which ASP.NET will use to connect to our database:

```
Dim connectionString As String = "server='(local)\netsdk'; " & _
                        "trusted_connection=true; Database='CAM'"
Dim sqlConnection As System.Data.SqlClient.SqlConnection = _
        New System.Data.SqlClient.SqlConnection(connectionString)
```

Next up we `Dim` the SQL string itself. We talked about the UPDATE command earlier, so it should be fairly familiar:

```
Dim queryString As String = "UPDATE [Discs] SET [Notes]=@Notes" & _
                    " WHERE ([Discs].[ReleaseDate] < @ReleaseDate)"
```

We then use the `queryString` and the connection to declare a `SqlCommand` object – this is what we'll use to actually tell the database what we want it to do.

```
Dim sqlCommand As System.Data.SqlClient.SqlCommand =
        New System.Data.SqlClient.SqlCommand(queryString, sqlConnection)
```

The next lines set up the name-value pairs of SQL variable names and the values we want to assign to them. Because they are variables we're passing to SQL, we call them parameters – just as we would if we were passing variables to a procedure or function:

```
sqlCommand.Parameters.Add("@ReleaseDate",
                    System.Data.SqlDbType.DateTime).Value = releaseDate
sqlCommand.Parameters.Add("@Notes",
                            System.Data.SqlDbType.Text).Value = notes
```

Next, the function declares an `Integer` to hold the number of rows affected by the operation:

```
Dim rowsAffected As Integer = 0
```

This is where the action happens. We open the connection, and run the query. We do this within a `Try` block so that, if something goes wrong, the `Finally` block still executes, and the connection is closed safely:

```
sqlConnection.Open
Try
   rowsAffected = sqlCommand.ExecuteNonQuery
Finally
   sqlConnection.Close
End Try
```

Finally we return the `rowsAffected` variable, and end the function:

```
    Return rowsAffected
End Function
```

If you didn't quite understand all that, it really doesn't matter. The reason the code builders exist is that you don't have to understand the details. They're worth getting to grips with, though, if you want to really understand how to get the most out of databases. There's a lot of theory behind all of these code builders that can get quite deep and complex, so for that reason, we recommend that you read *Beginning ASP.NET Databases using VB.NET, Wrox Press, ISBN: 1-86100-619-5* for a more in-depth discussion of what's actually going on behind the scenes.

# Data Binding to Other Types of List Controls

So far, we've only used one basic type of list control in our examination of using data to create output in our ASP.NET pages. We used a `DataGrid` control in this chapter. In the previous chapters, we used an `MxDataGrid`, but (as we discovered) this is just a cleverer version of the `DataGrid` designed for use within Web Matrix. In this remaining section of the chapter, we'll look at the other list controls that we can data-bind to a data source such as a database table.

## The ASP.NET List Controls

ASP.NET provides several types of list control that we can use to generate repeated content from a range of data sources:

❑ `CheckBoxList` – Creates a list of checkboxes, from which more than one can be selected. We can specify which column from our data source will be used to set the caption of each checkbox by setting the `DataTextField` property to one of the column names.

❑ `RadioButtonList` – Creates a list of radio (or option) buttons, from which only one can be selected. We can specify which column from our data source will be used to set the caption of each radio button by setting the `DataTextField` property to one of the column names, and which column will be used to set the value of each radio button by setting the `DataValueField` property to another of the column names.

❑ `DropDownList` – Creates a drop-down selection list, from which only one item can be selected. This is useful when we want to minimize the space used on the page. We can specify which column from our data source will be used to set the visible text of each option in the list by setting the `DataTextField` property to one of the column names, and which column will be used to set the value of each option by setting the `DataValueField` property to another of the column names.

❑   ListBox – Creates a list where more than one item is visible, and it can be configured so that users can select only one item, or so that they can select more than one item. We can specify which column from our data source will be used to set the visible text of each option in the list by setting the DataTextField property to one of the column names, and which column will be used to set the value of each option by setting the DataValueField property to another of the column names.

❑   Repeater – Repeats any type of content that we specifically define, without the control applying any of its own structuring or formatting to the content. It is simpler, lighter, and more efficient than the DataList or DataGrid, but has fewer features. Templates are used to define the format and layout of the content, and any line breaks, paragraph divisions, and so on, must be specifically declared within these templates.

❑   DataList – Lays out its content in the cells of a table, or repeated across or down the page in columns. This is a powerful list control, which is one step up from the Repeater in complexity and use of resources. By default, it lays out the content generated for each item in the data source within one cell of an HTML <table>, though it can also be used like the Repeater (without generating a <table> – called **flow layout** mode). It also provides a header and footer that can be formatted separately, and it can lay content out vertically or horizontally in columns when in table layout mode. Templates can be used to define the format and layout of the content, and any line breaks, paragraph divisions, and so on, must be specifically declared within these templates.

❑   DataGrid – As we've already seen, this control builds an HTML table where each value is in a separate column, so that it looks like a grid. It provides the most control over content, and the most extra features. As well as headers and footers, the control can divide the list of items across multiple "pages", provide automatic inline editing features, easily link code to events raised by controls in each row, and even automatically generate the columns based on the data source contents. A wide range of formatting options allows attractive layouts to be constructed.

In the next example, we'll use one of each of these controls (except the DataGrid, which we've already examined in enough depth). We'll bind them to the result of a method that we build with the SELECT Data Method code builder, as we did in the first *Try It Out* in this chapter. While we don't have room to examine all of the features of these list controls, it will show you how they can be used with server-side data binding.

## Using the ASP.NET List Controls

We start by creating the method that returns all the rows from the Publishers table in the example pubs database. The process is the same as we used in the first *Try It Out* in this chapter, just with a different table.

## Try It Out    Data Binding with List Controls

**1.** Start a new ASP.NET page called `ListControls.aspx`, and drag a SELECT Data Method into the editor window in Code view. Connect to the pubs database in the Connect to Database dialog. In the Query Builder dialog, select the Publishers table and then select the * entry in the list of columns to return all the columns:

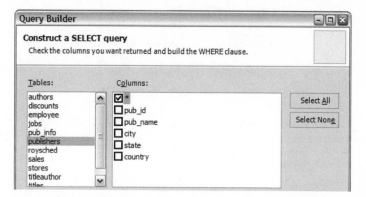

**2.** Click Next and test the query in the next page of the Query Builder dialog if you want to. Then click Next again, enter AllPublishers for the name of the method, and select a DataReader as the returned data object type. Then click Finish to create the data access method:

**3.** Switch to Design view, and drag onto the page a CheckBoxList control, a RadioButtonList control, a DropDownList control, a ListBox control, a Repeater control, and a DataList control, with each control on its own line, by pressing *Return*:

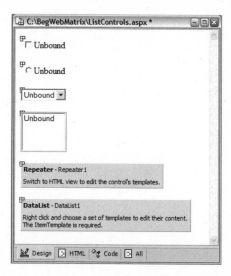

**4.** Select the `CheckBoxList` control in the page, and go to the **Properties** dialog. Enter the name of the data access method **AllPublishers()** for the `DataSource`, the name of the column containing the publisher's name, **pub_name**, as the **DataTextField**, and the name of the column containing the ID of the publisher, **pub_id**, as the **DataValueField** property:

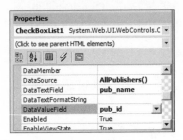

**5.** Now repeat these three property settings for the `RadioButtonList` control, `DropDownList` control, and `ListBox` control. You'll see as you do it that each control changes from displaying **Unbound** to **Databound**.

**6.** The `Repeater` and `DataList` controls don't have `DataTextField` and `DataValueField` properties, because they expect us to provide a template that defines the output to be created. However, we can set the `DataSource` property. Do this now by selecting them in turn and entering **AllPublishers()** for the `DataSource` property of each of these controls.

**7.** To generate output from a `Repeater` control, we have to define the templates that the control will use. There are no fancy UI widgets to help in this case; we have to resort to getting out hands dirty and typing it all into the HTML window. Switch to **HTML** view and enter the declaration of the `<HeaderTemplate>` and `<ItemTemplate>`:

```
<asp:Repeater id="Repeater1" runat="server"
              DataSource="<%# AllPublishers() %>">
  <HeaderTemplate>
    <b>Publisher List:</b><br />
  </HeaderTemplate>
  <ItemTemplate>
    <%# DataBinder.Eval(Container.DataItem, "pub_name") %>
    (ID: <%# DataBinder.Eval(Container.DataItem, "pub_id") %>)
    <font size="-1"><i>
    <%# DataBinder.Eval(Container.DataItem, "city") %>,
    <%# DataBinder.Eval(Container.DataItem, "state") %>,
    <%# DataBinder.Eval(Container.DataItem, "country") %> <br />
    </i></font>
  </ItemTemplate>
</asp:Repeater>
```

We're displaying some text in the header of the control, followed by a line break, and then for each item in the data source we're displaying the values of the five columns with some odd items of text, HTML formatting, and commas to make it look better. The `Repeater` control adds no layout or formatting itself so we have to define exactly what we want for each part of the output.

**8.** Switch back to **Design** view, and you'll see the layout we specified, and the fixed text content, rendered in the page. You can see how the declarations we use are literally translated into the output generated by the control:

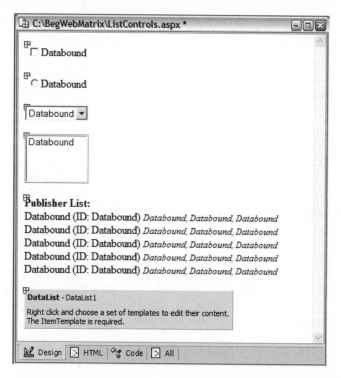

**9.** Select the `DataList` control in the page, as shown in the previous screenshot. In this case we have a couple of choices for how we define the content that the control will display. We can right-click on the control and create templates, or we can use the **Auto Format** and/or **Property Builder** Wizards (the links to which appear at the foot of the **Properties** dialog. The **Auto Format** and/or **Property Builder** are broadly the same as we saw used with the `DataGrid` control earlier in this chapter, so instead we'll use templates this time. Right-click on the `DataList` control and select **Edit Templates...** from the menu that appears:

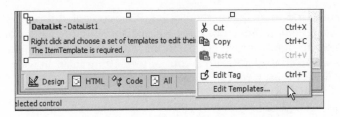

**10.** The Edit DataList1 Templates dialog appears. The two drop-down lists at the top allow you to select the template you want to edit, and the box below this is actually a design surface – the same as the ASP.NET page itself in Design view. So, you can drag-and-drop controls onto it, just as you do in the main editor window. Drag a `Label` control from the **Toolbox** onto it:

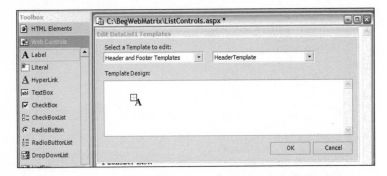

**11.** Go to the **Properties** dialog and enter **List of publishers:** for the `Text` property. You can also edit the properties that control the appearance of the `Label`. We've set the **Font Name** property to **Tahoma**, and specified that it should be displayed in bold italic font.

**12.** The `Label` control is automatically updated to show the results of these property settings. Drag a **Horizontal Rule** control from the **HTML Elements** section of the **Toolbar** onto the design surface as well, then select the **FooterTemplate** in the right-hand drop-down list of the template editor:

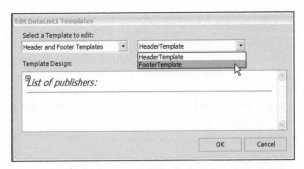

**13.** Drag a `Horizontal Rule` control onto the FooterTemplate, and then select ItemTemplates in the left-hand drop-down list:

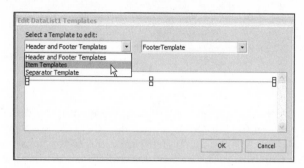

**14.** The ItemTemplate is the section that is repeated for each row in the data source. Add some text and drag five `Label` controls onto the surface as shown in the following screenshot. We'll be binding these `Label` controls to the five columns in the data source later on:

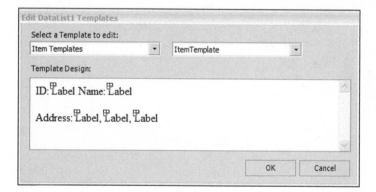

**15.** To separate the content generated by each ItemTemplate, we can specify content for the SeparatorTemplate. Select this from the left-hand drop-down list and drag a Horizontal Rule control onto it.

**16.** Now we can specify the data-binding properties that will display the values from the columns in the Label control we placed into the ItemTemplate. Switch back to the ItemTemplate, and select the first Label control (if it has seemingly disappeared, leaving just the three boxes at the top left corner, this could be a bug, and you will need to remove the labels, replace them with new labels, then work with these new labels). In the main Properties window, select the (DataBindings) entry and click the button that appears:

**17.** This opens the Label1 DataBindings dialog. We want to bind the Text property of the Label to the value in the pub_id column. Select the Text property in the left-hand list of Bindable Properties (we can bind other properties to the values in the row if we wish, as you can see from this list). The Simple Binding: list displays the objects in the data source that we can bind to:

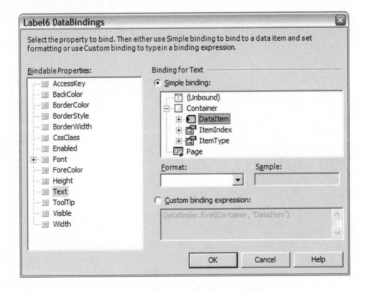

**18.** Because we are binding to a method, and not to a `SqlDataSourceControl`, the list cannot extract the actual column details. Instead, we can select the DataItem entry, then click the Custom binding expression: option button and edit the expression that this creates to suit our requirements. For the `Label` control that will contain the value from the pub_id column of the row, we need the following expression:

```
DataBinder.Eval(Container.DataItem, "pub_id")
```

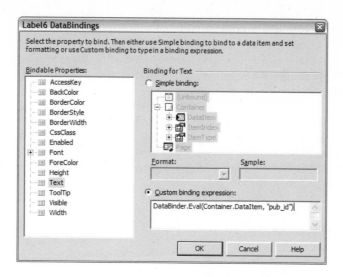

**19.** Now repeat this process for the other four **Label** controls. Select each one in turn in the **Edit Templates** dialog and bind the **Text** property to the appropriate column in the data source. The four data binding expressions required for this are:

```
DataBinder.Eval(Container.DataItem, "pub_name")
DataBinder.Eval(Container.DataItem, "city")
DataBinder.Eval(Container.DataItem, "state")
DataBinder.Eval(Container.DataItem, "country")
```

**20.** Now close the **Edit Templates** dialog. The `DataList` control in the page is updated to show the new layout and format:

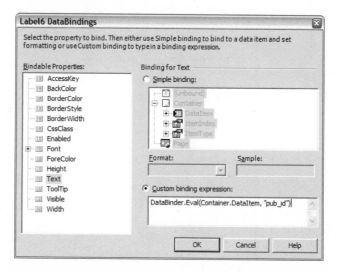

**21.** The final task is to tell the page that it should call the `DataBind()` method of all the controls when opened, so that the values returned by the `AllPublishers()` method are displayed in the controls. Select the entry for the **Page** from the drop-down list at the top of the **Properties** window, click the **Events** icon to show the events for the page, and double-click on the **Load** event.

**22.** In the outline event handler, we must add the calls to the `DataBind()` method for the controls. We could call the `DataBind()` method for each control in turn, but there is a quicker way. If we call the `DataBind()` method of the `Page` object itself, it automatically calls `DataBind()` for all the controls on the page. Enter the highlighted code shown below to do just this:

```
Sub Page_Load(sender As Object, e As EventArgs)
    Page.DataBind()
End Sub
```

**23.** Now click the **Start** icon to run the page, and you'll see the results appear in the browser. We'll look at the results next, and see what the various list controls have created.

## How It Works

The output from our example is a long page, so we'll examine it in sections. At the top of the page are the `CheckBoxList` and `RadioButtonList` controls. You can see that both display a list with one control for each publisher:

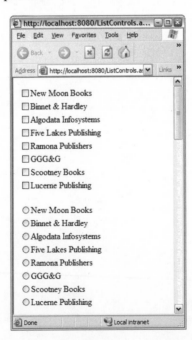

If you view the source of the page in the browser, you can see what the list controls have created. For the `CheckBoxList`, we get an HTML table that contains an `<input type="checkbox">` and a `<label>` in each cell. The publisher name, which we specified as the `DataTextField` property of the control, is used to populate the `<label>` elements:

```
<table id="CheckBoxList1" border="0">
  <tr>
    <td>
      <input id="CheckBoxList1_0" type="checkbox" name="CheckBoxList1:0" />
      <label for="CheckBoxList1_0">New Moon Books</label>
    </td>
  </tr>
  <tr>
    <td>
      <input id="CheckBoxList1_1" type="checkbox" name="CheckBoxList1:1" />
      <label for="CheckBoxList1_1">Binnet & Hardley</label>
    </td>
  </tr>
  ...
</table>
```

However, despite the fact that we specified the `pub_id` column as the `DataValueField` property, there are no `value` attributes on the checkboxes. Most HTML controls send their values to the server, when the `<form>` they are on is submitted, as *control-name=control-value*. However, by default, a checkbox submits only *control-name*=on if it is checked, or nothing at all if it is not checked. ASP.NET uses this default behavior, and doesn't bother filling it in.

### The Results from the RadioButtonList Control

The second control in the page is the `RadioButtonList` control. In this case, the `DataTextField` property sets the caption of each control, using the values from the pub_name column as we specified, and the `DataValueField` property sets the `value` attribute of each control:

```
<table id="RadioButtonList1" border="0">
  <tr>
    <td>
      <input id="RadioButtonList1_0" type="radio" name="RadioButtonList1"
             value="0736" />
      <label for="RadioButtonList1_0">New Moon Books</label>
    </td>
  </tr>
  <tr>
    <td>
      <input id="RadioButtonList1_1" type="radio" name="RadioButtonList1"
             value="0877" />
      <label for="RadioButtonList1_1">Binnet & Hardley</label>
    </td>
  </tr>
  ...
</table>
```

When the `<form>` containing this control is submitted, the single selected radio button sends the value `RadioButtonList1=`*control-value* to the server.

### The Results from the DropDownList and ListBox Controls

The next section of the page contains the `DropDownList`, `ListBox`, and `Repeater` controls:

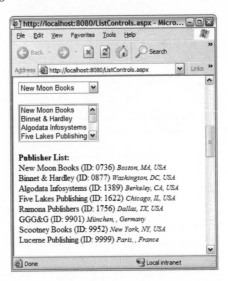

The output generated for the `DropDownList` control is exactly what we expect. The `DataTextField` property sets the text of each `<option>` element that is generated within the `<select>` element, using the values from the pub_name column. The `DataValueField` property sets the `value` attribute of each `<option>` element, using the values from the pub_id column:

```
<select name="DropDownList1" id="DropDownList1">
   <option value="0736">New Moon Books</option>
   <option value="0877">Binnet &amp; Hardley</option>
   <option value="1389">Algodata Infosystems</option>
   <option value="1622">Five Lakes Publishing</option>
   <option value="1756">Ramona Publishers</option>
   <option value="9901">GGG&amp;G</option>
   <option value="9952">Scootney Books</option>
   <option value="9999">Lucerne Publishing</option>
</select>
```

The `ListBox` control produces the same output with one exception. The opening `<select>` tag contains a `size` attribute set to the default value 4, so that four rows are displayed in the list:

```
<select name="ListBox1" id="ListBox1" size="4">
   <option value="0736">New Moon Books</option>
   ...
</select>
```

### *The Results from the Repeater Control*

The Repeater control output, shown at the bottom of the previous screenshot, contains only the elements we declared within the templates that we added to the control definition. All the repeater has done is output the content of each template – it adds no formatting or other content of its own. So, we get the heading **Publisher List:** enclosed in <b> tags and followed by the <br /> element we declared in the <HeaderTemplate>. This is followed by the values from each row in the data source, intermixed with the elements and text we declared in the <ItemTemplate>:

```
<b>Publisher List:</b><br />
New Moon Books (ID: 0736)
<font size="-1"><i>
Boston, MA, USA<br />
</i></font>
Binnet & Hardley (ID: 0877)
<font size="-1"><i>
Washington, DC, USA<br />
</i></font>
    ...
```

### *The Results from the DataList Control*

The third section of the page contains the output from the DataList control:

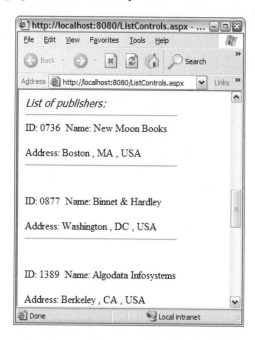

A `DataList` control (by default) generates an HTML table with one cell for each row in the data source, and inserts the values from the data source into these cells. It also adds some formatting to the table and its content, depending on the selections we make in the various style properties after we've added the control to our page.

In the following listing of the output generated by the `DataList` control, you can see the enclosing HTML table, and each row and cell in the table. The first cell is the content generated from our `<HeaderTemplate>` – the Label control we placed here creates a `<span>` element when the page is executed. The other cells contain a series of `<span>` elements generated by the five `Label` controls we placed in the `<ItemTemplate>` of the control declaration, each displaying the values from the rows in the data source:

```
<table id="DataList1" cellspacing="0" border="0"
       style="border-collapse:collapse;">
  <tr>
    <td>
      <span id="DataList1__ctl0_Label1" style="font-family:Tahoma;
            font-weight:bold;font-style:italic;">List of publishers:</span>
      <hr />
    </td>
  </tr>
  <tr>
    <td>
      <p>ID:
      <span id="DataList1__ctl1_Label1" style="font-weight:bold;">
        0736
      </span>
          Name:
      <span id="DataList1__ctl1_Label2" style="font-weight:bold;">
        New Moon Books
      </span>
      </p>
      <p>
        Address:
      <span id="DataList1__ctl1_Label3" style="font-weight:bold;">
        Boston
      </span>,
      <span id="DataList1__ctl1_Label4" style="font-weight:bold;">
        MA
      </span>,
      <span id="DataList1__ctl1_Label5" style="font-weight:bold;">
        USA
      </span>
      </p>
    </td>
  </tr>
  ...
</table>
```

# Summary

In this chapter, we moved away from using the two data controls that are supplied with Web Matrix, `SqlDataSourceControl` and `MxDataGrid`, to show you how we can use the more generic controls that are part pf the .NET Framework in our ASP.NET pages. We discussed why it is that we *need* to move up a gear, and *write code* to use data binding with the ASP.NET list controls.

To be able to write this kind of code, you have to know at least a *bit* about the .NET data-access objects. We looked at these in overview, as well as explaining the difference between the two types of object that we can return from a function or method – the `DataReader` and the `DataSet`.

As you saw, Web Matrix helps out where it can when we come to write data-access code by providing code builders that can do most of the work for us. We examined the **SELECT Data Method** code builder, and used it to generate a function that can extract data from a database table and return it to us as a `DataReader` object. Then, we bound this to a `DataGrid` control, and displayed the data. We also showed you how we can make the output more attractive using the **Auto Format** Wizard or by setting individual style properties.

The next stage was to see how we use the **SELECT Data Method** code builder to return a `DataSet` object, and at the same time select only the columns and rows we want. We built a simple page that allows you to enter a search string and find all the rows that match the criteria you specify.

Finally, we moved on to take a brief overview of the other .NET Framework list controls, and used them in an example page. We populated each one using data binding, and examined the output that they generate. All this should help you to choose the appropriate list control for your own pages.

In this chapter, we have covered:

- ❑ How ASP.NET exposes data that we can use with a range of standard .NET controls
- ❑ How we create code routines that can access a database and return data
- ❑ How we select individual columns and return specific sets of rows from a database
- ❑ How we can use some of the generic .NET Framework data controls to display data

In the next chapter, we'll take a look at linking pages together to form a web*site*, rather than a collection of individual web *pages*.

# CHAPTER 11

# Linking to Pages and Files

So far in this book, we've only really looked at single pages and responses to post-backs. As you know from browsing the web, one of the main features that it offers over traditional documents is the ability to link from one document to another using a **hyperlink**. Without hyperlinks, navigating around a website from one page to another would be very difficult. It would stop certain sites, such as search engines from being as useful as they are. For instance, browsing from a results page on a site such as Google to the results of a query would become a painful task – involving manually copying and pasting links at best.

In this chapter, we'll learn how to make use of hyperlinks that "glue" pages together in our own applications. We will:

❑   Learn how hyperlinks are formed and used for joining static pages to each other

❑   Examine how we can link to other types of files than just web pages, and how the requests for these linked files are dealt with

❑   Look at how links can not only be used to take us from one page to another, but can also pass data around between pages

❑   See how we can use hyperlinks for other functions, such as sending e-mails and running code within browsers

❑   Learn how to reuse client-side resources that we've written by linking to external documents from within a web-page

# Linking Your Pages Together

Although the World Wide Web is a fairly recent development, the idea for linking relevant pieces of content together to allow for easy navigation isn't a new one. In fact, it was originally proposed back in 1945 by Vannevar Bush. Bush was a distinguished scientist and scholar, serving as Dean at the school of engineering in MIT, chairing the President's National Defense Research Committee, and being a central figure in the development of nuclear fission and the Manhattan Project. He was also an inventor who recognised the limitations in the way that information was accessed – as the amount of information grows, there needs to be a way of simply relating one piece to others. To solve this problem, he described a machine called **The Memex** that would help someone find information based on association and context rather than standard categorical indexing. Without hyperlinks, we wouldn't have websites as we know them – all we'd be capable of developing is individual pages. Whenever we wanted to navigate from one page to another, we'd have to type in the new URL in the address bar, and displaying such links would break up the flow of text.

## HTML Anchors

**HTML anchors** are the basis for linking between web pages, relating them to each other and making it easier for a user to find the information they're interested in. There are several options we can make use of, and parameters we can vary, when we use anchors to add extra functionality. To start with, we'll keep things simple, before looking at the other features available to us shortly.

**Try It Out**     **Using HTML Anchors**

To show how we can make use of anchors (links) in our applications, in this *Try it Out* we'll create a homepage for the Cornflakes at Midnight site. This page will link to all of the pages that we're going to create in our site, such as the discography we've created in the previous couple of chapters, a biography of the band, and so on.

**1.** Within Web Matrix, create a standard ASP.NET page called `Default.aspx`.

**2.** Making sure that the HTML Elements tab is selected in the **Toolbox**, drag an `Anchor` control onto the page. Select the **Anchor** text that has appeared, and type **Discography**. Then from the **Properties** window on the right, change the `href` property to `Discs.aspx`, and the `title` property to `View Discography`.

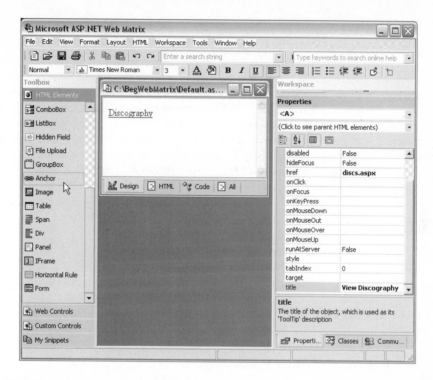

**3.** Click the Start button from the top toolbar to view our page, and when the browser window opens, you'll see the hyperlink appear in the top left. If you click on it, the browser should navigate to the Discs.aspx page (as long as it is in the same folder as Default.aspx), showing all of Cornflakes at Midnight's albums. The Discs.aspx page is included in the code download for this chapter.

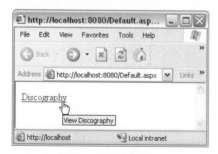

## How It Works

When you drag an Anchor onto the page, three things are inserted into the underlying HTML. The first is the text that is shown on the page, Discography in our case. The other two are a pair of opening and closing tags, <a> and </a>. If you look at the HTML view of the page we created, you'll see the following:

```
<a title="View Discography" href="Discs.aspx">Discography</a>
```

The `href` part is the most important attribute that has been specified in this tag; it is this that tells web browsers what to do when the text enclosed within the link is selected. When we're in the Design view, the Web Matrix environment acts a bit like a web browser, interpreting the `<a>` tag, and displaying the text in a different color to show that it is a link. The other attribute, `title`, displays a tool-tip when you hover over the link with a mouse (only when the page is properly browsed – this won't happen when you are working in design view). It is important to include this attribute for the benefit of visually impaired readers, who use tools such as screen-readers to browse the web. When a screen reader reads this attribute, it will read out the title attribute, informing the user where the link will take them if they click it.

## Folder Structures

In the example above, we linked from our homepage for the Cornflakes at Midnight site to another page located in the same folder – the `Discs.aspx` page. However, web sites are regularly split across several folders in order to separate files of different types, to help make the files more manageable, or for security reasons. When we need to link to a file in one of these folders, we obviously need a way of specifying a **path** to get there.

| Try It Out | Referencing Other Paths |
|---|---|

In this *Try it Out*, we'll see how to reference files in other locations, and how these references are used for all types of files, not just hyperlinks.

1. Open up the `Default.aspx` page, and make sure that you're in Design view. At the top of the page, enter the text Cornflakes at Midnight, select it, and choose the Heading 1 option from the toolbar at the top left-hand corner of the screen. This will be the title of our page, and your page will look like this:

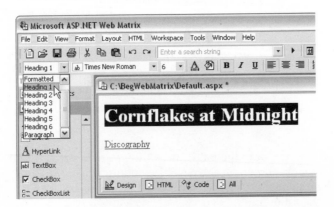

**2.** Beneath this title, drag and drop an Image control from the **HTML Elements** tab of the Toolbox. With this image selected, change the value of the `src` property to `Images/bandphoto.jpg`. Also, change the `alt` property to `Photo of the band`:

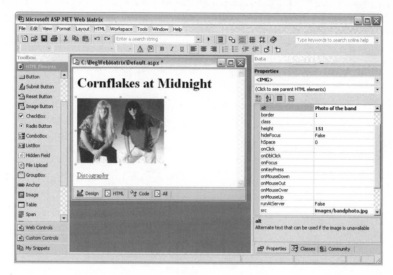

**3.** Now, when you run the page, you will see the photo of the band rendered in your browser.

## How It Works

In a similar way to the Windows folder system, websites can contain folder structures to physically (and logically) separate and group files. To see the folder structure of your local machine as an example of the **tree structure** that folder hierarchies create, click on the + symbol next to one of your drives in the **Workspace** panel in Web Matrix – this will display the folder tree on your local machine.

On a website, when we reference a file that is in a different folder from the document calling it, we must provide the necessary information to locate this folder. In the example above, this was relatively simple, as the `bandphoto.jpg` image was just in the `Image` subfolder of our current folder, requiring only the folder name, the file name, and a slash (/) character to separate the two. Depending on the location of the folder, other techniques may need to be used, as presented in the table below:

| Path | Referencing Method | Description |
| --- | --- | --- |
| Subfolder | `FolderName/FileName` | This is the simplest form of referencing a file, as shown in the example above. The `FolderName` precedes the `FileName`, separated by a slash (/) character. |
| Parent folder | `../FileName` | If, rather than accessing a file that exists in a subfolder of our current location, we want to access one higher up the folder tree (the **parent folder**), we must use the `..` symbol. This specifies "go up one folder". If we want to go up more than one, we can specify this multiple times. For example `../../` will take us up two folders. |
| Root folder | `/FileName` | Sometimes it's simpler to navigate down the folder structure from the top, rather than going up to the parent folder first. To do this, we must prefix the path we're interested in with a slash character. |

> The referencing of files on the Web is always done using a slash (/) character, rather than the backslash (\) character used in Windows file paths. Although Internet Explorer can accept locations specified in either manner, other browsers may not locate files in paths with backslash characters.

The items in the table above can be combined to reference any local path. We'll show this using the folder structure below as an example:

If the file that we were working on existed in the `Files` folder, and we wanted to reference a picture in the `Images` folder, we could specify either of the following two paths:

```
../Images/FileName
/Images/FileName
```

The first of these would take us to the directory above (`Root`), and then down to the `Images` folder. The second would take us straight up to the root (which also happens to be `Root`), and then back down to `Images`. If, instead of the `Images` folder, we wanted to reference an image in the `Photos` subfolder, we could append another folder name to either of the paths above, again separating them with a slash character:

```
../Images/Photos/FileName
/Images/Photos/FileName
```

## Linking to Other Sites

When we were looking at path structures above, we were using what are known as **relative** links. This is where all file and folder locations that are specified are given in relation to our current folder. As well as specifying files in this manner, we can also specify paths in **absolute** terms, as shown below.

### Try It Out      Referencing Absolute File-paths

**1.** Once again, open up the `Default.aspx` file within Web Matrix in **Design** view. Between the photo image and the **Discography** link, insert the text **Contents**, and set it to be **Heading 2** (from the menu on the toolbar, as we did before). Beneath the **Discography** link, insert another **Heading 2** item, this time named **Links**. These will be the section headings on our homepage.

**2.** Beneath the **Links** item, drag another `Anchor` link onto the design canvas from the **HTML Elements** tab of the **Toolbox**. The text for this should be changed to **Our favorite book**, the `href` property should be set to `http://www.wrox.com/books/1861007922.htm`, and the **title** property should be `Beginning Dynamic Websites`. When this is done, the properties and page should appear as in the screenshot:

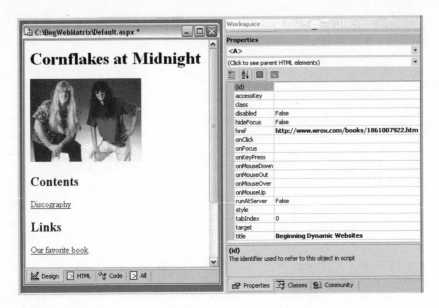

**3.** Press the Start button on the toolbar to show the page. When the Our favorite book link is clicked, Internet Explorer will navigate to the correct page on the remote Wrox site.

## How It Works

Unlike relative file paths, absolute file paths do not require (or expect) any knowledge of the current location to work. As a result of this, they must specify the exact URL required. This not only means that by definition they cannot begin with a / character or contain the parent folder reference (..), and they must start with the `http://` string. If this wasn't done, and the URL specified was `www.wrox.com/books/1861007922.htm`, then the browser would try and find the file in a folder named `www.wrox.com` within the current folder – it assumes it to be a relative path.

It's worth noting that there are advantages and disadvantages to both relative and absolute linking. As absolute linking requires the entire URL to be provided, if a site is moved to a different domain name, such as from `www.myDomain.com` to `www.myOtherDomain.com`, all of the links will require altering to point to this new location. However, if you always try to use relative links, then not only can it sometimes be difficult to see where they are linking to if many parent-folder (..) references are made, you can obviously only link to certain (local) resources.

## *Default Pages*

In the examples above, we've linked to specific files, whether they're on our local site (in the case of `Discography.aspx` and `BandPhoto.jpg`), or on a remote server (in the case of the book's page on the Wrox website). It isn't always necessary to link to a specific page on a site though, we can sometimes just link to the folder containing the files. Depending on how the server has been set up, this can present us with several different options, as we'll find out.

**Try It Out**       **Linking to a Default Page**

In this *Try it Out*, we'll add a link to a couple more of Cornflakes at Midnight's favorite sites, this time making use of default files for sites and folders, allowing the remote site to determine the appropriate page to display.

**1.** As before, open the `Default.aspx` file in **Design** view in Web Matrix. Beneath the **Our favorite book** anchor, drag and drop another `Anchor` element. The text of this should be set to **Our favorite search engine**, with the attributes for `href` and `title` set to `http://www.google.com` and `Google` respectively.

**2.** Repeat step one, dragging another `Anchor` onto the page, beneath the first. This time the text should be set to **A page that doesn't exist**, the `href` should be `http://www.microsoft.com/noSuchPage/`, and the title should be `No such page`.

**3.** Save the file and press the **Start** button in the top toolbar to view the page. When either one of these two newly created links is selected, not only will we now navigate to the site that we want, the default document will also be displayed for that site:

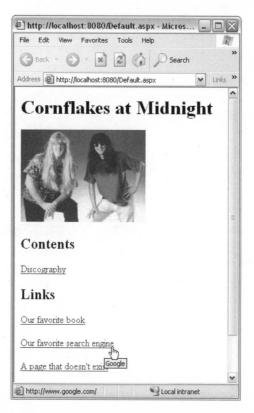

**4.** If you look at the address bar in the Internet Explorer window that has been opened (and in the screenshot on the previous page), you'll see that we're explicitly specifying the `Default.aspx` document to be viewed. If you edit this address, removing the filename so that all that is shown is `http://localhost:8080`, and then press *Enter* to navigate to the URL, you should see that exactly the same page is displayed; `Default.aspx` is already a default document for our site.

## How It Works

Default documents can be created for folders. When this is done, as well as being able to navigate to the file explicitly, the file will also be displayed if only the folder name is given. Microsoft's web servers (IIS and Personal Web Server) automatically treat certain files as default files without any configuration changes being made. In the preferred order, these are:

```
Default.aspx
Default.htm
Default.asp
index.htm
iisstart.asp
```

So, if both a `Default.htm` and `Default.aspx` file are specified, the `Default.aspx` file will be the one returned to the user.

As well as being able to display default documents, web servers can also display error pages and **directory listings**. These are shown when the specified file or folder doesn't exist, or no default document can be found for a folder. If we click on the No Such Page link, we'll be taken to the Microsoft page, and as the folder we gave doesn't exist on that server, a standard error page will be shown:

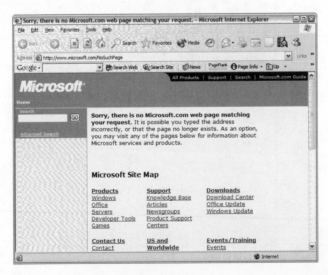

In the case of directory listings, details of all of the files and subfolders within a location are given, along with hyperlinks to navigate to them. If the `Default.aspx` file that we'd created weren't treated as a default document, or if it were deleted, then a directory listing, similar to the screenshot shown would be displayed:

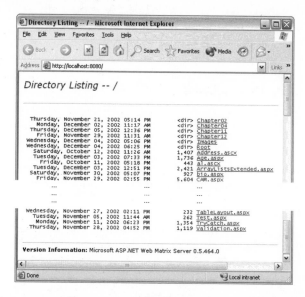

Depending on the web server that is being used, the settings that have been applied, and so on, several different results can be returned to the user if they try browsing to a folder without specifying a particular file. These are summarized below:

| Result | Description |
| --- | --- |
| Desired page is displayed | A default file has been specified for this folder, saving the user from having to specify the exact file desired. |
| List of folder contents is displayed | Directory browsing has been enabled, listing all of the contents of this folder. This usually allows the user to click on hyperlinks to each of the files in the folder, again removing the need for typing in the exact filename. |
| Permission denied message displayed | No default files have been set, and directory browsing is disabled. This message is often displayed by Microsoft web servers. |
| File not found message displayed | No default files have been set, directory browsing is disabled, and no permissions have been set. This message is usually displayed by web server software that is running on a platform other than Windows, for instance an Apache web server running on a UNIX variant. |

# Pop-up Links

In the previous example, we linked to two external locations (www.google.com, and a Microsoft page that didn't exist). When any of these links was clicked on within a web browser, the URL was navigated to within the current window. While that is probably desired when we're linking to a page within our site, if we're adding a reference to an external site, we may well want to allow the user to continue browsing our site, and view the referenced page/site separately.

### Try It Out     Creating Pop-up Links

In this *Try it Out*, we'll edit the three external links that we've got, specifying that they should all be opened outside the current Internet Explorer window.

**1.** Open the `Default.aspx` document in **Design** view once more from within Web Matrix. Select the first link (**Our favorite book**), and alter the `target` attribute in the **Properties** pane to `ExternalSite`.

**2.** Repeat step one for each of the other two external links (**Our favorite search engine** and **A page that doesn't exist**), setting each of their target attributes to `ExternalSite` too.

**3.** Click the **Start** button on the toolbar, and wait for the page to be displayed within your browser. If any of the bottom three links are now clicked on, it will open in an external window. You will notice that these all open in the same "new" browser window, however. Switching back to Web Matrix, we can change this so that each opens in an entirely new window. Selecting each of the links in turn, edit the `target` property, appending 1, 2, and 3 to the value respectively, so that we have targets of `ExternalSite1`, `ExternalSite2`, and `ExternalSite3`.

**4.** When the Start button is clicked now, and the page is shown again, each of the links will now open in a different window when clicked on. If any of them is clicked twice, however, it will be displayed in the same window that is first created for it each time.

## How It Works

When no `target` attribute is specified in a hyperlink, the page is opened within the current Internet Explorer browser window by default. This is usually the case with other browsers too. However, there is no rule stating that other third-party browsers shouldn't open all links within new windows. If we want to specify that a window is *always* opened within a new window, then we can specify a name for that window within the target attribute. The value for the window name should not contain any spaces or punctuation, other than the underscore character (_).

For each unique name that is specified on a page, all links targeting it will be opened within that window, navigating away from any content that was previously displayed there. If we want the page to ensure that this never happens, and that the page opens in a totally new browser window each time, we can specify _blank as the target (note the use of the underscore). This target is a special value that is understood by all commonly used browsers, including Internet Explorer, Opera, and any of Netscape's offerings.

> When specifying target window names for hyperlinks, the following values are reserved for special functions: `_self`, `_parent`, `_blank`, `_new`. In turn these open the link in the current window, the window that opened the current one, a new window, or a different window (which may override a previously opened one). If any of these values is entered, then it will always open in one of these predefined ways.

# How Web Servers Process Files

So far in this chapter, we've dealt with linking to two types of files – web pages, and images. From just these two, we can see that content is dealt with differently depending on its type. When a web page is returned from the web server, the HTML that it contains is interpreted and rendered in a browser window as a document containing links, tables, etc. If the file is an image file (not a web page that displays images, but an actual image file itself), then it is treated differently, being rendered as-is to the page without being searched for HTML tags as a web-page would be. Depending on the file type, other actions can be taken, too. It's important to note that no matter what the type of the file, it is transmitted to the browser in the same way, and referenced in an identical manner on a URL.

**Try It Out**    **Dealing with File Types**

We'll now add an extra page to our website where visitors can download samples of the "music" Cornflakes at Midnight have recorded. We'll create a new page and add links to allow them to select what format they'd like to download the music in to do this.

**1.** In your `Default.aspx` page insert a link (an HTML **Anchor** element) beneath the **Discography** called **Downloads**, just as we've done before. The **target** of this anchor should be `Downloads.aspx`.

**2.** Create a new **ASP.NET Page** called `Downloads.aspx`. This file will contain the links to each of our downloadable files. When this file opens, insert a **Heading 1** title of **Downloads** (in a similar kind of way to how we did earlier in the chapter) at the top of the page. Beneath this, drag and drop two HTML **Anchors**. The first of these should have a **href** of `Files/Sounds.wma`, the second should be set to `Files/Sounds.zip`. Also, change the text of the two anchors so that they match the following:

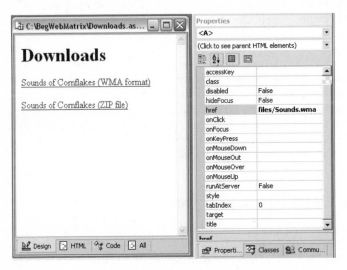

**3.** Save the file, and click the **Start** button in the toolbar. When the page is displayed in Internet Explorer, you should see different things happen when each of the links is clicked on. The ZIP file will always present the user with a dialog, asking whether the file should be opened or saved to disk. The WMA link behaves differently from this however. Internet Explorer presents a second dialog – stating that it recognizes the audio/video link that was clicked on. The option of playing the file in Internet Explorer is then given. If this is selected (by clicking the **Yes** button), the Media bar will be shown at the side of the screen, and the music will begin to play.

## How It Works

When a file is transmitted to a web browser from a web server, it contains extra information in addition to the file itself. One of the items that are included is the type of the content (known as a **MIME Type**), which is represented as a string in the form Type/SubType. The content-type string returned is calculated by the web server based upon the file extension. So, if a file with an extension of .htm or .aspx is detected, then the content type of text/html will be returned as the web server knows that this is a web page. Similarly, if a file with a .gif (Graphics Interchange Format) extension is found, the content type of image/gif will be returned.

So, if we renamed our Cornflakes.wma file to Cornflakes.htm and updated the hyperlinks to point to this, then it wouldn't be treated properly when it was returned to the browser; we'd see a load of garbage representing the data contained in the file displayed in the Window. If you like, you can try this out to see; just remember to change everything back again once you're done! As well as being used to control the content type that is sent down to the browser, the file extension is also used by the web server to determine what to do with the file *before* sending it across the web. In the case of most files, nothing at all is done. The main exception to this is with .aspx files – those that contain code that needs executing first. As with the WMA file, you can try renaming one of the .aspx files that contains server-side code (for instance Discography.aspx) so that it has an .htm file extension. When this URL is now requested in Internet Explorer, you'll see that any source code that was on the page (such as that for creating a DataGrid) is now returned.

# ASP.NET HyperLink Control

In all of the previous examples, we have made use of the HTML Anchor element, represented by an <a> tag. As well as being able to create a hyperlink by hand, we can also use an ASP.NET control to do this, allowing us to make use of more functionality based upon the underlying control. This is similar to the way that a DataGrid is rendered as a table, even though it provides much more functionality.

**Try It Out**    **Using a HyperLink Control**

In this example, we'll create a page that a presents a hyperlink to the user, which, when clicked on, will show them a different picture of the band depending on the time of the day. We'll do this by manipulating the target and text of the link at the server.

**1.** Open up the Default.aspx file within Web Matrix in **Design** view. This time, instead of selecting the **HTML Elements** tab from the **Toolbox**, select the **Web Controls** tab, and drag a HyperLink control onto the canvas, between the **Downloads** hyperlink and the **Links** title. From the properties panel, change the ID property to lnkTimeOfDay, so that we can reference it from within code easily.

**2.** Next, switch to **Code** view. Remove the two lines of code that being with a single quote ('), and enter the following text into the editor so that the link is altered when the page is loaded:

```
Private Sub Page_Load(ByVal sender As System.Object, _
                   ByVal e As System.EventArgs)
  If Now.Hour<12 Then
    lnkTimeOfDay.Text = "Cornflakes before lunch"
    lnkTimeOfDay.NavigateURL = "PhotoAM.aspx"
  Else
    lnkTimeOfDay.Text = "Cornflakes after lunch"
    lnkTimeOfDay.NavigateURL = "PhotoPM.aspx"
  End If
End Sub
```

**3.** Save the file, and click the **Start** button in the toolbar to display the file in a browser window. You should see that if the time is before midday, the text **Cornflakes before lunch** is shown, whereas **Cornflakes after lunch** will be displayed if it is after midday. When you click on the URL, it will also take you to a different file depending on the time of the day. The two files that are linked to – PhotoAM.aspx and PhotoPM.aspx – are both included as part of the setup package for the Cornflakes at Midnight application.

To see the text and link change, simply open up the system clock (by right-clicking on the taskbar, and selecting **Adjust Date/Time**), alter the time of day to the other side of midday (or midnight), and click **Apply**. Then switch back to Internet Explorer and click **Refresh**. Don't forget to change the clock back once you're finished playing!

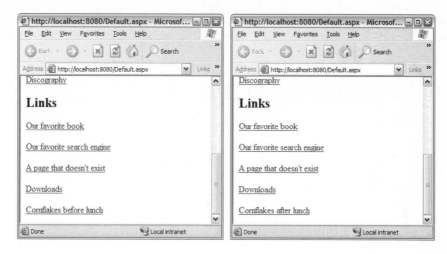

Clicking on this link will take you to:

## How It Works

Just like the data controls we've already looked at (such as the MxDataGrid), the Hyperlink control is processed by the web server and rendered into HTML before being returned to the client. The few lines of code that we entered in the file are called whenever the page is run – the .NET runtime knows to automatically execute the Page_Load routine every time the page is loaded.

The code itself does very little – it makes a call to the Now() function, finds out the hour of the day, and based upon that, sets the Text and NavigateURL properties of the HyperLink control. The Text property is that which is displayed on the screen to the end user – the text we can edit from within Design view. The NavigateURL property is the ASP.NET equivalent of the href attribute we set on the HTML Anchor element.

When the page is run, the hyperlink that is rendered in the browser is dynamically generated, with its text and target URL attributes being determined by those set in the Page_Load subroutine.

# Passing Data between Pages

Linking between static web pages allows us to group them into logical collections that allow for easy navigation. When we're dealing with dynamic pages, rather than just linking from one page to the next, we can also make use of the URL to send data between them. This is incredibly useful as it means that we can display data on one page based upon a choice that the user made previously.

**Try It Out**        **Passing Data Between Pages**

In this *Try it Out*, we'll edit the Discs.aspx page that is based on examples in Chapter 9, updating it so that whenever the title of a particular album is clicked on, we get taken to a second page that displays more details about it.

**1.** Open up the Discs.aspx page (which is included in the code download, and is based on the examples we looked at in Chapter 9). Ensuring that you're in **Design** view, select the MxDataGrid on the page. As in Chapter 9, click the ellipsis within the Fields entry on the **Properties** pane. As we're going to link to a second page on the Title, we'll want to remove the column that's already there, and create a new HyperLinkField. To do this, select entry 1 in the **Members** pane, and click the **Remove** button. Now click the arrow next to the **Add** button, and select the **HyperLinkField** option. Select the entry that has just been created in the **Members** pane, and click the up arrow until it appears just below the cover image field in the list (back at position 1 in the list).

**2.** The next step is to configure the field to display the Title, and to link to the DiscDetails.aspx page. To do this, update the values in the right pane, setting them as follows:

❑   HeaderText – Title

❑   DataNavigateURLField – DiscID

❑   NavigateURLFormatString – DiscDetails.aspx?DiscID={0}

❑   DataTextField – Title

The dialog should now appear like the one shown below:

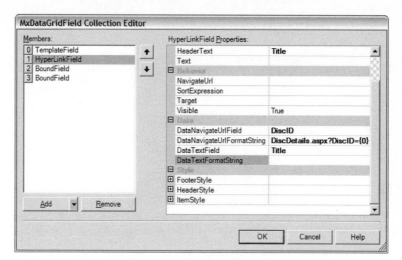

**3.** Set the visual styles to match the other columns as follows:

| HeaderStyle | Setting |
|---|---|
| BackColor | #668099 |
| BorderColor | #668099 |
| BorderStyle | Solid |
| BorderWidth | 2px |

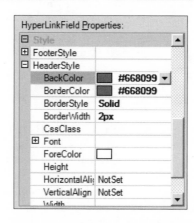

| ItemStyle | Setting |
|---|---|
| BorderColor | #668099 |
| BorderStyle | Solid |
| BorderWidth | 2px |

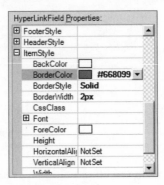

Click **OK** on the dialog to confirm the changes, and you should see the appearance change so that the Title column now appears in blue, showing that it is a hyperlink.

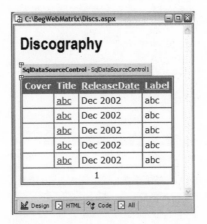

**4.** Save the Discs.aspx file, and create a new **ASP.NET Page** called DiscDetails.aspx. This page will be used for displaying the details of an album that is selected from the MxDataGrid – allowing us to show the cover image on the same page as the other details. In the **Design** view, drag a Repeater control onto the design canvas from the **Web Controls** tab of the **Toolbox**. Now, switch to the **All** view of the page so that we can both retrieve the data, and output it to the screen. Update the Repeater control, so that the following ItemTemplate declaration appears within its tags; this will define how our page looks:

```
<asp:Repeater id="Repeater1" runat="server">
  <ItemTemplate>
    <h1>Disc Details - <%# Container.DataItem("Title")  %></h1>
    <p><img src='<%# Container.DataItem("CoverImageURL") %>'
            align="center" vspace="4" /></p>
    <p><b>Notes:</b> <%# Container.DataItem("Notes") %></p>
    <p><b>Release Date:</b> <%# Container.DataItem("ReleaseDate") %></p>
    <p><b>Label:</b> <%# Container.DataItem("Label") %></p>
  </ItemTemplate>
</asp:Repeater>
```

**5.** Next, drag a SELECT Data Method from the Code Builders tab of the Toolbox onto the page. Enter the usual details for the Connect to Database dialog, and click OK. On the next dialog, select the Disc table in the left pane, and then check the * checkbox in the right pane to choose what data is returned. After that, click the WHERE button to so that we can specify the individual record to bring back. As this dialog defaults to the DiscID field, simply click OK on this dialog. The Query Builder should now look like the following:

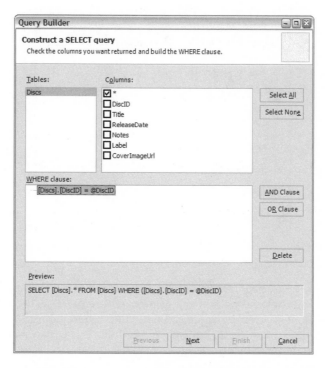

**6.** Click the Next button on this and the Preview page, and you will be presented with the Caption page. Replace the MyQueryMethod text with GetDiscDetails, ensure that the DataSet radio button is selected, and click Finish.

**7.** The final step is to tie the data returned from the GetDiscDetails() method to the Repeater control on our page. To do this, enter the following code above the GetDiscDetails() method:

```
Public Sub Page_Load()
  Repeater1.DataSource = GetDiscDetails(Request.QueryString.Item("DiscID"))
  Repeater1.DataBind()
End Sub
```

Save this file, switch back to the Discs.aspx file, and click the **Start** button on the toolbar. When the page is shown, you'll now see that the **Title** column contains hyperlinks. Clicking on one of these will take you to the DiscDetails.aspx page, displaying a page similar to the one below:

## How It Works

Whenever we call an ASPX page, we can append data to the URL that appears in the address bar in the browser. This data takes the form of **name-value pairs**; as their name suggests, each pair has a name to identify it, and a value associated with that name. They appear on the query string prefixed by a question mark (?). If we want to have more than one item passed to a page at once, we can separate them by an ampersand (&), as in the URL below:

```
http://localhost:8080/DiscDetails.aspx?DiscID=1&SecondDiscID=2
```

Whenever we pass data to a page in this fashion, we can retrieve it as we did on the DiscDetails.aspx page – by making a call to the Request object. This object allows us to retrieve information from the **querystring** (the extra information at the end of the URL after the question mark; our name-value pairs), from any forms that have been filled in, and from other data sources (such as cookies stored on the client's browser).

*Cookies are small text files that remember certain information relating to the user and to a specific site – we'll learn more about cookies in Chapter 15.*

By specifying the following code:

```
Request.QueryString.Item("DiscID")
```

we're asking for the value of the DiscID item that was passed in on the QueryString to be retrieved. In the example above, this value (which will be a number such as 1 or 2) is then passed into the GetDiscDetails method, which returns to us all of the information about a specific Disc. The Repeater control (which is a bit like a DataGrid, but allows us to define how we want the data to be presented more simply) then displays the details of the specified Disc.

**Try It Out     Encoding Data Being Passed on the Query String**

One thing that you'll notice if you do some experimenting with our DiscDetails.aspx page is that if the DiscID value on the query string is altered so that it's no longer an integer, for instance a value such as x, an error message is displayed. In this *Try it Out*, we'll create an error page that is displayed whenever this happens, and show how data can be encoded on the query string, allowing other values to be passed around.

**1.** In Web Matrix, open the DiscDetails.aspx page in **Code** view. Update the Page_Load routine at the top of the editor to match the code below, so that whenever an error occurs, the user is redirected to a different page:

```
Public Sub Page_Load()
  Try
    Repeater1.DataSource = _
      GetDiscDetails(Request.QueryString.Item("DiscID"))
  Catch
    Response.Redirect("Error.aspx?Message=" & _
      Server.URLEncode("Could not retrieve results for [DiscID] specified"))
  End Try

  Repeater1.DataBind()
End Sub
```

**2.** Create a new **ASP.NET** page called Error.aspx, ensure it's in **Design** view, and enter the text **Error** at the top of the canvas. Select this text, and set it to **Heading 1**, then enter the following text beneath it:

An error occurred while attempting to display the requested page

**3.** Next, switch to HTML view, and update the contents of the `<p>` tag to match the following:

```
<p>
    An error occurred while attempting to display the requested page:
    <%=Request.QueryString.Item("Message") %>
</p>
```

**4.** Finally, save both of these files, open the `Discs.aspx` file from within Web Matrix, and click the **Start** button on the toolbar. When the page is shown, click on one of the links taking you through to the `DiscDetails.aspx` page. Now alter the value in the address bar, so that the `DiscID` is set to X. When this URL is navigated to, the following screen should be displayed:

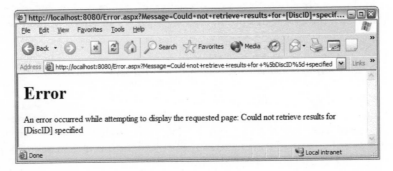

## How It Works

When the `DiscDetails.aspx` page is called, it tries to make a call to `GetDiscDetails()`, passing through the value of `DiscID` as a parameter. As this function expects a number as its input, it will cause an error to be raised if we pass through an invalid value (such as X). By wrapping this line of code up in a `Try ... Catch` block, we ensure that if an error occurs, then the `Response.Redirect()` line of code is called, sending the user to the `Error.aspx` page, and passing through a querystring parameter called `Message`.

Rather than simply passing the error message straight through, the `Server.URLEncode()` function is called first. Looking at the text in the **Address** bar in Internet Explorer when the `Error.aspx` page is displayed, you'll see that the message has been converted to:

Could+not+retrieve+valid+results+for+the+%5bDiscID%5d+specified

This is done because not all characters are valid in a URL. In fact, very few characters are valid – most symbols, such as the square brackets ([ and ]) in our message aren't allowed. When we pass text through to Server.URLEncode(), it replaces such characters with an encoded representation of them. Most characters get converted to a three-character string, beginning with a percent (%), followed by two hexadecimal (0-9/a-f) characters. Certain other values are treated differently, such as a space, which is converted to a plus (+) sign. If this encoding wasn't done, then an ampersand (&) in the middle of a string, for example, would cause a new name-value pair to be started.

> Whenever dynamic data is passed around on the query string, it is important to remember to call **URLEncode()** on it. Although datatypes such as integers are not altered when URL encoded, if the type of data is ever changed, then it could stop the system from working.

When the Error.aspx page is displayed, the line of code:

```
<%=Request.QueryString.Item("Message") %>
```

simply reads the value passed in on the query-string, and outputs it to the page for us. You'll notice that .NET takes care of decoding the text itself, re-inserting characters such as the square-brackets ([ and ]).

It should be noted that passing around server-side information via the client (either using the query-string, cookies, or any other means) is generally not considered good practice. This is because it leaves the system open to the malicious altering of these values in an attempt to gain access to parts of the system that shouldn't be accessible.

# Other Uses for Hyperlinks

In addition to being able to pass information around, we can implement other functionality using hyperlinks. While the href attribute was initially designed for linking to other files, it can also be used to send e-mails, call client-side scripts (such as JavaScript or VBScript), and link to much more than just web-based resources. In this section, we'll take a look at the first two of these situations – the most common alternative uses for hyperlinks – and then take a quick look at the other options open to us.

## E-Mailing

One of the most common uses for Anchor tags, after linking files to one another, is to initiate the sending of an e-mail. This is regularly included on a website whenever feedback or comments are wanted, as it saves the user from having to type in, or copy and paste the e-mail address from the page, and also removes the possibility of the user entering the address incorrectly.

## Try It Out       E-mailing the Band

In this example, we'll add a Contact Us page to the website, providing different means of getting in touch with the band. One of these options will be a hyperlink, which, when clicked, will bring up a window with which you can compose mail (depending on your system setup, this could be within Outlook, Outlook Express, or any other mail reader such as Pegasus).

**1.** Create a new **ASP.NET Page** called `ContactUs.aspx`, and on the design canvas, enter text to make the page look like the one shown below, using a **Heading 1** for the title, and the **Bold** button on the toolbar to highlight the methods of contact (to get the line breaks in the address, instead of paragraph marks that incorporate additional vertical spacing, press *Shift+Enter*, rather than just *Enter*):

**2.** Beneath the address, enter a section marked **E-mail:**, and follow it with a value of `cam@tempuri.org`. When you move your mouse cursor away from this line once it's complete, you'll see that Web Matrix has automatically converted this into a hyperlink. If you click on the link to select it, and look at the **Properties** panel, the `href` attribute will have been set to `mailto:cam@tempuri.org`. This is the method by which we can begin e-mails from links.

**3.** We can add to the `href` value so that it opens up the e-mail with certain fields filled in for us. To do this, amend the value so that it looks like the following:

```
mailto:cam@tempuri.org?Subject=Website%20Feedback&Body=Your%20site%20rocks!
```

You will find that once this value has been entered, the text on the canvas is also updated – this is due to Web Matrix linking the text that appears, and that `href` attribute. To correct this, switch to **HTML** view, locate the link, and amend the text between the `<a>` and `</a>` tags so that it says `cam@tempuri.org` once again.

**4.** Save this page, and click the **Start** button on the toolbar to show the web page in
Internet Explorer. When the page is shown, click on the `cam@tempuri.org` link at the
bottom of the page. A new e-mail message should be opened, with the **To**, **Subject**,
and **Body** already containing values, as shown below:

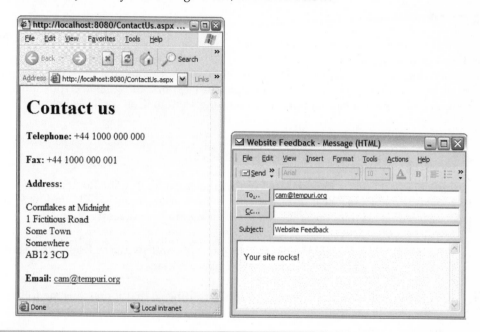

## How It Works

Whenever a hyperlink is clicked on, the browser first interprets the contents of the `href`
attribute, rather than just blindly navigating to a URL specified within it. If the value of the
attribute begins with one of a predefined list of items, including `mailto:`, then a special action
is taken. In this case, the browser tries to open a new e-mail. The program that is used to do this
depends on the web-browser itself. In Internet Explorer, this can be changed by selecting the
**Tools | Internet Options** menu entries, then altering the **E-mail** option on the **Programs** tab.

The rules for initiating an e-mail from within a link are very similar to those for passing data
between pages – the first parameter is prefixed by a question mark (?) character, and any
further ones are prefixed (separated) by ampersand (&) characters. The following parameters
can used in a `mailto:`

- ❑ `Subject` – Text to appear in the subject line of the message
- ❑ `Body` – Text to appear in the body of the message
- ❑ `CC` – Addresses to be included in the "cc" (carbon copy) section of the message
- ❑ `BCC` – Addresses to be included in the "bcc" (blind carbon copy) section of the message

Any of these parameters that are specified must follow the same rules as for normal (HTTP) query string parameters that we've already looked at. For instance, a less-than symbol (<) must be encoded as %3C, a greater-than symbol (>) as %3E, and so on.

# JavaScript

Another of the common uses for hyperlinks is the calling of client-side JavaScript (or VBScript) code. This is a very useful feature, as it allows for far more complex actions to be carried out than would otherwise be possible – such as the validating of fields that have been completed, the initiation of multiple actions at the same time, and so on. Calling JavaScript from a hyperlink can be done in a similar manner to sending an e-mail, as we'll see below.

## Try It Out — Using JavaScript in a Link

In this example, we'll update the pop-up window that we added to the homepage of the Cornflakes at Midnight site. We'll use JavaScript to open it in a fixed-sized window without menus, and so on, rather than the standard browser window it currently opens in.

**1.** Within Web Matrix, open the `Default.aspx` file and switch to **Code** view so that we can edit the links that are created based upon the time of day.

**2.** Amend the code within the `Page_Load` subroutine so that it matches the following:

```
If Now.Hour<12 Then
   lnkTimeOfDay.Text = "Cornflakes before lunch"
   lnkTimeOfDay.NavigateURL = "javascript:window.open(" & _
     "'PhotoAM.aspx', 'Photo', 'width=400,height=300');"
Else
   lnkTimeOfDay.Text = "Cornflakes after lunch"
   lnkTimeOfDay.NavigateURL = "javascript:window.open(" & _
     "'PhotoPM.aspx', 'Photo', 'width=400,height=300');"
End If
```

**3.** Save the file, and then click the **Start** button on the toolbar to display the page. When the page is displayed, click on the **Cornflakes before lunch**, or **Cornflakes after lunch** link, depending on the time of day. When you do this, you should see the photo open up in a new window, with the toolbars, menus, and so on:

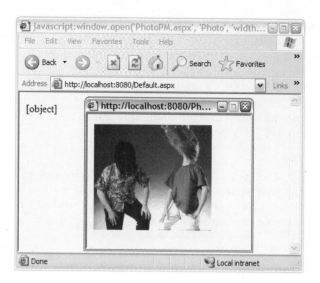

**4.** This will also update the original window as well, however, showing the value returned from the `window.open` call. To fix this, we can write our own JavaScript function to open a window that does not return a value. To do this, update each reference to `window.open` in the **Code** view to `openWindow`. Then switch to HTML view so that we can write our JavaScript function. Between the `<head>` and `</head>` tags at the top of the page, enter the following:

```
<html>
<head>
  <script language="javaScript">
    function openWindow(url, name, parameters) {
      window.open(url, name, parameters);
    }
  </script>
</head>
<body>
    ...
```

If this page is saved and viewed again, when the link is clicked, the original page will remain.

## How It Works

Just as with our `mailto:` example, if we prefix some code in an `href` attribute with `javascript:`, the browser detects this and knows to execute the instructions, rather than trying to navigate to a URL. The main differences between the two are that the `javascript:` protocol does not need to follow the same conventions of separating items with `?` and `&` characters, and the result of the code is returned and processed.

As with many JavaScript functions, `window.open` returns a value. In this example, a reference to the window that was opened is returned. It is very rare that we want to display this value in the window, so we must find a way of performing the action without getting a return value. The simplest way of doing this is writing a JavaScript function that makes the call for us, but ignores the result, and does not return anything. Other options include settings two attributes on the anchor – an `href` of `javascript:void`, and an `onclick` of the code that is to be executed. The problem with this is that the client-side `onclick` event (and associated attribute) is not supported by the ASP.NET `Hyperlink` control.

> When entering JavaScript statements in a hyperlink, be sure to use different quotation marks for delimiting the link from entering strings within the script. For instance `<a href="javascript:alert('ding');" />` is valid, but `<a href="javascript:alert("ding");" />` is not.

## Other Protocols

You may have noticed that there are some commonalities between the different functions we've used hyperlinks for, whether sending an e-mail or opening a web page; all the `href` links follow a similar pattern: `protocol:data`. For instance:

```
http://www.wrox.com
mailto:someone@tempuri.org
javascript:alert('hello');
```

This pattern continues with several other protocols that can be accessed from hyperlinks – most commonly for accessing different types of remote resources, rather than the special case of JavaScript. The majority of these follow the `http://` style, and include the following:

| Protocol | Example | Description |
|----------|---------|-------------|
| HTTPS | `https://www.microsoft.com` | The secure hypertext transfer protocol (HTTPS) is a communications protocol that allows information to be sent between computers on the Web in an encrypted format. HTTPS is HTTP using a Secure Socket Layer (SSL). A secure socket layer is an encryption protocol invoked on a web server that uses HTTPS. The HTTPS protocol is usually used for online purchasing, or the exchange of private information. |

| Protocol | Example | Description |
|---|---|---|
| FTP | `ftp://lcweb.loc.gov/` | The File Transfer Protocol (FTP) allows files to be transmitted across the Web. It is more appropriate for large files than HTTP, as it allows transfers to be resumed partway through, should they fail, among other features. |
| | | Explorer has a built-in FTP client that makes the transfer of files over the Internet as simple as between local folders. |
| Telnet | `telnet://locis.loc.gov/` | The TELNET protocol allows text-based programs to be run on remote computers, with your own computer acting as a terminal, taking keyboard input, and showing the results of any processing, and so on. |
| | | Windows comes with a Telnet client built into it that is launched whenever a telnet address is entered into Internet Explorer. |
| Gopher | `gopher://gopher.loc.gov/` | Gopher, made available in 1991, became an extremely popular service because it gave access to information and services on the Internet through a relatively easy-to-use menu system. |
| | | A third-party program is required to use the gopher protocol on Windows. |

Many of these protocols (Telnet, Gopher, and so on) are slowly dying out, with few new systems being developed for them. For this reason, and because of the large differences between them and web sites, we'll not cover them further in this book. It is worth remembering that hyperlinks aren't necessarily used for simply linking to resources that are related to websites (such as JavaScript, and other web pages), though.

# Linking to Resource Files

The final topic we're going to cover in this chapter is the way in which we can reference resource files from within our web pages. Such files include JavaScript files containing utility functions that are used throughout the site, and **stylesheets** that affect the appearance of the web pages rendered in browsers. Moving this kind of functionality into separate files provides us with two benefits:

❏ The contents of the resource file aren't included on each page, reducing the amount of data that the user has to download. This makes the pages load quicker, and also means that the web server can process more requests, as each one is smaller.

❏ As the contents of the resource file only exist in one location, whenever a change has to be made, it only needs to be done in that one place. If the JavaScript functions, stylesheet content, or any other such items were replicated on several pages, then every time a change was made, it would have to be done in several places.

## Try It Out — Linking to JavaScript Files

In the previous *Try it Out*, we edited our `Default.aspx` file so that the pop-up window was opened via JavaScript. As there are other places in the site where we may want to do the same, we'll now move the function that we used for doing this into a separate file that all of the others reference, allowing it to be used everywhere.

**1.** Within Web Matrix, create a **Text File** with the name `Functions.js`. This file should be in the same folder as all of the other ASPX files. When you click **OK**, the new file will open up with the number 1 in the top left hand corner – this is Web Matrix providing the numbering of lines for us.

**2.** Cut the `openWindow` function out of the `Default.aspx` file, and paste it into this new file. The opening and closing `<script>` tags are not required within this file:

Once this text has been entered, select the File | Save As... menu option as we need to rename the file (Web Matrix has appended a `.txt` file extension automatically, as shown above). Select the All Files (*.*) option from the Save as type: drop-down list, and make sure that the File name is `Functions.js`, before clicking Save:

**3.** Back in the `Default.aspx` file, update the `<script>` tag at the top of the document so that it links to this new file, by editing it to match the following:

```
<html>
<head>
  <script language="javaScript" src="Functions.js">
  </script>
</head>
<body>
```

**4.** Save both of the documents, and click the Start toolbar button with the `Default.aspx` file active to display the page in Internet Explorer. To the end user, nothing should appear different – the Cornflakes after lunch/Cornflakes before lunch links should perform exactly the same action as before.

### How It Works

Just like other HTML elements (such as the <a> tag), the <script> tag allows attributes to be specified altering its parameters. One of these is the src attribute that allows a URL to be specified that points to a text file that contains functions in the language specified by the language attribute. In our example, this was a local file, Functions.js. Any URL would work though, such as http://tempuri.org/someMoreFunctions.js.

## Linking to StyleSheets

In addition to JavaScript, other resources that are used by multiple pages can be linked in to a web-page, for the same reasons as you would in the example above. Most others use a standardized linking mechanism; the <link> HTML tag, as we'll see below.

### Try It Out          Linking to a Stylesheet

In the second example in this section, we'll reference a second type of document – a CSS (**Cascading StyleSheet**) file. CSS files allows us to alter the appearance of our pages, changing such things as the text size, paragraph spacing, colors, and so on, all without any need to update the content of the pages themselves. To implement this, we'll first embed the style definitions in our Default.aspx page until we've seen how CSS works, and we've come up with a look and feel for our site. Once this is done, we'll move it to a separate file that all of the others can reference.

**1.** Within Web Matrix, open the Default.aspx file, and switch to the HTML view. Beneath the </script> closing tag at the top of the document, but still within the <head> section, insert the following code:

```
<html>
<head>
  <script language="javaScript" src="Functions.js">
  </script>
  <style>
    h1 {
        font-family:    verdana;
        font-size:      22px;
        margin:         8px, 0px, 12px, 0px;
        padding:        0px, 8px, 0px, 0px;
        text-align:     right;
        border-bottom:  1px dashed #000000;
    }

    p, td {
       font-family:  verdana;
       font-size:    13px;
       margin:       0px, 0px, 2px, 16px;
```

```
    }
    </style>

</head>
<body>
    ...
```

**2.** Save the file, and then click the Start button on the toolbar to view the page. When the page appears, you'll see that two things appear differently – firstly the title at the top of the page has been right-aligned, with its font changed, and a dotted line beneath it. Secondly, the hyperlinks have had the line spacing between them removed and their font changed, and they're indented from the left of the window:

**3.** While this has made the layout of the text a little better – removing a lot of the unnecessary vertical spacing, we can go much further, and make the page appear far more professional. Back in the `Default.aspx` file, insert the following CSS definitions beneath those we've already entered:

```
h2 {
    font-family:        verdana;
    font-size:          16px;
    margin:             12px, 0px, 0px, 0px;
```

```
       background-color:  #668099;
       color:             #ffffff;
       padding:           2px, 2px, 2px, 4px;
   }

   body {
       background-color:  #c9d5d5;
       margin:            0px, 0px, 0px, 0px;
       padding:           0px, 0px, 0px, 0px
   }

   a {
       color:             #000099;
       font-style:        italic;
   }
```

**4.** As before, save the file and view it in your browser. You'll now see that, along with the change in background colour, the Contents and Links headings have been altered to fill up the entire line, and the hyperlinks have been altered slightly:

**5.** Now that we've got all of the CSS definitions that we need for our site, we can move them into a separate file. To do this, from within Web Matrix, create a new **Style Sheet** called `Style.css`:

Within this file, cut the style definitions that come between the `<style>` and `</style>` tags in `Default.aspx` (not including the `<style>` tags themselves. Next, paste this text into the `Style.css` document (overwriting anything that's already in the window).

**6.** The final thing that need's doing is updating our ASPX files to reference this stylesheet. We'll start with the `Default.aspx` file – within the **HTML** view, update the top of the file so that it matches the following:

```
<html>
<head>
  <script language="javaScript" src="Functions.js">
  </script>
  <link rel="Stylesheet" type="text/css" href="Style.css" />
</head>
<body>
```

With this done, all of the other files we've created (such as `ContactUs.aspx`, `Discs.aspx`, and so on) should be updated so that they use this file too.

**7.** Once all of the files in our site have been updated, everything should be saved. Next, click the **Start** button on the toolbar once more to show the site. All of the pages should now make use of our stylesheet, and should look much better for it!

## How It Works

CSS definitions allow us to alter the appearance of web page content, whether it's the background, text, tables, images, or whatever. CSS is a language in its own right, with its own rules for how to write definitions. The basic format of a CSS definition is:

```
tag/class name {
  item-entry: item-value;
}
```

As shown in our example above where we set the appearance of paragraph (<p>) and table-cell (<td>) tags at the same time, comma-separating items allows us to save time and space when several items need the same style applying to them.

Rather than include our CSS definitions within a <style> tag on every page, we can place them in a single external file. Then, within our individual web pages, we can reference the stylesheet using a <link> tag, which allows us to specify external resources that should be tied in to a web page. This tag must appear within the <head> of an HTML document, once for each document that should be referenced. The most important three attributes are those used in our example:

❑   href – Specifies the actual file to link to

❑   rel – Specifies the type of document (in this case, a Stylesheet)

❑   type – Specifies the MIME type of the document

There are other attributes available, such as hreflang. These are used far less often than the three above, and aren't usually necessary for including references to items such as stylesheets.

As this chapter is concentrating on the use of linking in websites, and CSS is such a large topic, we won't go into more detail about it here. We will be using stylesheets in later chapters of this book though, so if you need any more information then you can find more information at http://www.westciv.com/style_master/academy/css_tutorial.

# Summary

In this chapter, we've learned all about the different ways of linking between documents on the Web while adding to our Cornflakes at Midnight site. We started off with the simplest method – HTML anchors (<a> tags), showing how they can be used to organize individual web pages into sites.

Next, we learned how these pages can be arranged into folder structures, just like files on your local machine. This allows structure to be added to sites, making them more maintainable, and provides the basis for linking to other sites. We then saw how default documents can be used within websites to remove the need for typing in full paths to files, making it possible for us to navigate to sites such as http://www.wrox.com without needing to know that the actual file being displayed is default.htm.

Having seen how hyperlinks are formed and used, we started looking at more useful topics including learning how pop-up links can be used to allow a visitor to a site view extra information without losing their place on the current page.

After that, we covered more technical topics – the way that web servers process different types of file depending on their file extension, and the way that web browsers treat files differently depending on the MIME type that is returned to them by the server. Continuing with technical topics, we learned how a HyperLink control can be used to dynamically change the page that is being linked to, the text that is displayed to the user, and so on. Our last section on server-side code then looked at how we can pass information from one page to the next, how that can be retrieved on the page being linked to, and how this allows us to add far more functionality to a website, such as drill-downs from search-results.

Next, we saw that hyperlinks don't just have to be used for linking to other web pages; they can be used for sending e-mails, running JavaScript, or connecting to any number of other systems using different protocols such as FTP and HTTPS. Finally, we saw how links can be used within a web page so that resources such as JavaScript and CSS definitions can be shared across pages – saving time, and making site maintenance simpler.

# CHAPTER 12

# Reusable Content

In the previous chapter we looked at building websites, as opposed to single pages. We covered several important concepts about sharing and how this can make your life easier (you see, your Mom was right after all when she asked you to share your toys). Not only does sharing code make developing sites easier, but it also eases the burden if you have to change the site. None of us want to do more than is necessary, so doing it once is better than repeating it in several places.

A great feature of ASP.NET is that this technique can also be applied to parts of the interface, giving us the ability to not only avoid duplicating code, but also to bring consistency to our pages. In this chapter we're going to show you how:

- ❑ To create reusable content, using user controls
- ❑ That content can be easily used on multiple pages
- ❑ To customize reusable content
- ❑ To load content depending upon the user's choices

Although we're getting towards the end of the book, you can rest assured that user controls are just as easy as some of the topics we covered right at the beginning.

## What is Reusable Content?

This may be obvious, but it's important we explain what we mean when talking about reusable content. Simply put, it's content (including HTML, web controls, and code) that we want to use on multiple pages, or multiple times on the same page. We can wrap this content up within a special type of ASP.NET Page, called a **user control**. When creating user controls you use the same methods you've learned throughout this book – you drag web controls onto the design surface of the user control, you add code to interact with these web controls, and so on. We can then use this user control in the same way we use other web controls – by dragging it onto the design surface of other pages.

Creating a user control is just like creating an ASP.NET page – there's a template to help you. The main difference is that user controls have a different file extension. Standard ASP.NET web pages have an extension of `.aspx`, whereas a user control has an extension of `.ascx`. It's fairly easy to understand – the p stands for Page and the c stands for Control.

## When Should I Reuse Content?

Even though web pages within a site tend to be different, there are still plenty of examples of content that you'd want to use on more than one page. A really good example is the use of header and footer information. For example, consider the following pages:

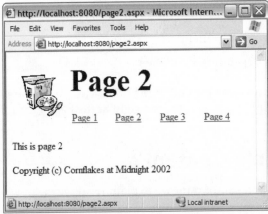

Notice that they look similar. The header area only differs with the header text, but the logo and links are the same. Likewise, the footer is the same. Both of these areas were created with a user control and just dragged onto the pages. Let's see how to do this.

## Try It Out    Creating a user control

**1.** First you need to add a new file. Instead of using the ASP.NET Page template though, you need to pick the ASP.NET user control. Call it `Footer.ascx`:

**2.** Now add the text you wish to display at the bottom of each page. I've used a copyright notice:

**3.** Save the page and close it.

**4.** Create another user control, this time calling it `Header.ascx`.

**5.** To get the layout we need for the header details we're going to use HTML tables. So, from the HTML menu (not the toolbox), select Insert Table…. From the dialog that appears, give the table 1 row and 2 columns, and leave the Width and Height as they are.

**6.** We want this table to stretch across the whole page, so select the table on the page. You'll have to hover the mouse pointer over the border of the table until the cursor changes (into a cross with arrows) before you select it. Once selected, set the **width** property to **100%** and delete the contents of the **style** property:

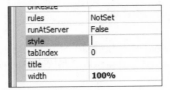

**7.** We also want to change the width of the first column, so click the mouse into the first cell. The **Properties** window will change to show properties for the **<TD>** element.

**8.** Change the **width** property to **15%**.

**9.** Drag an **Image** control from the Toolbox into this first cell, and set the **ImageURL** property to point to an image you want to use for the logo. You can copy the logo from the downloadable samples if you like. Resize the image, setting both the height and width properties to **90px**.

**10.** Drag a **Label** control into the second cell, delete the text from the **Text** property, and set the **ID** to **lblTitle**. You can also set the font size, perhaps to **XX-Large**.

**11.** Drag two **HyperLink** controls onto the page, putting them underneath the label. Add some spaces between each one so that they are easier to read. Change the **Text** properties to **Page 1** and **Page 2**, and the **NavigateURL** properties to **Page1.aspx** and **Page2.aspx**. Your control should now look like this:

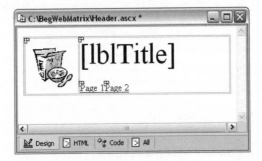

**12.** Now we need to add some code that will enable us to change the title in each page that uses the control. So, switch to **Code** view and add the following:

```
Public Property Title As String
  Get
    Return lblTitle.Text
  End Get
  Set
    lblTitle.Text = Value
  End Set
End Property
```

By adding a property to this control we allow it to be customized in the different pages on which it is used.

That's it for the controls, so save this page and close it. Now we need to see how to use them.

### Try It Out          Reusing Content

1.  Create a new ASP.NET Page called `Page1.aspx`.

2.  From the Workspace drag `Header.ascx` and drop it onto the page:

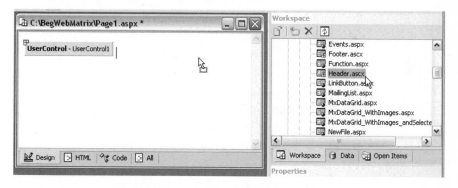

3.  Now type in some text – anything to identify this as page 1. Then drag `Footer.ascx` onto the page underneath:

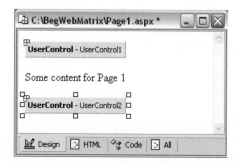

**4.** To set the title for the header we need to switch to HTML view (You can't change properties of user controls from the Property page in Web Matrix). The HTML for the header will look like this:

```
<uc0:Header id="UserControl1" runat="server"></uc0:Header>
```

When we created the control we added `Title` as a property, and this becomes available to us as part of the declaration, as an attribute. So change this HTML to:

```
<uc0:Header id="UserControl1" Title="Page 1" runat="server"></uc0:Header>
```

**5.** Save the page and close it.

**6.** Repeat the process with another ASP.NET Page, this time calling it `page2.aspx`. Use different title text so that it's easy to see the difference between two pages.

**7.** Now hit *F5* to run this, and click on the hyperlinks to flip between pages. See how the menu, logo, and copyright text appear on both pages, exactly the same.

## How It Works

There's actually very little to understand in regards to how user controls work. When you drag and drop them onto a page they act just like any other control, and their content is drawn along with the rest of the page content when the browser displays the page.

In our header control, the one thing that isn't automatic is the title, as we wanted to have the title different on each page. We needed a way of changing this, so we implemented this as a `Label` control. To gain access to this label we use a property. The user control is an object, so we can define properties on it. Since we only want one property, the `Title`, we added the following code:

```
Public Property Title As String
  Get
     Return lblTitle.Text
  End Get
  Set
     lblTitle.Text = Value
  End Set
End Property
```

Let's break this down. Firstly we have the declaration of the property. We define it as `Public`, so that it can be accessed from outside the user control. We need to do this to allow the property to be accessed when the control is used on another page.

```
Public Property Title As String
```

Next we define the `Get` part – this is how we can get the value of the title.

```
Get
   Return lblTitle.Text
End Get
```

Then we define the `Set` part, where we can set the title:

```
Set
   lblTitle.Text = Value
End Set
End Property
```

What's worth explaining is the use of `Value` in the `Set` part. This is a special object used in property declarations, and it's this object that contains the value being set. So, doing this:

```
Title="Page 1"
```

means that `Value` contains `Page 1`. When setting properties in the HTML declaration we use the attribute syntax:

```
<uc0:Header id="UserControl1" Title="Page 1" runat="server"></uc0:Header>
```

### Naming of User Controls

One thing that is worth mentioning is the way in which the user controls are linked into a page. When you drop a user control onto a page, Web Matrix adds the following line at the top of the page:

```
<%@ Register TagPrefix="uc0" TagName="Header" Src="Header.ascx" %>
```

This is only visible when you pick the All view from the editor, and it's this line that lets ASP.NET know which file the user control is using. This is worth mentioning because it allows you to understand how the control is named when it's used. If you think about the standard web controls, they are used like so:

```
<asp:TextBox ... />
<asp:Label ... />
```

The bit before the : is the prefix, and the bit after is the name. These are part of ASP.NET and so you don't need to tell the page where they come from. For user controls however, ASP.NET doesn't know where the control is, or what it should be called, so Web Matrix adds this line for us. This means that the control can be used on the page like so:

```
<uc0:Header id="UserControl1" runat="server"></uc0:Header>
```

Here uc0 is the TagPrefix and Header the TagName. When you drop a user control onto a page, Web Matrix assigns a tag prefix for you, and the tag name is taken from the file name of the user control.

## Making the Menu Dynamic

One limitation of this header control is that the menu is fixed. So if we wanted to change the menu we'd have to edit the header control itself. A far better way of implementing a menu is to use a data-bound control (such as a Repeater), and store the data elsewhere (such as a database or an XML file).

### Try It Out    Making the Menu Dynamic

1. Add a new item to your code directory. Pick XML File from the template list, naming it menu.xml. Add the following to the file that appears:

```
<menuItems>
    <menuItem Title="The First Page"    Src="page1.aspx" />
    <menuItem Title="Another Page"      Src="page2.aspx" />
    <menuItem Title="Last but not least" Src="page3.aspx" />
</menuItems>
```

2. Save the file and close it.

3. Open Header.ascx and delete the hyperlinks (and the spaces between them).

4. Drag a Repeater control into their place.

**5.** Switch to HTML view and change the repeater code so it looks like:

```
<asp:Repeater id="Menubar" runat="server">
  <ItemTemplate>
    <asp:Hyperlink id="Hyperlink1" runat="server"
            NavigateUrl='<%# Container.DataItem("Src") %>'>
      <%# Container.DataItem("Title") %>
    </asp:Hyperlink>
  </ItemTemplate>
  <SeparatorTemplate>
       
  </SeparatorTemplate>
</asp:Repeater>
```

Make sure you change the ID of the repeater control to `Menubar`.

**6.** Switch to All view, and add the following between the `Register` and `Script` parts:

```
<%@ import Namespace="System.Data" %>
```

It should look like this:

```
<%@ Control Language="VB" %>
<%@ import Namespace="System.Data" %>
<script runat="server">
```

**7.** Switch to Code view and add the following:

```
Public Sub Page_Load(Sender As Object, E As EventArgs)

  Dim dsMenu As New DataSet()

  dsMenu.ReadXml(Server.MapPath("menu.xml"))

  MenuBar.DataSource = dsMenu
  MenuBar.DataBind()

End Sub
```

**8.** Save the page and close it.

**9.** Open `Page1.aspx` and press *F5* to run it. Notice how the menu now shows what's in the XML file:

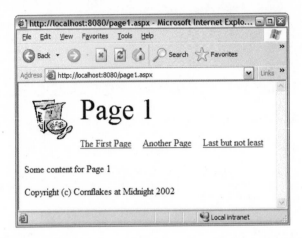

The really important point about this is that if you want to change the menu you can do so easily by changing the menu structure in the XML file, without worrying that you might accidentally change something in the user control. The user control is really just an ASP.NET page so it can run code as well as just being a place to hold content. In the above example the `Page_Load` event is used to read the XML file containing the menu items, and use this data to fill the `Repeater`.

# Make Reusable Content Clever

The previous example shows how code can be part of user controls, and you can take this even further. We added a property to the previous user control, allowing us to alter the content. Since the user control is an object we can also add methods. For example, think back to our dice game that we first introduced in Chapter 2. We first started with `Label` controls for the dice, and then we swapped the labels for images so it looked better. Thinking about what we know of reusable content, wouldn't it be sensible to use this technique for each of the dice? The dice user control could then take care of rolling itself, and displaying the right image.

Let's modify the dice program so that each of the dice is a user control. We'll give it a `Roll` method, so we can just drop one of our dice onto a page and tell it to roll itself.

## Try It Out — Dicing with User Controls

**1.** Add a new User Control, calling it `onedice.ascx`.

**2.** Add an Image to the new page.

**3.** In Code view add the following:

```
Public Function Roll() As Integer

    Dim diceValue As Integer

    diceValue = Int(Rnd() * 6) + 1

    Image1.ImageUrl = "images/" & diceValue.ToString() & ".gif"

    Return diceValue

End Function
```

**4.** Save the control and close it.

**5.** Open `dice.aspx` and delete the existing images used for the dice.

**6.** Drag two copies of `onedice.ascx` onto the page, in place of the existing images.

**7.** Rename these two controls `dice1` and `dice2`.

**8.** In Code view, change the code that runs when you click the roll dice button. It should now look like this:

```
Sub Button1_Click(sender As Object, e As EventArgs)

    Dim d1 As Integer
    Dim d2 As Integer

    d1 = dice1.Roll()
    d2 = dice2.Roll()

    Label3.Visible = False

    If d1 = 1 And d2 = 1 Then
        Label5.Text = Label4.Text
        If CInt(Label5.Text) > CInt(Label6.Text) Then
            Label6.Text = label5.Text
        End If
        Label4.Text = 0
        Label3.Visible = True
```

```
    Else
       Label4.Text = CInt(Label4.Text) + _
               d1 + d2
    End If

End Sub
```

**9.** Save the page and run it.

## How It Works

Let's first look at the code for the user control, starting with the function:

```
Public Function Roll() As Integer
```

Notice that it's a `Public` function – this is what makes it available to other pages.

Next we roll the dice, using exactly the same code to get the dice number.

```
Dim diceValue As Integer

diceValue = Int(Rnd() * 6) + 1
```

We then use this dice number as part of the filename for the image to display.

```
Image1.ImageUrl = "images/" & diceValue.ToString() & ".gif"
```

Finally we return the number thrown from the function.

```
    Return diceValue

End Function
```

The code here is no different from how it was before, except that it's now encapsulated within the dice control. This means that the die is entirely self-contained. Now we can use this die on the page – the only bit of code we need to look at is this:

```
d1 = dice1.Roll()
d2 = dice2.Roll()
```

Remember that when we dropped the dice controls onto our page we renamed them dice1 and dice2. So here, we are just calling the Roll method on each die. There are two dice, and each is rolled independently. We don't have to bother with how the die rolls itself, or how it shows the correct image – we just roll.

This reinforces the concept of reusability. If we suddenly want to change the game so that it uses 12-sided dice, we only have to change the Roll method. The game page itself doesn't need to change. We could also easily add a third die by just dropping another copy of the user control onto the page.

# Contain Yourself

With the Header control you saw that a user control is just a special ASP .NET page, and can contain other controls. You also saw with the above dice example, how you can have multiple copies of the same user control on one page. The question you might ask is how, if you have multiple copies of a control, you access the controls within it? For example, consider online purchasing, where you have to fill in both a home address and a delivery address. The fields for both addresses are exactly the same, so this is a good case for a user control.

Let's assume we have a user control that contains three TextBoxes – txtAddress, txtCity, and txtPostalCode. We drop that onto our page and call it HomeAddress. One would expect that you should be able to access these inner controls like so:

```
HomeAddress.txtAddress.Text
```

However, if you try that what you get the following compiler error:

**Compiler Error Message**: BC30390: 'ASP.Address_ascx.txtAddress' is not accessible in this context because it is 'Protected'.

This is because you can't access the controls with the user control directly. We have to do what we did with the header control and use a property as an intermediary between the inner control and the page that the user control sits on. Let's look at how we do this, especially when we use multiple copies of the same control.

**Try It Out**     **Containing Multiple Controls**

1.  Create a new ASP.NET User Control from the Add New File dialog, called
    `address.ascx`.

2.  Add some `Label` and `TextBox` controls so it looks like this:

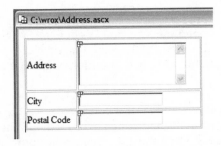

3.  Change the ID properties of these controls to `txtAddress`, `txtCity`, and
    `txtPostalCode`. Set the TextMode property of `txtAddress` to MultiLine.

4.  Switch to Code view and add the following:

```
Public Property Address As String
  Get
    Return txtAddress.Text
  End Get
  Set
    txtAddress.Text = Value
  End Set
End Property

Public Property City As String
  Get
    Return txtCity.Text
  End Get
  Set
    txtCity.Text = Value
  End Set
End Property
```

```
Public Property PostalCode As String
  Get
    Return txtPostalCode.Text
  End Get
  Set
    txtPostalCode.Text = Value
  End Set
End Property
```

**5.** Save the control and close it.

**6.** Create a new **ASP.NET Page** called `purchase.aspx`.

**7.** Drag two copies of `address.ascx` onto the page. You might like to use an HTML table to line them up next to each other, perhaps with some header text. Change the **ID** properties to `HomeAddress` and `DeliveryAddress`.

**8.** Add a **Button** underneath the address controls, and change the **Text** property to `Show Addresses`.

**9.** Finally add two **Label** controls. You should have something similar to the following:

**10.** Double-click the **Button** and add the following code:

```
Sub Button1_Click(sender As Object, e As EventArgs)

    Label1.Text = "Home address is:<br />" & _
        HomeAddress.Address & "<br />" & _
        HomeAddress.City & "<br />" & _
        HomeAddress.PostalCode

    Label2.Text = "Delivery address is:<br />" & _
        DeliveryAddress.Address & "<br />" & _
        DeliveryAddress.City & "<br />" & _
        DeliveryAddress.PostalCode

End Sub
```

**11.** Save the file and run it.

**12.** Add some details into all of the text fields and press the button:

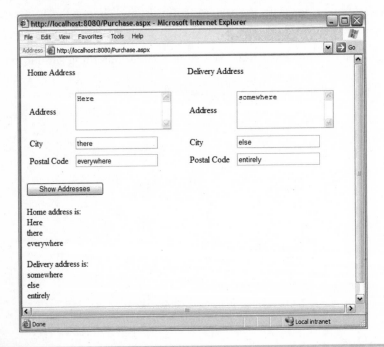

## How It Works

The important point about how this works is to remember that to provide access to controls within a user control you have to add public properties. Hence the property for each of the TextBox controls:

```
Public Property Address As String
...
Public Property City As String
...
Public Property PostalCode As String
...
```

This technique has the added benefit of hiding the internal implementation of the user control, allowing access to its functionality through easy-to-understand names.

The second stage is the use of two copies of the user control. Because there are two distinct copies, with separate names, the internal controls and properties are also distinct. This allows us to access them as individual controls, even though they are based on just one control description:

```
Label1.Text = "Home address is:<br />" & _
      HomeAddress.Address & "<br />" & _
      HomeAddress.City & "<br />" & _
      HomeAddress.PostalCode

Label2.Text = "Delivery address is:<br />" & _
      DeliveryAddress.Address & "<br />" & _
      DeliveryAddress.City & "<br />" & _
      DeliveryAddress.PostalCode
```

To understand what this is doing, let's take another look at the property for the `Address`:

```
Public Property Address As String
   Get
      Return txtAddress.Text
   End Get
   Set
      txtAddress.Text = Value
   End Set
End Property
```

This stores and retrieves values in the `TextBox` called `txtAddress`. When we fetch the address (as we do to display it on our main page), we are actually calling the `Get` part of the property, which 'gets' the value stored in the `TextBox`. We could do the opposite to set the address:

```
DeliveryAddress.Address = "4 High Street"
```

This would call the `Set` part of the property, which pushes the `Value` we've supplied into the `TextBox`.

**399**

# Dynamic Content

Another way of using content in this way is not so much to promote reuse, but for convenience. Let's consider the case where we have a page that displays several pieces of information, but we don't want them all displayed at once. One way we could achieve that is by wrapping each segment of information in a Panel control, and hiding them or making the visible when appropriate. The disadvantage with this is that the page gets quite long and is harder to edit.

Another issue is that you might like different people to be responsible for those different segments. Having several people responsible for a single page gives too many possibilities for errors as people invariable take copies, and overwrite others' content. So, if we have different people, then wouldn't separate pages be better? Yes, but this might not quite achieve what you want, perhaps keeping a unified look to parts of the page. One way around this is to have each segment of information in a user control, which you can then load on demand.

Let's consider an example using the downloadable sample case study, which is the website of the Cornflakes at Midnight fictitious band that we met previously. Here the band members each have a biography, detailing their ineptitude on a variety of instruments, and their love of strange music. We want the whole biography page to look the same, no matter which bio is being shown, but we also want the members to be able to update their own bio.

## Try It Out    Loading User Controls at Run Time

1. Create a new user control, called dave.ascx.

2. Add some content to make a biography for Dave. You can copy the one from the samples, or just make up something – he's fairly thick skinned so you can say anything you like about him 8)

3. Save this page and close it.

4. Create another user control, called al.ascx, and do the same with the content to create a biography for Alex.

5. Save this page and close it.

6. Add a new ASP.NET Page called bio.aspx, and add some title text:

   Band Biography

7. Underneath that, add two LinkButton controls. Change the Text properties to Alex and Dave.

**8.** Underneath the LinkButtons add a PlaceHolder control.

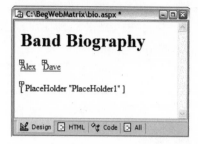

**9.** Double-click the first LinkButton (Alex) and add the following code:

```
PlaceHolder1.Controls.Add(LoadControl("al.ascx"))
```

**10.** Back in Design view, double-click the second LinkButton (Dave) and add the following code:

```
PlaceHolder1.Controls.Add(LoadControl("dave.ascx"))
```

**11.** Save the page and run it. Initially it will look like this:

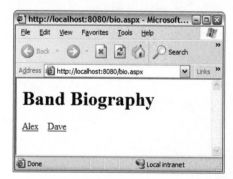

**12.** Click Alex and see how the content of the Alex user control is shown:

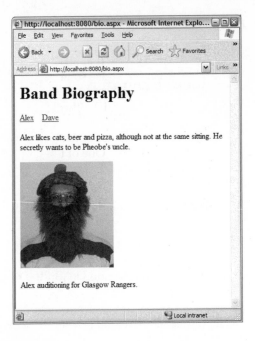

**13.** Do the same for Dave:

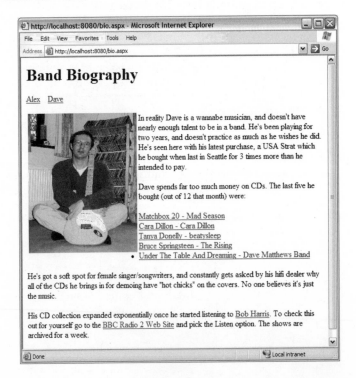

This code is extremely simple, relying on the fact that all controls can be created dynamically at run time and added to the page. This works because some controls can contain other controls (these are called Container Controls). The `PlaceHolder` is one of these, and is designed just for this purpose – as a holder in the page into which other controls can be added.

Container controls have a property called `Controls`, which is a collection (see Chapter 6 for more on these) of all of the controls they contain. One of the methods on this collection is `Add`, which allows us to add controls to the collection. To get the control to add we just use the `LoadControl` method and pass in the name of the user control:

```
PlaceHolder1.Controls.Add(LoadControl("al.ascx"))
```

So, this code simply loads a user control and adds it to the place holder.

You might wonder why we'd use this method instead of storing the content in a database. The simple reason is that databases aren't great at storing free-form content. They are very good at rigid structures, but not if you want each piece of information to differ in structure. Using the method shown above, the user controls can contain anything – there's no reason why each has to be similar to (or even the same as) the others.

# Summary

This chapter has been all about saving time. It may not seem that obvious, but it really is. I once saw a statistic that said developers spend 60% of their time maintaining old code. There are many reasons for this – badly designed systems, badly written code, inadequate development tools, and so on. Without rewriting completely is hard to rectify this for existing applications, but that shouldn't be the case for new applications.

The goal of all developers should be to write bug-free, easy-to-maintain code, and part of the way of doing that is to reuse existing code and content. The reason is simple – existing code and content has already been tested. This means that you not only save time during development, but also during testing, and your application will be more stable. More stable means less time going back to fix old code at a later date.

In this chapter we've explored just one method of reuse – that of user controls. These encapsulate both code and content, and allow you to quickly share common features between pages. In particular we've looked at how to create user controls to share parts of the interface, and then how to extend that model to include shared code. We then went a step further, showing how user controls can be used dynamically, allowing their display to be customised depending upon user actions.

# CHAPTER 13

# Case Study Part 1: Extending Your Web Application

In this chapter, we're going to begin to allow interaction with our website. As it's a site for a band, we want to develop a sense of community with our fans so that they feel as if they "belong" when they use the website.

To provide this interactivity, we're going to develop a **guest book** for users. Users will be able to come to the website and post comments for other users and band members to view and respond to.

In creating the guest book in this chapter, we'll cover the following topics:

❑   Using a datagrid for the guest book entries

❑   Customizing the grid so only the required columns are shown

❑   Adding custom text formatting to the grid, so that our user text is formatted correctly

❑   Creating a separate **component**, or **custom class**, where we can put the formatting code, so it can be use in more than one page

Most of this has been covered in earlier chapters, so what we're doing here is showing you how to bring it all together. Let's start by looking at what we need for our guest book.

## Creating a Guest Book

The guest book we're creating will allow users to post entries online. Here is a list of the functionality we're going to provide:

❑ They will be able to provide their name, a subject for their messages, and the message itself.

❑ Each entry will be logged with the date and time when it was created.

❑ The list of entries can be sorted by the user by name, subject, and posted date.

❑ The message can have multiple lines, can contain bolding and italics, and will have emoticons converted to graphics.

## Create the Guest Book Database Table

First of all, we need to create the data table for the guest book. We're going to call the table `GuestBookEntries`. We looked at creating tables back in Chapter 8, so we're going to use the same technique here. The columns we are going to need are:

| Column Name | Data Type | Properties | Value |
|---|---|---|---|
| GuestBookEntryID | Int | Required: | Yes |
| | | Primary Key: | Yes |
| | | Auto-increment: | Yes |
| | | First Value: | 1 |
| | | Increment: | 1 |
| Author | VarChar | Required: | Yes |
| | | Field Size: | 50 |
| Subject | VarChar | Required: | Yes |
| | | Field Size: | 100 |
| Message | Text | Required: | No |
| PostedDate | DateTime | Required: | No |
| | | Default: | getdate() |

Create the new table with the above columns and properties, using the same CAM database you created in Chapter 8. This gives us enough details to store user comments.

## Create Some Guest Book Entries

The first part of our guest book is going to show existing entries, so we need some data in the table. Add the following two rows of data – remember you shouldn't add anything to the ID column, as this will automatically be filled in for you:

| Author | Subject | Message | PostedDate |
|---|---|---|---|
| Brian Berry | First Message | I am the first poster. Cool :). I am the man! | 10/15/2002 10:33 |
| Nicole Malseed | I'm next | Yes, Brian, you ARE the man! | 10/16/2002 8:54 |

Don't worry if the dates turn into `null` values. In the early version of Web Matrix this is a bug, as the default value doesn't get inserted. When we enter dates from the web page this will work fine.

# Centralizing Database Configuration

Before we go ahead and build the guest book page, it's worth thinking about the rest of our site, and the other pages that access data. All of these will get their data from the same database. Near the end of Chapter 8 we used a connection string to contain the details of our database server, and this connection string was in the actual page. Think about the situation of lots of pages that need the same connection details – you have to have the connection string in *each* page. There's nothing wrong with that, so don't worry if you've done it elsewhere, but what would happen if you wanted to use a *different* database? You'd have to edit *all* of the pages to change the connection string for each one individually, and that would be a pretty repetitive and boring process!

The solution to this is to store the database connection details in a central location. That way, if we want to change it we only need to do so in *one place*. The location we are going to use is the ASP.NET configuration file, which is called the `web.config` file. This is an **XML text file**, and is easy to read and create. However easy it is, Web Matrix makes it easier by creating a template for us, so let's give it a go in the next *Try It Out*. We will encounter the `web.config` file again in Chapter 15 and XML when we discuss Web Services in Chapter 16.

### Try It Out      Creating a Configuration File

1.  Create a new file in Web Matrix, but instead of choosing an **ASP.NET Page** as we have been doing for most of the book so far, pick **Web.Config** from the (General) templates. Keep the file name as `web.config` (all lowercase) and then click **OK** to create the file.

2.  Change the first section of the XML file so that it looks like this:

```xml
<?xml version="1.0" encoding="UTF-8" ?>

<configuration>

  <!--
    The <appSettings> section is used to configure application-specific
    configuration settings.  These can be fetched from within apps by
    calling the "ConfigurationSettings.AppSettings(key)" method:
  -->

    <appSettings>
      <add key="cam"
       value="server=(local)\NetSDK;trusted_connection=true;database=cam"/>
    </appSettings>

  <system.web>
```

**3.** Save the file and close it, and that's it; our application now has a centralized connection string.

### How It Works

The configuration file is automatically handled by ASP.NET, and can contain lots of things (we'll see how it can be used for security in the next chapter, when we implement logging into our site and controlling who has access). All we want it for at the moment is to centrally store the database connection, and we can use the `<appSettings>` section for this. This section allows us to specify a custom string, and then fetch that later from our code. When ASP.NET starts, it reads the configuration file so we can access this from any code in any page.

When the file is created by Web Matrix, some sections are commented out. In XML, comments start with `<!--` and end with `-->`. Looking at the above configuration file, what we've done is to move the comment so that it only surrounds the text, which means the `<appSettings>` section is now live (and not commented out). We then change the values for key and value, substituting our values for what was there. We've just added the details of our database server (which is the MSDE instance installed with the .NET Framework samples).

Now that we've centralized our database details, let's crack on with creating the guest book page.

## Displaying Guest Book Entries

To start with, we'll display the entries on a web page. In the next *Try It Out*, we're going to create a page from a template that displayed the guest book entries. We'll explore the kind of decisions that you as a programmer will have to make as you begin to develop your own web sites.

**1.** Create a new Data Page file of type Data Report with Paging and Sorting and name it GuestBook.aspx:

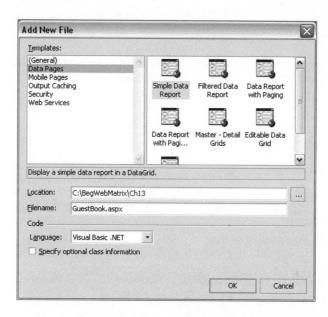

**2.** In the code that is generated, you will need to remove the ConnectionString object in the BindGrid() subroutine. The template code suggests we should update it, but since we don't need it any more, you can just delete it. This means the start of this routine (in the Code view, of course) should look like this:

```
Sub BindGrid()

   Dim CommandText As String
```

**3.** Now find the line where the connection object is declared:

```
Dim myConnection As New SqlConnection(ConnectionString)
```

and replace the use of connection string with the setting the web.config file, so that the line looks like the following:

```
Dim myConnection As New _
   SqlConnection(ConfigurationSettings.AppSettings("cam"))
```

**4.** The next thing we want to do in the `BindGrid()` subroutine is change the SQL commands. We want to show the author, subject, message, and posted date in the grid. So, we'll change it as shown below:

```
' TODO: update the CommandText value for your application
If SortField = String.Empty Then
    CommandText = "select Author, Subject, Message, PostedDate" & _
        " from GuestBookEntries order by PostedDate desc"
Else
    CommandText = "select Author, Subject, Message, PostedDate" & _
        " from GuestBookEntries order by " & SortField
End If
```

**5.** Now save the page. When you run the page for the first time, you should see something like the following:

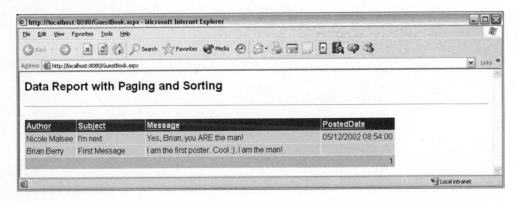

*As we pointed out earlier, don't worry if the **PostedDate** column is empty – it just reflects on the behavior when we inserted these two rows in the first place.*

## How It Works

The first thing we did was change the way we connect to the database. Instead of using an explicit connection string we now use the connection details stored in the configuration file. To access these we used the following line of code:

```
Dim myConnection As New _
    SqlConnection(ConfigurationSettings.AppSettings("cam"))
```

This simply reads in the value for the supplied key – in this case the key is `cam`. It returns the string from the `value` part of the configuration setting, and we used that in place of the `ConnectionString` variable.

Next, we changed the text used to fetch the data from the database. The default template text doesn't fit our database, so we just supplied our own table and column names:

```
If SortField = String.Empty Then
  CommandText = "select Author, Subject, Message, PostedDate" & _
    " from GuestBookEntries order by PostedDate desc"
Else
  CommandText = "select Author, Subject, Message, PostedDate" & _
    " from GuestBookEntries order by " & SortField
End If
```

The template that we used automatically allows sorting on columns, and our code caters for this. If no sorting is being done, then the SortField property will be empty, so we pick a default sort order of the PostedDate in descending order. If SortField has a value, then we sort by that instead.

## Fixing the Bug... What Bug?

We've got a bug in the page we just created though – try sorting by the different column headers. They all work except for the **Message** column. You'll get a SQL exception like the following:

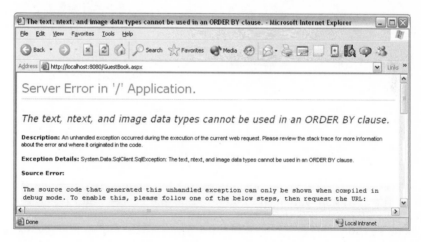

SQL doesn't allow sorting by columns of type Text, as the error clearly explains. Therefore, we need to turn off the ability to sort by that column. We also need to provide some enhanced formatting, which you'll see later in the chapter, so let's change the datagrid to use **templated columns**.

In the following example, we're going to take our existing page and explicitly tell ASP.NET which columns we want to display, and how we want to display them. This puts us in charge of the page, rather than relying on ASP.NET.

**Try It Out**     **Preventing Sorting for Columns**

**1.**  Go to the `GuestBook.aspx` page's **Design** view and pull up the properties for the datagrid. Click on the ellipsis (...) within the **Columns** property to pull up the **DataGrid1 Properties** dialog.

**2.**  Uncheck the **Create columns automatically at run time** box, and then add a **Template Column** to the right-hand listbox, by highlighting it in the left-hand column and clicking the > button once. Both the **Header text** and **Sort expression** should be set to **Author**:

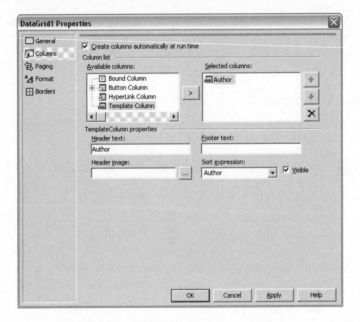

**3.**  Next, add another **Template Column**, setting the **Header Text** to **Subject** this time. For the **Sort expression**, you need to set it to **Subject, PostedDate**. This is due to the fact that several people might have posted entries with the same subject – it is nice to have a second field to sort on as well. This way, for example, if several people post entries with the subject of **Hello**, they'll be in chronological order.

**4.**  Next comes the **Message** template column. We only need to set the **Header text** box to **Message**. We don't want people to be able to sort on this column, so we'll leave the **Sort expression** blank.

**5.**  Finally, we have the **PostedDate** template column, with **Header text** set to **Posted Date** and the **Sort expression** set to **PostedDate**.

**6.**  Click **OK** to close the dialog, and in **Design** view the grid should now look like the following:

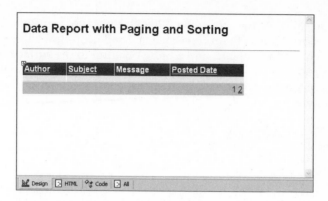

**7.** Right-click on the grid and choose **Edit Templates...** from the context menu. Then, choose to edit the **ItemTemplate** of the **Author** column. To do this, simply select the relevant option from the right-hand drop-down list:

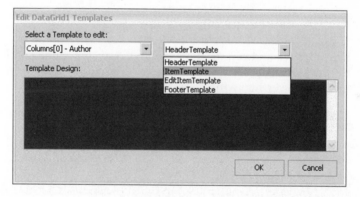

**8.** Drag a `Label` control onto the template's surface, right-click on it, and select **Edit Tag**. By default, Web Matrix, generates the following tag:

```
<asp:Label id="Label1" runat="server">Label</asp:Label>
```

Modify it to look like the following:

```
<asp:Label id="Label1" runat="server">
<%# Container.DataItem("Author") %>
</asp:Label>
```

We're using a `Label` control in this template to display the value of the **Author** field from the table.

*The template design dialog box is a bit bugged in the current release of Web Matrix. Most of the time, you can see the* Label *control graphically represented. However, sometimes, you'll only see a small glyph, and sometimes you won't see anything at all!*

**9.** Do a similar thing for the remaining **Subject**, **Message**, and **Posted Date** columns. Select the appropriate column from the left-hand drop-down list, select **ItemTemplate** from the right-hand template, add a `Label` control to the surface, right-click on it and select **Edit Tag**, and finally modify the tag. As a reminder, you should be including these lines in the tags for the labels in the different columns (changing the `id` of the label each time):

```
<asp:Label id="Label2" runat="server">
<%# Container.DataItem("Subject") %>
</asp:Label>
```

```
<asp:Label id="Label3" runat="server">
<%# Container.DataItem("Message") %>
</asp:Label>
```

```
<asp:Label id="Label4" runat="server">
<%# Container.DataItem("PostedDate") %>
</asp:Label>
```

**10.** Now, when you save and run the page, you will see something similar to before, except that the **Message** column is no longer a hyperlink. This means that this column no longer supports sorting, which is exactly what we wanted:

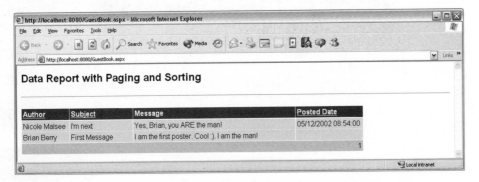

### How It Works

What we've actually done here is change the default behavior of the grid. By default, the grid automatically shows all columns, and because the template page we used allows sorting, we automatically get sorting on all fields. However, since the `Message` column is a `Text` column, we can't sort on it, so we needed to remove the sorting.

If you look at the HTML for the data grid, you should now see the following. First of all, there is the declaration of the grid and the styles:

```
<asp:datagrid id="DataGrid1" runat="server" AllowSorting="True"
              OnSortCommand="DataGrid_Sort" AllowPaging="True"
              PageSize="6" OnPageIndexChanged="DataGrid_Page"
              ForeColor="Black" BackColor="White" CellPadding="3"
              GridLines="None" CellSpacing="1" width="80%"
              AutoGenerateColumns="False">
  <HeaderStyle font-bold="True" forecolor="White"
              backcolor="#4A3C8C"></HeaderStyle>
  <PagerStyle horizontalalign="Right" backcolor="#C6C3C6"
              mode="NumericPages"></PagerStyle>
  <ItemStyle backcolor="#DEDFDE"></ItemStyle>
```

Next, we have the columns, each of which is a `TemplateColumn`. This means that the grid doesn't automatically display any content for it – we have to provide the content. For each column we are using a `Label`, and within that `Label` we are binding to a column in the database:

```
<Columns>
  <asp:TemplateColumn SortExpression="Author" HeaderText="Author">
    <ItemTemplate>
      <asp:Label id="Label1" runat="server">
        <%# Container.DataItem("Author") %>
      </asp:Label>
    </ItemTemplate>
  </asp:TemplateColumn>
  <asp:TemplateColumn SortExpression="Subject, PostedDate"
                      HeaderText="Subject">
    <ItemTemplate>
      <asp:Label id="Label2" runat="server">
        <%# Container.DataItem("Subject") %>
      </asp:Label>
    </ItemTemplate>
  </asp:TemplateColumn>
  <asp:TemplateColumn HeaderText="Message">
    <ItemTemplate>
      <asp:Label id="Label3" runat="server">
        <%# Container.DataItem("Message") %>
      </asp:Label>
    </ItemTemplate>
  </asp:TemplateColumn>
  <asp:TemplateColumn SortExpression="PostedDate"
                      HeaderText="Posted Date">
    <ItemTemplate>
      <asp:Label id="Label4" runat="server">
        <%# Container.DataItem("PostedDate") %>
      </asp:Label>
    </ItemTemplate>
  </asp:TemplateColumn>
</Columns>
```

# Entering New Guest Book Entries

Now that we can display guest book entries, we need to allow users to *create* them. A user will need to be able to enter their name, a subject for their message, and the message itself. When designing functionality like this where the user can view a list of records and also add new ones, you have to decide whether to keep the view and edit functionality on one page, or split the functionality into two separate pages. There are many decision points to determine which is best, and it's beyond the scope of what we're doing. For the purposes of our example, we'll leave everything on the same page, since a guest book can be sort of a conversation. As a result of this, it's good for the user to be able to refer to the previous entries while creating a new one.

First, let's design the graphical user interface for this functionality.

## Try It Out     A User Interface for the Guest Book

We're going to be reusing the `GuestBook.aspx` page we created just now, so open it if you haven't already got it open, and go to the **Design** view. Now do the following:

1. Under the **DataGrid** on the page, place an HTML table (**HTML | Insert Table...**) onto the page and then place the following controls and text, and set the appropriate properties for them:

| Control type | Property | Value |
|---|---|---|
| Label | ID | lblStatusMsg |
| | Text | |
| Textbox | ID | txtAuthor |
| | MaxLength | 50 |
| RequiredFieldValidator | ControltoValidate | txtAuthor |
| | ErrorMessage | You must enter your name! |
| Textbox | ID | txtSubject |
| | MaxLength | 100 |
| RequiredFieldValidator | ControlToValidate | txtSubject |
| | ErrorMessage | You must enter a subject! |
| Textbox | ID | txtMessage |

| Control type | Property | Value |
|---|---|---|
| | TextMode | MultiLine |
| | Rows | 5 |
| | Columns | 50 |
| Button | ID | btnOK |
| | Text | Create Entry |

You should also add some text in the table so that your page should look like the following:

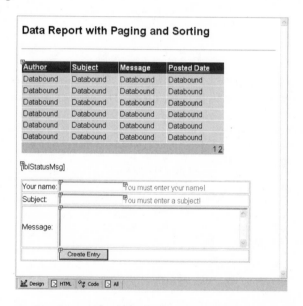

So that's our graphical user interface completed we'll now move on to the code that saves the new entries on the page to the database.

2.  Double-click on the **Create Entry** button to create a handler for the button's `Click` event, which fires, of course, when the button is pressed. Add the following code to the currently empty handler:

```
Sub btnOK_Click(sender As Object, e As EventArgs)
  Dim NumRecords As Integer = 0

  If IsValid Then
    NumRecords = _
      InsertGuestBookEntry(txtAuthor.text, txtSubject.text, txtMessage.text)
    If NumRecords = 0 Then
      lblStatusMsg.visible = True
      lblStatusMsg.text = _
        "An error occurred while trying to create the entry."
    Else
      lblStatusMsg.text = _
        "Entry created successfully. " & _
        "Thanks for letting us know what you think."
      InitPostForm
    End If
    BindGrid
  End If
End Sub
```

**3.** You now need to add the following function, which is called from the `btnOK` button's event handler and saves the details entered by the user into the guest book:

```
Function InsertGuestBookEntry(ByVal author As String, ByVal subject _
  As String, ByVal message As String) As Integer
  Dim conn As New _
    SqlConnection(ConfigurationSettings.AppSettings("cam"))
  Dim queryString As String = _
    "INSERT INTO GuestBookEntries (Author, Subject, Message)" & _
    " VALUES (@Author, @Subject, @Message)"
  Dim cmd As New SqlCommand(queryString, conn)
  Dim rowsAffected As Integer = 0

  cmd.Parameters.Add( _
    "@Author", System.Data.SqlDbType.VarChar).Value = author
  cmd.Parameters.Add( _
    "@Subject", System.Data.SqlDbType.VarChar).Value = subject
  cmd.Parameters.Add( _
    "@Message", System.Data.SqlDbType.Text).Value = message

  conn.Open()
  Try
    rowsAffected = cmd.ExecuteNonQuery()
  Finally
    conn.Close()
  End Try

  Return rowsAffected
End Function
```

**4.** The final function we need to add will initialize the form to allow the user to post another message after they have just created a new one:

```
Sub InitPostForm()
    txtAuthor.text = ""
    txtSubject.text = ""
    txtMessage.text = ""
End Sub
```

**5.** Test the page out now. When you create entry, you should see it appear at the top of the grid, and you should see the status message stating that it was successfully created.

**6.** Add the top three entries. For the **Message** for **Peter Armore** just enter <g>. Also, for the **Ryan Amburgy** entry make sure you press the *Return* key between the two lines – between the ! and the **I listen** should do it. You'll see why later, but the fact that the <g> doesn't show up should give you some clue.

Your screen should look like this now:

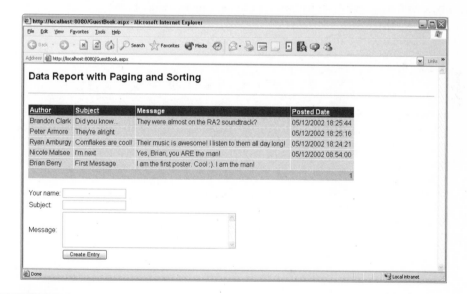

## How It Works

Everything about the user interface form should be fairly straightforward. We've set the maximum lengths on the name and subject `TextBoxes` to match the maximum field lengths in the database. Also, since the database requires name and subject, we've put `RequiredFieldValidators` next to them to ensure that the user specifies them. The `lblStatusMsg` label will be used to provide textual feedback to the user as they attempt to create new entries.

Let's now look at the button's click event handler.

First, we initialize the NumRecords object to 0 – this object will hold the function's return value. Then, we need to make sure the user has entered their name and the subject of the message:

```
Dim NumRecords As Integer = 0

If IsValid Then
```

The InsertGuestBookEntry() function is going to return the number of records created. We can use this to ensure that a record did get successfully created. Here, we call the InsertGuestBookEntry() function. We pass the author's name, the subject, and the message itself to the function:

```
NumRecords = _
    InsertGuestBookEntry(txtAuthor.text, txtSubject.text, txtMessage.text)
```

If NumRecords is 0, no record got created. If this is the case, we want to alert the user to this problem by displaying error information in the status message label:

```
If NumRecords = 0 Then
    lblStatusMsg.visible = True
    lblStatusMsg.text = _
        "An error occurred while trying to create the entry."
```

If a record was created, we'll let the user know that as well. Since it *was* created, we can call InitPostForm(), which will clear the form. We'll also reload the grid from the database through a call to BindGrid():

```
Else
    lblStatusMsg.text = _
        "Entry created successfully. " & _
        "Thanks for letting us know what you think."
    InitPostForm
End If
BindGrid
End If
```

Now, let's take a look at the InsertGuestBookEntry() function.

The parameters we expect are strings that contain the values for the author, subject, and the message. We will return an integer to the calling function. This integer will contain the number of records created by our insert statement, as we'll see in just a minute:

```
Function InsertGuestBookEntry(ByVal author As String, ByVal subject _
    As String, ByVal message As String) As Integer
```

We create a SQL connection using the connection string from the configuration file.

```
Dim conn As New _
    SqlConnection(ConfigurationSettings.AppSettings("cam"))
```

Next, the `queryString` object is set to the SQL statement:

```
Dim queryString As String = _
    "INSERT INTO GuestBookEntries (Author, Subject, Message)" & _
    " VALUES (@Author, @Subject, @Message)"
```

In this case, we're inserting a new record into table `GuestBookEntries`. We will set the `Author`, `Subject`, and `Message` fields to the values contained in the `@Author`, `@Subject`, and `@Message` parameters. Remember that when we created the `PostedDate` field, we set the default value to `getdate()` – this allows SQL to default to the current date, so we don't need to set it to anything here.

Next, we create a new command object and initialize it with the `queryString` and SQL connection created earlier:

```
Dim cmd As New SqlCommand(queryString, conn)
```

The `rowsAffected` integer will contain the number of rows created by the `INSERT` statement, and we default it to 0. This way, if the execution of the `INSERT` statement in the `Try ... Finally` block below fails, 0 will be returned to the calling function, indicating that no row was created:

```
Dim rowsAffected As Integer = 0
```

The three-parameter objects containing the values for the author, subject, and message are as follows:

```
cmd.Parameters.Add( _
    "@Author", System.Data.SqlDbType.VarChar).Value = author
cmd.Parameters.Add( _
    "@Subject", System.Data.SqlDbType.VarChar).Value = subject
cmd.Parameters.Add( _
    "@Message", System.Data.SqlDbType.Text).Value = message
```

Now we open the connection to the database and then execute the command:

```
conn.Open()
Try
    rowsAffected = cmd.ExecuteNonQuery()
Finally
    conn.Close()
End Try
```

Since we don't expect anything back from the INSERT statement that's being executed, we use the ExecuteNonQuery() method. We determine the number of rows created by setting rowsAffected to the return value from ExecuteNonQuery(). Regardless of whether the statement successfully executed or not, we want to close the connection, and this is done in the Finally block.

Finally, we return the number of rows created:

```
Return rowsAffected
```

Lastly in the code for the page, we have the InitPostForm() function, which simply resets all of the text fields to empty string values.

## Formatting the DataGrid Text

Now that we're allowing users to create entries, we can add some additional functionality to enhance the formatting of the values within the grid. In Chapter 5 you learned about the need to use HTMLEncode() to allow the display of special characters such as < and >. You also learned about converting carriage returns in SQL text fields into <br /> HTML tags so that multi-line text values would display correctly. Let's build a single function that can handle doing both of these things. That will help keep our code more concise.

**Try It Out**     **Formatting Our Entries**

**1.** Add the following code to GuestBook.aspx:

```
Function MyCstr(ByVal o As Object, Optional ByVal EncodeText As Boolean = _
    False, Optional ByVal ConvertCRToBR As Boolean = False) As String
    Dim str As String

    If o Is Nothing Then
        Return Nothing
    ElseIf o Is System.DBNull.Value Then
        Return Nothing
    Else
        str = CStr(o)
        If str = String.Empty Then
            str = Nothing
        Else
            If EncodeText Then
                str =server.HtmlEncode(str)
            End If
            If ConvertCRToBR Then
                str = Replace(str, ControlChars.CrLf, "<br />")
                str = Replace(str, ControlChars.Cr, "<br />")
                str = Replace(str, ControlChars.Lf, "<br />")
```

```
        End If
      End If
      Return str
    End If
End Function
```

2. Modify the `Author`, `Subject`, and `Message` template columns to call the `MyCstr()` function with the `Container.DataItems` as parameters. You can do this by simply going to the **HTML** view for the page and modifying the code as follows:

```
<Columns>
  <asp:TemplateColumn SortExpression="Author" HeaderText="Author">
    <ItemTemplate>
      <asp:Label id="Label1" runat="server">
        <%# MyCstr(Container.DataItem("Author"), True, True) %>
      </asp:Label>
    </ItemTemplate>
  </asp:TemplateColumn>
  <asp:TemplateColumn SortExpression="Subject, PostedDate"
                      HeaderText="Subject">
    <ItemTemplate>
      <asp:Label id="Label2" runat="server">
        <%# MyCstr(Container.DataItem("Subject"), True, True) %>
      </asp:Label>
    </ItemTemplate>
  </asp:TemplateColumn>
  <asp:TemplateColumn HeaderText="Message">
    <ItemTemplate>
      <asp:Label id="Label3" runat="server">
        <%# MyCstr(Container.DataItem("Message"), True, True) %>
      </asp:Label>
    </ItemTemplate>
  </asp:TemplateColumn>
  <asp:TemplateColumn SortExpression="PostedDate"
                      HeaderText="Posted Date">
    <ItemTemplate>
      <asp:Label id="Label4" runat="server">
        <%# Container.DataItem("PostedDate") %>
      </asp:Label>
    </ItemTemplate>
  </asp:TemplateColumn>
</Columns>
```

You can pass `False` to `ConvertCRToBR` because they are single-line values. Also, we pass `True` for `Message`.

3. We have already inserted some extra test rows into the table as part of the previous *Try It Out*. All we need to do to test our latest modifications is to rerun the page, remembering to refresh the page if need be. You should see something like this:

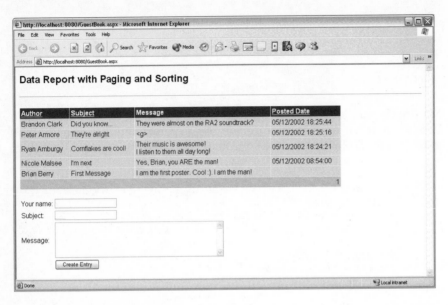

Note how the entry that spans multiple lines is now displayed correctly. Also, the <g> has been formatted and displayed correctly too. Let's talk about the function we created.

## How It Works

We call the function `MyCstr()` and we pass three parameters to it:

```
Function MyCstr(ByVal o As Object, Optional ByVal EncodeText As Boolean = _
    False, Optional ByVal ConvertCRToBR As Boolean = False) As String
```

O is an object we pass to be formatted. We make it type `Object` because `Container.DataItem` could return several different types of values, including a null value if the field value in the database doesn't contain anything. If we made O to be of type `String`, we couldn't handle this situation.

`EncodeText` is a Boolean flag specifying whether or not we want to `HTMLEncode` the string. Here, we've used the `Optional` keyword, so that we can skip this parameter if we want to. If we don't specify a value for the parameter, the default will be used.

`ConvertCRToBR` is another Boolean flag. This one specifies whether we want to search out the carriage-return and linefeed characters, and replace them with the `<br />` HTML tag (which is the HTML equivalent of a return).

Now let's look at the code. If we pass an object that is `Nothing`, we want to stop immediately. There's no need to continue any processing, and many text functions will raise an exception when one is passed to them:

```
If o Is Nothing Then
   Return Nothing
```

If the value in the database is `System.DBNull.Value`, we also want to stop immediately, and we'll return a string that is `Nothing`. We might get this value if the entry from the database doesn't have a value:

```
ElseIf o Is System.DBNull.Value Then
   Return Nothing
```

We then convert the passed object to a `String`:

```
str = CStr(o)
```

If `str` is `Empty`, we return `Nothing`. This indicates that we didn't have a string to process:

```
If str = String.Empty Then
   str = Nothing
```

Now that we are sure that we have some text, we need to see if the text *is* to be encoded. If so, we use `HTMLEncode` (see Chapter 5 for more details). Note that we have to do this before converting the carriage returns to <br />s, because if we did it in the reverse order, the <br /> itself would be encoded by `HTMLEncode`:

```
If EncodeText Then
   str =server.HtmlEncode(str)
```

You've seen the next part in Chapter 5 – this is where we use the `Replace()` function to replace one set of characters in a string with another:

```
If ConvertCRToBR Then
   str = Replace(str, ControlChars.CrLf, "<br />")
   str = Replace(str, ControlChars.Cr, "<br />")
   str = Replace(str, ControlChars.Lf, "<br />")
```

Here, we are replacing several things, all with the <br /> tag. We are replacing the carriage-return/linefeed combination (`CrLf`), then carriage-return (`Cr`), and then linefeed (`Lf`) – these are all possible entries for producing a new line. Note that you need to search for both together (`CrLf`) before searching for each individually, or you might get multiple <br />s.

## *More Formatting Options*

Now that we can ensure what's been entered into the field is displayed correctly, let's take it a little further. A little formatting goes a long way to letting users express themselves. So, to give them more flexibility when entering messages into the guest book, let's support the three most common formatting options: italics, bolding, and underlining. We know that the HTML for these are <i> and </i>, <b> and </b>, and <u> and </u>.

Let's allow the users to enter these tags into the message entry box. We also want to allow users to add emoticons to their messages. Emoticons are the keyboard characters that we use in messages to symbolize the way we feel. The most common is :), which represents a smiley face. When a user enters this emoticon or any of several others in their messages, we'll convert them to images to be displayed in the actual message.

**Try It Out**    **Formatting and Emoticons**

Let's see how to implement this functionality:

1.  Create the following function, called `ConvertEmoticonsAndFormatting()`, in the `GuestBook.aspx` page we've been using throughout the chapter:

```
Function ConvertEmoticonsAndFormatting(ByVal str as String) as String
    str = Replace(str, "&lt;b&gt;", "<b>")
    str = Replace(str, "&lt;/b&gt;", "</b>")
    str = Replace(str, "&lt;i&gt;", "<i>")
    str = Replace(str, "&lt;/i&gt;", "</i>")
    str = Replace(str, "&lt;u&gt;", "<u>")
    str = Replace(str, "&lt;/u&gt;", "</u>")
    str = Replace(str, ":)", "<img src=""Images/smiley.gif"">")
    str = Replace(str, ";)", "<img src=""Images/wink_smiley.gif"">")
    str = Replace(str, ":(", "<img src=""Images/sad_smiley.gif"">")
    str = Replace(str, ":o", "<img src=""Images/omg_smiley.gif"">")
    str = Replace(str, ":D", "<img src=""Images/big_smiley.gif"">")
    str = Replace(str, ":p", "<img src=""Images/tongue_smiley.gif"">")
    return str
End Function
```

2.  Modify the `Message` template column in the datagrid to call this function:

```
<asp:TemplateColumn HeaderText="Message">
  <ItemTemplate>
    <asp:Label id="Label3" runat="server">
      <%# ConvertEmoticonsAndFormatting(
          MyCstr(Container.DataItem("Message"), True, True)) %>
    </asp:Label>
  </ItemTemplate>
</asp:TemplateColumn>
```

3.  Now refresh the page and you should see the following:

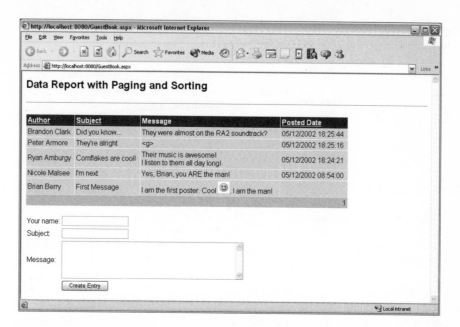

See how the :) characters have been converted into a smiley. You might like to try adding some more messages, using the underline or bold options, just to see these working too.

## How It Works

This function takes a `String`, modifies it, and returns the modified string to the calling function:

```
Function ConvertEmoticonsAndFormatting(ByVal str as String) as String
```

We search the strings for the encoded versions of the formatting tags. We then replace them with their unencoded versions. We do this because we encode the message text before passing it to this function – encoding the message is a good thing to do as it stops people adding potentially harmful HTML code into our application. If what the user types in is encoded, then it's safe for us to display. However, we do want the HTML formatting to show correctly, so we convert these from the encoded form back to HTML. The strings you see above (&lt;b&gt;, and others) are what the encoded versions look like. All of the other special characters in the message stay encoded, but these get put back to their original state, meaning that they will the formatting will be correctly displayed within the data grid:

```
str = Replace(str, "&lt;b&gt;", "<b>")
str = Replace(str, "&lt;/b&gt;", "</b>")
str = Replace(str, "&lt;i&gt;", "<i>")
str = Replace(str, "&lt;/i&gt;", "</i>")
str = Replace(str, "&lt;u&gt;", "<u>")
str = Replace(str, "&lt;/u&gt;", "</u>")
```

Next, we search for the emoticon characters and replace them with an HTML image tag that points to the GIF that we want to display to represent the emoticon:

```
str = Replace(str, ":)", "<img src=""Images/smiley.gif"">")
str = Replace(str, ";)", "<img src=""Images/wink_smiley.gif"">")
str = Replace(str, ":(", "<img src=""Images/sad_smiley.gif"">")
str = Replace(str, ":o", "<img src=""Images/omg_smiley.gif"">")
str = Replace(str, ":D", "<img src=""Images/big_smiley.gif"">")
str = Replace(str, ":p", "<img src=""Images/tongue_smiley.gif"">")
```

# Creating a Custom Class

We've now created a couple of functions, `MyCstr()` and `ConvertEmoticonsAndFormatting()`, that could be useful on more than just the guest book page. It's important to reuse your code as much as possible so that you're not reinventing the wheel each time you write a new application, as we saw in the previous chapter. Now, you could just copy and paste this code to each new page that needs it, but what happens if you enhance the functionality of the code, or if you fix a bug? If you do use the copy and paste method, you'd have to go to each page where the code existed and make the changes more than once. The better way is to create a **custom class** that is compiled and can be reused as needed.

When creating a custom class, we need to organize it into a namespace. A namespace is a logical method of organizing the functionality within applications. The .NET Framework has hundreds of classes. Without the ability to organize them somehow, there would be naming conflicts with the class names, and finding the functionality you needed would become unwieldy.

You will see namespaces and classes all throughout .NET, and you have seen some in the book already. `System.Data.SqlClient` and `System.Data.OleDb` are examples of namespaces. Within `System.Data.SqlClient`, there are many classes, such as `SqlError` and `SqlCommand`. All of .NET is organized in this way. When you come up with your own namespaces and classes, you can name them just about anything you want. We're going to create a namespace and class now. The namespace will be `CAM` and the class will be `Formatting`.

*We covered namespaces way back in Chapter 6 so if you've forgotten some of the details then please refer back to that chapter.*

---

**Try It Out**      **Creating a Class and Namespace**

**1.** Create a new Class file using Web Matrix, name it **CAM.vb**, and specify **CAM** for the Namespace and **Formatting** for the Class:

**2.** Move (cut and paste) the `MyCstr()` and `ConvertEmoticonsAndFormatting()` functions from `GuestBook.aspx` to the skeleton code that was generated by Web Matrix in the `CAM.vb` file, as shown below:

```
Imports System

Namespace CAM

  Public Class Formatting
    Public Sub New()

    End Sub

    ' Place MyCstr() and ConvertEmoticonsAndFormatting() functions here

  End Class
End Namespace
```

**3.** Change the function declarations by placing the keywords `Public` and `Shared` in front of them:

```
Public Shared Function MyCstr(ByVal o As Object, _
    Optional ByVal EncodeText As Boolean = False, _
    Optional ByVal ConvertCRToBR As Boolean = False) As String
...
Public Shared Function ConvertEmoticonsAndFormatting( _
    ByVal str as String) as String
```

**4.** At the top of the page, we need to import a couple of other namespaces. Add the two `Imports` as follows:

```
Imports System
Imports Microsoft.VisualBasic
Imports System.Web
```

**5.** Modify the following line in the `MyCstr()` function:

```
If EncodeText Then
    str = HttpUtility.HtmlEncode(str)
End If
```

**6.** That's it; our custom class is finished so just save the file for the time being.

## How It Works

Let's first look at the changes to the function declarations. The `Public` keyword allows us to call this function from *outside* the class itself. We didn't need this when the functions were within the ASP.NET page, but now that we've moved them into their own class we need a way to allow them to be accessed externally to the class.

The `Shared` keyword allows us to call the function without creating an instance of the class. Normally, when you have a class you create an 'instance' of it, which gives you access to properties and methods. However, our class is only a container for our formatting functions, and these don't need any properties – they run standalone. Making them `Shared` allows them to be called directly.

Next, we added two `Imports` statements. The `Microsoft.VisualBasic` namespace contains, among many other things, the `Replace()` function and the `ControlChars` enumeration. The `System.Web` namespace contains the `HttpUtility` class, in which is contained the `HttpEncode()` function.

Finally, we changed the way in which we called `HtmlEncode()`. The `HttpUtility` class contains the `HttpEncode()` function. When we had the function on the ASP.NET page itself, we could use the server object to call the `HttpEncode()` function, because the server object is intrinsic to all ASP.NET pages. Our new class, however, doesn't have this automatically available, so we have to use the `HttpUtility` class directly.

## Compiling the Custom Class

Now we need to compile this class. Before code within the .NET Framework can be run, it must be compiled from the high-level language code we write to instructions that the machine can understand and execute. Up until now, we've placed all code and objects onto distinct ASPX pages. The .NET Framework is very helpful with this type of development. It will compile ASPX pages on the fly, as, and when, they are requested by the web server. Once we get outside of this scenario, however, we must take the responsibility for compiling our code. When we compile code, a file is returned to us that contains the compiled instructions. Since we're compiling a class, we will get something called a **Dynamic Link Library** or a **DLL** for short.

Any supporting DLLs have to be accessible to whatever application will use them. The ASP.NET Framework requires that DLLs be placed into a directory called bin under the root of your application.

### Try It Out — Compiling and Using the Class

**1.** Create a new folder called bin *within* your current working folder. This is probably C:\BegWebMatrix\ if you've used the same directory structure as we described earlier in the book, so you will now also have a C:\BegWebMatrix\bin folder.

*The folders used in the code download separate out the code into chapter-by-chapter folders, so the root folder may in fact be C:\BegWebMatrix\Chapter13 on your system. The simple method to remember is to create the bin directory within the folder you use to run your examples.*

**2.** Create a new text file, either using Web Matrix, or Notepad, and enter the following code:

```
Set PATH=%SystemRoot%\Microsoft.NET\Framework\v1.0.3705
cd c:\BegWebMatrix\
vbc CAM.vb /t:library /r:System.Web.dll /out:bin\CAM.dll
pause
```

*Important – if you have installed the .NET Framework version 1.1, the version number of the Framework will be different. Navigate to your system directory, which will be either C:\Windows, or C:\WINNT, for example, then navigate to the Microsoft.NET\Framework folder, and look for the sub-folder with the highest number, and use that number in the path instead of v1.0.3705. Also, if your code root isn't C:\BegWebMatrix, you need to change that line too.*

**3.** Save this file as Compile.bat within your code directory, and double-check in your code folder to make sure this has been saved with the correct file extension (make sure a .txt hasn't been added to the end of the file name!)

*A .bat file, referred to as a **batch file**, is a way of processing a series of commands on the operating system.*

**4.** To compile `CAM.vb`, simply double-click the `Compile.bat` file and you will see a screen similar to the following:

Press a key when complete to close the window. We'll look at what this did in just a moment. This is all we need to create our DLL. Once we've done this, we need to change the `GuestBook.aspx` file. Let's do this now.

**5.** Change the template columns as shown below:

```
<Columns>
  <asp:TemplateColumn SortExpression="Author" HeaderText="Author">
    <ItemTemplate>
      <asp:Label id="Label1" runat="server">
        <%# CAM.Formatting.MyCstr(
            Container.DataItem("Author"), True, False) %>
      </asp:Label>
    </ItemTemplate>
  </asp:TemplateColumn>
  <asp:TemplateColumn SortExpression="Subject, PostedDate"
                      HeaderText="Subject">
    <ItemTemplate>
      <asp:Label id="Label2" runat="server">
        <%# CAM.Formatting.MyCstr(
            Container.DataItem("Subject"), True, False) %>
      </asp:Label>
    </ItemTemplate>
  </asp:TemplateColumn>
  <asp:TemplateColumn HeaderText="Message">
    <ItemTemplate>
      <asp:Label id="Label3" runat="server">
        <%# CAM.Formatting.ConvertEmoticonsAndFormatting(
            CAM.Formatting.MyCstr(
            Container.DataItem("Message"), True, True)) %>
```

```
      </asp:Label>
    </ItemTemplate>
  </asp:TemplateColumn>
  <asp:TemplateColumn SortExpression="PostedDate"
                      HeaderText="Posted Date">
    <ItemTemplate>
      <asp:Label id="Label4" runat="server">
        <%# Container.DataItem("PostedDate") %>
      </asp:Label>
    </ItemTemplate>
  </asp:TemplateColumn>
</Columns>
```

We now have to specify the fully qualified path to the function. In this case, it's
CAM.Formatting.*functionname*.

## How It Works

Let's look at how the compilation process worked by taking apart our batch file line-by-line:

```
Set PATH=%SystemRoot%\Microsoft.NET\Framework\v1.0.3705
```

The first part of our command creates a temporary shortcut to a location containing the file that
compiles our code, which is a file called vbc.exe. The %SystemRoot% bit of the path refers to the
directory Windows is installed in, which could be C:\Windows, or C:\WINNT. The final location is
version-specific, so you may need to alter this path if you install .NET version 1.1 when it's released.

```
cd c:\BegWebMatrix\
```

The next line changes the working directory for the compiler to match the working directory of
our web application.

```
vbc CAM.vb /t:library /r:System.Web.dll /out:bin\CAM.dll
```

The next line is where the compilation actually occurs. Notice that we are using the vbc
command, which runs the vbc.exe file we mentioned earlier. Let's look at the options we
specify in the compilation command:

| Parameter | Description |
|-----------|-------------|
| CAM.vb | This is the file we're compiling. |
| /t:library | Next, we specify the type of file we're creating. In this case, we're creating a DLL, which is specified as a library. |

*Table continued on following page*

| Parameter | Description |
|---|---|
| /r:System.Web.dll | We use functionality contained within System.Web.dll. This parameter tells the compiler that it should be referenced. |
| /out:bin\CAM.dll | We're naming and saving the DLL to a file at the specified location. Since our working directory is C:\BegWebMatrix, the file will be saved to the bin directory we created earlier within this location. |

The final statement "pauses" the window that displays our progress, so that it doesn't simply disappear once execution of the file is completed:

```
pause
```

This gives us a chance of seeing any error messages that may be generated. This line also gives us the "Press any key to continue . . ." prompt.

This may seem like a lot of work, and it definitely is more involved than simply keeping the code on the same page where it's going to be used. However, as your websites get more sophisticated, you'll save tremendous amounts of time by reusing your code in this manner.

## Finishing the Guest Book

The last thing we need to do is fit the guest book into the rest of the site. To do this, we need to put the menu user control on the page and add a reference to the site's style sheet.

### Try It Out     Tidying up the Guest Book

1.  First, let's add a <Head> tag to the page that contains the stylesheet link (make sure you have Style.css from Chapter 11 available in your code directory):

```
<html>
<head>
<% = "<link href=""Style.css"" type=""text/css"" rel=""stylesheet"" />" %>
</head>
```

One thing to note is that you need to put the link to the stylesheet inside <% %> tags. This is because there's a bug in Web Matrix at the time of this writing that prevents design mode from working correctly on some systems when a stylesheet reference is in the header section. The design mode will show glyphs for controls instead of the controls themselves. (We've seen this bug earlier in the chapter, when editing item templates.)

2.  Now we need to add the menu control. First, add the @ Register page directive for

the user control to the top of the page in the **All** view:

```
<%@ Page Language="VB" %>
<%@ Register TagPrefix="CAM" TagName="Menu" Src="Header.ascx" %>
<%@ import Namespace="System.Data" %>
<%@ import Namespace="System.Data.SqlClient" %>
```

You need to make sure that Header.ascx from Chapter 12, and its associated XML file, menu.xml, are both in your code directory.

**3.** Back in the **HTML** view, add the user control itself to the page in place of the default title:

```
<h2>
    <CAM:Menu id="Menu" title="Guest Book" runat="server"></CAM:Menu>
</h2>
```

**4.** Finally, we need to change the XML file that defined the links, menu.xml, to point to the available pages in our site. Amend the file so that it contains the following code:

```
<?xml version="1.0" encoding="utf-8" ?>
<menuItems>
    <menuItem Title="Home" Src="Default.aspx" />
    <menuItem Title="Discography" Src="Discs.aspx" />
    <menuItem Title="Biography" Src="Bio.aspx" />
    <menuItem Title="Download" Src="Download.aspx" />
    <menuItem Title="Guest Book" Src="GuestBook.aspx" />
</menuItems>
```

That's it. When you run your page now, it will look consistent with pages we have created earlier in the book:

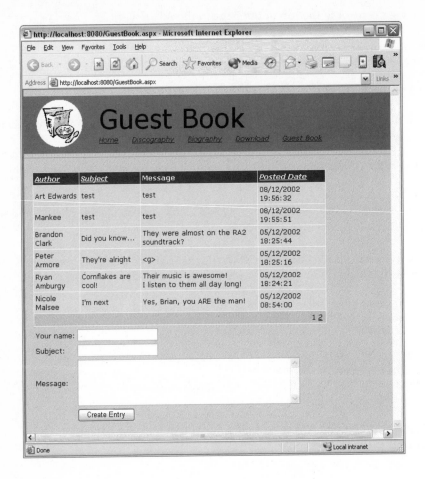

## Summary

Most of what you've seen in this chapter hasn't been new – it's been covered elsewhere in the book. What we've started to do however, is to pull many of the techniques you've learned together, showing how to create integrated pages. In particular we've looked at:

- ❑ Creating a database table – We created a new table for our guest book entries, to allow the fans of the band to leave messages.

- ❑ Centralizing database connection details – Here, we used the ASP.NET configuration file (web.config) to store the connection string for our database. This allows us to have these details in only a single place, allowing them to be maintained more easily.

- ❑ Displaying guest book entries – We looked at using the default properties of the grid, and then we customized them to only show the columns we required, and to ensure that we could only sort on the columns we needed to sort on.

❑ Adding new guest book entries – Here, we showed how to call a SQL statement to insert a fan message into the guest book.

❑ Formatting a guest book message – Here, we used some custom formatting within our data-binding expressions to show some nicer formatting. This sort of ability brings a more human touch to the guest book, and makes it more enjoyable to use.

❑ Centralizing code – Next, we moved our formatting functions into a central location, to allow them to be used elsewhere in our application. This saves having to duplicate code at a later point.

At the end of the chapter, we integrated the guest book into our existing website, giving the fans a great and easy way to communicate with the band. Now we're going to look at the flip side – a way for the band to communicate with their fans by adding a tour diary, and some security so that only the band members can log into the diary pages.

# CHAPTER 14

# Case Study Part 2: Identifying Your Users

In this chapter, we're going to create a **tour diary** for our Cornflakes at Midnight application. This is where band members create entries much like the guest book entries you saw in the previous chapter. They can talk about how the tour is going, harass the other members publicly, and just generally talk about whatever comes to mind that they think their fans would be interested in knowing.

Here's a specific list of what we're going to provide with the tour diary:

- The band members will be able to log on **securely** to the diary.

- They will be able to create entries with a subject line, and the message text itself. The name will be set to the same value as their logon name.

- Each entry will be logged with the date and time when it was created.

- The list of entries can be sorted by the username, subject, and posted date.

- The message will have the same formatting as the guest book.

# Security

Obviously, we need to secure this part of the website so that only band members can access it. There are several ways of providing security in .NET. Here's a quick rundown:

❑ **Windows** – You are prompted for your Windows username and password. Your entry is checked against the Windows user account database. If you are a valid user in Windows, you are allowed access to the site. There are many advantages to this method in an intranet environment. One advantage is that if they already have Windows accounts, they're logged on to their workstation with that account, and they're using a Microsoft browser, it's possible for users to access the secure website without ever having to re-enter their credentials. Instead, the credentials with which they're logged onto the workstation are passed through to the web application. This is very convenient.

❑ **Forms** – A user enters their username and password on a login page. It is then up to you, the developer, to determine whether or not the user is valid. .NET provides a basic authentication method, which we'll utilize in a moment.

❑ **Passport** – This mode uses Microsoft's Passport security mechanism to allow or disallow access to the site. Passport is the security mechanism used throughout Microsoft and other vendor's web presences. An example of where it's used by Microsoft can be found within Microsoft's MSN Messenger. Other third-party sites such as eBay.com and Buy.com allow you to sign into their sites with it as well.

For more info on it, check out http://www.microsoft.com/passport.

In our example, we're going to use the Forms-based authentication. There are several reasons for this:

❑ It doesn't require the users to have Windows accounts. Using Windows accounts is great if you're in an intranet environment where your users already have accounts. Setting up security is a little more complicated using this method, because you have to set file-level permissions on the website.

❑ Passport is overkill. It's much more complicated to add Passport security to your site, and many users wouldn't want to sign up for a Passport account anyway. You'll see that most non-Microsoft sites that allow you to sign in with Passport also provide an alternative sign-in method as well.

❑ Forms-based authentication is the most flexible. You can set it up very quickly to use the Web.config file (we'll talk about this file in a minute) to store credentials, or you can get much more complex and use a database to store credentials and role information that specifies exactly what a user can and cannot do within the application.

## The Configuration File

As mentioned in the previous chapter, the Web.config configuration file contains configuration for ASP.NET applications. We used it for the database connection string details, but it has many sections, one of which allows setting the security options. What we'll be doing here is using the security sections to define which parts of the site are secure, and who can access those secure sites.

Each ASP.NET application on your web server can have its own Web.config file. It should be placed in the root directory of the application you're configuring. If you are using IIS to access this sample, you'll need to make sure that the virtual root is configured as an application. See Appendix A for more details on this.

# Configuring a Secure Site

We're going to go the simple route and store our **credentials** in the Web.config file. We can do this in our situation because the members of the band shouldn't change very often. Therefore, there won't be much administration of these accounts required. If you had a situation where you were changing users a lot, it would make more sense to have a database-driven security model.

We need to set up a configuration file for our secure section of the site.

**Try It Out**     **The Web.config File**

1. If you haven't already got one, create a file called Web.config using the built-in Web Matrix template.

2. Insert the following configuration XML as shown below. You can delete any existing authentication and authorization sections:

```
<configuration>

  <system.web>
    <authentication mode="Forms">
      <forms name=".ASPXAUTH" loginUrl="Secure/Login.aspx">
        <credentials passwordFormat="Clear">
          <user name="john" password="passjohn" />
          <user name="al" password="passal" />
          <user name="dave" password="passdave" />
          <user name="colt" password="passcolt" />
          <user name="james" password="passjames" />
        </credentials>
      </forms>
```

```
      </authentication>

      <authorization>
         <allow users="*" />
      </authorization>
   </system.web>

   <location path="Secure">
    <system.web>
       <authorization>
          <deny users ="?" />
       </authorization>
     </system.web>
   </location>
</configuration>
```

## How It Works

As we've talked about, the way you authenticate a user with Forms-mode authentication is totally up to you. One method is to include the users' credentials in the Web.config file itself, as we did above. This is great for simple applications like ours that have few users, and whose users don't change very often. As you can imagine, if you had lots of users, and you needed to make changes to them often, constantly editing this configuration file would get very repetitive and dull! It could also be error-prone. If you break the XML schema of the Web.config file, your application will throw exceptions.

Here is an explanation of our Web.config file. We have to set up the authentication section, which specifies the attributes of your users and the method of logging in, and the authorization section, which specifies what the authenticated users can access and what their levels of permissions are.

The following line specifies we're using Forms-mode authentication:

```
<system.web>
  <authentication mode="Forms">
```

The name attribute specifies the name of the cookie that's used to track the user's authentication status. The default is .ASPXAUTH. You should change this if you have more than one secure directory using different credentials on the same website:

```
<forms name=".ASPXAUTH" loginUrl="Secure/Login.aspx">
```

The loginURL is the page the site redirects a user to when they try to access a page when they're not authenticated. In a minute we'll create the Login.aspx file itself.

The next line is the beginning of the section that has the users' credential information stored. The `passwordFormat` specifies how the passwords are encrypted. There are several possibilities that allow a password to be stored in a way that prevents viewing of the password itself in the configuration file. We're using `Clear`, which simply means we'll type the password in a standard textual format:

```
<credentials passwordFormat="Clear">
```

Next are the users themselves. We simply specify a name and password, and the user will use these combinations to gain access to the site:

```
<user name="john" password="passjohn" />
<user name="al" password="passal" />
<user name="dave" password="passdave" />
<user name="colt" password="passcolt" />
```

The authorization section is unique in that it's actually possible to have multiple sections for different locations. First, we specify the default permissions:

```
<authorization>
  <allow users="*" />
</authorization>
</system.web>
```

This section specifies what kind of users can gain access to the site. There are two tags, `allow` and `deny`. You can specify usernames specifically within either tag by using a comma-delimited list, or you can use wildcards. There are two wildcards. The ? represents users that aren't authenticated. The * represents all users, authenticated or not. When you have multiple `deny` and `allow` tags, the system checks the user against each tag from top to bottom. As soon as the user matches one of the tags, they are either allowed or denied based on the tag type.

What we do next is override the settings for the location specified, in this case the `Secure` directory. You can also specify a specific file if you want. For this location, we are denying unauthenticated users. This will force them to log in using the `Secure/Login.aspx` page specified earlier in the `Web.config` file:

```
<location path="Secure">
  <system.web>
    <authorization>
    <deny users ="?" />
    </authorization>
  </system.web>
</location>
</configuration>
```

You should note that, in general, storing passwords in a text file is a *bad* idea, especially if they *aren't* encoded. This is because if anyone gets access to the text file, they then get your passwords. For this example, this is safe enough, but for commercial applications it's best to use another form of storage, perhaps a database. In the online version of the samples running at **http://alanddave.com/books/7922/cam/** the user details are stored in SQL Server. The login page on that site details and code of how this is done.

## Creating the Login Page

Now that we've got the security for the site configured, we need a way for the user to log on. Fortunately, Web Matrix provides a template for this, so it will be nice and easy to implement.

**Try it Out**     **The Login Page Template**

1. Create a new directory in your current working directory, and call it `Secure`.

2. Add a new page to the `Secure` directory, choosing the **Login Page** template from under the list of **Security** templates, and name the file `Login.aspx`:

3. In the Code view, change the code that's generated to look like the following:

```
Sub LoginBtn_Click(Sender As Object, E As EventArgs)

   If Page.IsValid Then
     If FormsAuthentication.Authenticate(Username.Text, UserPass.Text) Then
       FormsAuthentication.RedirectFromLoginPage(UserName.Text, true)
     Else
       Msg.Text = "Invalid Credentials: Please try again"
     End If
   End If

End Sub
```

**4.** If the `Web.config` file doesn't already live in the `Secure` folder, along with `Login.aspx`, then move it now. You can now save and run the login page, and here is what you will see:

One of two things will happen now if you try to log in on this page.

If you submit incorrect credentials in the textboxes, then you will see this screen:

Note the helpful error message that is returned.

If you submit the correct credentials as dictated by the `Web.Config` file, then you will come across the following error screen:

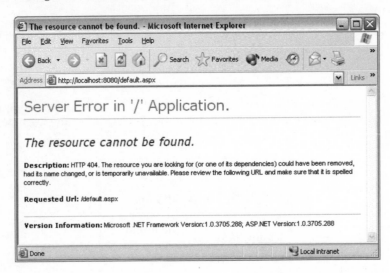

This is because we have not yet created the `Default.aspx` page that the web application looks for after a user logs in. We have already seen in Chapter 11 how to do this but you will see a quick recap on this, after we have seen how the code works.

## How It Works

The page contains two textboxes, one for the user to enter their username and the other for them to enter their password. When they click on the **Login** button, the code above is executed. Let's take a look at it now:

```
If FormsAuthentication.Authenticate(Username.Text, UserPass.Text) Then
```

The `Authenticate()` function in the `FormsAuthentication` class takes a username and password as parameters. It then compares these to whatever credentials you've provided. In this case, we provided credentials in the `Web.config` file, so the function checks to see if the username and password are in it. If the username and password combination is in the credentials, it also checks the `Authorization` section of the `Web.config` to make sure the user is allowed to access the requested content. If the user is allowed to access it, the function returns `True`. If not, it returns `False`.

If the user was authenticated, we call the `RedirectFromLoginPage()` method:

```
FormsAuthentication.RedirectFromLoginPage(UserName.Text, True)
```

The first parameter above specifies the user's name. This can technically be anything you want, but it usually corresponds to the user's logon name. The second parameter specifies whether the cookie should remain valid across browser sessions. If set to `True`, the cookie will remain valid even if the browser is shut down and restarted. Therefore, the user won't have to log on again. This is great option for sites that need minimal security, but for others, I would set this to `False`. This is because when you set this value to `True`, you take the chance that someone might use your workstation after you and access the site under your name.

We have a message label on the page that we can use to provide feedback to the user as they attempt to log on. In this case, we let them know that their credentials are invalid:

```
Else
    Msg.Text = "Invalid Credentials: Please try again"
```

## Creating the Options Page

As we mentioned at the end of the previous *How It Works* section, we need to have a page that a band member sees when they first log on. This will show them all of the things they can do within the secure site. This concept is similar to the linking to a default page functionality we saw in Chapter 11, but this time we are tying it in with security concerns.

---

**Try It Out**     **Where to go after Logging in?**

**1.**  Create a new page called `Default.aspx`, within the `Secure` directory:

**2.**  In the Design view for the page, add the following controls and set their properties:

| Control Type | Property | Value |
|---|---|---|
| Label | ID | lblWelcome |
| | Text | Welcome |
| Hyperlink | NavigateURL | TourDiary.aspx |
| | Text | Tour Diary |
| Hyperlink | NavigateURL | Logout.aspx |
| | Text | Log Off |

You should have something similar to the following. It's not pretty, but it serves our purposes:

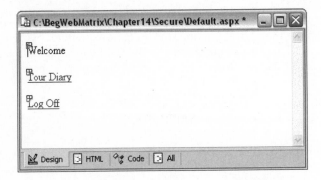

Now you should be able to login through your Login.aspx page and once authenticated, you should see Default.aspx we just created.

## Creating the Logout Page

Before we create the tour diary functionality, let's complete the security of the site by allowing the user to log off. Fortunately, there's a template for this too.

---

**Try It Out**     **Logging Out of the Site**

**1.** Create a page called Logout.aspx using the **Logout Page** template under the **Security** option in the **Add New File** dialog:

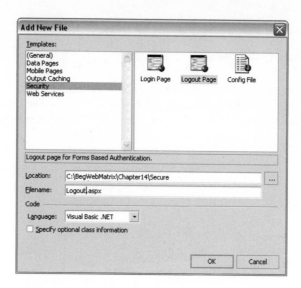

2. Try to log in to the website, view the `Default.aspx` page, and then choose Log off from the list of options on `Default.aspx`. After you click the Log Off button, you will see the following page:

It's interesting to note that when you first click the Log Off button on the `Logout.aspx` page, you'll see the message stating that you're not authenticated. If you click the button a second time, however, you'll be redirected to the `Login.aspx` page. This is because you can't even access the `Logout.aspx` page after the `FormsAuthentication.SignOut()` method has been called.

That's it. Let's look at the simple code that's generated and see how it's working.

## How It Works

The intrinsic `Request` object has an `IsAuthenticated` property that specifies whether or not the user has been validated against a set of credentials:

```
Sub Page_Load(Sender As Object, E As EventArgs)

   If (Request.IsAuthenticated = true) Then
```

If the user is authenticated, we display their username and the fact that they are logged in. The User object contains several properties and methods. The one we're utilizing here is Name, which returns the same value we passed to the FormsAuthentication.Authenticate() method above:

```
Status.Text = "User " & User.Identity.Name & " is currently logged in."
```

To log the user out, call FormsAuthentication.SignOut():

```
Sub LogOffBtn_Click(Sender As Object, E As EventArgs)

   FormsAuthentication.SignOut()
   Status.Text = "Not authenticated."

End Sub
```

The user's authentication cookie will be removed and they will have to log on again.

# Creating the Tour Diary Page

We're going to get really lazy here and reuse most of the GuestBook.aspx page's functionality, which we created in the previous chapter. Using the **Data** window, create a new table in the CAM database, and call it TourDiaryEntries. Use the following columns:

| Column Name | Data Type | Property | Value |
|---|---|---|---|
| TourDiaryEntryID | Int | Required: | Yes |
| | | Primary Key: | Yes |
| | | Auto-increment: | Yes |
| | | First value: | 1 |
| | | Increment: | 1 |
| Author | VarChar | Required: | Yes |
| | | Field Size: | 50 |
| Subject | VarChar | Required: | Yes |

| Column Name | Data Type | Property | Value |
|---|---|---|---|
| | | Field Size: | 100 |
| Message | Text | Required: | No |
| PostedDate | DateTime | Required: | No |
| | | Default: | getdate() |

The `TourDiaryEntries` table is structured exactly the same as the `GuestBookEntries` table that we created in the previous chapter.

## Try It Out    Creating the Tour Diary

Ever feel like wanting to cut corners on an assignment? I do, right now, so here's what we're going to do:

**1.** First of all, you need to copy `GuestBook.aspx` from the previous chapter into a new file called `TourDiary.aspx` in the `Secure` directory. The easiest way to do this is using Windows Explorer to manipulate the files as you would with any other files.

**2.** Open `TourDiary.aspx` and display the All view.

**3.** Remove the `Register` directive at the top of the page for the menu. We're not going to use the `Menu` user control on this page since we're not using that look and feel for our secure site. We're going with the "barren" look!

**4.** Next, we need to change the `Page_Load` subroutine. Instead of asking the user for their name, we're going to display their name based on their login. So here, we'll set the new label that will display the user's name:

```
Sub Page_Load(Sender As Object, E As EventArgs)

  If Not Page.IsPostBack Then

    ' Databind the data grid on the first request only
    ' (on postback, rebind only in paging and sorting commands)

    lblAuthor.text = User.Identity.Name
    BindGrid()

  End If

End Sub
```

**5.** Edit `BindGrid()` to read records from the `TourDiaryEntries` table instead of `GuestBookEntries`:

```
Sub BindGrid()

  Dim CommandText As String

  ' TODO: update the CommandText value for your application
  If SortField = String.Empty Then
    CommandText = "select Author, Subject, Message, PostedDate" & _
                  " from TourDiaryEntries order by PostedDate desc"
  Else
    CommandText = "select Author, Subject, Message, PostedDate" & _
                  " from TourDiaryEntries order by " & SortField
  End If
```

**6.** Rename the `InsertGuestBookEntry()` method to `InsertTourDiaryEntry()` and modify the query string to insert into the correct table:

```
Function InsertTourDiaryEntry(ByVal author As String, ByVal subject _
  As String, ByVal message As String) As Integer
  Dim conn As New SqlConnection(ConfigurationSettings.AppSettings("cam"))
  Dim queryString As String = _
    "INSERT INTO TourDiaryEntries (Author, Subject, Message)" & _
    " VALUES (@Author, @Subject, @Message)"
  Dim cmd As New SqlCommand(queryString, conn)
  Dim rowsAffected As Integer = 0
```

**7.** Modify `btnOK_Click()` to call `InsertTourDiaryEntry()`. Also, instead of passing `txtAuthor.text` as the author name, pass `User.Identity.Name`:

```
Sub btnOK_Click(sender As Object, e As EventArgs)
  Dim NumRecords As Integer = 0

  If IsValid Then
    NumRecords = InsertTourDiaryEntry( _
    User.Identity.Name, txtSubject.text, txtMessage.text)
```

Since we require the band members to log in, we don't need them to enter their name each time they post a message. Instead, we're using the intrinsic `User` object to determine who they are and we store their name from the `User` object in the database.

**8.** Change the status message we display in `btnOK_Click` when the entry is created successfully:

```
  Else
    lblStatusMsg.text = "Entry created successfully."
    InitPostForm
  End If
```

Take out the `"Thanks for letting us know what you think."` It just doesn't seem appropriate when you're talking to the other band members!

9. Next, you need to change the `InitPostForm()` subroutine. We change `txtAuthor` to a label in the code later, so we don't need to initialize it after a message is posted. Simply delete the following line:

```
txtAuthor.text = ""
```

10. Change the top of the HTML as shown here. We're removing the style sheet reference and the menu control:

```
<uc0:Menu id="UserControl1" title="Tour Diary" runat="server"></uc0:Menu>
```

11. Change the textbox where we asked the user for their name to a label, and remove the `RequiredFieldValidator` for it:

```
<asp:Label id="lblAuthor" runat="server" MaxLength="50"></asp:Label>
```

12. We're utilizing `CAM.dll` on this page. As mentioned in the previous chapter, any DLLs that you utilize in your pages must be placed in a directory called `bin`. Since we had to configure the `Secure` directory to be a new IIS application in order to set up security, we'll also need to create a `bin` directory within this directory, and place the `CAM.dll` file in there. It'd be nice to utilize the DLL in one place, but it makes sense from a security standpoint. This way, one application on a server can't maliciously make calls into DLLs on other applications. This is especially important for web hosting companies. So, create a `bin` directory within the `Secure` directory and copy `CAM.dll` to it.

> A `bin` directory must always reside within the root of a web application in order for ASP.NET to locate the DLL, and the classes it contains, correctly.

13. Now we can test the `TourDiary.aspx` page to ensure that it works. Here's my first successfully posted entry:

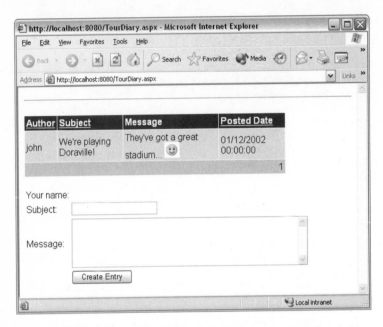

If this page doesn't work for you immediately then there are a couple of things that you need to bear in mind when constructing this functionality.

First of all, you may get a complaint about not being able to connect to the database with which you are working. If you have created a new Web.config file especially for this chapter, then you may have forgotten to add the connection properties with the connection string details:

```
<appSettings>
  <add key="cam"
      value="server=(local)\NetSDK;trusted_connection=true;database=cam"/>
</appSettings>
```

Also, you may find that the emoticons don't work. This is because you may have forgotten to have an Images folder within the Secure folder. This is where all the emoticon image files are stored so that the application can find them when a user uses them, as we discovered in the previous chapter.

## How It Works

There's not really much to explain here since we're using a copy of the page we created in the previous chapter. We can do this because the data and layout is essentially the same. All we've done is change the name of the SQL statements so that they point to the correct table, and renamed the functions. We've also removed a little of the code and design that's not necessary.

# Creating a Data Access Tier

We have just given the ability for band members to post messages about their experiences on the road, but it doesn't do any good if their fans can't read them. So, we need to create a page in the public website to display them.

We have two choices for reading the tour diary records to be displayed. We can copy the code that reads the records from the `TourDiary.aspx` page, or we can create a class to do this, and reuse it between the two pages. You know the right answer – it's always the right answer! We don't ever want to have to copy and paste code, so, let's move the data-access code we have in `TourDiary.aspx` to a class. The way to do this is very similar to what we did with the text formatting functionality in the previous chapter.

**Try It Out      Moving the Code to a Custom Class**

**1.** Create a new class file called `TourDiaryDB.vb` in the `Secure` directory. Specify `CAM` for the namespace and `TourDiaryDB` for the class.

**2.** Delete the default constructor (the `Sub New()` routine), and you should now have the skeleton as shown.

```
Imports System

Namespace CAM

   Public Class TourDiaryDB
   End Class
End Namespace
```

**3.** Add these `Import` statements to the top of the page as follows:

```
Imports System.Data
Imports System.Data.SqlClient
Imports System.Configuration
```

We'll be performing data access, so that is why we need these namespaces.

**4.** Move the `InsertTourDiaryEntry()` function from `TourDiary.aspx` and make it public:

```
Public Function InsertTourDiaryEntry(ByVal author As String, _
    ByVal subject As String, ByVal message As String) As Integer
```

**5.** Create a new function called `ReadTourDiaryEntries()`. Take the database code from the `BindGrid()` function and move it into the new function:

```
Public Function ReadTourDiaryEntries(ByVal SortField As String) As DataSet

    Dim CommandText As String

    If SortField = String.Empty Then
        CommandText = "select Author, Subject, Message, PostedDate" & _
                   " from TourDiaryEntries order by PostedDate desc"
    Else
        CommandText = "select Author, Subject, Message, PostedDate" & _
                   " from TourDiaryEntries order by " & SortField
    End If

    Dim myConnection As New _
            SqlConnection(ConfigurationSettings.AppSettings("cam"))
    Dim myCommand As New SqlDataAdapter(CommandText, myConnection)

    Dim ds As New DataSet()
    myCommand.Fill(ds)
    return ds

End Function
```

We're now passing the `SortField` value in as a *parameter*, since this class can't read the `SortField` value from the datagrid directly any longer.

**6.** Going back to the **Code** view in `TourDiary.aspx`, modify the `BindGrid()` function as shown here:

```
Sub BindGrid()

    Dim TDDB As New CAM.TourDiaryDB()

    DataGrid1.DataSource = TDDB.ReadTourDiaryEntries(SortField)
    DataGrid1.DataBind()

End Sub
```

We have to create an instance of the `TourDiaryDB` object with the `Dim` statement. Then, we use it to call the `ReadTourDiaryEntries()` function, passing the `SortField` string to it.

**7.** Now modify the `btnOK_Click` function as follows:

```
Sub btnOK_Click(sender As Object, e As EventArgs)
    Dim NumRecords As Integer = 0
    Dim TDDB As New CAM.TourDiaryDB()

    If IsValid Then
        NumRecords = TDDB.InsertTourDiaryEntry( _
          User.Identity.Name, txtSubject.text, txtMessage.text)
```

Again, we create an instance of the object and use it to call the `InsertTourDiaryEntry()` function.

**8.** Now, we need to compile the class. Make sure there is a `bin` directory within your `Secure` folder. Copy over `Compile.bat` from the previous chapter, and alter the following lines:

```
Set PATH=%SystemRoot%\Microsoft.NET\Framework\v1.0.3705
cd c:\BegWebMatrix\Secure
Set references=System.Web.dll,System.dll,System.XML.dll,System.Data.dll
vbc TourDiaryDB.vb /t:library /r:%references% /out:bin\TourDiaryDB.dll
pause
```

Save the file, then double-click `compile.bat` to compile the class.

### How It Works

There is one new line in our compilation statement that we need to look at, and one other modified line:

```
Set references=System.Web.dll,System.dll,System.XML.dll,System.Data.dll
vbc TourDiaryDB.vb /t:library /r:%references% /out:bin\TourDiaryDB.dll
```

The first line creates a temporary variable for our compilation file, and in this variable it stores all of the `.dll` files that need to be referenced for the compilation to be successful. These DLLs contain the actual classes that we'll be using, for example, the `SqlConnection` class. ASP.NET pages automatically refer to these DLLs when they run, but custom classes have to be explicitly told where to find the classes we need. Using a temporary variable means that the actual compilation statement is shorter, and now includes the following statement:

```
/r:%references%
```

Which simply says "Take the values stored in the variable called references, and use them here." The `/r:` statement in our compilation references the dlls we require.

Refer to compiling `CAM.vb` of the *Creating a Custom Class* section in the previous chapter for more information on what the other options mean. Notice we have to have references to `System.Data`, `System`, and `System.XML`. `System.Data` is for the data access we're performing; `System` is required because many objects rely on functionality within it; and `System.XML` is required because datasets are actually XML under the surface.

That's it. Your page should now work exactly as it did before.

# Create a View Page

Now that we've given the band members the ability to create tour diary entries, we need a page for the fans to see them. We're going to create a view page in the public site. Fans will be able to view all entries, or just entries by their favorite band member.

**Try It Out**     **Viewing Tour Diary Entries**

1. Create a page called `Diary.aspx` in the CAM directory. Use the **Data Pages | Data Report with Paging and Sorting** template.

2. Most of the steps below are the same as, or borrow heavily from, the examples you have already seen, both in this chapter and the previous chapter. First, let's modify the page so that it uses the menu control and styles for the public site. View the **All Web Matrix** tab.

```
<html>
<head>
  <% = "<link href=""Style.css"" type=""text/css"" rel=""stylesheet"" />" %>
</head>
  <body style="font-family:arial">
  <h2>
    <uc0:Menu id="UserControl1" title="Guest Book" runat="server"></uc0:Menu>
  </h2>
    <hr size="1">
    <form runat="server">
```

3. Now we need to add the menu control. First, add the @ `Register` page directive for the user control to the top of the page:

```
<%@ Page Language="VB" %>
<%@ Register TagPrefix="uc0" TagName="Menu" Src="Header.ascx" %>
<%@ import Namespace="System.Data" %>
<%@ import Namespace="System.Data.SqlClient" %>
```

4. Modify the `BindGrid()` function as shown here:

```
Sub BindGrid()
  Dim TDDB As New CAM.TourDiaryDB()

    DataGrid1.DataSource = TDDB.ReadTourDiaryEntries(SortField)
    DataGrid1.DataBind()

  End Sub
```

We have to create an instance of the `TourDiaryDB` object with the `Dim` statement. Then, we use it to call the `ReadTourDiaryEntries()` function, passing the `SortField` string to it.

**5.** Add an import statement to the top of the code, in the **All** view, for the `CAM` namespace. That's the namespace in which we placed the `TourDiaryDB` class above:

```
<%@ import Namespace="CAM" %>
```

**6.** Now, we have a running site, but as with the guest book and tour diary in the private site, we need to use templated columns for the datagrid so that we can have formatting, and so that we can turn off sorting for the `Message` column. Here's exactly the same datagrid HTML we used for the diary datagrid in the private site. Replace what is on `Diary.aspx` with this:

```
<asp:datagrid id="DataGrid1" runat="server" AutoGenerateColumns="False"
              AllowSorting="True" OnSortCommand="DataGrid_Sort"
              AllowPaging="True" PageSize="10"
              OnPageIndexChanged="DataGrid_Page" ForeColor="Black"
              BackColor="White" CellPadding="3" GridLines="None"
              CellSpacing="1" width="80%">
  <HeaderStyle font-bold="True" forecolor="White"
               backcolor="#4A3C8C"></HeaderStyle>
  <PagerStyle horizontalalign="Right" backcolor="#C6C3C6"
              mode="NumericPages"></PagerStyle>
  <ItemStyle backcolor="#DEDFDE"></ItemStyle>
  <Columns>
    <asp:TemplateColumn SortExpression="Author" HeaderText="Author">
      <ItemTemplate>
        <asp:Label id="Label2" runat="server">
          <%# CAM.Formatting.MyCstr(
              Container.DataItem("Author"), True, False) %>
        </asp:Label>
      </ItemTemplate>
    </asp:TemplateColumn>
    <asp:TemplateColumn SortExpression="Subject, PostedDate"
                        HeaderText="Subject">
      <ItemTemplate>
        <asp:Label id="Label1" runat="server">
          <%# CAM.Formatting.MyCstr(
              Container.DataItem("Subject"), True, False) %>
        </asp:Label>
      </ItemTemplate>
    </asp:TemplateColumn>
    <asp:TemplateColumn HeaderText="Message">
      <ItemTemplate>
        <asp:Label id="Label1" runat="server">
          <%# CAM.Formatting.ConvertEmoticonsAndFormatting(
              CAM.Formatting.MyCstr(Container.DataItem(
              "Message"), True, True)) %>
```

```
          </asp:Label>
        </ItemTemplate>
      </asp:TemplateColumn>
      <asp:TemplateColumn SortExpression="PostedDate"
                        HeaderText="Posted Date">
        <ItemTemplate>
          <asp:Label id="Label1" runat="server">
            <%# container.dataitem("PostedDate") %>
          </asp:Label>
        </ItemTemplate>
      </asp:TemplateColumn>
    </Columns>
  </asp:datagrid>
```

**7.** Before we're done with this, however, let's change the `Author` column to display an image of the band member. We'll assume that we have set up the website so that there is a GIF image of each band member in the `Images` directory off of the public website, and that it's named the same as their logon name. Based on this, change the `Author` template column above to what's shown here:

```
<asp:TemplateColumn SortExpression="Author" HeaderText="Author">
  <ItemTemplate>
    <asp:Label id="Label2" runat="server">
      <img src=
        "Images/<%# Container.DataItem("Author") %>.gif"><br />
        <%# CAM.Formatting.MyCstr(
            Container.DataItem("Author"), True, False) %>
    </asp:Label>
  </ItemTemplate>
</asp:TemplateColumn>
```

What we've done here is dynamically built an image tag, using the author's name, as it is stored in the database as the first part of the image name. So, a message by John would be converted by the line `<img src="Images/<%# Container.DataItem("Author") %>.gif">` into `<img src="Images/john.gif">`. So now, we have what's shown opposite:

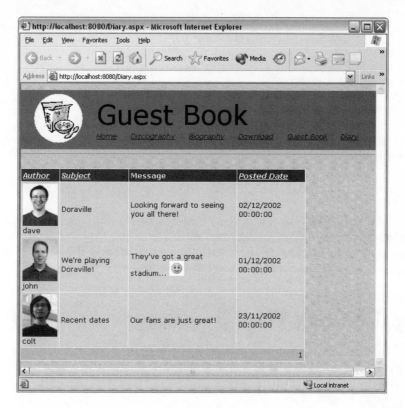

*Web Matrix can sometimes do more harm than good when switching to and from **Design** mode. For me, it kept changing `<%# Container.DataItem("Author") %>` into `<%# Container.DataItem("Author") % />`. Be careful to recheck your pages after you use the **Design** mode.*

## How It Works

Most of this you've seen before, but there are a few steps that are new or worth repeating. The first of these is the use of our data class. Remember that this was compiled and the DLL placed into the `bin` directory. ASP.NET automatically loads that for us, so all we have to do is reference it in our page:

```
<%@ import Namespace="CAM" %>
```

To use the data layer, we simple create an instance of the `TourDiaryDB` class, which contains the data code. We then call the `ReadTourDiaryEntries()` method of that class, and use the results from this as the source of data for our grid. This is the way you'll see most data access code being used:

```
Sub BindGrid()
  Dim TDDB As New CAM.TourDiaryDB()

    DataGrid1.DataSource = TDDB.ReadTourDiaryEntries(SortField)
    DataGrid1.DataBind()

  End Sub
```

The use of images as part of our column is worth mentioning too. We're showing an image of the band member, as well as their name. The important line is:

```
<img src="/Images/<%# Container.DataItem("Author") %>.gif"><br />
```

This simply creates an HTML image, and uses the author name column (which is the name of the band member) as part of the image name. What's important about this is that it shows you can use data binding within an existing HTML tag. That's because the data binding happens before the HTML is formed, so it can be used to make up part of the HTML.

# Filtering the Diary View By Author

Now, let's do one final thing. Fans are extremely loyal to their favorite band members, so let's provide a way for them to click on their favorite member's name to display only entries that they've created.

## Try It Out          Filtering the Diary Entries

1.  First, we need a method of selecting the author whose entries we want to view. Let's create a set of LinkButton controls to do this. Each button will represent a different band member. When the member's button is clicked, only that member's entries will be displayed. Add six LinkButton controls above the DataGrid, all in a row, one after the other. We'll have a button for each band member, plus one to display all entries. Here are the properties for the buttons:

| Control | Properties | Values |
|---------|-----------|--------|
| btnNoFilter | CommandName | Filter |
| | CommandArgument | NoFilter |
| | Command (from events tab) | FilterButton_Command |
| | Text | All Entries |

| Control | Properties | Values |
|---------|-----------|--------|
| btnAl | CommandName | Filter |
| | CommandArgument | Al |
| | onCommand | FilterButton_Command |
| | Text | Al |
| btnColt | CommandName | Filter |
| | CommandArgument | Colt |
| | onCommand | FilterButton_Command |
| | Text | Colt |
| btnDave | CommandName | Filter |
| | CommandArgument | Dave |
| | onCommand | FilterButton_Command |
| | Text | Dave |
| btnJohn | CommandName | Filter |
| | CommandArgument | John |
| | onCommand | FilterButton_Command |
| | Text | John |
| btnJames | CommandName | Filter |
| | CommandArgument | James |
| | onCommand | FilterButton_Command |
| | Text | James |

All buttons will call the same Command() method on the page. To know what to filter by, we'll use the CommandArgument property.

**2.** Add a FilterValue property to the page:

```
Property FilterValue() As String
  Get
    Dim o As Object = ViewState("FilterValue")
    If o Is Nothing Then
```

```
      Return "NoFilter"
    End If
    Return CStr(o)
  End Get

  Set(ByVal Value As String)
    ViewState("FilterValue") = Value
  End Set
End Property
```

This property will store the filter value we pass via the CommandArgument property on the link button. In turn, we'll use this property when we bind the data in the DataGrid.

**3.** Next, we need the event handler for when a LinkButton is clicked. The command event is fired when the button is clicked. Here's our handler:

```
Sub FilterButton_Command(sender as object, e as CommandEventArgs)
  FilterValue = e.CommandArgument
  BindGrid()
End Sub
```

This event passes the object that was clicked and the CommandEventArgs property. The latter contains the command name and command argument that was specified for the control that was clicked. Note that in this case, we only have one command on the page, so we don't need to put any conditional logic to check for the command name. We simply utilize the command argument to set the FilterValue. Then we reload the grid.

**4.** Now, we need to modify the BindGrid() subroutine to filter the data when appropriate. We have two options: we can change the CAM.TourDiaryDB class to allow passing of the filter value, or we can filter after the dataset has been returned to our page. There's no right or wrong answer. If you have a lot of data, it's often more efficient to let the database do the filtering so that you're not passing so much data from the database to the calling object. On the other hand, a lot of times in a real programming environment you may not have the option of changing the data-tier classes, so you have to work around their limitations. Or, you might be caching the data on the web server so that you don't have to do database accesses each time you display data on the page. In this case, I'm going to filter after the dataset has been returned.

Unfortunately, the dataset doesn't allow itself to be filtered directly. Instead, you need to get the data view you want to filter on, and then perform the filter itself. Here's new BindGrid() code:

```
Sub BindGrid()
  Dim TDDB As New TourDiaryDB()
  Dim dv As DataView

  dv = TDDB.ReadTourDiaryEntries(SortField).Tables(0).DefaultView
  If FilterValue <> "NoFilter" Then
```

```
    dv.Rowfilter = "author = '" & FilterValue & "'"
  Else
    dv.RowFilter = ""
  End If
  DataGrid1.DataSource = dv
  DataGrid1.DataBind()

End Sub
```

That's our code sorted out. Now, when you recompile and run the page, and when you click on the John LinkButton, say, you'll see only his entries, like the following:

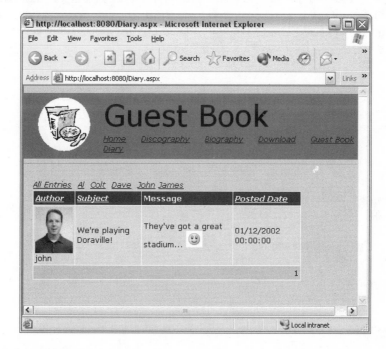

When you click on All Entries, you'll clear the RowFilter and see all of the entries again.

## How It Works

One of the most important points about this example is that we have five link buttons, but only one event procedure. In previous examples we've had an event procedure for each button, but that would be wasteful here, since we want to perform the same action from each button. This is possible because we set the onCommand event property for all of the buttons to the same event procedure, so the same procedure will run whichever button we click. The second parameter of the event procedure contains specific details of which button was pressed – ASP.NET automatically passes this information to us, and since we set the CommandArgument property for each button (to the name of the band member), we can use this in the event procedure:

```
Sub FilterButton_Command(sender as object, e as CommandEventArgs)
  FilterValue = e.CommandArgument
  BindGrid()
End Sub
```

Here, we just extract the `CommandArgument` and use that as the value for the filter. We can then bind the grid to the data.

In the `BindGrid()` routine, we take that filter value, and we use it to show only those records. We can do that with a `DataView`, which is a sortable, filterable view of the data. Each table in a `DataSet` has a `DefaultView`, which is the unfiltered view of the data – normally we bind directly to this default view, but we want to filter the data so we create a `DataView` variable, and set this to the `DefaultView` of the first table in the `DataSet` (there is only one table):

```
dv = TDDB.ReadTourDiaryEntries(SortField).Tables(0).DefaultView
```

If the `FilterValue` is `NoFilter`, we clear the `DataView`'s `RowFilter` by setting it to empty as well. If it's not empty, then we build the filter criteria string, which in this case means searching the `Author` field for records that have the same name as `FilterValue` itself:

```
If FilterValue <> "NoFilter" Then
  dv.Rowfilter = "author = '" & FilterValue & "'"
Else
  dv.RowFilter = ""
End If
```

Finally, we set the data source to this filtered `DataView`:

```
DataGrid1.DataSource = dv
```

# Summary

Creating the tour diary functionality has shown us how to implement several useful ideas. We first looked at creating a secure area of the site, by creating a new directory and adding our secure pages to it. The ASP.NET configuration file (`Web.config`) was used to store the access details for that secure area. The really great thing about ASP.NET is that once security is configured, you don't have to worry about doing security checks in each page. ASP.NET knows whether you've logged in or not, and if you haven't, it automatically redirects you to the login page. This means less coding for you, and a simple way to implement secure sites.

We also looked at moving code into a data-access layer – it's something we've said before (and no doubt will again!), but this is a sensible design choice. It means the data code is separate from the ASP.NET pages, and allows you to easily change the code if you need to.

The final example looked at filtering data, giving the user a much more friendly page, allowing them to concentrate on their favorite band members.

In the following chapter, we will be looking at how to include functionality in your site to remember your visitors and keep a track of who is logged in and when they did so.

# CHAPTER 15

# Remembering Your Visitors

It's always nice to be remembered, whether you're at work, at a social gathering, or somewhere else. It also nice to be remembered when you visit a website as well. Seeing something as simple as "Good to see you again, John" upon your return is a nice touch. In this chapter, we'll give our website something akin to a memory. Not only will it remember who you are, it will know when you're visiting again after a time away. Finally, it will track the band members that are online and display them to the fans.

In creating this functionality, we'll cover the following:

❑   Using cookies to remember a user

❑   Using application state to track online band members and display their status to fans

## Cookies

Normally, a web application is **stateless**. This means that no data is kept as the user navigates between one page and another in a website. In a **thick client**, such as a Windows application, the client remains running and data the application needs is stored in memory until the client is closed. However, with a web-based application, a connection is made to the website, the page content is downloaded, and the connection is ended. So, there's no constantly running client to maintain state. However, there are workarounds we can utilize to let our web application work as if it can maintain state.

The first technique is **cookies**. Cookies are name-value pairs that get sent to and from the browser with each HTTP request. They contain information about your visit that the developer of the website you're visiting wishes to track. They can either be designed to be **volatile**, lasting only for the duration of your current visit to the website, or they can be **persistent**, lasting for an extended period of time, which is determined by the developer. We're going to use cookies below to remember a user's name.

# Security

Cookies have gotten a bad reputation as being insecure. Many say that a user's privacy will be compromised if they allow sites to place cookies on their computer. The most important things to know about cookies are:

❑ They only contain data. They aren't programs, and can't run programs, so they aren't going to delete files, or mail your credit card details back to the authors.

❑ The only site that can access a cookie is the site from which it was created . So, someone can't create a malicious site and read all of your cookie data at will. This makes cookies relatively secure.

*There have been some browser bugs that do allow this sort of unauthorized cookie access between sites. Patches exist, but keep in mind that some of your users may not have applied these patches, and also that new bugs to exploit could be found in the future.*

Now, if your browser stores cookies in files, and someone can gain access to the cookie file on your computer, they could view the data contained within, or possibly copy it to another computer and utilize it there. The best strategy is to use cookies *only* to store information that isn't overly sensitive. Many websites use cookies to recognize a user, but still require the user to log on in order to view their sensitive data. This is a good compromise.

Different operating systems store cookies in different ways. With Windows XP, they are stored as files in a directory specific to each user of the system. Most of the time, the path will be C:\Documents and Settings\\*username*\Cookies, where *username* is the logon name you use to log onto your operating system. The cookie files on XP are named as username@domainname[uniquenumber].txt. The domain name is the URL domain you accessed the site with. The unique number is used in the case where a site has more than one cookie.

*Cookies are limited to 4,096 bytes in size.*

# Implementation

ASP.NET provides two accessible collections of cookies, both returned as type HttpCookieCollection. The first one is accessible via the HttpRequest.Cookies property. This collection contains all of the cookies returned from the browser with each request. This collection is used to read cookies. The second collection is accessible via the HttpResponse.Cookies property. This collection is sent to the browser with each request. This is the collection you use to create cookies.

The HttpCookieCollection contains objects of type HttpCookie. The HttpCookie object has the following commonly used properties. For other properties, refer to the documentation:

| Property | Description |
|----------|-------------|
| Domain | The name of the domain with which the cookie is to be associated. By default, it's the name of the current domain. The domain is the root of the URL you're accessing. So the domain for `http://www.msn.com/news` would be `www.msn.com`. |
| Expires | The date and time when the cookie should expire. |
| Name | The name of the cookie. By default, it's set to `Nothing`. |
| Path | This is the URL virtual path where the cookie originates. In the example `http://www.msn.com/news`, the path is `/news`. If no path is specified, this cookie will be sent to all pages on the server. If it is specified, this cookie will only be sent to pages under the `/news` path. |
| Value | The value of the cookie. A simple example is:<br><br>`MyCookie.Value = "abc"` |
| Values | A `NameValueCollection` of values for the current cookie. This is convenient if you want to store more than one value within the current cookie. An example is:<br><br>`MyCookie.Values("FirstValue") = "abc"`<br>`MyCookie.Values("SecondValue") = "def"` |

Here's some example code that creates a cookie and sends it along with the page to the browser.

First, you create a new `HttpCookie` instance, with the name `FavoriteBand`:

```
Dim MyCookie as New HttpCookie("FavoriteBand")
```

Set the value of the cookie to `Cornflakes at Midnight`:

```
MyCookie.Value = "Cornflakes at Midnight"
```

Set the cookie to expire 30 days from now:

```
MyCookie.Expires = today.AddDays(30)
```

Add the cookie to the response object's cookie collection so that it will be sent to the browser along with the rest of the page:

```
Response.Cookies.Add(MyCookie)
```

As mentioned above, different browsers will store these cookies in different ways. Regardless of how the browser stores them, it will return them each time a request to the site is located, as long as the cookie is determined to be valid for the domain and path of the URL the user is requesting. To use the cookie value on our page, here is the kind of code we need:

```
If Request.Cookies("FavoriteBand") Is Nothing Then
   txtField.Text = ""
Else
   txtField.Text = Request.Cookies("FavoriteBand").Value
End If
```

If it is Nothing, then the cookie doesn't exist and if it doesn't exist then set the text field to nothing. Otherwise, set the text field to the value of the cookie name FavoriteBand.

Cookie values are always stored and returned as strings, so you'll need to cast your types appropriately when setting and returning non-string values.

OK. Now that you've seen a quick example, let's implement cookies in our band's website. The perfect place for it is on the page where fans can make a guest book entry. Instead of making them type their name in each time, we'll remember their name after they post their first entry. After that, we'll pre-populate the name textbox from the cookie's value.

## Try It Out     Adding Cookies

**1.** Open the GuestBook.aspx page we created in Chapter 13 and add the following method to the code:

```
Sub SaveNameToCookie()
   Dim MyCookie As New HttpCookie("Name")
   MyCookie.Value = txtAuthor.Text
   MyCookie.Expires = Today.AddDays(30)

   Response.Cookies.Add(MyCookie)
End Sub
```

**2.** In the btnOK_Click event handler, add the following line:

```
Sub btnOK_Click(sender As Object, e As EventArgs)
   Dim NumRecords As Integer = 0

   If IsValid Then
      NumRecords = _
         InsertGuestBookEntry(txtAuthor.text, txtSubject.text, txtMessage.text)
```

```
    If NumRecords = 0 Then
       lblStatusMsg.visible = True
       lblStatusMsg.text = _
          "An error occurred while trying to create the entry."
    Else
       lblStatusMsg.text = "Entry created successfully. " & _
                            "Thanks for letting us know what you think."
       SaveNameToCookie()
       InitPostForm()
    End If
    BindGrid()
   End If
End Sub
```

Now, when the entry is saved successfully, the user's name will be stored in the cookie.

**3.** Next, change the `InitPostForm()` method as follows:

```
Sub InitPostForm()
   If Request.Cookies("Name") Is Nothing Then
      txtAuthor.Text = ""
   Else
      txtAuthor.Text = Request.Cookies("Name").Value
   End If
   txtSubject.text = ""
   txtMessage.text = ""
End Sub
```

We check to see if the cookie named `Name` contains a value. If it does, we set the `txtAuthor` to the value of the cookie. Otherwise, we set it to an empty string.

**4.** Change the `Page_Load` event handler to initialize the post form:

```
Sub Page_Load(Sender As Object, E As EventArgs)

   If Not Page.IsPostBack Then

      ' Databind the data grid on the first request only
      ' (on postback, rebind only in paging and sorting commands)

      InitPostForm()
      BindGrid()

   End If
End Sub
```

This causes the name to be loaded from the cookie when the page is first loaded.

Now, after you create your first entry, the name you entered for yourself should be pre-populated into the Your name: field. If you haven't used the site for 30 days, however, the cookie will be deleted and you'll have to enter your name again. I created an entry with the name of Art Edwards, closed the browser, opened it up and navigated back to the guest book.

To test the cookie's deletion after a certain time, you can always set the expiration date to say 1 day and then go back to the site a couple of days later to see if the page still remembers you.

## How It Works

This is pretty simple code. First we created a `SaveNameToCookie` routine, so save the user name into a cookie:

```
Sub SaveNameToCookie()
   Dim MyCookie As New HttpCookie("Name")
   MyCookie.Value = txtAuthor.Text
   MyCookie.Expires = Today.AddDays(30)

   Response.Cookies.Add(MyCookie)
End Sub
```

This simply stores the user's name (`txtAuthor.Text`) into a cookie named, appropriately enough, `Name`. Their name will be stored for 30 days.

We now need to call this routine, and the best time to do this is when the guest book entry is saved successfully. We don't want to store it if the save fails, because for all we know, it could be the name itself that caused the failure. So, if the entry was successfully written to the database, we just call the above routine:

```
SaveNameToCookie()
```

What we next need to do is modify the `InitPostForm` routing, which resets the Subject and Message textboxes. Instead of just clearing the name, we check to see if the cookie has a value, and if so we use that value as the value for the author name textbox:

```
If Request.Cookies("Name") Is Nothing Then
   txtAuthor.Text = ""
Else
   txtAuthor.Text = Request.Cookies("Name").Value
End If
```

Finally we make sure this routine is called when the page is first loaded, so that their name will be filled in when they return to the site at a later date. We simply added a call to `InitPostForm()` in the `Page_Load` event:

```
InitPostForm()
```

# Session State

Cookies are a way to maintain state, but they have several limitations:

- ❑ They can only store strings. No other object types can be stored within them.

- ❑ Cookies can only hold 4k of data.

- ❑ Some web browsers don't support cookies, and even with those that do, most give the user the option of turning cookie support off.

- ❑ Since the information within cookies is stored on the client, it is possible with some clients for an unauthorized user to access the data in the cookies, either by physically accessing the client, or by exploiting browser bugs.

These limitations are overcome through the use of server-side sessions. **Server-side sessions** give you the ability to save values on the server side for each user accessing your site. A session is started when the user first access the site, and it ends when they close their browser. A new browser instance causes the start of a new session. So, the session values will exist until the user's session times out or they close their browser. Values on the server are associated with the client by use of one of two methods, described below under the Cookieless option text.

The values are not stored on the user's browser. Instead, you can configure the server to store them in one of three places. You configure your choice in the Mode attribute, shown below.

The Web.config file, which we looked at in more detail in previous chapters, is used to configure session state on your server. You need to place the settings in a <sessionstate.../> tag, which must, in turn, be placed within the <configuration><system.web> tag. Here is the syntax required:

```
<sessionState mode="Off|InProc|StateServer|SQLServer"
              cookieless="true|false"
              timeout="number of minutes"
              stateConnectionString="tcpip=server:port"
              sqlConnectionString="sql connection string" />
```

and here is an explanation of each option:

| Attribute | Value | Description |
|---|---|---|
| Mode | Off | Session state is disabled. |
| | InProc | Stores the session state in memory within the website process. This is the fastest mode. |
| | StateServer | Stores the session state in memory via the use of a process running out of the website's process. This mode is fast, yet will still work with web farms. |
| | SQLServer | Stores the session state in a SQL Server. This method is the most reliable, since the web server can crash without losing session state, but it is slower than the other methods. |
| Cookieless | true or false | The session state values are associated with the browser by one of two methods you choose when you configure your website. The first method uses a cookie to uniquely identify the user's session (false). Each time they access the site, this unique key is used to retrieve the session values. The second method is by having the unique key automatically appended to the URL each time the user accesses the site. This method is good for those times when the user doesn't allow cookies on their system (false). Note that you can only use one method or the other. |
| Timeout | Integer value | Number of minutes of inactivity before the session times out and the values are cleared on the server. Each time the user accesses the site, the number of minutes before timeout is reset to this value. |
| stateConnection String | tcpip=server: port | When using the StateServer mode, you must specify the server and port that the remote state server is listening on. |
| sqlConnection String | SQL connection string | When you use the SQLServer mode, you must specify the connection string to the SQL server that is storing the session state. |

As shown above, session state is keyed to the user's browser through the use of a cookie, or, in the case of cookieless operation, through the use of a modified URL. This technique is called **URL rewriting**. Either way, a unique session key is used to relate the client to the session data. In the case of cookies, the key is stored within the client's cookie. With cookieless operation enabled, any URLs within the HTTP stream that is returned to the client are modified to include the session key within the URL itself. This key then serves to relate the client to the stored session information. Here's an example of a URL when cookieless operation is used:

http://localhost/(srivxx55mux14fngwbxadz45)/GuestBook.aspx

Unlike with cookies that you create, session state *cannot* be persisted between browser visits. Session state times out after the period of inactivity defined above, no matter what – it is *meant* to be temporary. If you need to permanently track user information, use a database. Also, realize that if you restart the web server, or update the website in such a way that a new application instance is created, you will have a new instance of session state for your users as well, unless you use the StateServer or SQLServer mode. The bottom line is that you shouldn't count on session state being there in your application. Session state is very useful to enable advanced features within a website, but you should always build logic into your application to handle those times that session data isn't available.

## Global Functions

All of the code we've used so far in the book has either existed within a page, or within a separate component class. The latter of these allows code to be shared among pages. Sometimes, ASP.NET also needs to have code that's not part of a page, but which isn't shareable among pages. An example of this is code that can be run when a session starts or ends. To achieve this you have a special file, called Global.asax, which can be created in the root directory of your web application. It's an ASP.NET page, but only contains code for these global event procedures. Web Matrix has a template for this file.

There are two events in the Global.asax file that you can use when a new user session is started and when it ends. Their code shells as generated by Web Matrix are shown below:

```
Sub Session_Start(Sender As Object, E As EventArgs)
    ' Code that runs when a new session is started
End Sub

Sub Session_End(Sender As Object, E As EventArgs)
    ' Code that runs when a session ends
End Sub
```

Data is stored in key-value pairs. You add data to the session state via the following statement:

```
Session.Add("MyData", "Testing")
```

or:

```
Session("MyData") = "Testing"
```

There are many properties and methods for the Session object. Here are the most commonly used:

| Property/Method | Description |
| --- | --- |
| Count | The number of objects contained in the session state. |
| IsCookieless | Used to determine whether the session is being tracked with a cookie or with the URL identifier. |
| IsNewSession | Determines if the session was created with the current request. If this property always returns True, then the client isn't able to persist the session key across requests. |
| Item | Allows you to get or set values in the session. |
| Keys | The collection of keys in the object. |
| Timeout | Gets or sets the number of minutes before the session will timeout. |
| Add() | Adds a new value to the session. |
| Clear() | Clears all objects from the session. |
| Remove() | Removes a single object from the session. |
| RemoveAll() | Same as Clear() – removes all objects from the session. |
| RemoveAt() | Removes a session object at the specified index. |

# Application State

Session state is great for storing data that is unique to each user session. Data from another user or a later session is not visible in the current session. However, if you have a lot of users, and you're storing session state values in memory, as opposed to using a database, you might run out of memory on the server. If, for example, you have 1,000 users, and each user stores 100KB of session data, that's 100MB of memory used.

**Application-level state** is where you can store information that is shared among *all* the web application's users. Anything stored here can be viewed and modified by *any* user. It can be accessed by any page within the application, so it is a great place for storing global data, but you need to understand that you can't count on the data in the application state sticking around for any definite period of time. If the website code is updated, a new instance of the website will be created, which means that the application state starts with a clean slate. The same thing happens if you restart the web server, so use it judiciously.

Application state works similarly to session state. You store data via key-value pairs. Here are the commonly used properties and methods:

| Property/Method | Description |
| --- | --- |
| Count | The number of objects contained in the application state. |
| Item | Allows you to get or set values in the session. |
| Keys | The collection of keys in the object. |
| Add() | Adds a new value to the application state. |
| Clear() | Clears all objects from the application state. |
| GetKey() | Returns the name of the key at the specified index. |
| Lock() | Locks the application state until the Unlock() method is called – this allows you to make updates to objects in the application state while preventing others from doing so. Without this, two users might attempt to update the same object at the same time, causing integrity issues. |
| Unlock() | After you call Lock() and make your updates, you should call Unlock() to allow other users access to the application state. |
| Remove() | Removes a single object from the application. |
| RemoveAll() | Same as Clear() – removes all objects from the application. |
| RemoveAt() | Removes an application object at the specified index. |
| Set() | Updates an existing value based on the name of the key. |

Data is stored in key-value pairs, so you would add data to the application state via the following statement:

```
Application.Lock()
Application.Add("GlobalData", "Testing")
Application.Unlock()
```

or using:

```
Application.Lock()
Application("GlobalData") = "Testing"
Application.Unlock()
```

It's important to call `Lock()` and `Unlock()` both when updating existing data, and when you're adding a new value as well. Otherwise, as pointed out in the table, two people might try to add the same key-value pair at the same time.

An application starts when the first request to a web application arrives after the web application has been started or restarted. An application ends when the `Global.asax` page is changed or the web server is shut down. As with session, we have two methods in `Global.asax` that execute when an application starts and ends:

```
Sub Application_OnStart(Sender As Object, E As EventArgs)
    ' Code that runs on application startup
End Sub

Sub Application_OnEnd(Sender As Object, E As EventArgs)
    ' Code that runs on application shutdown
End Sub
```

An example of what code might be used here is some database cleanup code. Some applications keep temporary data throughout the life of an application, so if the application restarts it's a good idea to clean this up.

## Tracking Online Band Members in Application State

Let's give the fans the ability to see which band members are online. We'll do this by storing online information in the application state and displaying the information to the fans on a public page within the site.

**Try It Out        Using Application State**

When the band member logs on, we'll add their name and logon time to a hashtable in the application state. We do this by performing the following steps:

**1.** Open the `Secure/Login.aspx` page you created in the previous chapter and change the `LoginBtn_Click` handler to the following:

```
If Page.IsValid Then
    If FormsAuthentication.Authenticate(Username.Text, UserPass.Text) Then
        Application.Lock()
```

```
      If Application("OnlineUsers") Is Nothing Then
        Dim ht As New HashTable()
        ht.Add(username.Text, Now())
        Application("OnlineUsers") = ht
      ElseIf Not CType( _
        Application("OnlineUsers"), HashTable).Contains(Username.Text) Then
        CType(Application( _
          "OnlineUsers"), HashTable).Add(Username.Text, Now())
      End If
      Application.Unlock()
      FormsAuthentication.RedirectFromLoginPage(UserName.Text, False)
    Else
      Msg.Text = "Invalid Credentials: Please try again"
    End If
  End If
```

**2.** Now open the page used for logging out, `Secure/Logout.aspx`, and change the `LogOffBtn_Click` handler to the following:

```
Sub LogOffBtn_Click(Sender As Object, E As EventArgs)

  Application.Lock()
  If Not Application("OnlineUsers") Is Nothing Then
    CType(Application("OnlineUsers"), hashtable).Remove(User.Identity.Name)
  End If
  Application.Unlock()

  FormsAuthentication.SignOut()
  Status.Text = "Not authenticated."

End Sub
```

This won't show anything yet, but is the groundwork that will allow us to see who is logged on.

## How It Works

First, let's look at the modifications we have made to the login code.

We lock the application variable to ensure that two changes to the application state aren't attempted at the same time:

```
    Application.Lock()
```

If `Application("OnlineUsers")` hasn't been initialized, then we need to do so next:

```
    If Application("OnlineUsers") Is Nothing Then
```

We're storing information about online band members in a hashtable. The key will be the band member's login name, and the value will be the time they logged in. Here, we're initializing the application object the first time with a new hashtable that contains the user's info:

```
Dim ht As New HashTable()
ht.Add(username.Text, Now())
Application("OnlineUsers") = ht
```

If the application object has already been initialized, we check to see if the band member is already in the hashtable:

```
ElseIf Not CType( _
    Application("OnlineUsers"), HashTable).Contains(Username.Text) Then
```

If the band member isn't already in the application object, we add them now. If they are, we don't need to change anything:

```
CType(Application( _
    "OnlineUsers"), HashTable).Add(Username.Text, Now())
End If
```

Finally, we can unlock the application state object:

```
Application.Unlock()
```

After we have unlocked the application state object, we change the `FormsAuthentication` to not be persistent:

```
FormsAuthentication.RedirectFromLoginPage(UserName.Text, False)
```

This way, the band member has to log in each time they open the site in their browser. It helps us get more accurate information on when the band member is actually online.

Now, let's look at the logout code.

We first lock the application object before making changes:

```
Application.Lock()
```

We check here to make sure `Application("OnlineUsers")` has been initialized:

```
If Not Application("OnlineUsers") Is Nothing Then
```

You might be asking why it wouldn't be, since the user had to log in before being able to log out, and we've initialized the variable in the login page. Well, as mentioned earlier, the application state can get wiped if the website changes or the application is restarted, so you should always verify the application state data before attempting to use it.

Next we remove the current user's key-value pair from the hashtable here:

```
CType(Application("OnlineUsers"), hashtable).Remove(User.Identity.Name)
```

Finally, we unlock the application object again:

```
End If
Application.Unlock()
```

## Displaying Online Band Members

Now, let's display the online band members in a new page.

### Try It Out    Displaying the Band Members

**1.** Create a new page called `ShowOnlineUsers.aspx`. using the standard ASP.NET page template provided by Web Matrix.

**2.** Drag a label control onto the page and name it `lblOnlineUsers`.

**3.** Add the following `Page_Load` code, which will display all of the online users:

```
Sub Page_Load(sender As Object, e As EventArgs)

   Dim key As String

   lblOnlineUsers.text = ""
   If Not Application("OnlineUsers") Is Nothing Then
     For Each key In Application("OnlineUsers").Keys
       lblOnlineUsers.Text &= key & " - Logged in at " & _
         CType(Application("OnlineUsers"), hashtable)(key) & "<br />"
     Next
   End If

End Sub
```

That's it! To test it, you will need to open two browsers and do the following:

**4.** Log on to the secure site in one browser as john.

**5.** In the second browser, view the `ShowOnlineUsers.aspx` page, and you should see the following:

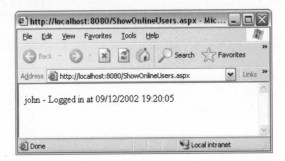

**6.** Now, you can open a third browser window and log on as `Al`. Refresh the second browser showing the `ShowOnlineUsers.aspx` page, and you'll now see both member's information:

Note that if you try to log off John, and refresh this page, you will see some strange behavior – don't worry, all will be explained in just a moment!

## How It Works

In the code, we first initialize the variable `key` and clear the text in the label:

```
Dim key As String

lblOnlineUsers.text = ""
```

We check to make sure `Application("OnlineUsers")` has been initialized:

```
If Not Application("OnlineUsers") Is Nothing Then
```

We enumerate through the keys in the hashtable. As a reminder, the keys are the band members' login names:

```
For Each key In Application("OnlineUsers").Keys
```

We add the band member's login name, a dash, and their login time to the label text:

```
lblOnlineUsers.Text &= key & " - Logged in at " & _
    CType(Application("OnlineUsers"), hashtable)(key) & "<br />"
```

At the end of this example, if you are running all these browser windows on the same machine, you will notice something strange happening if you try to log off John (the user who was first to log in to the application). Because your machine can only remember one user at a time, you can only log Al off! You may want to try this out for yourself using these three windows. The solution is that these files will work fine when hosted on a proper web server machine (one running IIS, for example). You are unlikely to want to log in to the site as more than one person from the same machine, and when this application is hosted on a full web server and browsed to by different users on different machines, you can then log off users one by one. This leaves you with a simple task of refreshing `ShowOnlineUsers.aspx` in your browser to see who's logged on. If we logged off John, in this example, we would then be left with just `Al` in the list:

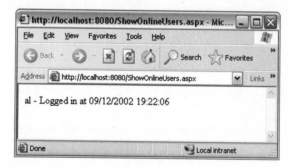

Of course, instead of having this as a separate page, you could add this code to the existing diary page. That way when fans view the diary, they could see if and band members were logged on:

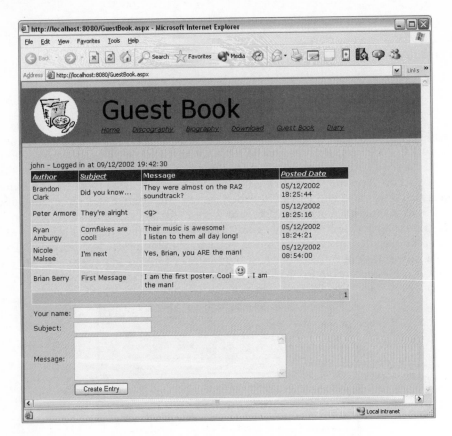

This would give the fans a way to get instant contact with band members.

# Summary

This chapter has been all about the personal touch – or personalization, the act of customizing a site to individual users. It's functionality that doesn't apply to all sites, but for any site that has a degree of user interaction it's a worthwhile addition. Simple things like remembering who the user is make the site much more approachable – users don't have to retype their name, and you can customize content depending on who they are.

Cookies are a simple way of doing this, by simply storing some simple details, and fetching them on each page where required. You can also use sessions to keep track of details for a particular user in the site. An example of this is perhaps a shopping basket, although this leaves you open to the basket disappearing of the user closes the browser. To cure this you can use application state to keep a more permanent store of a users details.

All in all these are simple techniques to keep track of users as they navigate around your site. Anything that makes the site easier to use is a good thing, and will ensure that users come back again and again.

# CHAPTER 16

# Web Services

What do Amazon, Google, and Microsoft MapPoint, among many other sites and products have in common with each other? And is there anything out there that would allow you to leverage their functionality in your own websites? Well, yes there is – **web services**, of course! Web services are the Internet's hot new technology that everyone is talking about. However, few people really understand what they are or how to use them correctly. In this chapter of the book, we'll look at just what a web service is, what encompasses the overall vision for web services, and how to create and leverage existing web services effectively.

## What is a Web Service?

Let's begin with the question, what are web services? At a high level, the technology is much simpler than might seem possible considering how much hype there is regarding their power and the possibility of their changing the entire face of the Web. Web services enable two different applications, no matter whether they are within the same building or on opposite sides of the planet, to talk to each other. They can do this through using a common language and syntax.

Prior to web services, (for those of you who are thirsty for a bit of history!), there had been other attempts to provide a way for different, or distant systems to communicate with each other. Among these were technologies called **Distributed COM**, or **DCOM**, and **CORBA**, and others were tried, too. However, none of these attempts ever gained critical acceptance or implementation in the industry. They were too complicated to set up, and the various technologies couldn't work together.

Then, along came web services, which allowed applications to happily talk to each other, wherever they were. The biggest problem with web services for our purposes, though, is the heap of acronyms and buzzwords that go along with them. In this chapter, we'll be exploring things called XML, HTTP, SOAP, and WSDL. These are all important to web services so we're going to make sure that you gain a full understanding of them, putting some meaning behind the letters!

The best way to learn about the stuff that makes web services work is to build one ourselves. We're going to create a page from which we can allow the fans to search for music on Amazon's site. We'll give them a textbox to enter a keyword to search for, and then return some matching music. We'll display the artist's name, the name of the album, and Amazon's price.

## Accessing Amazon's Web Services

Amazon has a Web Services Developer's Kit that you can download to get documentation and samples for their web services. To find this, type in the following URL http://associates.amazon.com/exec/panama/associates/join/developer/kit.html. It is worth reading the documentation as it'll be important when you need to know the values that are valid when you're using web services. We'll go through just a small subset of the full functionality provided by Amazon, but for if you want to know some more, keep reading through that documentation!

OK, so now we need to download our developer's kit. Amazon states that you will need to get a developer's token before you can use their web services, and the URL above will give you a link to requesting one. This token is your unique identifier as you access Amazon's services. You will pass it every time you access any Amazon web service. Fortunately, it's free, so go ahead and get one – you'll need it to try out the examples.

## Generate the Proxy Class

The first thing we need to do is create something called a **proxy class** through which we can access Amazon's web services. In general terms, a **proxy** is something that acts as an intermediary between one item for another. For instance, if you can't vote, you could get someone to vote for you. That person would then be your proxy, acting on your behalf. For our web service, we need something to act as a proxy between our application and the web service. Using this will mean that we don't need to understand the complexities of the web service.

Web Matrix makes this really quite easy to do. Most websites that provide web services have a document available, called a **WSDL (Web Service Description Language)** document, which describes the methods, properties, and other behavior provided by the web service. Web Matrix has a tool called the XML Web Service Proxy Generator that takes this WSDL document and creates a class that acts as a proxy for the web service.

| Try It Out | Creating a Proxy Class for Amazon's Web Service |
| --- | --- |

In Web Matrix, choose Tools | WebService Proxy Generator from the toolbar at the top, and you will be presented with the XML Web Service Proxy Generator dialog. This dialog has a number of textboxes, which you need to fill in to match the following:

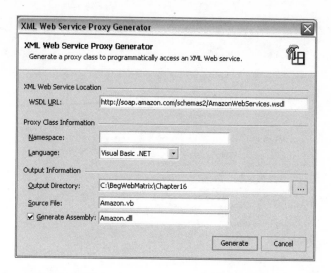

Hit the **Generate** button and that's it! Your proxy class with all of the code necessary to talk to the Amazon web service is generated and placed in the location you specified.

## How It Works

The Web Matrix proxy generator does a lot of work behind the scenes. It reads the WSDL document, which it locates from the URL we give it in the dialog box above (http://soap.amazon.com/schemas2/AmazonWebServices.wsdl). It then actually creates the methods you'll need to access the available web service functionality.

The screenshot that follows is of the first portion of Amazon's WSDL document. If you'd like to view this for yourself, you just need to point your browser at the URL we gave to the proxy generator:

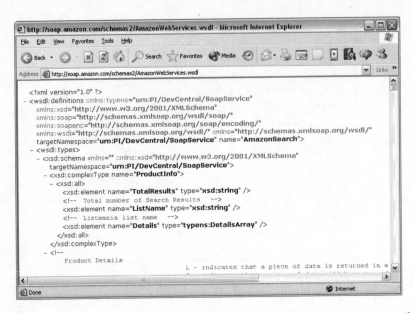

This document describes everything the proxy generator needs to know to access the services. The language it is written in is XML, which is a markup language, like the HTML that we have seen already in our applications. What makes it so useful to web services, however, is that it provides strict rules to everybody who uses it on what they can write and how it should be written. This standardizes what is sent and received to a format that everything can understand.

While a proxy class means that you don't need to actually go in and view the WSDL directly, it's good to get in and have a look at what is going on.

The proxy generator takes this information and creates a Visual Basic .NET file, called `Amazon.vb`, which contains methods and classes you can use. It also goes one step further if we tell it to do so, and compiles this class for us into a DLL. It places this DLL into the `bin` directory under the output directory we specified, in a similar way to that which we have seen in previous chapters when compiling class libraries. In our example, it created a DLL called `Amazon.dll` under `C:\BegWebMatrix\Ch16\bin`. There are many classes and methods created, but we're only interested in three of them.

Let's take a look at `Amazon.vb`. There is a lot in here, and a great deal of it is information for formatting the requests sent to and from the web service. (This is taken care of by a technology called **SOAP**, or the **S**imple **O**bject **A**ccess **P**rotocol. It works by providing a standard syntax for the data being sent back and forth to ensure that both our application and the web service understand one another. If you'd like more information on SOAP, take a look at http://www.w3.org/2000/xp/Group/).

We don't need to worry about this as we want to look at the methods themselves. What I've done is take the code in `Amazon.vb` and strip it of the extra detail. This is only to clarify what's in the file, so DON'T do this with real code!!

What you have is a class called `AmazonSearchService` in a namespace called `Amazon`:

```
Option Strict Off
Option Explicit On

Imports System
Imports System.ComponentModel
Imports System.Diagnostics
Imports System.Web.Services
Imports System.Web.Services.Protocols
Imports System.Xml.Serialization

Namespace Amazon

    Public Class AmazonSearchService
        Inherits System.Web.Services.Protocols.SoapHttpClientProtocol
```

It has a property that contains the URL that is used to interact with the web services. In this case, Amazon has placed the web services at http://soap.amazon.com/onca/soap2:

```
Public Sub New()
  MyBase.New
  Me.Url = "http://soap.amazon.com/onca/soap2"
End Sub
```

The following is one of the many provided functions. This function, `KeywordSearchRequest()`, takes an object of type `KeywordRequest` as its parameter, and returns an object of type `ProductInfo`:

```
Public Function KeywordSearchRequest _
  (<System.Xml.Serialization.SoapElementAttribute("KeywordSearchRequest")> _
   ByVal KeywordSearchRequest1 As KeywordRequest) As _
   <System.Xml.Serialization.SoapElementAttribute("return")> ProductInfo
  Dim results() As Object = _
    Me.Invoke("KeywordSearchRequest", New Object() {KeywordSearchRequest1})
  Return CType(results(0),ProductInfo)
End Function
```

We're going to need to use this method, and to do so, we need to know more about the `KeywordRequest` type and the `ProductInfo` type. They can both be found towards the end of the `Amazon.vb` file.

The `KeywordRequest` type is shown here, again stripped of excess detail that we don't need:

```
Public Class KeywordRequest
  Public keyword As String
  Public page As String
  Public mode As String
```

```
      Public tag As String
      Public type As String
      Public devtag As String
      Public sort As String
   End Class
```

Here's a rundown of the properties in the `KeywordRequest` class:

| Property | Description |
| --- | --- |
| keyword | This is the keyword you are searching for. |
| page | Some searches could return a tremendous amount of results. Amazon limits each search to ten results per call. You pass the page of results you want returned with this property. If you want the first ten results, you pass a "1". For the second ten results, pass a "2", and so on. |
| mode | This is the area of Amazon you're searching. A couple of examples are "music" and "books". |
| tag | This is the associates tag. To be honest, I don't know the significance. I do know that you need to set it to "webservices-20". |
| type | This signifies the amount of detail returned. "lite" signifies that only essential information such as name, artist, and prices are returned. "heavy" signifies that additional information such as customer review data is returned. |
| devtag | This is your developer token. |
| sort | This is the way you want your results sorted. See the Amazon documentation for the possible values. We'll sort our items alphabetically, which is "+titlerank". |

The return value we receive when we call `KeywordSearchRequest` is of type `ProductInfo`. Here's the stripped version:

```
   Public Class ProductInfo
      Public TotalResults As String
      Public ListName As String
      Public Details() As Details
   End Class
```

Here are the properties and their descriptions:

| Property | Description |
| --- | --- |
| TotalResults | The total results available based on the search criteria. |
| ListName | Undocumented, but don't worry, we don't use this in our application! |
| Details() | This is an array of the results of type Details. |

The Details type contains all pertinent information for each returned item. If you look in the generated class, you'll see that this type has many, many properties. I won't show you all of them, but here is a description of the ones we'll use:

| Property | Description |
| --- | --- |
| URL | A link to the item on Amazon's site. |
| ProductName | The name of the item. |
| Artists() | A string array of all the involved artists. |
| OurPrice | Amazon's price for the item. |

## Create an Amazon Search Page

Now that we have a better understanding of the classes we'll utilize, let's create an example.

**Try It Out**     **Searching Amazon.com**

1. Create a new ASP.NET page and call it AmazonSearch.aspx. This page needs to be in the same folder as the one you generated your Amazon.vb file into.

2. Add the text **Search Amazon for:** and add a textbox with ID of txtSearch to the right of it.

3. Hit *Return*, then add a button and set its ID to btnSearch and the text to Search.

4. Finally, add a label control at the bottom of the page, with the ID of lblResults and clear its Text property. This is where we'll place the returned item list.

5. While still in design mode, double-click on the btnSearch button and add the following code in the click event handler:

```
Sub btnSearch_Click(sender As Object, e As EventArgs)
   Dim amazonsrch As New Amazon.AmazonSearchService()
   Dim productinfo As Amazon.ProductInfo
   Dim keyrequest As New Amazon.KeywordRequest()
   Dim details As Amazon.Details

      keyrequest.keyword = txtSearch.text
      keyrequest.page = "1"
      keyrequest.mode = "music"
      keyrequest.tag = "webservices-20"
      keyrequest.type = "lite"
      keyrequest.devtag = "xxxxxxxxxxxxxx"
      Try
         productinfo = amazonsrch.KeywordSearchRequest(keyrequest)

         If cint(productinfo.TotalResults) > 0 Then
            lblResults.text = ""
            For Each details In productinfo.Details
               lblResults.text &= "<a href=""" & details.URL & """>"
               If ubound(details.artists) >= 0 Then
                  lblResults.text &= details.artists(0) & " - "
               End If
               lblResults.text &= details.ProductName & " - " & _
                  details.OurPrice & "</a><br />"
            Next
         Else
            lblResults.text = "No results found"
         End If
      Catch
         lblResults.text = "There was an error with this search."
      End Try
End Sub
```

Now you can try the page out. You should be able to search for any music that has the text you specify as part of the author, title, or keywords. I've searched for Cornflakes below, but unfortunately, I guess our CD is too new to be listed yet! Here are the results of using the web service:

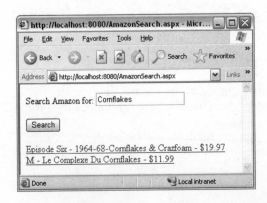

## How It Works

Let's look at the code we inserted in the click event handler for our button.

First, we need an instance of the `AmazonSearchService` object. We name ours `amazonsrch` and this is the class in which the web service's methods are located:

```
Dim amazonsrch As New Amazon.AmazonSearchService()
```

As we've discussed, the results are returned in an object called `ProductInfo`:

```
Dim productinfo As Amazon.ProductInfo
```

The next object is what we pass to the web service to specify the properties of our search:

```
Dim keyrequest As New Amazon.KeywordRequest()
```

The details of the search results are held in the following object:

```
Dim details As Amazon.Details
```

Next we specify our search properties:

```
keyrequest.keyword = txtSearch.text
keyrequest.page = "1"
keyrequest.mode = "music"
keyrequest.tag = "webservices-20"
keyrequest.type = "lite"
keyrequest.devtag = "xxxxxxxxxxxxxx"
```

The keyword is set to the value that the user types into the textbox on the page. We are only going to return the top 10 results, so we can just display page 1 of the results. The `mode` is set to `music` as that's what we're searching for. Next, we are only going to use the values we can get from the `lite` return results. Finally in the above code, we have to enter the token string in the `devtag` property. As I said earlier, you need to get your own token from the Amazon link. (At the time of writing, it was possible to carry out this example without actually using your developer's token but there is every chance that Amazon will start checking these so it's probably better to use it!)

We need to gracefully handle errors, especially when dealing with web services. Even if your code is perfect (which, of course it is!), you can't always count on the Internet being available, and then, even if it is, you can't count on the web service provider being available and bug-free.

So, we start off with a `Try` block declaration so that we can trap and deal with any errors. Then, we get the `ProductInfo` object after calling the `KeywordSearchRequest()` method. We pass our `keyrequest` object to the method so that the web service knows what to search for:

```
productinfo = amsrch.KeywordSearchRequest(keyrequest)
```

We need to check to see if any results are returned. Since `TotalResults` is a string property, we need to convert it to an integer first:

```
If cint(productinfo.TotalResults) > 0 Then
```

Next, we're saying that if we've got some results, let's clear `lblResults`, because we're going to add stuff into it:

```
lblResults.text = ""
```

Then we run through all of the results details:

```
For Each details In productinfo.Details
```

We're placing hyperlink HTML in `lblResults`. First, we set the a tag's `href` attribute to the returned URL. This URL is a link to the product details on Amazon's website:

```
lblResults.text &= "<a href=""" & details.URL & """>"
```

If any artists are returned, they'll be displayed as the first part of the link text:

```
If ubound(details.artists) >= 0 Then
    lblResults.text &= details.artists(0) & " - "
End If
```

Finally, we show the product's name and Amazon's selling price, and then we close the a tag.

```
lblResults.text &= details.ProductName & " - " & _
    details.OurPrice & "</a><br />"
```

If the `TotalResults` is 0, we let the user know that there were no results, using the following line:

```
lblResults.text = "No results found"
```

If there are any errors at any point, we handle them by letting the user know:

```
Catch
    lblResults.text = "There was an error with this search."
End Try
```

# Creating Our Own Web Service

Wouldn't it be cool if fans could display tour diary entries on their own websites? Well, with web services, they can. Let's make a web service available from our website that fans can tap into. We'll provide one method to return all tour diary entries.

As usual, Web Matrix makes the process of providing a web service simpler through the use of a template file. We'll use this template to provide our web service, and then customize it.

**1.** Using the **Web Services | Simple** template, create a new file called `TourDiary.asmx` (`asmx` is the extension for web services). Use the namespace `CAM` and the class `TourDiaryWS` for this file:

**2.** The template file that is created now has an example method that adds two integers together and returns the result. Remove this and add the `ReadTourDiaryEntries()` method below so that the file contains the following:

```
<%@ WebService language="VB" class="TourDiaryWS" %>

Imports System
Imports System.Web.Services
Imports System.Xml.Serialization
```

```
Imports System.Data
Imports CAM

Public Class TourDiaryWS

  <WebMethod> Public Function ReadTourDiaryEntries( _
               ByVal SortValue As String) As DataSet
    Dim TDDB As New TourDiaryDB()

    Return TDDB.ReadTourDiaryEntries(SortValue)
  End Function

End Class
```

That's it – we now have a completed web service.

ASP.NET provides an easy way to test your web service. You can browse to your .asmx page in the usual way as you have seen throughout this book, and see the methods provided, like the following:

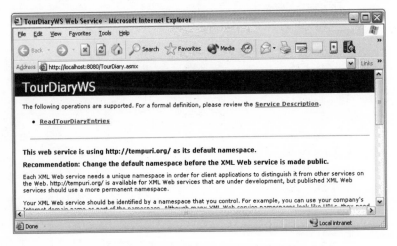

If you click on the ReadTourDiaryEntries link, you can even invoke the method (of course, this is only for testing – you normally access these services from websites or other applications). The page will now prompt you to provide values for the parameters:

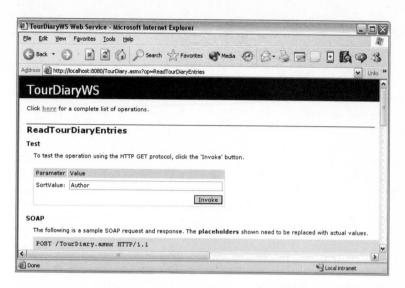

If we invoke the method with **SortValue** set to **Author**, we'll get something like the following XML returned, depending on what is in the tour diary of course:

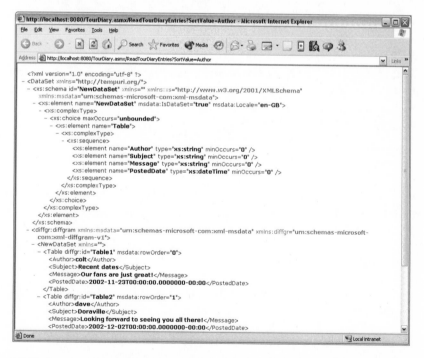

This is the XML that comprises the returned dataset. In the next *Try It Out*, we'll use it in a fan's web page, where their ASP.NET code will call and utilize the returned data from this web service. Firstly, though, let's look at the code to see what is going on.

## How It Works

The `WebService` directive declares this file as providing web service functionality. You must also specify the language within the page, and the class that will be providing the web services. In this case, the class within our page named `TourDiaryWS` is providing the functionality:

```
<%@ WebService language="VB" class="TourDiaryWS" %>
```

We utilize several namespaces to provide web service functionality. The first three that are placed in the code by Web Matrix are always required for a web service. The two that we add are needed because we're providing functionality that returns datasets, and we use functionality within the CAM namespace to provide the data:

```
Imports System.Data
Imports CAM
```

Methods within a class providing web services are only available to the web service if they are marked with the `<WebMethod>` attribute. You should only enable the functions you explicitly want available to the users of your service. Your application will be more secure this way:

```
<WebMethod> Public Function ReadTourDiaryEntries( _
             ByVal SortValue As String) As DataSet
```

We're using our `TourDiaryDB` class to provide a dataset containing all of our tour diary entries, sorted by the value contained in the `SortValue` property:

```
Dim TDDB As New TourDiaryDB()

Return TDDB.ReadTourDiaryEntries(SortValue)
End Function
```

Now that we've created our web service and tested it, let's actually use it, or to put it another way, **consume** it.

## Try It Out    Consuming our Web Service

1. Create a new directory called `Fan`. Then, in Web Matrix, choose **Tools | WebService Proxy Generator**.

2. Enter the following parameters in the proxy generator dialog:

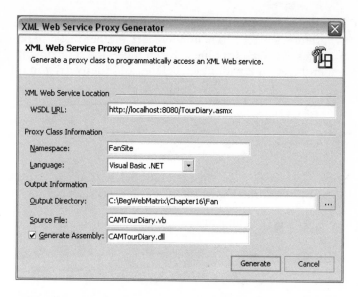

Hit **Generate** to have Web Matrix generate the proxy.

**3.** If the above works, you should have two files created. The first, CAMTourDiary.vb, contains a proxy to our ReadTourDiaryEntries() method. The second, bin\CAMTourDiary.dll, is the compiled assembly.

**4.** Now create a fan page in the Fan directory using the **Data Pages | Simple Data Report** template and call it CornflakeDiary.aspx.

**5.** Change the Page_Load method to match the following:

```
Sub Page_Load(Sender As Object, E As EventArgs)

    Dim TDWS As New FanSite.TourDiaryWS()

    DataGrid1.DataSource = TDWS.ReadTourDiaryEntries("PostedDate")
    DataGrid1.DataBind()

End Sub
```

This works by creating an instance of our generated proxy from Step 3 above. We used the namespace FanSite, and the web service class we created a proxy for was called TourDiaryWS. We call the ReadTourDiaryEntries() method to set the data source for the grid on our page.

Of course, to finish up the page, you should encode the returned data for display as we've done with the other examples in this chapter and the previous few chapters.

I have the band's website running on my workstation on port 8080, so I'm going to run the fan site on port 8081. Therefore, we need to manually start another instance of the Web Matrix web server. In order to do this, we have supplied a batch file in the code download that you can copy to your system and then run by double-clicking. Alternatively, you can create one yourself by creating a new text file and entering the following code:

```
cd c:\Program Files\Microsoft ASP.NET Web Matrix\v0.5.464
webserver /port:8081 /path:c:\BegWebMatrix\Chapter16\Fan
pause
```

Save the file as StartWebServer.bat, then double-click it to run the commands. This starts a new instance of the web server listening on port 8081 and serves the content in the Fan directory.

Now load http://localhost:8081/CornflakeDiary.aspx and you should get the following result:

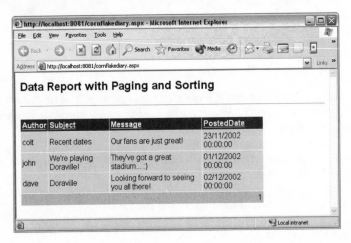

We're done! We've just consumed our own web service. Now our fans can provide our tour diary entries on their own websites. We didn't have to know any XML, SOAP, or any of the other complex technologies to make it happen.

# Summary

In this chapter, we've utilized existing web services, which are the hottest topic in web development these days, as well as creating and consuming our own. Hopefully, this gives you a taste for the work it takes to make real sites utilize each other's services. We've just touched on the tip of the iceberg in the functionality we have seen in this chapter and more and more sites out there are enabling third-party use of their functionality through web services each day. There is a huge opportunity for application designers to create sites that utilize these services in new, creative ways – using Web Matrix and web services, you can do this cheaply, simply, and effectively.

# CHAPTER 17

# Beyond Web Matrix

The previous chapters in this book have looked at everything from the initial installation of the environment required to create our applications, through the development of web pages, and on to more advanced tasks such as creating web services. Now that we've covered most of the functionality offered to us by Web Matrix, in this final chapter of the book, we'll see what options are open to us going forwards, and how Web Matrix fits into the big picture of developing web applications. There are obviously many aspects and issues involved in the provision of such applications, but we'll focus on those that are most relevant at this point, rather than those that only apply to large-scale or uncommon projects. The topics that we'll concentrate on are:

- ❑ The limitations of Web Matrix when compared to other web development software

- ❑ How we can move applications from our local machine, where we develop them, to live web servers where they can be made visible to the public

- ❑ The resources available to us on the Web to give us extra information and support when creating our applications

## Other Development Environments

As you've probably gathered by now, Web Matrix is the new kid on the block; it's only been around for a very short time, even when compared with ASP.NET, which itself is relatively young in comparison to many other ways of developing web applications (such as classic ASP and Perl). Obviously, there were other tools around before, both for developing on this platform, and for others such as those mentioned above. As the list of primary functions that a web-development environment has to perform is fairly short, we can compare Web Matrix to other development tools in general to see how it compares with the competition.

## Limitations of Web Matrix

Web Matrix is a great product for many reasons – not least because it costs us nothing. The ease of use, range of features, and amount of support available for it all add up to a first-class development tool. There are limitations to the product, though. As you start to create larger-scale, and more complex applications than we've worked on through this book, there are tools and options available in other products that offer more support in development:

❑ The application is only a 1.2MB download, and while this is great for our bandwidth, it does mean that a lot of the features available to other development environments are unavailable to Web Matrix. In contrast, Microsoft's Visual Studio .NET (Matrix's big brother) is several CDs in size, which means that a lot of different functionality has been added to Visual Studio .NET.

❑ Web Matrix was developed by a small team of developers at Microsoft in their spare time, and while they're a talented team, it's not quite the same as a product that's been developed full-time, with a large budget, by a larger team. Also, Web Matrix is still a technology preview, and as such, it contains a few bugs.

❑ Web Matrix has been designed as a way for individual developers to create individual web-pages quickly and simply. Other tools have been designed with teams of developers working together in mind.

Due to these factors, the following features that are often found in other products are not included:

❑ **Manuals and greater on-line help** – Although the Community tab provides us with many links to useful resources, it isn't a replacement for good basic documentation that is integrated with the environment, or presented in a book. In other tools, it's often possible to simply select a piece of code, click a button, and have help displayed for it, making tracking information down much simpler.

❑ **Source-control** – We all make mistakes that cause existing code to stop working when we're developing. The ability to undo such mistakes when they're finally detected is important, even if the file has been saved many times since. There are several tools, such as Microsoft's Visual Source Safe that integrate with other development environments, and allow code to be reverted to an old version at any time.

❑ **Application design** – This isn't very important with the size of the sites that we've developed so far, but with bigger projects the ability to visually model how your system is going to work, and then have the environment take care of a lot of the work for you can be a God-send.

❑ **Deployment** – Once an application has been created, it's important to be able to move it to another location so that it can be accessed by others, leaving you free to use your machine to develop your next masterpiece.

❑ **Modularization of applications** – Similarly to source-control, this is not so important when we're creating small websites. When the application grows in size, it becomes increasingly important to be able to take existing bits of code and reuse them elsewhere in a site without physically copying the chunk of code and pasting it wherever it's needed. Also, we can split up applications into different sections to make it easier for teams of developers to work on them We'll look at this more later in the chapter, but you can think of it as being like linking to a JavaScript file so that its functions were available everywhere, as we did in Chapter 11.

❑ **Creation of Windows applications** (as well as other types) – In addition to creating web applications, .NET caters for standard Windows applications to be created in a similar environment. Web Matrix itself is such an application that was written in .NET.

That is not to say that none of these features will ever make it into Web Matrix. Features such as the creation of Windows applications are obviously not a priority for a web development tool, but features such as deployment are a concern for all developers, as we'll see later in the chapter. For now though, if Web Matrix isn't king of the hill, what are our alternatives when we're creating applications in .NET?

If you're willing to spend a little more time getting to know an IDE (and a little money purchasing one!) then there are several alternatives available. There are few .NET development environments that offer many great advantages in functionality over Web Matrix, the main being Microsoft's own product major offering – **Visual Studio .NET** (www.microsoft.com/vstudio). However, if you prefer to write code rather than use WYSIWYG editors such as those in Web Matrix, then there are a number of options, most of which are listed on the following web-page:

http://www.dotnetcoders.com/web/Articles/ShowArticle.aspx?article=49

## Visual Studio .NET

Visual Studio .NET (alternatively known as Visual Studio 7) has a long history, with certain previous versions being both praised and cursed. It is widely agreed that this latest version of this IDE, while keeping a lot of the features that have made it popular worldwide (**IntelliSense** for instance, which we explain in a little while), has also remedied a lot of the problems of earlier versions (such as poor deployment tools). Web Matrix borrows many aspects of development from Visual Studio .NET, including:

❑ Drag-and-drop Design view

❑ HTML and Code views for ASPX pages

❑ Property panes for setting object attributes

❑ Web service development

❑ Integrated data designers

There are some features present in Web Matrix that are not found in Visual Studio .NET though, such as code-snippets and the built-in web server. Due to such constraints as time, money, and complexity, Web Matrix does *not*, however, include the following core features that are present in Visual Studio .NET:

❑ **Built-in Debugging of code** – This allows you to execute one line of code at a time, and see where problems are occurring.

❑ **IntelliSense** – When writing HTML or code, this presents the user with a drop-down list of all of the options currently available, (available properties or methods of an object, for example) meaning developers have little to remember.

❑ **Improved database management** – Visual Studio .NET provides many more features when it comes to managing any SQL Server or MSDE database, rather than just the ability to maintain tables and stored procedures as in Web Matrix's **Data** view. Among other things, this makes moving databases from one server to another far simpler.

❑ **Windows application development** – The ability to create standard Windows programs, such as Web Matrix itself.

Visual Studio .NET comes in several different versions, all of which incorporate the features listed above. In its simplest form (the *Standard* edition), Visual Studio .NET can be purchased as individual language tools, such as Visual Basic .NET and Visual C# .NET. The next model up is Visual Studio .NET *Professional* edition, which allows us to create applications in both VB.NET and C#, as well as enabling many other features unavailable to the Standard editions of Visual Studio .NET. In addition to this, extra functionality is included with two further *Enterprise* editions. The differences between the versions can be summarized as follows:

| Version | Features |
|---|---|
| *Standard* edition | ❑ Available as single language-only packages<br><br>❑ Restricted functionality so that only certain types of application can be built (including web applications, windows applications, and command-line executable applications).<br><br>❑ Restricted database functionality. Can only view existing database tables, views, stored procedures, and so on. Ability to create and delete using SQL statements only. |
| *Professional* edition | Has all the features of the Standard edition, plus:<br><br>❑ Includes the ability to create database tables, stored procedures, views, and so on, using visual tools and wizards.<br><br>❑ Can create a greater range of applications, including class libraries, custom control classes, windows services, and so on. |

| Version | Features |
|---|---|
| *Enterprise Developer* edition | Has all of the features of the *Professional* edition, plus:<br><br>❑ Includes SQL Server (licences only for test and development)<br>❑ Backup and version control of code<br>❑ Application Center Test software for performance testing, and so on |
| *Enterprise Architect* edition | Has all of the features of *Enterprise Developer* edition, plus:<br><br>❑ Graphical database and application modeling |

While the *Standard* edition costs only $100 US Dollars or so, the *Enterprise Architect* edition retails for $2,500. On a large project, the extra cost of the development can usually be readily offset by the time savings its extra features offer. On smaller projects, this may not be the case, and these features may not be required at all, leaving the cheaper editions being far more cost-effective. The version of SQL Server that is included with the *Enterprise* versions does allow you to manage MSDE databases using the **Enterprise Manager** tool that's included with it, though, as well as integrating better database management into the Visual Studio IDE itself. This can lower the cost of developing a project considerably, as it means that development SQL licenses may not need to be purchased (though you will still need to purchase SQL Server licenses for deploying the applications if you intend to host them yourself).

To get a feel for Visual Studio .NET, the following is a screen shot from the *Enterprise Architect* edition:

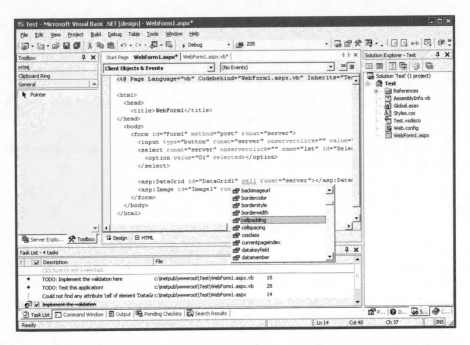

As you can see, not only does the environment list all of the options available for our
`DataGrid` tag, it also underlines the `cell` attribute, to tell us that it's not valid (just like
Microsoft Word underlines an invalid spelling), and gives us a list of tasks that need
completing at the bottom of the screen. As well as including tasks that we define ourselves in
this pane, it also includes lists of errors that the IDE has detected with our application that will
need correcting before it functions correctly. Fixing these is known as **debugging** an
application, as we saw in Chapter 7.

# Web Hosting Server Software

It's all very well being able to view our sites and see that they work, but if they are intended for
others to view, such as our Cornflakes at Midnight site, we usually want to put them online so
that they're visible just like any other website, rather than having them confined to just those
who can peer over your shoulder at your screen. To allow us to do this in a live environment,
we usually need two main things:

❏ **Web server software** – The software that takes the requests for pages such as
www.mySite.com, processes the ASPX file for the page, and returns the result to
the end user.

❏ **A database management system** – This is only necessary if our application makes use
of a database, and could be a product such as MSDE, SQL Server, Oracle, or MySql.

Once we've configured our live environment – the database software, the web server software, and any other programs required – we need to transfer the application we've developed and move it to this environment from wherever it was created – usually our local machine. We'll come back to that in a while; for now let's take a look at server software, starting with web-servers.

## Dedicated Web Server Software

One of the main limitations with the environment that Web Matrix gives us is the ability to host pages. The built-in web server that is started when the Start button is clicked on the toolbar only allows the web pages developed to be viewed on your local machine. If your computer is on a network, no users on other machines could view it, let alone people across the Internet. That's not to say that the web server included with Web Matrix isn't useful; when developing, it provides us with most of the features we need to view and test our websites. Obviously, if a site is to be made visible to other people once completed, we need to find an alternative.

Thankfully, Microsoft is a step ahead of the game on this one, and included with all versions of Windows 2000, the *Professional* edition of Windows XP, and Windows .NET Server (all editions), is **IIS** (or **Internet Information Services**). IIS has been Microsoft's software platform for hosting web applications since the mid-90s, originally catering for classic ASP applications, and now providing us with a means of publishing our ASP.NET websites.

The version that is included with *Professional* (desktop) editions of Windows is very similar to the version that comes with *Server* editions. The main differences are the inability in the former to create more than one website at once (multiple applications can be hosted within a single site though), and the limit of five simultaneous requests to the site. For individual or group development, and testing purposes, the *Professional* edition is great. In a live environment, an installation of Windows 2000 Server or the soon to be released **.NET Server** really is necessary for sites to be hosted.

One further difference between IIS and the web server included with Web Matrix is the ability of the former to make use of security features, such as **SSL** (Secure Sockets Layer). SSL allows us to secure our applications by encrypting the data sent between the web server and the web browser. If ever you've been to a website where Internet Explorer shows a padlock in the status bar, you'll have been making use of SSL certificates, possibly without knowing it. These certificates can be bought from companies such as VeriSign (www.verisign.com), and installed on a web-server, allowing data such as credit card details to be transferred securely.

The screenshot below shows us just some of the options provided by the Internet Services Manager tool that comes with IIS (more information on IIS can be found in Appendix A):

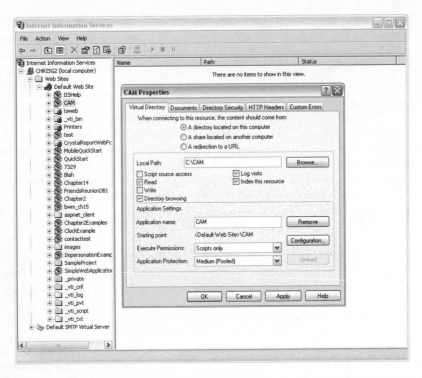

When compared with the dialog that is shown by clicking on the system-tray icon for Web Matrix's server, this should make it clear just how much can be configured with a full-blown web server:

If you are running one of the versions of Windows that was listed above that includes IIS, then you can refer to Appendix A of this book for details on how to set it up to host your web applications. If not, then unfortunately there are (at time of writing) few other pieces of Web server software available that provide a good platform for hosting ASP.NET applications.

# *Alternative Database Servers*

When we've been working with the **Data Explorer** in Web Matrix, we've always been connecting to the database server that we installed at the start of the book – the freely available MSDE. This is by no means the only database product available, though. Microsoft itself has several other offerings, including Access, FoxPro, and **SQL Server**. Other companies produce yet more products, such as Oracle, Informix, and MySQL. While each of these performs a very similar function – storing and allowing the retrieval of data in tables, very similarly to MSDE – each has its own benefits and drawbacks. For instance, MySQL is free and supported on operating systems other than Windows, while Oracle is widely accepted as being the most suitable for enterprise-level usage (where whole corporations are relying on the one database).

Like the other options, MSDE has its own list of pluses and minuses. It its favor, it's free, it's widely available, it integrates exceptionally well with tools such as Web Matrix, and it provides a wealth of features. As Microsoft already has its own enterprise-level database software in SQL Server that sells for a few thousand US dollars, it obviously didn't want MSDE to detract from its sales. In order to stop this from being the case, it's added limitations to the operation of MSDE. The most important three of these are:

❑ **Restricted number of connections** – MSDE has been optimized for up to 5 simultaneous users, with performance dropping off if there are more. In a large system, this will cause a drop in performance, potentially making it unsuitable for applications that have hundreds of users at once.

❑ **Maximum database size** –MSDE only allows databases of up to 2GBs in size. All but the largest database will fit within this. For instance, our CAM database is only around 1MB in size.

❑ **No management utility** – Included with SQL Server is a tool called **Enterprise Manager**. This allows for the database to be backed up, data to be imported into it, security settings to be altered, as well as providing a more advanced way of doing all of the database operations we carried out within Web Matrix. A sample of the interface (and multitude of options) that SQL Server provides is shown in the screenshot overleaf:

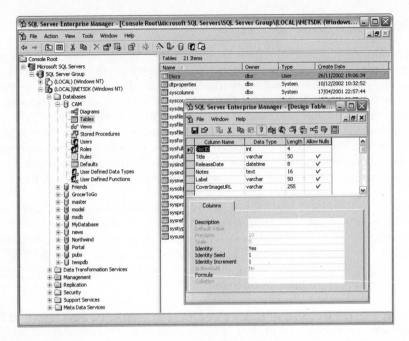

Besides being a very capable database server, MSDE has one other feature that puts it head and shoulders above other budget Microsoft database products, if not those of other companies – it is directly compatible with SQL Server. This means that you can develop applications using MSDE, and move them to SQL Server at a later date if there ever becomes any need to do so, because MSDE stands for Microsoft SQL Server Desktop Engine. It is essentially just the database server portion of SQL Server, with the limitations we listed above, as well as licensing restrictions.

> *The license with MSDE restricts how you are allowed to use it. While it's great for testing applications, if you want to let your clients access the database, you need to consider client-access licenses. For more information, you may want to check out the following page: http://www.microsoft.com/sql/howtobuy/msdeuse.asp*

Another major benefit of using MSDE and SQL Server is their integration with Web Matrix, as mentioned above. As a result of this, when we were developing our Cornflakes at Midnight site, we didn't have to leave the development environment in order to create our database, create stored procedures on it, and so on. These two products are the only ones that can be managed in this manner from within Web Matrix – other third-party tools would have to be run to achieve the same effect with alternative database server software

So, when upgrading from MSDE as a site becomes more popular, or needs to use some advanced features, SQL Server is the natural choice. Not only is it a very competent product, it is also directly compatible with MSDE itself, and is catered for by the development environment too. If this migration is ever performed, the Enterprise Manager tool can be used to connect to your existing database, and move it across to SQL Server. The only change that will have to be made to the application is usually the connection string specifying what to use as the database server.

One other point to note about database servers that we've not seen yet is their location. So far, we've always had our database running from the same machine as the web server. In a real-world application, the database server software is regularly running on a separate machine. One of the main reasons for this is that it allows the machine to be optimized with a specific hardware configuration that can provide the best possible performance. Since this hardware can be very expensive, it is more economical, in some cases, to put all the databases on one machine. Additionally, security settings can be applied so that the database server is only accessible from the web servers, and only for certain functions making it more difficult to gain unauthorized access to any sensitive information stored on it (such as credit card numbers).

> When talking about databases, the terms database, server, and database server regularly get confused with one another. Technically speaking, a *database* is a store of information (such as **pubs**) that is provided by a *database management system (DBMS)*. This management system is also known as a *database server*, but this term regularly implies the hardware that it is running on, as well as the software itself. The server – the machine that hosts the DBMS, is often a separate machine from that hosting websites, for reasons discussed above.

Due to the usefulness of Enterprise Manager and other such tools, there have been attempts at creating free versions of software that perform a similar function. Possibly the best known application that is available for maintaining MSDE in this manner is the ASP Enterprise Manager, which provides a web interface to management, and is available from www.aspenterprisemanager.com.

# Deploying Applications

Now that everything is set in place for unleashing our applications on the world, there's only one task remaining – moving the site to the web and database server(s) that are going to host it. We've already seen that Visual Studio .NET has some features to offer us here, but before taking a quick look at them, we'll see what's available to us with just Web Matrix.

## Hosting Websites with Web Matrix

Moving a website to a live environment in .NET is a very simple task; using either the web server built into Web Matrix, or IIS, it's simply a matter of copying the relevant files to a folder that has been **web-published** (made available via an `http://` web address). The .NET Runtime then deals with compiling these files when they're first requested, and executing them, before the web server returns the output back to the browser. If the application makes use of databases, specifically referenced folders for storing files, or other external resources, then settings stored in files such as `Web.config` may also need amending. Compared to earlier Microsoft technologies, this is a vast improvement. In the past, deploying an application could be fairly torturous as although classic ASP files could similarly just be copied to the target folder, other resources required a more in-depth knowledge to carry out a lot of custom actions.

Deploying the site is only part of the issue, however. Maintaining a server – ensuring it has a permanent connection to the Internet, checking for security updates, and performing all of the other necessary tasks – to enable the smooth running of a hosting environment can take a lot of resources, both time and money. Rather than setting up your own web server so that you can publish applications, there are many other companies that provide this service, allowing you to use their servers. Examples of these can be found on Microsoft's site at the following location:

```
www.microsoft.com/vstudio/partners/webhosters/default.asp
```

Most of these companies charge a fee for the hosting, and can take care of other tasks such as registering domain names to use for your site. There are other companies that provide hosting for free, as long as you allow them to place advertising banners on your sites.

Obviously, if the web server is located remotely, copying the necessary files to it may not be as simple as dragging and dropping files between the two; they may not be on the same network, there may be security details that need entering, and so on. As mentioned earlier in this book, we have FTP, the **File Transfer Protocol**. This is designed specifically for copying files to remote locations over the Internet using FTP software. Web Matrix *does* support this feature, making life much simpler if the provider has already configured the live environment. Even if you're doing the hosting yourself, this method can be used for transferring files to a live server.

To do this from within Web Matrix, select the **Add FTP Connection...** option from the **Workspace** menu once you've set up an FTP account. This will bring up the following dialog:

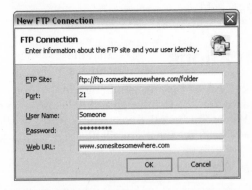

Once this has been filled in with the details of either your own FTP server, or those of an account with one of the sites such as those listed by Microsoft, click the **OK** button, and a new entry will appear in the **Workspace** pane in Web Matrix. Right-clicking on this will bring up a menu allowing new items to be added directly to this remote location:

Alternatively, files can be dragged and dropped from the local drives to the FTP server from within the tree, copying them to the web server.

As well as the FTP software built into Web Matrix and Windows itself, there are many other utilities available that have been developed for this task, and include such functionality as timed uploads, and automatic retry when errors occur. Two of the most popular tools for this are Cute FTP (www.cuteftp.com), and Bullet Proof FTP (www.bulletproofftp.com), both of which are sold for a small charge and have trial versions that can be downloaded.

## Deploying Databases

Deploying databases can quite often be the most difficult part of moving an application to a live environment. This is especially true if we're simply making updates to a database that we've already deployed previously, as the chances are that the data stored in the live version has been updated and needs keeping, while the table structures and stored procedures need overwriting. Solving this problem depends on the specific circumstances encountered, but the general task of transferring a database is a topic worth looking at here.

If we are using a full SQL Server installation, then this can all be done graphically through the Enterprise Manager, given a little experience and patience. If we're using MSDE then the task can be much harder. If we're using MSDE, and have an Enterprise edition of Visual Studio .NET, then the development edition of SQL Server is included with it, along with Enterprise Manager. As SQL Server and MSDE are virtually identical, Enterprise Manager can also be used for administering an MSDE database, making it just as simple as a full-blown SQL Server.

If we don't have access to these tools, then things start to get far more involved as the process has to be carried out manually. This requires a fairly in-depth knowledge of SQL to inform the database of the operation to perform, a copy of the specific file that MSDE uses for storing that particular database's information in, the location where that file is to be placed, and so on. This is one reason that other database engines, such as Microsoft Access, are still being used – not all of them require the same amount of effort in deployment. Microsoft hasn't left developers totally stranded, though. MSDE comes with a command-line tool called `osql.exe`, which allows SQL statements to be executed against a database server. As well as being able to run SQL code such as `SELECT` statements that manage data, there are commands such as `BACKUP` and `RESTORE` that operate on the database as a whole. More details on these are available in the SQL Books online, which can be downloaded from:

http://www.microsoft.com/sql/techinfo/productdoc/2000/books.asp

There are also articles available on the Web that show how these commands can be put together into tools, and called from `osql.exe` in order to help us copy our databases around. The first of the following links gives information on the `osql.exe` tool itself, with the second being an article on backing up databases using it:

http://msdn.microsoft.com/library/default.asp?url=/library/
en-us/coprompt/cp_osql_1wxl.asp
http://support.microsoft.com/default.aspx?scid=kb;en-us;241397

## Deployment Packages in Visual Studio .NET

As mentioned, Visual Studio .NET helps us out when it comes to deploying a project. This is done via special types of programs that can be created in the environment – **Setup and Deployment Projects**. These make the process of transferring our applications to the hosting environment much simpler. Using such a setup project, we no longer have to manually put all of our files in the right location on the server, alter the necessary settings on the machine, amend files such as `Web.config` by hand so that they point to the right database server, and other such essential, but monotonous tasks.

Instead, we create one of these projects, then drag-and-drop all of the required files into Visual Studio .NET, along with any other information that is required to make changes to system settings on the servers. When the application that this generates is distributed and run, it presents the user with a standard installation interface, just like the one that was shown while Web Matrix was installing.

Setup projects are especially important if the person who developed the application isn't the one deploying it, or the application is being deployed on a regular basis (possibly to multiple machines). Otherwise, knowledge of all the settings that need to be changed would be required by whoever is installing it, and these changes would have to be made every time the application was installed by hand.

In addition to the deployment packages that we can create in Visual Studio .NET, there are other commercial products available that have been around for much longer, and include greater functionality and ease of use. Two of the most popular examples of these are InstallShield (www.installshield.com) and Wise (www.wise.com), and both have devoted followings.

# Further Resources

At this point, the first iteration of our development cycle has been completed. By this point in any project, there are usually dozens of ideas for extra features that can be added, problems that can be fixed, and ideas that can be tried out. To help incorporate these, and possibilities that others have come up with, into future versions of our applications there's a wealth of information available on the Internet to help us out. Of course, there are those provided by Wrox; in addition to books such as this one, there are the online resources of:

- ❑ http://p2p.wrox.com – Online technology discussions with tens of thousands of other programmers, all categories, and with the ability to subscribe to topics.

- ❑ http://www.asptoday.com – A solutions library for ASP and ASP.NET developers, containing around a thousand professionally written articles and case studies covering almost all relevant topics.

- ❑ http://www.csharptoday.com – A site similar in style to ASPToday, but focusing solely on .NET. The content here is provided in C#, rather than Visual Basic .NET, but most of the information given is relevant to this language, also.

- ❑ http://www.wroxbase.com – Wroxbase allows subscribers to have online access to books published by Wrox Press. This allows for searching on specific information across all books, as well as real-world features such as annotation of texts, and bookmarks.

There are also many other sites out there, which contain everything from short articles and how-tos that describe specific pieces of functionality and aspects of development, right the way through to comprehensive online documentation of .NET in its entirety:

- ❑ http://www.asp.net – The main Microsoft site for ASP.NET, which includes many useful articles, links, and downloads.

- ❑ http://msdn.microsoft.com – Microsoft's Developer Network site, which contains online documentation for all of its programming languages and technologies, along with downloads, articles, and other resources.

- ❑ http://www.asp101.com – An introductory site, giving information on ASP and ASP.NET, including reviews, articles, and forums.

- ❑ http://www.15seconds.com – A site dedicated to all development for all Microsoft technologies, not just ASP.NET, covering more in-depth and advanced topics than ASP101.

❑ http://www.4guysfromrolla.com – Another site containing similar information to 15 Seconds and ASP101, with the complexity and detail of articles pitched somewhere between the level of the other two.

❑ http://www.123aspx.com – A resource site that indexes ASP.NET-related articles in a fully-searchable database.

Failing all of the popular sites such as those above, try entering important terms related to the subject you're interested in into a search-engine (such as *Google* – http://www.google.com). This will usually turn up some information on the topic due to the vast number of newsgroups, forums, magazines, and articles that are dedicated to .NET and Microsoft development in general – the chances are that you're not the first person to come across a particular problem, and it's likely to have a resolution on the Web.

# Summary

Throughout the course of this book we've learned how to create dynamic web applications based upon ASP.NET technology, using the Web Matrix tool. This is available free of charge, and when combined with the MSDE database, it includes everything we need in order to create our own dynamic websites using the latest technologies. If we want to introduce more complex functionality, work in teams, or publish the sites we've created so that others can use them, then we need to start thinking about extra software and processes too, though. At the very least, this involves an installation of one of the *Professional* rather than *Home* edition version of Windows, so that IIS can be used. Usually, a server version such as Windows 2000 Server will be installed. To make hosting dynamic sites more manageable, either the database server usually runs a full-blown installation of SQL Server instead of MSDE, or some other way of managing MSDE deployment is found.

In this chapter, we looked at the other products out there that we may want to look at when scaling up our applications. We also saw that there are many resources available on the Web, from well-known names such as Microsoft and Wrox, through to other independent sites. Due to the size of following ASP.NET has, these provide a wealth of information that can not only fill in the blanks on specific topics, but also provide new ideas on what to do and how to do it.

You're probably full of ideas for creating your next sites now. If not, then how about a personal site that allows you to update content via an administration section, or a database of your own records or photos? Alternatively, you could develop a site for any club or group that you're a member of, including updateable features such as calendars. As one last piece of advice, when creating a site, take some time to look around and see what ideas others have that you can incorporate and expand upon. Whichever project you decide to tackle next, good luck and happy coding!

# APPENDIX

# Microsoft Internet Information Server

Microsoft Internet Information Server (IIS) is the industrial-strength web server supplied by Microsoft. Unlike the Web Matrix web server, IIS is designed to serve entire sites, and it contains many more features. If you are using a server product (Windows 2000 Server for example), then IIS is installed by default, but it's not installed by default on the Professional versions (for Windows 2000 and XP). It is, however, included on the CD that comes with the Professional versions, so you can just install it as an add-on, as shown below. If you are using the Home version of Windows XP, then IIS is not included on the CD, and not supported on XP Home, and you are limited to using the Web Matrix web server.

## Installing IIS

To install IIS you pick **Add or Remove Programs** from the **Control Panel**. From the next screen select **Add/Remove Windows Components**:

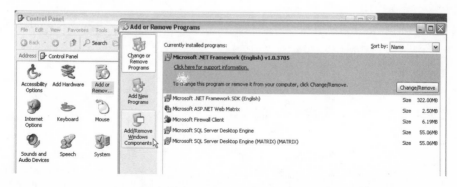

You now have the option to install extra components of Windows. Just tick the Internet Information Services (IIS) option:

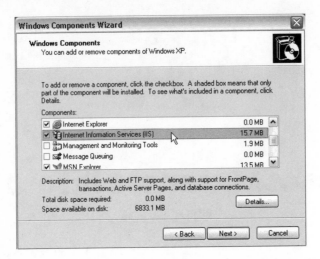

Press **Next**, and go make some coffee. It's either that or sit and look at the dialog that tells you it'll take 'just a few minutes'. You can click **Finish** when the installation is complete. Once done, you then need to make sure you can get to the IIS admin tool.

# Viewing the Administrative Tools

By default the installation of Windows XP doesn't show the **Administrative Tools** menu, where the link to the IIS is held. To view these you need to right-click over the **Start** button and select **Properties**. You then need to click the **Properties** button. If you're using the **Classic Start Menu** you'll see a list of **Advanced Start menu options** – just check **Display Administrative Tools** and press **OK**:

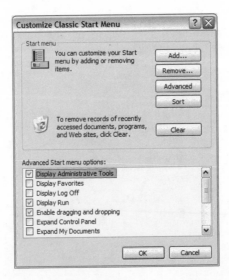

If you're using the fancy XP menus, you need to select the Advanced Tab, and then scroll the Start menu items all the way to the bottom to show the System Administrative Tools option. Select the first of these, Display on the All Programs menu and press OK:

# Configuring IIS

Now that you can see the admin tools, select Internet Information Services from the Administrative Tools menu. Expand (local computer), and then expand Web Sites. Right-click on Default Web Site, and from the New menu select Virtual Directory...:

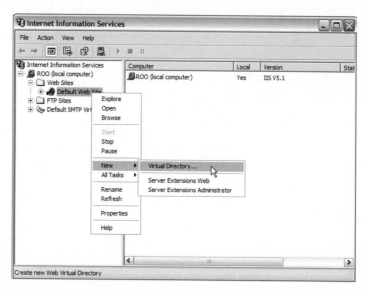

This starts the wizard to create web applications. A Virtual Directory is simply a link from IIS to a directory on your disk – it doesn't physically create a new directory. Enter the name of your application here – we've used wrox in this example:

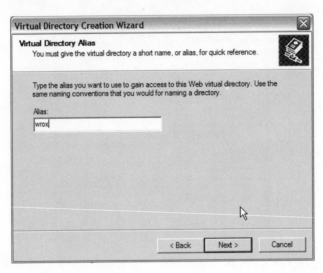

Press **Next**, and now enter the physical directory where this web application will point:

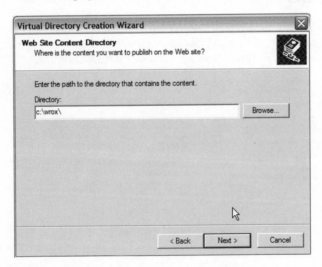

Press **Next** to get to the permissions screen:

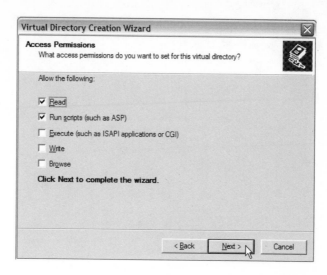

You can leave these as they are, so just press Next and finish the configuration.

Now that this directory is configured as a web application, you can browse files using Internet Explorer, by using //localhost/wrox in the address bar. Substitute wrox for another name if you've used a different one.

# Security

One very important point to note is that if you are connected to the Internet via a permanent connection, such as DSL, then your computer can be seen from the Internet. This could leave you exposed to potential hacks. Installing IIS means that if other users can see your machine, they will be able to browse to IIS applications that you create.

The best way to protect yourself is to have some sort of firewall, which limits what comes into your machine from outside. You can buy specialist firewall products, or with Windows XP you can use the built-in features. This topic is outside the scope of this book, but it's worth mentioning in case you are unaware of it. For a starting point head to http://www.microsoft.com/security/ – there's a section titled 'for home users', which contains several links worth reading.

# INDEX

# Index

## Symbols